1948

This book may be kept

N

CERVANTES ACROSS THE CENTURIES . . .

A QUADRICENTENNIAL VOLUME EDITED

BY ANGEL FLORES AND M. J. BENARDETE

THE DRYDEN PRESS · NEW YORK · 1947

I F we take as his birthday September 29, 1547, the date usually given by the chroniclers, it is exactly four hundred years ago today since he first saw the light, he who was to become, in after life, the writer of one of the supremely excellent masterpieces, the creator of two of the most alive and inspiring characters ever imagined, a heroic fighter in battle, an unflinching endurer of the terrible lot of a prisoner of war, a great and gallant genius whom fame never spoiled and misfortune never cowed—the Spaniard Miguel de Cervantes, author of *Don Quixote*. Thus the anonymous writer for "Topics of the Times" (The New York Times, Sept. 29, 1947) admirably summarized the perennial values embodied in the masterpiece of Cervantes.

Don Quixote is perhaps the most seminal novel ever written. We know for a certainty that Flaubert and Dostoyevsky owe to the one-armed hero of Lepanto the germinal ideas of their *Madame Bovary* and *The Idiot*. But Cervantes' secret, however lucid and plastic his prose, cannot be readily discerned. For at least three centuries scholarship has been attempting to plumb the depths of this first great modern novel that purported to destroy the infantile books of chivalry. In the eighteenth century critics discoursed on the epic qualities of *Don Quixote* which affiliated it with the Homeric poems. The scholars of Romanticism emphasized the social and spiritual implications of Cervantes' approach to the theocratic world of Spain—that civilization which deliberately walled itself off from nascent seventeenth-century Europe. (A remarkable instance of this Romantic attitude appears in the annotations made by Herman Melville in his copy of *Don Quixote*, which Professor Harry Levin of Harvard University has discussed in the present volume.) Impressionism and the Symbolist approach to literature enabled the irascible, dynamic Unamuno to see in *Don Quixote* the incandescent life-story of the Knight of La Mancha for whom the poverty-stricken Cervantes was an inadequate and prejudiced biographer. In a like manner have the critics of our own century studied the masterwork of the great Spanish novelist to find new meanings and new reflections significant for the life of our time.

As the literature of the sixteenth century came to be better understood, scholars and scholarly critics began to make separate studies of the various problems posed by *Don Quixote*. Sensitive objective criticism assumed the leadership, and thanks to the work of a whole brotherhood of students and lovers of Cervantes, we are now in a position to discern some of the meanings of Spain's first genius. Samples of this rich harvest are offered in English for the first time in the pages of this book. The serious reader, the student, the teacher, and the critic will find in the essays of Menéndez-Pidal, Joaquín Casalduero, and Helmut Hatzfeld analyses of the first order centering around the possible original idea which developed into the work we know as *Don Quixote*. For the first time these readers will experience the pleasure of surprise in discovering the architectural design and style of a literary monument.

We should require a whole essay to discuss the studies contained in the present volume, in order to point out the signficance of such contributions as those by Américo Castro, Waldo Frank, Jean Cassou, and others. Let the essays speak for themselves. However, it may be worth observing that the following pages fall into three main categories: the purely interpretive, the scholarly explanations of values and ideas, and the influences exerted by the work of Cervantes upon the literature of the world.

In a volume of this kind, composed of essays by a wide range of authorities, it has been deemed best to forego the usual editorial procedure with respect to spelling and punctuation. Each contributor's essay has been presented in the author's own manner. The editors have not imposed stylistic uniformity on the contributors, believing themselves chiefly responsible for the integrity of each contribution. Especially did this seem desirable in view of the considerable disagreement in interpretation among a number of the scholars included in this work.

For special permission to use certain material included in this volume, the editors make grateful acknowledgment: To Mario Casella, for the excerpt from his *Cervantes, Il Chisciotte,* first published in Florence; to Jean Cassou, for selections from his *Cervantes,* published by Editions Sociales; to Benedetto Croce, for the essay which appeared in his *Poesia antica e moderna* (second edition), published by Bari at Laterza, Italy; to Waldo Frank, for the passage taken from his *Virgin Spain,* published by Liveright, New York; to Alfred A. Knopf, Inc., publishers, for "The Spirit of Castile" by Miguel de Unamuno, from *Essays and Soliloquies* by Miguel de Unamuno, copyright 1925 by Alfred A. Knopf, Inc., New York.

October, 1947 A. F.
New York M. J. B.

TABLE OF CONTENTS

LVCEM POST TENEBRAS SPERO

REPRODUCTION OF THE DESIGN APPEARING ON THE TITLE PAGE OF
THE FIRST EDITION OF "DON QUIXOTE," 1605

PART ONE

PART ONE

An Introduction to Cervantes

JEAN CASSOU

CHILD of the Renaissance, Miguel de Cervantes was born in 1547 during the most brilliant period of the Golden Age. He was eight years old when Charles V abdicated his Empire and Philip II came to the throne of Spain. And it was midway through the reign of Philip III that he died, in 1616. Chronologically, he was the contemporary of El Greco and Lope de Vega, taking his place a little after St. Theresa and St. John of the Cross, who both belong entirely to the sixteenth century. Later than Cervantes came Quevedo, Gracián, Velázquez, Calderón, and Murillo, who were to mark the period of decadence, characterized by extreme "conceptism,' extreme realism and satire, and even an occasional lapse into the formalism of the past.

In this new world, with its widened horizons, where the rigid traditional framework of the Middle Ages had been broken, Cervantes entered upon the nomadic existence shared by so many of the vivid personalities in that dawn of modern times—among them, Columbus, Camoëns, Lope, and El Greco. Similarly, the humanists of the Renaissance became travelers who could not conceive of their resting-places as other than temporary abodes. "Knight-errant of theology," Menéndez y Pelayo called Miguel Servet; and Bonilla y San Martín dubbed "knight-errants of literature"[1] those wandering stars: Erasmus, Vives, Thomas More, and the Cretan, Demetrius Ducas. Ducas, who followed the same course of intellectual development as that taken by El Greco, became a member of Aldus Mantius' Platonic Academy at Venice, and later was summoned to Spain by Cardinal Ximenez to teach at the University of Alcalá de Henares. There he collaborated on the famous polyglot Bible with Nebrija, and with the Toledan, Hernán Nuñez, known as El Pinciano, as well as with Hellenists and converted Hebraists.

In the work of the European pacifist, Juan Luis Vives, it is shown that these various peregrinations and exchanges were the first step toward the establishment of an intellectual Europe, independent of princes and populations, an

3

ideal concept that has continued to excite generous imaginations up to our own time.

The odyssey of Cervantes had its beginning in the very midst of centralized Castile: on October 9, 1547, he was baptized in the Church of Santa María la Mayor in Alcalá de Henares. He was the fourth of seven children of a physician, himself the son of a lawyer who had held civil office in various provincial towns. These were his small middle-class origins. The family moved to Valladolid, then to Madrid, then to Seville, and back again to Madrid. It was in this last town that he is known to have studied with Juan Lopez de Hoyos, under whose direction he composed poetry, and in particular some eulogistic verses for the funeral of Queen Isabel de Valois.[2] Toward the end of 1569 he took service as a valet in the household of Cardinal Acquaviva at Rome. This contact with humanist Italy must have had a certain influence on his intellectual and cultural development.

Shortly afterward, he became a soldier, and on October 7, 1571, in the company commanded by Diego de Urbina, which formed part of Moncada's regiment, he fought in the naval battle of Lepanto, where he lost his left hand "for the greater glory of the right." That was his great day—just as it was the great day for Christianity and Christian Spain. A resounding victory, pompous and spectacular, it marked the unity of Mediterranean Christendom in a sacred cause; and the paladin Don Juan of Austria was its most striking figure. But it was a day without a tomorrow for Christianity, and also for Spain and Cervantes. Its effect was short lived, for actually the Christian nations sought only one another's destruction. Politics prevailed over the epic, and the crescent continued to shine in the heraldic azure of the sky.

Cervantes, mutilated but covered with glory, spent the winter in the hospital at Messina. At the end of his recuperation he resumed the King's service and took part in new engagements. Returning to Spain to solicit the rank of captain, Cervantes' galley was attacked by Barbary pirates and he was taken prisoner. For five years he was held captive in Algiers. His flattering letters of recommendation from Don Juan of Austria and from the Duke of Sessa, Sicilian viceroy, implied that he was one of the noblest of princes, when he was actually a poor nobody. Ironically this prevarication only increased his misfortune; nevertheless, he mustered his courage and put a good face on the affair.

As a slave of the renegade Dali-Mami he organized an unsuccessful revolt and found himself sold out by Hassan Pasha, Dey of Algiers, and thrown into prison as a dangerous character. He called upon his country to help him, and appealed to the Minister, Mateo Vásquez, in verses extolling the Holy Crusade. Later, numerous plans for escape—assisted, if one is to believe his plays and novels, by the loyal hearts and secret sympathies of lovely Moorish girls—were defeated by the treachery of a priest. All these efforts show his unfaltering struggle toward freedom, the while inspiring his companions with his unshakable faith, refusing to denounce them, and taking sole blame when discovered.

Meanwhile in Spain the poor members of his family were working in his behalf. They finally got together the sum demanded for his ransom. Trinitarian monks negotiated the affair, and thanks to their devotion Cervantes was freed and restored to his country on September 19, 1580.

Here ended the epic period of his career. Now no more than a ransomed soldier, defeated, one-handed, beggared, he again resumed the King's service; had a few plays performed; and published the *Galatea*. Finally, in the village of Esquivias, near Madrid, he married Catalina de Salazar, who brought him a small dowry. In the same year, a daughter, Isabel de Saavedra, was born to him out of wedlock, by Ana Franca de Rojas. In 1585 he was living in Seville, engaged in some obscure occupation.

At that time Spain was occupied with a new and erratic enterprise: the equipment of the Invincible Armada. This was an immense undertaking that abounded in profit. Cervantes obtained employment in a commissary of provisions, and traveled through Andalusia, requisitioning oil and wheat. But this was inevitably a business full of contention and chicanery, and eventually he fell foul of the Inquisition, which excommunicated him for laying hands on certain stores belonging to the Church. He continued to make his abode in Seville, where he resorted to various expedients to supplement his salary in order to live. In 1590 he tried to enlist for service in the Indies—"usual refuge for the poor in heart"[3]—but he was rejected. Nevertheless, he kept his positions and managed as well as he could. Then irregularities were discovered in his accounts and he was imprisoned at Castro del Rio. In 1594 he held office as tax collector, still in Andalusia. (Such jobs as these were held in popular contempt at that time and Cervantes calls attention to this in his *Novelas Ejemplares*.) Again convicted of fraud, he was sentenced to three months' imprisonment at Seville; his quarrels with the revenue officers began once more, his books were reexamined, and he was again thrown into jail. At last he was sent to Valladolid, where the Court was in residence, for a final settlement of his accounts. There in the suburbs, Cervantes settled down to a sordid and meager existence with those of his family who had accompanied him: his two sisters, Andrea and Magdalena, his natural daughter Isabel, and his niece Constanza, daughter of Andrea. His wife had apparently remained in Esquivias. His officer-brother Rodrigo, who had shared his captivity in Africa, had met his death in Flanders.

In September 1604, Cervantes obtained a permit to print the first part of *Don Quixote*. The book was published in Madrid in 1605, when Cervantes was fifty-seven years old.

Several months later a young nobleman was killed near Cervantes' house in mysterious circumstances reminiscent of those frequently reproduced in his works. Everyone in the house (which today is known as 14 Calle del Rastro) was alarmed, and the alcalde came to suspect that the cause of the murder might well have been one of the women—either Cervantes' sister, Magdalena, or his daughter, Isabel. Eleven of the tenants, including Cervantes and his family, were imprisoned. The Cervantes were finally cleared of all suspicion and set free.

In 1606 the Court returned to Madrid. There Cervantes lived the rest of his life. He had finally married off Isabel, although the husband died almost at once. Isabel remarried, but under fairly complicated conditions, especially in the matter of dowry, which Cervantes guaranteed, thereby adding to his difficulties. He became a member of some religious fraternities, joined a literary academy, and published his last works: *Novelas Ejemplares* (1613), *Viaje del Parnaso* (1614), *Ocho Comedias y Ocho Entremeses Nuevos,* and the second part of *Don Quixote* (1615). On April 19, 1616,—the year Shakespeare died— he dedicated *Persiles y Sigismunda* to the Count of Lemos:

> I could wish that that old once-famous song which begins:
>> "With one foot in the stirrup"
> did not fit so aptly and, as it were, so opportunely into my own epistle.
> For I could well have begun in almost the same way, saying:
>> "With one foot in the stirrup,
>> With the anguish of death in my heart,
>> Noble lord, I write this to you."
> Yesterday I was given extreme unction, and today I write this to you.
> Time is short, anguish grows, hope flies away . . .

He died on April 23rd and was buried in the Trinitarian convent in the Calle de Cantarranas, today known as Calle Lope de Vega.

What literary fame had he known? The theatre that he persisted in writing for had brought him no success. If we consider contemporary opinion, he would seem to have been little esteemed on the whole. Even in the latter part of his life, when he published his masterpieces, he enjoyed scant satisfaction. Nevertheless his name spread abroad, especially in France, where the Spanish fashion was then at its height. Well known is the story of Marquez Torrez, official licenser of the second part of *Don Quixote:* he meets some gentlemen in the French Ambassador's retinue who, as soon as Cervantes is mentioned, hasten to ask: Who is this man? How old is he? What is his profession, his rank and fortune? Before such eager curiosity the Spaniard bows his head.

> I saw myself, he says, obliged to reply that he was old, a soldier, a gentle-man, and poor . . .

Critics have often tried to make Cervantes into a "child of nature," a poor, ignorant fellow who from time to time quotes the classics of literature just to be in the fashion, without understanding them at all. Unquestionably Cervantes is neither learned nor intellectual—certainly not systematic. But he does have within him that receptive quality, that sensitive wealth of the unconscious in which many have seen the very essence of genius. Unamuno has gone to the length of completely ignoring the character of Miguel de Cervantes Saavedra, the more vividly to emphasize the character of Don Quixote—and that of Sancho as well. *Life of Don Quixote and Sancho* is the title he has given to his magnificent exegesis of the sacred book. But this is a purely personal theory without any claim to objectivity, and is valuable only in relation to his own views.

Actually Cervantes, like Shakespeare, or Victor Hugo, or any other creative artist, was entirely aware of what he was about. The variety and subtleties of meaning discovered in his work by the readers of his own century and ever since, were not there by accident; Cervantes expressed these ideas because he felt them, if not explicitly in our terms, at least in his own. Above all, he was clearly a "modern" man who fully participated in contemporary life. The ideas and opinions as well as the conflicts of his time are all embodied in his work, authentic and convincing. We might suppose that he had scarcely time to read. Yet he was not uneducated, and had more or less direct access to the works of Erasmus, Castiglione, León Hebreo, Juan de Valdés, and other celebrated humanists and neo-platonists. He read the moralists, and certainly the great Spaniard, Seneca. Finally, if we read his works without looking for the precise literary sources, we receive the impression of an intelligent, thoughtful man who has learned less from books than from life itself, but who has not been ignorant of literature; and who, like all representative figures, offers us an extensive mirror of the philosophy of his era. We must see Cervantes first as a Renaissance figure, in accordance with the general conception of that period and its typical achievements. Later, we may consider the special influence that his personal life and profound experience, his genius and his masterpieces, have impressed upon our idea of the Renaissance.

It is to the opposite pole of the Spanish Empire, in the home of its antagonists, where I would go to select an illuminating example of the Renaissance spirit. I would borrow this symbol from Pieter Breughel, true man of the Renaissance, philosopher of Nature and *amateur* of folklore. For it is in his painting, *The Land of Cockaigne,* where that characteristic of the new age—the variety of perspective—is shown more strongly than in any other of his works.

Man does not take his place in the universe by divine dispensation. He has emerged from order. He has laid his hands on the planet and made a tour of inspection around it. His emancipated spirit observes and experiences phenomena. He reclassifies them according to the criteria of reason and the dictates of experience. But reason is specific, and experience limited. By a curious boomerang trick, reality becomes less certain the better it is known. Man has discovered Nature but he is also discovering his own mental powers. And God, who used to establish a fixed bond between the two, has retired from the scene.

So the mind projects different views onto Nature. Free examination evokes infinitely varied perspectives. In *The Land of Cockaigne* there is no longer a single eye contemplating the roundness of the globe from a central position, but many eyes. Each dining table, within each separately balanced plane, provides the setting for a different appetite. And there the sleepers lie, each in his own dimensions and his own space, each dreaming his separate, personal dream. These dreams that pursue each other beyond the frontiers of neighboring dreams; these contradictory appetites that open their yawning jaws across worlds to be conquered, while the views over these worlds are varied and opposed; all these elements, sublimely orchestrated, were to produce a new instrument of knowledge, a complex and supple art, even a social weapon: the novel, of which Cervantes gave us the prototype.

Reality changes with the eye of the beholder. The critical mind, freed from the weight of revelation, begins to examine this changing reality, and its first judgment and first assertion will be a doubt. Whom shall I believe, Don Quixote or Sancho? The dukes or Samsón Carrasco? Each to his own truth, Pirandello was to say later.[4] Thus is reality shattered into manifold illusions. What conception of this looking-glass game did Cervantes himself have? An occasional hint slips through to show that he is aware, and is smiling—a word murmured in his sleeve, a lightning flash in the dark. Don Quixote tells Sancho: "What seems to thee a barber's basin seems to me Mambrino's helmet, and to another it will seem something else." (I, 25)

Does Don Quixote here reveal himself in his true colors? Does he actually realize that everything he sees and describes is the stuff of dreams? Does he really believe in the glib fantasies he says he has seen in the cave of Montesinos? And does not even Sancho seem to learn that living, thinking, speaking, and acting are only synonymous with lying? Returning from his celestial journey on the magic horse he tells of a thousand wonders. At one point, when he has finished his story and won a most gratifying response from his audience, his master comes up to him and whispers softly and seriously to him with (perhaps) a very slight wink:

"Sancho, as you would have us believe what you saw in heaven, I require you to believe me as to what I saw in the cave of Montesinos; I say no more." (II, 41)

In *Persiles,* one of the characters, telling his story, claims to have jumped on horseback from the top of a cliff onto a glacier.

> With regard to that leap which he made without any injury, the story seemed a little hard for Mauricio to believe. He would have thought it more natural if the horse at least had broken three or four of its legs, or if Periandro had not left the belief in such a formidable jump up to the courtesy of his audience. But the authority they all accorded Periandro made them dismiss their doubts then and there . . . (II, XX).

We should note that this humorous tone appears in the most serious of Cervantes' work—wherever he yields most completely to his personal demon.

We have only to read the flights of the neo-platonists to see to what mystical heights pure thought can be raised: León Hebreo's *Dialoghi d'amori,* for example; or the sublime ecstasy in the speech of Castiglione's Cardinal Bembo, in the last pages of *Il Cortegiano.* The creation of Dulcinea, and all the adorable and touching vagaries woven around her, which set Don Quixote and Sancho against each other, resulted in this, the highest, most supremely burlesqued form of such metaphysics. Don Quixote knows that Dulcinea is an image and nothing more. Sancho, both ingenuous and shrewd, knows it too. As for Miguel de Cervantes, he knows what extraordinary force dwells within him—a demon, we have called it—and it does indeed appear to be a demoniacal power. In his *Viaje del Parnaso,* he describes himself as "rare inventor," and further on declaims: "I, who surpass all in invention." Yet what rivals he has! How familiar is the realm of invention to the fecund writers of the Golden Age! But Cervantes is confident of surpassing them all.

"Oh, imagination," he exclaims in one of his comedies,[5]
"Imagination, which reaches the most impossible things!"

This free use of the imagination, which the idealist Renaissance, with its golden precepts, its flights of fancy, employed as an educational force, was to be turned by Cervantes into an instrument of joy.

In the meantime it becomes in his work an intellectual means toward his evaluation of truth. He declares that the world is not really what it seems on the whole, for each man views it individually, with the power to embellish and enhance what he sees according to his personal vision. So who is right? The madmen are often wiser than those who believe themselves sane. Who was ever more sensible, nobler, or more human than the madman Don Quixote, or than all the other madmen that people the work of Cervantes, each pursuing his own fantasy: the Licenciado Vidriera, who is full of such witty observations of men and things; or the lovers, who cannot be convinced of their error even when it is obvious to all the world. Then reality gives illusion a peremptory reply, in the face of which the insistent subtleties of madness and imagination are futile. Error is found guilty. Error is punished. In the end the madmen are "proven" wrong.

Once their conception of the universe is destroyed, the madmen cannot rebuild it according to their caprice. And from this emerges a great melancholy, the disillusionment of the new age that is dwelt upon in Dürer's *Melancholia* and symbolized in the blows and insults that rain upon poor Don Quixote and Sancho. The time has not yet come when the mind can accept the diverse views of an endlessly changing universe, thereby to rise above the melancholy contradiction and in it find cause for joy. Later, Leibnitz resolved these diverse conceptions into an affirmation of harmony and hope.[6] But this was a brief, illusory interlude, abruptly to be broken by Voltaire's cynical sneer. This sneer, coming as it did at the end of the "modern" age, on the eve of crises and revolutions, corresponds to the Cervantine bitterness.

However, there was not only bitterness in this moment of dawn. Blows were not the sole reward in this adventure through the myriad contradictions of a divided universe that the intellect embarked upon. Without going as far as the blissful satisfaction of Leibnitz, there was the hope that the abyss between the mind and the object might be bridged one day. It now became possible for identification and adjustment to enter the picture. The Renaissance discovered the capricious powers of the mind, but it also discovered ways to reach reality by using analysis and recognizing the real by means of experience. A great hope arose from the ruins of the Middle Ages.

A reticent and modest wisdom is implied when, like Erasmus and Montaigne, one comes to the conclusion that one knows nothing, and that this fact must be stoically accepted. But Nature does not remain completely deaf to our inquiries. She is not merely an untameable shrew who replies to all our advances with blows; for when that happens it is because we have not known how to approach her. The madmen are wrong, as we have said. But to some others, wise in other ways, Nature can appear a magnificent and generous bride. In such guise she reserves her mysteries for the bold lovers—for such princes of the Renaissance as Giordano Bruno and Rabelais. And her voice is heard throughout the works of Cervantes.

Coming between Erasmus and Montaigne, and Rousseau, Cervantes took up the theme of the Golden Age spoilt by society and civilization. Don Quixote, seated under the trees and holding a handful of acorns, preaches to the goatherds: there *is* a natural order: there *is* harmony between man and nature. In the *Galatea* man is described as "a world in little." And twice—in the same passage in the *Galatea,* and again in *Persiles*—nature is called the "majordomo of God." Then too, in his predilection for love affairs which he conceived according to nature's laws rather than society's, and for the free judgment of the heart, portrayed in his fleeing couples who take refuge in the highway inns and seek the perils of the forest, Cervantes anticipated Molière and that happy theme of youth avenging itself on authority, which often inspires the classical drama and the novel. Secret marriages had been forbidden by the Council of Trent in 1563, but Cervantes frequently abandons formalities and celebrates nocturnal weddings that fulfill nature's vow.

> "Give me your hand, Don Rafael, as a token that you are mine; here I give you my hand and promise you to be yours. And let the sky, the sea, the sand, and this silence be our witnesses . . . " Thereupon Leocadia let him embrace her, and gave him her hand, Don Rafael gave his, and these strange and nocturnal marriage rites were celebrated by the tears which joy drew from their eyes, even though their sad times were over.[7]

And in *Persiles:*

> "Take me in your arms," replied Ruperta, "and you will see that my body is no fantastic illusion, and the soul in it that I yield to you is simple, pure, and true." Croriano's servants, who had come in with the lights, were the witnesses of this embrace and the hands given in troth as man and wife; this night saw the triumph of sweet peace over harsh war, the battlefield was transformed into a bridal bed . . . Day came and found the newly wedded pair in each other's arms. (III, 17)

—A wonderful sleep, secure in the arms of Mother Nature, whom we may view at last with eager and confident eyes, and discover her deep and kindly wisdom. Even in Sancho's everlasting proverbs that he strings together to the despair of Don Quixote, can excellent truths be found, when everything is considered. And if there is something rather touching in the perpetual dialogue between Don Quixote and Sancho, it is perhaps not so much unconscious good nature that makes the realistic Sancho unbend, and finally wins him over to the cause of the ridiculous, as the loyal and brotherly humanity of Don Quixote who makes himself the equal of his lowly squire, and shares with him his time, his trouble, and his discourse.

The reader who is familiar with the diapason of ideas and attitudes of the Renaissance will find its echo through all Cervantes' work. The play of ideas and the hope they give the spirit, the challenge and irony they arouse in the face of the relativity of opinions and the reality of things; on the other hand, a new enthusiasm for nature, instinct, common sense, and freedom: all these opposing elements are evoked at every turn and put to the test in this extraordinarily vivid work. With Cervantes we are perpetually in the presence of ambiguity. "Cervantes' thought," Américo Castro has written,[8] "works like a great pendulum."

Cervantes tells us what is true, both for Don Quixote and for Nature. As for himself, truth swings back and forth—just as it did for society and the universe in that confused period of ruin and dawn. What is his real opinion on the great problems of his day: sorcery, lycanthropy, the miracles, religious orthodoxy, freedom of thought, the expulsion of the Moriscoes? He alludes to all of these in this work, and each time it appears that his judgment hovers between the popular or orthodox opinion and one more thoughtfully reserved and humane. He agrees with official opinion on the expulsion of the Moriscoes, for instance, but he depicts them in a sympathetic and favorable light. Besides, when we know about the innocent jokes the Inquisition suppressed in his work, we can understand his caution. On one occasion, it was a question of hyperbole about some rosary beads; on another, the exchange of harness between two donkeys was compared to the *mutatio caparum*[9] of two cardinals. The rough draft of the "El celoso extremeño" shows that in the first sketch of the plot Carrizales was well and truly cuckolded—a conclusion close to merciless reality. But for publication Cervantes had to temper his realism, and so contrive it that the lover Loaysa does not succeed in conquering the beauty's virtue, but exhausts himself in the struggle and finally falls asleep: a conclusion which cannot fail to appear unlikely but which is certainly moral.

We have said that the thought of the time took refuge in hypocrisy. Cervantes wore a more or less conscious mask before Descartes did. The old man Mauricio in *Persiles* is to Cervantes what Prospero is to Shakespeare: the magician and sage, in whose guise the poet bids farewell to his fantasy, to his imaginative powers, to his winged genii and his enchantments. And Mauricio, in recounting the story of his life, calmly tells us:

> "I followed my country's customs, at least those which seemed the most
> reasonable. As for the others I went through the motions of observing
> them, for dissimulation can be profitable." (I, 12)

One of the pieces in which the critical interplay of reality and illusion reaches its most lively and intoxicating height is undoubtedly the story of "El curioso impertinente," which is introduced into *Don Quixote,* and which for narrative power and psychological depth is one of the marvels of universal art. Anselmo believes blindly in the absolute virtue of his wife. Her virtue is to him an article of faith. But then he is seized by doubt. Would this abstract, unproven virtue withstand trial? Doubt grows into torment, until Anselmo conceives it absolutely necessary for a friend—his best friend, himself a very model of virtue—to put it to the test. The friend at first angrily refuses. But Anselmo insists, his peace of mind at an end. After various vicissitudes the test is made: the woman's virtue is lost. The resulting circumstances carry the story to a tragic close. Then we are assailed and bewildered by a multitude of questions: if experience nullified Anselmo's faith it was surely because his wife was not as virtuous as he believed? Yet we may be sure that when he married her she was perfection itself, and if he had never courted this disastrous trial, the evil would never have occurred. So he should have continued to cling to his illusion—which really *was* only an illusion? For after all, the woman must have carried within her her virtual sin, her fallibility, and therefore was not essentially perfect at all. In this maze of contradictions we must look for the central thought of Cervantes, which is prudent, reserved, and essentially dialectical. There is no absolute transcendental truth. Truth is always relative to a specific reality, to a condition or circumstance, and is verified by life, but not by experience artificially provoked. True experience, or truth that has been lived, consists of a fragile and precious harmony which must be treated with the most charitable reverence, beyond which it is fatal to venture.

It is easy to imagine the enthusiasm that such a complex and subtle art could arouse among the German Romantics. But these idealists could judge it only on the intellectual plane, and appreciate the play of a sovereign mind entertained with reality, and opposing experimental philistinism with continual deceptions. Tieck, in his commentary on "El curioso impertinente," holds that Anselmo came to grief because he wanted to "realize the ideal," and in the attempt "he destroyed the ideal of moral treasure itself." I do not think that in Cervantes' eyes Anselmo was guilty of wanting to realize the ideal. His very century pushed him in that direction. There is no way of resisting a period which is no longer satisfied with the ideals of a preceding age, and which wishes to grasp palpable and verifiable realities. Experience must be sought, but we must also know at what point it becomes dangerous, and meet it then with a tranquil heart and a simple confidence in nature and the future. The young wife of Anselmo is certainly no abstract idea. She is a creature of flesh and blood. But life must be given time to adapt itself to the passing days, and to the temptations and errors which can arise. The ideal and the real do not have to be imposed brutally on each other. A gradual harmony should be born from their interaction. Experience, accepted and integrated, should produce a new wisdom.

A crumbling and disintegrating society takes on a legendary aspect in the mind. Feudalism came to be transformed into fable; and a painful nostalgia grew in the hearts of those who experienced the change. Cervantes the soldier, the hero of Lepanto, the captive of Algiers, carries the appeal of a time when adventurous exploits were considered gratuitous, fabulous, and all-powerful. But Cervantes also came up against a very unpleasant reality, and there was no magician to let him out of the prisons into which he was thrown for absurd and paltry offenses.

Through the dialectical working of history it was an invention of the new age—the printing press—that helped to establish and illustrate the chimerical symbol of the Dark Ages. Printing gave wings to the modern spirit, but at the same time crystallized the past under a seductive form, palpitant with regret and appeal. What did the men who were destined to transform the thought of mankind do with their energy? They read novels of chivalry. Listen to this passage from the *Diálogo de la lengua,* by the arch-heretic Juan de Valdés:

> *Marcio.* You have read them?
> *Valdés.* Yes, indeed.
> *Marcio.* All of them?
> *Valdés.* All of them.
> *Marcio.* How is it possible?
> *Valdés.* During the ten years, the best of my life, that I spent in palaces and courts, I busied myself with no more virtuous occupation than reading these lies, and I found so much to relish in them that I ate my own hands (in the process).

I translate this Spanish idiom literally so as not to rob Valdés' statement of any of its passionate tone. It is strange to consider this powerful union of a new invention especially designed for change, with the nostalgic urge toward an illusory past. The power of the printed word, before being applied to reality and transforming it, created an ideal zone beyond reality, where all the wild fancies of the heart are given free rein. Innumerable bewitching fantasies are unfolded there, containing their own validity, their connections and consequences—as well as their own internal logic, necessity, and irresistible pleasure. While the will slumbers, the eyes of the heart follow the hallucination with insatiable demand; and when one is over, another immediately begins again. This is in truth a fascination comparable to that of another marvelous invention of our own time—the cinema.

The chivalric novel sprang from a union of very ancient fantasies: Milesian fables, Byzantine stories, the remains of the Arthurian romances, becoming more and more fragmentary and reduced to lays, and the Carolingian epics, equally disintegrated into romances or transformed into prose chronicles. But we should note one thing, as historians of Spanish literature particularly Menéndez y Pelayo, have already pointed out: that, of these two great streams, Spain was open particularly to the second, the Carolingian cycle. She resisted the matière bretonne except in Galicia and Portugal, which are Celtic countries and whose characteristics allying them to Britain have often been noted. In these countries the messianic nature of Arthur is confused with the myth of

King Sebastian and his future return. It is indeed very probable that *Amadís* came from the Atlantic region of the peninsula: in fact, the Portuguese origins of this romance are almost certain.

Bonilla y San Martín, confirming the observation of Menéndez y Pelayo, notes that the Carolingian element is predominant over the Breton in Don Quixote's library. Similarly, we may say that the commonplace predominates over the mysterious, the artificial over the real, and the simple over the complex. The *Baladro del Sabio Merlin,* which the French call *Brait de Merlin,* is certainly far from unknown to Don Quixote, who quotes it. The famous enchanter even appears in the more or less farcical phantasmagoria for which the Dukes' castle and park provide an obliging setting. But there are curious and vivid inconsistencies in the Merlin legend which resist the simplifications that a fascinated imagination looks for in the chivalric stories. To satisfy the mind's automatism we need a narrative that may certainly be complicated in its details but which must be very elementary in its general lines, and based simply, in the last analysis, on the well-defined opposition of good and evil. It was for good versus evil, for the Cross versus the Crescent, that Cervantes fought at Lepanto. The living complexities of politics certainly contradict this rigid manichaeism, and in the maelstrom of real causes and effects the minute figure of Cervantes, as chivalric a hero as one could wish, actually counts for very little. But his imagination comes into its own in the childish, unfathomable, enchanting, and magic dream where the good, pure, innocent knight triumphs over the forces of evil.

A clear example of this manichaeism appears at the beginning of the *Baladro de Merlin,* where the *Primera Parte de la Demanda del Sancto Grial* opens with a council of demons organizing themselves against good and creating Merlin to oppose Jesus Christ. But everything immediately becomes confused and ambiguous. The Breton tradition contains secrets profoundly different from the simple ideas of good and evil. Beyond the dualism we can detect an idea of unity underlying the infernal doctrines. Merlin is not, as one might superficially suppose, the simple incarnation of evil, but represents an equivocal power, capable of a curious good nature under his many disguises. Alchemy, on numerous material and moral levels, gives an account of variously complex conflicts opposed to the hieratic concept of good and evil; and I should not be surprised if this symbolic tradition were expressed in certain passages of the Baladro.[10] But the romance reader's imagination does not thirst for these forbidden secrets. It wishes to remain among the elementary struggles between angels and devils, between the forces that are willing to give miraculous help and those that can be gloriously defeated: the two hosts that Loyola dreamed of when, wounded and lying in his chair, he read romances and envisioned the glories of future exploits. I find the same symbol of Jesuit polemics in the prologue of the *Palmerín de Inglaterra:*

> "And although some people attack and deprecate these stories of chivalry, saying that they are a bad example to those who read them, it is necessary for them to learn, as the sage says, that there are two hosts in the world . . . ."

Stripped of their profundities, the successful romances will become mere compilations, rich in matter and poor in spirit, that satisfy simple, naïve tastes: such are the romances that make up the series of the *Palmerín* and *Amadís,* or the prolix creations of Feliciano de Silva, "the great manufacturer of literature" whom Menéndez y Pelayo compares with Alexandre Dumas *père*. Such creations provide facile food for dreams, and a setting that no longer conceals any allegorical significance. Pompous and formula-ridden as befits a mechanical literature, their style was to be developed later in newspaper serials and melodramas and generally in the conventional, standardized literature designed for mass production and popularization. The picture of life that these novels present is one of daily ritual, when each day is set apart from the ordinary run of living and becomes a festival, for the celebration of nothing but tournaments, masses, feasts, rites, and ceremonies.

Between this popularized form and the romance of mythical origin, heavy with obscure organic secrets, at the crest of the two slopes of religion and mechanization, of obscure collective mystery and facile collective method, art has its seat. There is one masterpiece of art among the chivalric romances, a living creation where the myth is accepted and submitted to, but kept in the background with its train of ancient enigmas; where the mind is not given up to passive and common day-dreams, but where the material is deliberately controlled by an individual genius that gives it form, decides its scope, embellishes it, and endows it with order and harmony. The mass, the majority of people, will undoubtedly achieve their identity with the unified whole, but at the same time they will have experienced the individual fantasy of the artist. This book is *Amadís*.[11]

Amadís is one of the great events in literary history: it is the synthesis in artistic form of all the aspects under which a new age dreams of the preceding one. We will set aside the problem of the first version of the book—an obscure problem which, as we have mentioned in passing, seems to be resolved in favor of Portugal. Let us select the edition published in 1508—the *Amadís* of Montalvo —the earliest we have—and let us consider its artistic perfection, its style, its conception of the world, and its fame and significance as a cultural phenomenon. In particular, let us direct our attention to that apotheosis of Amadís, the prophecy of Urganda in Book IV, proving that the idealism of chivalric romance

reaches the same delirious abandon as that of the humanist neo-platonic literature. In this connection Menéndez y Pelayo has also evoked Vives and Erasmus,
the knight-errants of humanism and morality. We will hear, too, the echo that
this speech produced in the mind of Don Quixote.

Don Quixote, child of the Middle Ages, is also born of the Renaissance. It is
his desire to revive the former, but at the same time he aspires to create for himself a new life. He knows that the ways to glory are numerous now. It is true
that he gives the palm to arms above letters; nevertheless his age teaches him
that the latter can also be a royal road to fame. And then the pastoral life too
is heroic and beautiful. How often have he and Sancho dreamed of abandoning
dragons and battles in order to become shepherds and to sing ballads! In this
nostalgic look backward towards chivalry, the important thing is to show the
power of ideas, and that man creates his own glory. This theme of fame, with its
theological and metaphysical implications of life after death, is stressed by
Unamuno in his commentary. But let us listen to Urganda's prophecy:

> Lead a new life and take care to rule rather than to fight battles as you
> have done up to now . . . Leave arms for him to whom the supreme
> judge grants great victories . . . For your high feats of arms, so renowned
> in the world, will be dead among his; in the same way many ignorant
> people will say that the son killed his father, but I, I say that it had
> nothing to do with this natural death to which we are all bound, but a
> death that passes over all other worse dangers and all other worse tor-
> ments, and wins so great a glory that the glory of men past is forgotten,
> and if anything remains to them it is neither glory nor renown but their
> shadow. (IV, 52)

In *Amadís* and its idealism the chivalric novel reached its zenith, achieving a
synthesis where the themes of the past were reborn in the ambitions of the
present. Later poets utilized the work as material for their art, combining its
idealistic themes with irony or melancholy, according to the temperament of the
artist—of Ariosto, perhaps, or Tasso—and the spirit of the time: the jubilation
of the Renaissance, or the contradictory and decadent lyricism of the baroque
period. The artist no longer believed in the fables: he used them because they
entertained or consoled him.

But art was not enough to satisfy Don Quixote. He was not a contemplative
man, neither was he a sybarite or a dilettante. He was a tormented man, who
wished to be diverted and intoxicated. He really loved these naïve and artificial
romances far more than prose masterpieces or poems, and more than the melancholy oracles from the very beginning. He longed for the enchanting vistas of
that fantastic fiction-land where his critical spirit could sleep and his somnam-
bulant imagination browse. Did not his creator, Cervantes, spend his full and
restless lifetime dreaming that one day he himself might be able to write a novel

of chivalry better than all the rest—yes, even more fantastic, more extravagant! It is true that in *Don Quixote* Cervantes has written a satire on the romance, but at bottom he was primarily a writer of chivalric romances. He lacked only the courage—and perhaps the time. For it is possible in time to satirize the things we love—that is, to adjust to life. But to confess what is loved is fatal, because we dare not expose our secret in the face of ridicule, and so shatter our self-respect. In fact, Cervantes did not write his real book until the eve of his death, and he was dead before it was published: "With one foot in the stirrup, with the anguish of death in my heart . . . " Then he released his secret in *Trabajos de Persiles y Sigismunda*.

Much has been said in our own time about automatic writing. Real automatic writing is found in this fascinating and inspired literature of chivalry, which perhaps made it flow the more freely. These fancies, as the canon says in *Don Quixote*: " . . . offer a wide and spacious meadow through which the pen may run without any hindrance."

And while he lets his pen run dizzily on, Cervantes makes his adventures live: not those he can contemplate from this point in his real life, not even the exploits of Lepanto and the Algerian captivity, for they were followed by the imprisonments in La Mancha and so many petty and even ludicrous misfortunes; but the past adventures of fabulous times. Past? Now Don Quixote is annoyed and exasperated. But it is true—they are past! Are not the giants windmills, and the castle an inn whose host exacts his reckoning in ringing coin? Impossible! Don Quixote will make the past live again, revive it in all its reality, seize the mechanism and set it going in reverse, accomplish that miracle that another somnambulist was to try in our time—he who also wavered on the verge of two epochs, and who called his work *A la Recherche du Temps Perdu*.

A seventeenth-century author tells the following story, illustrating the eagerness with which readers of both sexes entertained themselves with knighterrantry and the adventures of olden time:

> A gentleman on his return home found his wife and daughters and their maids in tears. He was much surprised, and asked anxiously if some child or relative of theirs was dead. They said "No" through their sobs. His perplexity growing, he cried, "But why do you weep, then?" They replied, "Sir, Amadís is dead."[12]

A bitter-sweet taste is left by those stories which are witnesses of the passing of one epoch into another quite different. In the same way there lingers in the memory the enigmatic tale of the mariner of antiquity who heard of the great Pan's death. Don Quixote has donned his armor, and dreams of launching forth again on the exploits to which the chimerical spirit calls him from the depth of time. But it is a new age that he would strive against. Amadís is dead, even as the great Pan died. The time is forever lost.

The hierarchical order of a society characterized by feudalism and guilds gave place to a freer, wider world, where the impetus of capitalism encouraged the growth of individual personality. Just as everyone from then on had his own point of view, so everyone had his own destiny: each had his intellectual view of the world, and found his own way to attack this world or to submit to it. The adventures that befell the knight-errant going off to war took place only according to predestined ritual. Don Quixote, in Chapter XXI of Part I, recites it with his eyes shut to the astonished Sancho: "Thou needst not doubt it, Sancho, for in the same manner, and by the same steps as I have described here, knights errant rise and have risen to be kings and emperors . . . " (I, 21)

For the characters of medieval literature are not individuals but types. For them too their paths are laid out. There is the monk, the merchant, the hermit and the saint. Tristan, alone, perhaps—a Celt, again—escapes the ready-made molds, and his passion, destroyer of order, is revolutionary.[13]

From now on, mankind, violently dislodged by centrifugal force, wanders across a planet it has discovered to be huge and in motion, and finds itself confronted by reality. And while the nostalgic fancy of Cervantes recreates adventures that happen automatically, on the other hand, his personal experience leads him to create the kind of novel where varied and contradictory destinies play their game with and against reality.

For the formulation of this new realist philosophy, Cervantes borrowed Stoic maxims, revived by the moralists of the time, who continually held forth on the question of how far we are masters of our fate. Cervantes' emphasis on this theme, which recurs frequently in his work, together with what we know of his personal history, and what we know from other sources of how strongly he felt the attraction of the past, all lend his declaration a special value. This is where the true heroic character of Cervantes becomes apparent, his *amor fati,* as well as his constant faith in man.

When a moralist asserts that man is the master of his fate—"artífice de su ventura," as Don Quixote says (II, 66)—we have a truism that has no meaning apart from the caliber of the speaker. When the speaker is Cervantes, whose genius is essentially dialectical, the saying takes on a positive vitality. Cervantes dreamed of giving himself up to the soothing and sleep-walking movement of the past. But he also suffered and submitted to the blows of fate with patience and steadfastness. So we must listen to him with especially respectful attention when he says in *Persiles:* "We mold our destiny ourselves, there is no soul that is not capable of raising itself to its rightful place . . . " (II, 12)

And in the *Viaje del Parnaso,* which is, I repeat, his personal confession, and where he speaks most freely about himself, we may hear him describe himself as a poet, with all the humility that the term implies:

> Poets are made of gentle stuff
> Smooth, flexible and tender . . .
> . . . .
> Absorbed in their fantasies . . .
> Weeping over wars or singing over loves,
> Life passes for them like a dream
> Or as time does for players . . .

It was this dreamer and player, this weak and defenseless poet, who was to wander through the wide theatre of the world (as it was to be known henceforth), proclaiming the merit of mankind, and matching his will against unconquerable circumstances:

> Against my brief fate I do not fret
> But seeing myself upright as I do
> And in such a place, I weigh my loss against its gain . . .
> . . . . . .
> Perhaps a happy state,
> When chance refuses it without reason,
> Confers honor when more deserved than attained.

Apollo speaks. And then comes a superb Spanish gesture:

> . . . You yourself have forged your adventure.
> . . . But if you wish to leave your quarrel,
> Joyfully, unashamed and reconciled
> Fold up your cloak and sit upon it.

When Apollo has finished his speech, Poetry appears, apparelled in the bright tints of Spring, and offers the poor poet laurels and consolation. But poetry, more than mere consolation or compensatory illusion, is the sublime expression of shared experience, echoing recognition in the hearts of men. Cervantes projected his desires outside himself but he also connected them with the reality of his intimate experience. His work is that of a man who was both constrained and a vagabond, and is fabricated out of this very opposition. The ancient social order was broken, and with it the religious order, the bond which united the whole animate and inanimate world. The new man saw himself compelled to doubt. "To be or not to be" he asks in Hamlet's words. As long as he was part of the given scheme of things he did not have to ask himself that question. But now he exists, an entity, by himself. If he is unable to find a place for himself in the new system, he consequently sinks into oblivion and exists no more. However, let us grant that he exists. What then? He exists alone. The new man is alone.[14] Alone with his destiny, alone with the peculiar conditioning which binds him to an exhausted and dying world. Alone and poor. As soon as man is led to ask himself the metaphysical question about his existence, he immediately has to leave metaphysics and add an attribute to his verb to be, an attribute that is physical, real, and economic. What is this new, modern man? Poor and lonely. When Don Quixote is separated from Sancho and finds himself in the guest chamber in the Dukes' castle, he feels poorer and more lonely than ever. (II, 44)

"Wonderful conjunction," here exclaims the commentator Unamuno, "that the historian has wished to establish between the solitude and poverty of Don Quixote! Poor and lonely! We can still endure poverty if we have company or solitude if we have wealth, but poor and lonely! ... "[15]

From this poverty and solitude, from this terrible reality with which he had felt, lived, and fought, Cervantes draws the substance of his work. Realism, certainly; but it is not enough to understand by this word the artistic formula of observing external reality, for it is in fact a lyrical realism, that implies a constant relationship—a constant engagement—between the poet and reality. If he had not been so deeply involved with this reality, he would not have displayed so much eagerness in escaping from it. He denies it, he opposes it with his fantasies, with the return to the past, with the charms of his imagination. But he also plunges back into it, for the *alguaciles* are there, the bailiffs of the Holy Office, the treasury agents and the alcaldes, as well as the aspirant to knighthood, Sansón Carrasco, with his common sense, the priest with his good faith, the niece who has to be fed, and the farthing that falls out of the poor hidalgo's stocking when he finds himself in the castle-of-riches and cries: "Oh poverty, poverty!" His destiny rejoins the destinies of other men, each with its own pattern: Sancho, the honest, good, lovable Sancho; Maritornes whose heart is really as tender as it is gay: who else? Those men who pass by in chains: Who are these men? What is their fate? Are they not also constrained, obliged, forced? Yes, they are convicts, "gente forzada del rey"—a chain of prisoners on their way to the galleys *by force of the King's orders.* "How by force?" asked Don Quixote; "is it possible that the king uses force against any one?" (I, 22)

If his consideration of constraining circumstances and his naturistic impulse do not yet lead Cervantes to the conception of justice, at least his work is the first in the history of modern literature that seems to have felt a breath of universal sympathy, simply because of this perpetual sense of the inescapable attachment of man to his fate. Even though this destiny does not manage to triumph over circumstances, even though it is a defeated destiny, it is still man's destiny, miserable perhaps but never servile, where man knows himself and which grows fat on resistance and pride. If we go back with Américo Castro to the gamut of ideas through which Cervantes declared himself to be a new man, we will see in his theory of sin—a theory no longer applied on an intellectual level, but on a moral and practical one, on the level the Marxists call "praxis"—that sin is still an expression of man, and that suffering is inherent to him. Similarly with the idea of honor; we notice that this idea, which was so rooted in the primitive social and religious system of Spain, loses its ritual and transcendental rigidity with Cervantes. This rigidity is found again fifty years later in the plays of Calderón, works of a retrogressive, reactionary, and decadent genius that resemble revivals of the miracle plays in all their primitive and hieratic splendor. But Cervantes—discounting the reservations dictated by prudence, and without trying to make him into a bold thinker or a philosopher ahead of his time, but rather allowing him his position as a man of his age who expressed his temporal experience with supreme force—Cervantes, then, does not submit to any transcendental demand, but only recognizes the conflict wherein man moves and has his being, acted upon by the real and reacting upon it. And so in the idea of honor—a mystical idea—he sees simply the opinion that a man forms of his personal dignity and of the merit of his own actions. Everywhere Cervantes, freed from superstition—without fanfare or parade, with scarcely any theoretical explanation, and by nothing more than the way in which he communicates his experience—shows himself to be the first of the moderns.

He does not mention justice, then, nor pity, nor revolt. His maxims are borrowed from the moralists who were more or less generally read at the time. But there is the breadth of universal sympathy in his creations, there is tremendous animation, a fresh and virginal sense of life, and an irresistible affection for independence, a leaning toward the happy life led by gypsies, lovers, shepherds, madmen, adventurers, thieves, and rogues.

With a mincing air the little gypsy raises her fragile, dancing silhouette, taps her tambourin, and sings her pretty song to the four winds of freedom. This love of the bohemian life was to provide haven for another vagabond a few years later: Jacques Callot, an artist with a Cervantine strain, who sought refuge in his turn from the sadness of his age and from the horrors of war. From the same source springs a complete Romantic tradition: the bohemian myth—to which I would not hesitate to add the names of Lenau and Liszt, and which found its classic expression in Spain in the famous (if not too famous) *flamenquismo*. The caprice, the unpredictable nervousness of gesture, the improvisations, the art of having a reply to everything, the indomitable fantasy, the impetuous irrepressibility, the deep song—*cante jondo*—the free song, the song quivering with all the trills, vibrations, and everything that the inalienable personal temperament can abandon itself to, together with the walk in the sunshine when the eye is forever intoxicated by a horizon that forever recedes, the wandering path, the rest by the stream, the refusal, the flight and counterflight, the denial and reply, the blessed indifference: all these themes already have their first draft in Cervantes. There we are aware for the first time of the attraction of this music.

Cervantes' naturism, his opposition to the constraints of society, is two-faced like the other attitudes of this ambiguous genius. From the intellectual part springs the joy of knowledge, the discovery that reality can be experienced, participation in that spirit that penetrates the hidden forces of matter and is imbued with its principles. But simultaneously there appears on the ideal plane that same need for escape from the reality of a disorganized narrow and cruel society, that had led Cervantes toward the novel of chivalry, and which now leads him toward the pastoral novel.

Nature is a new source of both knowledge and action. But she is also a refuge. That is how she appears to Don Quixote, and to so many lovers who have gone mad. Even in the Middle Ages the two characters who (as we have seen) had broken with the categories and social norms of the system—Merlin and Tristan—have known this state of wild delirium, anarchic rebellion, despairing solitude, and the frenzy that seizes the soul when it is removed from human conflicts and renews its contact with rocks, springs, and woods. They went mad in the hearts of forests, just as do the characters of the opulent Renaissance: Orlando Furioso, the melancholy Jacques in *As You Like It,* the Ragged One of the Sierra Morena (*Don Quixote,* I, 23–24), and Don Quixote himself, who gives himself up to the extravagant penances that affect Sancho so greatly (I, 25 *passim*). Here the naturism of the Renaissance shows itself in literary themes: madness in the forest, the Golden Age, pastoral lyricism. And Montemayor's *Diana,* also of Portuguese origin, plays the same rôle as *Amadís:* it is the greatest artistic transcription of these themes.

But Cervantes understood the new reality more deeply and more completely. Throughout his life, and in the more sanguinary and carnal parts of his book, he communicates the chief experience of contemporary Spain, an experience that originated there: the picaresque.

Here there is no recourse, no changing over to a spiritual plane: we are concerned only with a man involved with reality, with a hard and terrible reality, a man buffeted about and defending himself, and extracting from this struggle and torment, a vital philosophy, an expression of life. He is no longer escaping. He is no longer dreaming. He is caught. He embraces his destiny and tries to understand it.

Miguel de Cervantes was not a "pícaro." But during his sad career he came fairly close to being one. He knew the wisdom of rogues. He lived among them. The mysteries of Seville held no secrets from him. He understood the jargon of these people and their tricks and dodges. He spent many long hours in Monipodio's hide-out.

Here too, in order to understand properly the genius of Cervantes, that "rare inventor," we must look at his background and consider that if he has invented a great deal he has also acted as an extraordinarily sensitive mirror of his age. The picaresque, like the chivalric or the baroque, is a way of life, a way of thinking and feeling that is peculiar to the age, and we must look for signs or proofs of it outside Cervantes. The admirable thing about Cervantes is that he has brought together all these varied modes in his work without omissions, and, with an emphasis that is all his own, he has blended them into an extraordinarily original symphony. Cervantes is both a rare inventor and a complete symbol of his century.

The picaresque ethos was compounded of a mixture of stoicism and cynicism; we shall consider it now as it appears in a great book of the time, Mateo Alemán's *Guzmán de Alfarache,* the first part of which was published in 1599.

"I, Sir . . . " Guzmán begins, and it is with these words that all picaresque novels begin. A man speaks and tells the story of his fate. And what a fate! What a world he sees himself involved in! He has no illusions about this society. "Everyone steals, everyone lies . . . You will find nobody who will act as man to man . . . " (I, 2, 4)

No literature has been more cruelly lucid, nor more deliberately pessimistic than the picaresque. "This road traverses the world . . . Let no one hope for better times, nor start imagining that the past was better . . . The first father was dishonest . . . " (I, 3, 1).

We are reminded of Breughel again, for the pícaro is close to him when he speaks of the fish: "The big ones eat the little ones" (II, 2, 7). In the midst of this hell a man can only follow his destiny, extricate himself as well as possible, imitate others, keep himself in hand, and understand—as the pícaro says so splendidly—how to be "the usufructuary of his life." This indeed is the lesson that the new and formidable power, reality, teaches man. Be the usufructuary of your life, it tells him, for it will not be restored by a transcendental providence whose patterns follow a comprehensible end. Your life is dependent wholly on circumstances. Either divorce it from them or come to terms with them. Work with them. You and reality. You and the world. You are alone. It is up to the two of you now.

To the two of you! the rogue says. The same cry was repeated later by another hero of fiction, Rastignac, who also sprang from a disintegrating society. But the sixteenth-century rogue is not out for success. To be able to eat is enough for him, and to avoid the gallows in particular. Otherwise he is happy: he does no work; he sings *seguidillas,* he busies himself occasionally with a few operations that are "non sanctas."

"Sir," Rinconete politely asks the porter he met in the Seville marketplace, "are you perhaps a thief?" "Yes, to serve God and the good people . . ."[16]

It is with a sort of pious resignation that one must accept all the necessities of this hazardous but marvelous existence—marvelous because it brings great happiness with it. "To enjoy liberty, to live content . . . " are the opening words of a contemporary sonnet entitled "Description of a Poor Pícaro's Life"[17]. And how well Cervantes understands those two students in his story "La Ilustre Fregona," who, instead of going to Salamanca to study, as the old fogies, their fathers, commanded, leave their tutor on the way, turn their bridles and take the road to that magic world that spread its net over all Spain and which Cervantes has mapped so clearly for us!

> Oh kitchen knaves, filthy and shining with grease, false paupers, sham cripples, thieves of Zocodover, feigned blindmen and sayers of prayers, porters of Seville, pimps and vagabonds and the whole innumerable train of those who go under the name of "pícaro"! Lower your flag, surrender arms, and do not pride yourself on this title unless you have taken a two years' course at the academy of tunny fishing; that is where work triumphs through laziness, there you see real society, plump fatness, prompt hunger, abundant satiety, unmasked vice, gambling always, quarrels now and then, murder from time to time, abuse at every step, as many balls as at a wedding, plenty of *seguidillas,* tales of chivalry, unrestrained poetry. Here they sing, there they curse, further on they argue, elsewhere they gamble, and everywhere they steal; here liberty is encamped and work sparkles; there more than one famous father goes or sends someone to find his children, and finds them as sorry to be torn from this life as if they were being led to their death.

Under Cervantes' pen the hell that Guzmán de Alfarache plunged into becomes a paradise. Beneath the crude reality, where society exhibits its most voracious and pitiless practices, there appeared a new refuge. The golden age that Cervantes projected in the pastoral ideal, the chivalric dream, and the heroic fantasies are found again here; but this time it is confident, possible, and really free in the picaresque life. Order reigns there finally, and harmony, and a just and humane law. We pass from the cave of Montesinos to that of Monipodio, and we find happiness. Is Cervantes joking—or being sarcastic? Is this a new form of irony and ambiguity? But everything goes so well in Monipodio's den! The customs are so gentle under appearances that are occasionally rather violent . . . Everything comes right there. The *alguacil* himself is reconciled to the thieves. And after all, the principles, codes, points of honor, and superstitions that are important among the robbers are worth as much as the maxims and morals that an honest society is founded on. Are not all things relative? The theme is familiar, it is one of the most famous in the critical irony of the Renaissance, but with the golden pen of Cervantes it takes on extraordinary life and zest.

In any case, we have come to the end of the dialectical experience that we undertook with this indefatigable companion. The ideal, the illusion, the sleep-walker's vision, the sprightly dream, the pastoral romance, are rejected and abolished. They are no more than shadows, or smoke. Cervantes is merely a poor man, very poor and very lonely, facing a terrible reality that drags him from prison to prison with his family, his paltry worries, his bickerings, his perpetual stories of ducats and maravedis. The wretched lodgings, the comedies that failed, the unanswered petitions, the shameful existence: a sad world, this new one that so many others hailed with such joy, and which heralded the knowledge of the globe, of the human body, of matter and life; the liberation of thought, the reign of nature and reason. A sad world, which one penetrates even further as one sinks to the lower ranks of society, among those who have nothing except their ingenuity and lack of scruples. Illusions are dead indeed. What could Amadís do in the infamous den of Monipodio? And yet at the core of this true reality the imagination awakens again, and smiling, resumes its dreaming. All is well; if the chivalric ideal is no longer possible there is still the picaresque—the golden age of adventurers and beggars . . .

Opening *Don Quixote* at random, I come upon a passage of conversation between Don Quixote and Sancho. I can hear their voices, see their gestures and faces. It is little enough to remark that this book is alive, evocative, and sug-gestive. Speaking for myself I know that I have known Don Quixote and Sancho forever, and will go on knowing them until I die. It seems to me that none of the people who have been my companions all this time have ever comforted me with words so full of kindness and humanity as these two have.

The other things which interest Cervantes are depicted no less truly and nobly than his hidalgo and his squire. The roads, the very walls, the verdure, the sun-light, and the night—all Spain, in fact—capture and take full possession of our senses when Cervantes mentions or describes them. Animals also have their characteristic features and their place. Because of all this we can say that Cervantes was an extraordinary artist, the greatest artist, with Velázquez, that his country has produced. He was not a thinker, philosopher, nor mystic, neither was he a one-sided man carried away by his speculative thoughts and unbalanced by them, straining to construct strange things outside himself. He was certainly (as he himself boasted) a rare inventor who outdid all his colleagues on Parnassus in imagination. But this imagination, recaptured by reality, set out to

contrive real forms, to place solid objects against a vast blue sky similar to the one the great Andalusian painter was to depict later in Madrid, and finally to make human beings talk to other human beings. And all this after the manner of the surest and wisest of professions: as a poet who understands the subtleties of language, the appropriateness of terms, the elegance of rhythms and word order, the impact and enhancement of a word well placed, the word that gives light and shade, that touches the reader's skin, rings in his ear, comes back to his tongue, tucks itself into his memory and takes root there.

This knowledge Cervantes possesses and uses with unique sureness of touch. Nothing is ever superfluous in his work. He expresses himself seriously, solemnly, and bombastically, in the Spanish manner. But this bombast is never unpleasing as it is with many Spanish authors. Some mystery of economy sees to it that it is not branded as useless. Nothing, I repeat, is gratuitous or superfluous in Cervantes, not even superabundance; for the extravagance of his style provides an element of contrast, and consequently of comedy. There is always this organic dualism of his mind that is so intimate and admirable. The style is always fine, often too fine; but in that excess dwells a hidden purpose. We must watch, then, follow the twisting phrases attentively, and finally listen with all our ears to the pause in the music.

A great artist reveals himself by demanding a constant vigilance of this sort; we always have to pay attention to him. If he used this word it is because he meant to; and that turn of phrase, because he thought it fine. If he mentions something, it is necessary and significant. There is nothing more delightful than the cadence, harmony, and fulness of a Cervantine sentence. Reading aloud in Spanish the description of the armies drawn up in the plain that Don Quixote sees from a hilltop, instead of a flock of sheep, is one of the highest oratorical and musical treats that can be enjoyed. (I, 18)

I speak of the musical pleasure that Cervantes gives. It should really be emphasized that this creator and conjurer of concrete things, of figures and landscapes, this elder brother of Velázquez is a musician as well. His work presents a completely musical organization with its long sentences, the tempo of which opens majestically, and sweeps forward according to the circumstances. And in the pastoral interludes the lyrical flow is joined by the indefinable symmetry of ballet or opera as the characters introduce themselves vocally, singing a romance. Here Cervantes and Shakespeare meet; Sancho gives a real Shakespearean answer to the Duchess, who is surprised to hear the unusual sound of an orchestra in the forest: "Where there is music, lady, there can be no evil." (II, 34)

Since there is always music in Cervantes we shall never find anything evil in his work. Even when the poor man complains of life, it is without bitterness or hatred. His smile is the passive smile of understanding: it stops short of the sarcasm of the grimace, at the boundary which would be leaped by the terrible, gnashing Quevedo in the realm of the picaresque. The filth and nausea, all the magnificent color of bile and excrement that satirical Spain uses in its painting, is present in Cervantes, but moderately, and never shocking. He is humorous, true, familiar, courageous; a master of irony and even of cynicism; yet at the same time he covers his world with a veil of exquisite delicacy. I take him for a man of better company than Rabelais, Montaigne, and Shakespeare, more of a gentleman—yes, more gentlemanly, more elegant, noble, and discreet (in the contemporary Spanish sense of the word—*discreto*—implying all the delicacies of the heart and mind). And this gentlemanliness enables him to appear good without being ridiculous—ideally good. The *goodness* of Cervantes is his most striking characteristic. It is a brotherly, Christian goodness that illuminates every one of his characters. Maritornes is good when she brings Sancho a jug of water after he has been tossed in the blanket. And Sancho is divinely good when he weeps for his donkey. Beneath the self-interest and passion there is always the possibility for charity. Cervantes is not deceived. He knows there are evil and ungrateful people. As soon as Don Quixote's back is turned, the cruel farmer begins whipping his victim again, in spite of his sworn promise (I, 31); and the freed galley slaves stone their liberator (I, 22). But Cervantes still maintains his calm; he is not at all disillusioned, but full of confidence in the resources of universal sympathy and in the radiating strength of the heart. Don Quixote resumes his tireless career, offering afresh to anyone who will listen the teaching of his gentle and crazy wisdom. In a century that was as sanguinary as it was golden, Cervantes ignores to a surprising extent the violence and vengeance that are the pleasures of dominion and cruelty.

Nothing can prevent Cervantes' delightful spirit from dreaming, even in the midst of his worst misfortunes. He is the first to have discovered reality, and the shock left a lasting impression on him. All the blows that are constantly inflicted on Don Quixote's bony carcass resound in him. Everywhere he knocks against things. When he is wandering at night in Toboso looking for the palace of the incomparable Dulcinea, we see that great scarecrow of a figure, too big for the pigstys and stables that make up the village, come suddenly into a tower. "It's the church we have lit upon, Sancho . . . " (II, 9). Cervantes sometimes runs into the Church, the Holy Office and its bailiffs, the social code, the authority, wealth, egoism, and incomprehension of the real world. His dreams were no longer of this world. Other dreamers were to come, and their dreams are still not of it.

Cervantes does not look to the future. He remains content in the present, which he endows with amazing life and integrity. This is where his experience is exemplary and revolutionary, a constant object lesson that will be perpetually relived. At every turn he puts an aspect of reality before us, and then balances it with a dream, a regret, a sigh, or a smile. Reality wins, of course, but the situation remains. Other dialecticians will teach us to draw a reason for action from this play of ideas.

Cervantes does not act. He dies, broken, after he has exhausted his greatest dream and his sleepwalker's art in *Persiles*. A year earlier he had made Don Quixote die—after he had really made him live. Don Quixote dies disillusioned, restored to reality—but to the reality of his priest and his niece, the reality of the aspirant Sansón Carrasco. He dies resigned.

The secret of all life and rebirth lies in the experience of reality that is followed to its logical conclusion, and accompanied by a dream directed chiefly toward the future, rather than by a dream that is retrogressive and extravagant. The fact that ideas have power inspires a healthy confidence, and Don Quixote's generous and noble idea is one that can be used effectively, especially when this personal code and caprice of a sublime madman are joined by the countryman's instinct. For Sancho, the humble and practical peasant, was the only one who would consent to follow the madman and submit to his fantasies. Sometimes even poor Sancho is afraid of the boldness of these fantasies: "What devils have possessed you to set you on against our Catholic faith?" (I, 52).

This was the devil that impelled Don Quixote to free the galley slaves from their chains. One day Sancho will not need to ask what the devil is. And Don Quixote himself will have understood what it is called.

True culture is that collaboration through the centuries of expression and meaning, which establishes a clear dialogue between the situations of today and the past, not by searching for texts but by taking the most famous of them in all the living richness of their content. Our sufferings find an echo in those of Don Quixote: and we may, without falsifying his idiom, lend it certain meanings from our own vocabulary, just as he lends ours some of the inflections of his noble speech. The constellation under which he was born, lived, and acted is compared to the pattern the stars make in our century: and immediately the mind sees the track of routes already traveled; reconstructs the paths in the celestial air that were the signs of the earthly destiny of our species and the heralds of its future. But in order that this understanding between generations may be possible, the texts and fortunes considered must be of the calibre of Cervantes and his works, of Don Quixote and his story. If we are to draw inspiration from the powers of a great mind, this mind at its height must have been extraordinarily vital, and aware, with particularly dramatic lucidity, as it engaged in the struggle with reality where it had pushed resistance to the limit, and exhausted its affirmative power. And it must have known how to embody this resistance and affirmative power in a complete and organic work, where all parts are firmly rooted and all vibrate and speak.

Some of these great men have expressed the dialectic of their time theoretically, as if they were leaving us passwords for the future. These are the moralists and philosophers who remain on the sidelines of action, and who have directly criticized ideas and overthrown the gods. But since ideas and gods are easily recognizable under the various aspects they assume when they reappear in the course of time, the passwords of these men—the splendid gladiators of history—can be used again by new teams with hardly any change in form or content. It is easy to show what is still exciting, long-lived, and revolutionary in Lucretius, Voltaire, or Marx. The situation becomes more subtle in the case of artists whose qualities cannot be satisfactorily transmitted by a certain aggressively explicit formula, but whose entire passion must be relived, and their flesh and blood partaken of, in order to receive their stirring virtues.

Cervantes, who echoed so clearly a particularly critical age, was especially an artist—tremendously so. And to follow him in an adventure from which he draws no general formula, which he merely brings alive—but with what power of transcription, what tragic intensity, what completeness in the test of happenings and the consciousness of men and things!—to follow Cervantes we must expend all the sympathy and disinterestedness which are the burnt offerings due great artists. In return we shall get the invigorating reward that admiration brings. For we shall feel in our hearts the awakening of a marvelous person, full of the most delicate and refined elements that go to make up human nature.

The Spaniards have a delightful expression to describe a charming person. They say: "to have something of the angels." It means a kind of lively and spiritual kindness that is at the same time ingenuous and on its guard, and whose charm no one can resist. Cervantes had "something of the angels." His nature is angelic, not in an abstract way like a carefully kept creature who has never dipped the tip of his wing in a drop of water; but his is an innocence that is pure and proud because it has been tested. Nothing was unknown to the lucid mind of Cervantes. When a man has gone through the dungeons of Algiers, and the prisons of Andalusia and Castile, there is nothing he does not know. He may be an angel, but he is no longer a child, neither is he a monk or a servant. We can never be sufficiently grateful for the amazing fact that he could keep his soul so luminous and so fertile after such experiences. We must love Cervantes, we must love Don Quixote and Sancho Panza, we must follow all three, throughout their vicissitudes. All three of them were, and always will be, the best and most human of men.

(*Translated by* Muriel Kittel)

NOTES

[1] *Luis Vives y la filosofía del Renacimento*. Madrid, 1903.

[2] Philip II's third wife who died October 3, 1568.—Ed.

[3] Cervantes: "La española inglesa" (*Novelas ejemplares*).

[4] *Cf.* Américo Castro on Cervantes' Pirandelloism in *Santa Teresa y otros ensayos*. Madrid: "Historia Nueva," 1929.

[5] *Pedro de Urdemalas*.

[6] *Cf.* his *Monadologie*, §§ 57 and 58: "And as the same city seen from different sides seems quite different and as if multiplied by its perspectives, so it happens that, owing to the infinite number of simple substances, there seem to be as many different worlds as there are different viewpoints of each monad, when these are really only the aspects of a single world. And this is the way to have as much variety as possible with the highest possible amount of order: that is to say this is the way to have as much perfection as possible."

[7] "Las dos doncellas" (*Novelas Ejemplares*).

[8] *op. cit.,* p. 61.

[9] At Whitsuntide the cardinals and prelates exchanged the fur-lined hood and cloaks worn in winter for lighter ones of silk. (Ed.)

[10] As in Chaps. XLVI and following, where we find the tower, the battle of dragons and other alchemic symbols. "Know" it is said further on (Chap. XLVIII) "that white honors red, and know that there will be great labor and very great significance therein."

[11] "We may even claim," writes Menéndez y Pelayo, "that chronologically this is the first modern novel, the first example of long prose narrative conceived and executed as such, since the stories in the Breton cycle are poems put into prose, amplified and degenerated. They are consequently an immediate derivation and corruption of the epic narratives whose objectivity and traditional basis they retain; that is why they do not appear singly, but are grouped in huge cycles, interlocking and mutually dependent, forming together a poetic world which is not the special creation of anyone, but has arisen from the contact of two races, the French and Celtic. The case of *Amadís* is quite different. In spite of the huge number of characters which occasionally form a bewildering labyrinth, its organic unity is evident, no longer in a cyclic sense, but in that of a norm or internal law which regulates all the happenings of a tale cleverly put together." (*Orígenes de la novela,* Vol. I, pp. ccxxiii, ccxxiv.)

[12] Francisco de Portugal: *Arte de Galantería*, 1670, quoted by Menéndez y Pelayo: *Orígenes de la Novela,* Vol. I, p. ccxxxvi.

[13] See a curious book on the subject of Tristan's significance: Adrienne Salinque: *Les Dogmes Sexuels*. Paris, Alcan, 1932.

[14] I have observed elsewhere ("Les nocturnes de Cervantes" *Revue de Paris*, March 15, 1935) that this feeling of solitude that appeared with modern times was expressed in various places by the theme of night—a theme that was to appear again later in another time of attacks of conscience: the Romantic period. Night plays a predominant part in Cervantes. He chooses it as a background for the moments of greatest stress or highest romance in his hero's adventures. Of all the nocturnes that mark the work of Cervantes in this way, I would like to mention again here that the most beautiful, moving, and musical is surely the beginning of Chap. IX (Part II) of *Don Quixote*, which describes the entry of Don Quixote into Toboso, where he expects to find the palace of Dulcinea; the occasion consequently for Cervantes to go all out in playing his most distant dream against the nearest reality.

[15] *Vida de Don Quijote y Sancho*. Madrid, 1905. 2nd. ed. Madrid: Renacimento, 1914, p. 344.

[16] Rinconete y Cortadillo, *Novelas Exemplares,* p. 147.

[17] Damón de Henares: *Testamento del Picaro Pobre*.

The Genesis of "Don Quixote"

RAMÓN MENÉNDEZ-PIDAL

IN the twelfth century France, relying in general on Breton legends, set the
model for the versified romance of chivalry, a taste for which spread
throughout Europe due both to the charm of works like "Tristan,"
"Lancelot," "Perceval," "Merlin" of Chrétien de Troyes or Robert de Boron and
to that of a complete later literature in prose which made its appearance in the
first half of the thirteenth century. Heroic verse, reflecting old political and martial ideas replete with commonplace austerity and to which love as a poetic
theme was unknown, is now succeeded by a new kind of narrative poetry which
like the lyric assumes essentially the character of poetry of love wherein the
scenes unfold in a polite, elegant world far removed from the gloomy feudalism
of the epic.

The varied and new emotions which enriched these poems of adventure were
cultivated in very different ways. France, through the famous works of Béroul,
Chrétien, and Thomas, felt especially the poetry of a fatal and turbulent love
which with poisoned dart wounded the heart of Tristan. Germany, in the poem
by Wolfram von Eschenbach, contemplated the battles of inner purification
fought in the soul of Parsifal, battles which won for him the kingdom of the
mystical city of the Holy Grail. Spain filtered the Breton inspiration into the
anonymous "Amadís," conceiving the fresh first love of the Doncel del Mar and
the lady Oriana which was destined to last from childhood until death, despite
the temptations and afflictions which tenaciously conspire against the lovers "in
such a wise that not for one hour did they cease to love."

Amadís, whose stout heart beats comfortably only at the surprise of danger
and during the struggle against mortal attacks, trembles and becomes a coward
in the presence of his lady at whom he hardly dares to look; he becomes senseless merely on hearing the name of Oriana and would fall from his horse were
it not for his faithful squire Gandalín who supports him. But although the
romance of chivalry inherits this trait from the poetry of love, since the latter
originates at a time immediately subsequent to that of the epic, it is not strange

32

that both it and the later novels of chivalry should possess some points of contact with the ancient heroic poems. Like these, the romances of chivalry for example conceive their heroes within very similar ideals of chivalrous perfection, they surround them with a world made up of two groups only, the noble and the wicked, in perpetual conflict with one another, and the struggle between them is settled in combats which are subjected to the same technique and described with the same narrative formulas in the novels of chivalry as in the epics.

But in addition to the inspiration of love other very profound differences in the conception of poetic life separate the new productions from the old. In the romance of chivalry the struggle between the two groups before mentioned is not fought out in an organized manner as in the epic, generally before the king and his court, nor does it extend to entire nations; but is rather purely personal. The life of the ancient vassals surrounded by a powerful family group and faithful to or rebellious against their lord, abandons its national and political interest to assume human but merely individual interest in the new knights-errant who wander alone in search of adventures, moved by caprice and chance. The horrible "vengeances of inherited hate" of which the epic treated are replaced now by those which the "Amadís" calls "beautiful vengeances," which as if guided by a professional technique the knight executes in the name of justice without himself being concerned with the wrong he wishes to punish; the knight-errant fights ferociously for any reason whatever, to prevent the harmful enchantments of Archelaus as well as merely to compel an unknown knight to declare his hidden name. *Heroic effort* is replaced in the romances by *arbitrary effort;* arbitrary and superhuman both in the brutal acts of violence of wicked knights and in the lance thrusts of just knights who always pierce the strongest coats of mail of perversity. The heroic *deeds* of the epic develop slowly within a social life lived by people dwelling in thickly populated communities, while the *adventure* of the romance of chivalry takes place roughly and rapidly within a solitary landscape: the extensive forest wherein the laments of the wronged one go unheeded until the avenging knight hears them. If on the edge of the forest there rises the well turreted castle inhabited by some powerful being or by a giant or enchanter, now kindly, now malign, it is only for the purpose of introducing further involved adventures which the good knight untangles with blows of his invincible arm; if farther on a king's court is to be found it is because in it awaits the valient knight-errant who by himself alone is more powerful than all the kingdom. How far removed is all this from the "Lay of the Cid!" The Corpes woods are not the center of heroic life; the greatest of affronts committed against the hero in the oak woods is not avenged there on the spot as the romance of chivalry would demand it, but under the authority of the court of Toledo.

However, the romance of chivalry is not so far removed from the later epic, the decadent epic, were the vassal repudiates his king and the entire nation.

This medieval novel had in Spain a very tardy reflowering. Garci Ordóñez de Montalbo, about 1492, adapted and added to the old "Amadís" with such opportuneness, with such fortune, characteristic at that time of all Spanish enterprises, that the work which for two centuries had lived locked up in the Peninsula was now launched forth brilliantly and impetuously into universal literature, achieving translations and repeated editions in a multitude of foreign languages. And then it was that the romance of chivalry, which during the Middle Ages had scarcely produced any original works in Spain and which in France was completely forgotten, had in the full maturity of the Renaissance a copious flowering which from the Peninsula spread all over Europe; then there were composed a series of continuations of the "Amadís" in which were recounted the lives of the sons and grandsons of the fortunate Doncel del Mar, Esplandianes, Lisuartes, Floriseles; further series of Palmerines, Primaleones and a hundred knights more, who came from the strangest and most archaic kingdoms of fiction to distract the minds of those generations worthy of the most refined art of Bembo, of Garcilaso, of Ronsard, of Sidney. The last highly successful romance of chivalry, the one which survived longest, was "El Caballero del Febo" by Diego Ortúñez de Calahorra (1562) whose adventures furnished plots to the courtly theater of Queen Elizabeth of England and inspired Henry Pettowe and perhaps Shakespeare himself.

Based in part on fact but also in part on exaggeration which has been justified by the exuberance of popular opinions it has been denied that the knightly and adventurous ideal was in conformity with the Spanish spirit and character; an unsurmountable abyss has been placed between the Spanish gestas and the books of chivalry, and these books are even denied a true popularity among us. It is true that the romance of chivalry is not derived from the Spanish epic, but it is nevertheless united to it though only by a fine thread; it is true that it is in the main a reflection of foreign models, but this fact neither prohibits its popularity nor hinders the intimate españolismo of the "Amadís," a happy adaptation of a French current to the Spanish spirit. And if the literature of chivalry captivated the public from the remote times of King Don Pedro to those of Philip III filling bulky tomes for the more cultured classes, descending in the form of small, popular, cheaply-bound books to the humblest classes, and occupying a part by no means the least beautiful of the Romancero; if it inspired the Hispano-Portuguese theater; if it filtered into seignorial emprises and into public fiestas; if its enormous novels were absorbing reading capable of filling with bitter remorse the conscience of the old chancellor Ayala, of Juan de Valdés, of Santa Teresa, and of keeping preoccupied the solicitors in the Cortes of the kingdom, the moralists, Luis Vives and Fray Luis de Granada, we must grant that this literary genre was not only popular but exceedingly so. The novels of chivalry were not successful as some believe because they were the only novels available in the sixteenth century, but rather they were practically without competition because their adventures had long been triumphing in the Spanish imagination. These books grew into second parts and continuations because the imagination wished to prolong the pleasure of living a life of exciting adventure and victorious and avenging endeavor.

And this literature was not dying of old age even in 1602 when Don Juan de Silva, lord of Cañadahermosa, published his "Crónica de don Policisne de Boecia." Then came the well known moment when Cervantes wished to benefit the literature and moral state of his fatherland by discrediting the books of chivalry.

"Don Quixote" is thus born with a special literary purpose, stated repeatedly by the author, and according to this it may be believed that it bears only a negative relation to those books and to the chivalrous spirit which gives them form. Lord Byron (in his "Don Juan") thinks that Cervantes ruined the Spanish feeling for chivalry and thus caused the ruin of his country; likewise Léon Gautier (on dedicating his monumental volume on the chivalrous life to Cervantes himself) laments bitterly at seeing how the ancient chivalry, his love of loves, is ridiculed and put to death by the great novelist; to spare the author of the imperishable and destructive pages of "Don Quixote" he is obliged to think of the heroic soldier of Lepanto, preferring the man to the book. But, quite the contrary, Menéndez y Pelayo maintains that Cervantes did not write a work antithetical to chivalry nor one of dry and prosaic negation, but a work of purification and completion; he came not to kill an ideal but to transfigure it and exalt it; all that was poetic, noble and human in chivalry had been incorporated in the new work with the loftiest meaning, and in this way "Don Quixote" was the last of the books of chivalry, the definitive and perfect one.

Between this point of view, which seems paradoxical, and the other simpler and more generally accepted one we shall be able to guide our judgment concerning the fundamental meaning of "Don Quixote," taking a genetic point of view.

"Don Quixote" appears as the last terminus of a series as far as the injection of the comic element into the heroic element is concerned. This mixture had existed in literature for centuries, since the very time of the epic's splendor; it is sufficient to recall as the most notable example the cantar of the "Pélerinage de Charle Magne." The Renaissance accentuated this manner of viewing heroic poetry, for this period which went deep into the contemplation of serene classic beauty must have seen the characters of the *chansons de geste* as extremely simple poetic fictions, monotonous in their turns of thought and in the extraordinary slashes of their swords. Spirits which were nourished in the ideas of Roman antiquity understood the empire of Charlemagne still less than that of Augustus, and they were unable to feel deeply the simple grandeur of the medieval epic. Thus the Italian Renaissance from the end of the fifteenth century, with Pulci and Boiardo, finding itself confronted with the Carolingian and Breton poetic material which the tradition of northern Italy was transmitting to it could not sincerely look upon it in seriousness. Boiardo in causing Roland to be in love takes pleasure in presenting the unconquerable paladin as an unskillful and timid lover, a stupid fellow, a *babbione* ever deceived by Angelica. Later, Ariosto (1516, 1532) continues this ridicule of the hero, making him a scorned lover, and tracing the furious madness of his jealousy with enlarged tragicomic characteristics; round these culminating scenes the poet, quizzically and whimsically, intermixes the knights of Charlemagne and Marsilio in a tangle of adventures—adventures marvelous in affairs of love, combats and enchantments, each one being overtaken and interrupted by the following one like the peaceful waves of the sea, always continuous, always monotonous, always teeming with playful novelty.

Almost a century after Ariosto, Cervantes again treats of the adventures of chivalry from a comic point of view. The Spanish author knew and admired both Boiardo and Ariosto; he frequently imitated the "Orlando Furioso," and even Don Quixote prided himself in singing some stanzas of this poem, but nevertheless Cervantes, face to face with his much admired predecessors, assumed a strange originality. While Pulci, Boiardo, and Ariosto continued with jesting humor the tradition of the old poems in verse, Cervantes imitated satirically other narratives in prose; he was not going to write a poem then but a novel, which fact carried him into an artistic world very different from that of the Italians. However Cervantes did not seek the first source of his inspiration in their works, encumbered with artifices and niceties of monumental effort, but, rather, sought it, following the instincts of his Spanish race, in a simpler, more popular literature.

Along with the comic scenes of the old French epic and the incredulous narrative of fictions of chivalry composed by the Italians of the Renaissance there had long existed in works of lesser literary magnitude another more frankly hostile manner of regarding chivalry: that of incarnating the ideals of the latter in a poor madman whose fancies were dashed to pieces against the hard realities of things. For example, in the second half of the fourteenth century the Italian novelist Sacchetti presents to us a figure of quixotic appearance, that of Agnolo di Ser Gherardo: an eccentric, afflicted with a chivalry monomania in spite of his seventy years, he goes from Florence to a nearby town to attend certain jousts, mounted on a tall, lean horse which was the image of hunger. At the time of putting his helmet on him and giving him his lance, mischievous wags place a thistle under the tail of his nag which begins running with great leaps and curvets, not stopping until it reaches Florence; there amid the laughter of everybody a woman takes the ill-treated horseman in, puts him to bed to treat him for the bruises from his helmet and armor, and upbraids him for his foolish chivalrous madness. Not only the comic foundation but the details themselves are similar to those of "Don Quixote." Who does not recall the old Manchegan hidalgo on his lean Rocinante on the beach at Barcelona where he was going to certain jousts, arousing wonder among the people on holiday by his strange bearing; and the boys who place a bundle of furze beneath his horse's tail, and the curvets of the animal which send Don Quixote to the ground?

Cervantes could have known the tale of Sacchetti or a similar one, or have been familiar with some of the various stories which were then in circulation concerning comic hallucinations suffered by readers of books of chivalry, like that of the student of Salamanca who because of them abandoned his studies and one day interrupted the solitude of his reading with loud shouts and knife thrusts in the air in defense of one of the characters in the novel he was reading which absorbed his brains to such a point.

While Cervantes could have known narratives of this sort, he conceived the first episodes of "Don Quixote" only through the stimulus of a contemptible "Entremés de los Romances" whose importance in my opinion has not yet been understood by critics. Adolfo de Castro happened to exhume this poor theatrical composition, affirming that Cervantes himself was the author of it, and he attracted to himself the most just and general discredit. But this foolish affirmation ought not to prevent us from examining the question without prejudice.

The "Entremés" must have been written about 1597; it seeks to make fun of the excessive vogue of the Romancero which had been reedited unceasingly for half a century, and especially the "Flor de Romances" which was reprinted and added to from 1591 to 1597.

The "Entremés" introduces us to a poor peasant, Bartolo, who from "reading the Romancero so much" goes crazy as Don Quixote did from reading the books of chivalry; he insists on imitating in a ridiculous manner the knights of the ballads. His ravings bear the most striking similarity to those of Don Quixote in the first adventure undertaken by him, that of the Toledan merchants. Bartolo, having become a soldier, through his madness believes himself the Almoradí or the Tarfe of the Moorish ballads, and he wishes to defend a shepherdess annoyed by her shepherd companion; but the latter takes possession of Bartolo's lance and with it maltreats him, leaving him stretched out on the ground, in like manner Don Quixote is beaten with his own lance by one of the merchants' muleteers. Bartolo, without being able to get up, consoles himself by thinking that not he but his horse was to blame for such a misfortune; Don Quixote says the same thing without being able to rise from the ground: "it is not through my fault that I lie here, but through that of my horse."

Resemblances increase also when Bartolo, recalling the well known ballad of the "Marqués de Mantua," believes himself to be the enamoured Valdovinos who lies wounded in the deserted woods and exclaims:

> "¿Dónde estás, señora mía,
> que no te duele mi mal?"

> ("Where art thou, my lovely lady,
> Feel'st thou not my cruel pain?")

and Don Quixote believes himself likewise to be Valdovinos and breaks forth recalling these very verses.

Meanwhile members of Bartolo's family arrive and he thinks that it is the Marqués himself arriving and so greets them with further verses of the ballad:

> "¡Oh noble Marqués de Mantua,
> mi tío y señor carnal!"

> ("O noble Marquis of Mantua,
> My carnal kinsman and my lord!")

verses which Don Quixote also repeats when a peasant from his own town approaches him.

The Entremés continues stringing together excerpts from the ballad, first in the mouth of Bartolo, then in the mouths of the other characters who, humoring the madman, give themselves over to a foolish parody in action of the very famous history of the "Marqués de Mantua." Cervantes, as was natural, rejected such a grotesque parody and reduced it to a short narrative in which he told us that to all the questions of the peasant Don Quixote only replied by continuing with verses of his ballad and recounting as his own the misfortunes of Valdovinos. But even in this short narrative Cervantes allows himself to be carried along by the system of the entremés parody; he recalls that the Marqués on approaching the wounded knight,

> "desque le quitó el almete,
> comenzóle de mirar . . .
> con un paño que traía
> la cara le fué a limpiar,
> desque la ovo limpiado,
> luego conocido lo ha"

("From his head and face his helmet
 And his beaver first he drew;
Then with gore beheld him cover'd,
 All of one ensanguin'd hue.

With his handkerchief he wipes him;
 When his face from blood was clean,
Then, alas! too true the story,
 Then too plain the truth was seen")

and he tells us that the peasant on approaching Don Quixote, "taking off the visor of his helmet . . . he wiped off the dust that covered his face, and presently knew the gentleman. . . ." This parody made by Cervantes without any burlesque intent is a charming remnant of unconscious imitation suggested by the "Entremés."

Bartolo and Don Quixote are carried in the same fashion to their respective villages, and on the way the madness of both takes a violent leap from the ballad of the "Marqués de Mantua" to the Moorish ballads. Bartolo now imagines that he is the alcaide of Baza who laments with his friend Abencerraje the falsity of Zaida, and Don Quixote fancies that he is the captive Abencerraje who tells the alcaide of Antequera of his love affair. Both madmen finally reach their homes and being put to bed fall asleep; but both in a short time again alarm their afflicted relatives, disturbing them with new follies; Bartolo with the burning of Troy and Don Quixote with the tournaments of the twelve peers.

"May the devil take the Romancero which has put you in such a plight!" says Bartolo's neighbor. "A hearty curse . . . light upon those books of chivalry that have put you in this pickle," says Don Quixote's housekeeper when he reaches home. The "Entremés" wishes to make sport of indiscreet readers of the Romancero and treads its ground firmly when it makes Bartolo believe that he is some character of the ballads. Cervantes wishes to censure the reading of books of chivalry and he is quite out of his field when he repeatedly makes Don Quixote rave with the same ballad characters as Bartolo; it can well be seen that the first idea of the madman who dreams that he is Valdovinos belongs to the "Entremés" and that only by undue influence of the latter is it found in the novel. If we should claim to suppose for an instant that the "Entremés" was later than and made in imitation of "Don Quixote" we should strike against the argument which touches the very foundation of the two works.

And still we ought to add another substantial consideration in behalf of the precedence of the "Entremés." The madman in whose head the idea of his own personality vanishes in order to be substituted by that of any other famous character is the common and sole type which always governs the "Entremés," mindful only of provoking the laughter of the spectators; but in "Don Quixote" such a sort of madness appears only in the first adventure, in the fifth and seventh chapters of which we have been speaking, and it is a madness moreover discordant with that which is always maintained by Don Quixote whose personality remains on all other occasions steadfast and erect in the presence of those heroes who are the cause of his madness. One must think then in examining the foundations of that which is quixotically comic in the adventure of the Toledan merchants, that Cervantes did not conceive the idea of the episode by combining the characteristic resources of his imagination but that the imagination was as if confined and limited by the indelible recollection of the "Entremés de los Romances" which had produced a vigorous comic impression in his mind. This tenacious, immoderate impression imposed on the novelist not only an unconscious and incomprehensible substitution of the ballads for the books of chivalry as the cause of the madness of Don Quixote but also a form of madness and a procedure of parody quite foreign to the free conception of the novelist.

This is the fundamental fact in the incubation of "Don Quixote." Cervantes discovered a fertile humor in the "Entremés" which poked fun at the mental "upset" caused by indiscreet reading of the Romancero. This literary satire seemed to him to be an excellent theme, but he separated it from the Romancero, an admirable poetic genre, in order to transfer it to a literary genre execrated by many, that of romances of chivalry which were as popular as the Romancero. There were authors, too, who like Lorenzo de Sepúlveda wished to apply a corrective to the old ballads "full of many lies and very little fruit," but Cervantes could not think like Sepúlveda nor like the writer of the "Entremés."

As soon as Don Quixote arrives home and goes to sleep, resting from the madness of being Valdovinos of the ballad, the priest and the barber proceed to the scrutiny of the sick hidalgo's library. In it besides the great multitude of novels of chivalry there appear the "Dianas," the "Galatea" and other pastoral novels; there appear heroic poems in the Italian style and the "Tesoro de varias poesías," but with surprise we observe that there does not appear any of the many "Cancioneros," "Flores de Romances" or "Romanceros" which had been in course of publication for more than half a century. The little poems contained in these collections were, as it were, the work of all the Spanish people and they could not be the cause of the madness of the very noble knight of la Mancha, nor should they be subjected to the judgment of the priest and the barber. What really drove Don Quixote mad were those bulky old books of chivalry which were condemned to the fire, the intractable "Don Florisel de Niquea," that voluminous tome of "Don Olivante de Laura"; however, the first moment of the immortal madness did not begin with any of these but with that of a thin, little, cheaply-bound book containing the "Romance del Marqués de

Mantua" which does not figure at all in the pleasant and great scrutiny because it entered not into the plans of Cervantes but into those of the commonplace writer of the "Entremés."

Solely through the immediate influence of the latter can we find ballads in the groundwork of "Don Quixote" instead of books of chivalry. And this not only in the adventure of the Toledan merchants but also in other passages of the second chapter. At dusk of that hot July day which saw the first longed-for sally of Don Quixote through the fields of Montiel, when the knight arrives at the inn where he is to be dubbed knight, he is contented with the poor lodging which the innkeeper offers him, recalling the words of the mysterious ballad on Constancy:

> "Mis arreos son las armas;
> mi descanso, el pelear"

> ("My armour is my only wear,
> My only rest the fray")

and when the women of the inn help him remove his armor, he continues his madness by imitating verses of the ballad of Lancelot:

> "Nunca fuera caballero
> de damas tan bien servido
> como fuera Don Quijote
> cuando de su aldea vino."

> ("Oh, never, surely, was there a knight
> So served by hand of dame,
> As served was he, Don Quixote hight,
> When from his town he came.")

But all this changes completely as soon as Cervantes puts the "Entremés" out of his mind.

The study of literary sources which is always excellent for understanding human culture in the aggregate serves when it is a question of a superior work, not to see what the latter copies and to discount it from the original (for that can be thought of only by one who does not comprehend what truly constitutes artistic invention), but to catch the origin and development of an idea, to see how the thought rises above its sources, how it surpasses them and emancipates itself from them.

Cervantes, even when he follows the "Entremés" most closely, is very original. Of that fresh, keen and profound comic delicacy which makes the episode of the Toledan merchants one of the best in the novel not one bit of it derives from the "Entremés" which imposes on Cervantes' imagination only an occasional one of the most external details of the adventure. The grotesque and rustic Bartolo resembles Don Quixote in the literalness of some actions, but only in this small matter, for he lacks totally the mysterious inner charm which accompanies Don Quixote from the start. The "Entremés," after arousing the generative idea in Cervantes, rather than aiding him finally served as a hindrance to him since it forced him to a task of correction which we are able to observe in part since it was in part carried out not in the moments of generation but in the very course of execution.

There can easily be observed in "Don Quixote" several inconsistencies in the sequence and connection of the episodes. This fact causes some to speak of the genial hurriedness of Cervantes in writing his work, while others believe that that is more than a commonplace phrase since it is known that Cervantes corrected and gave more than one form to his productions. Evidently there is a trace of everything in the contradictions which have been observed: there are evident inadvertencies, there are corrections half made, there are bold manifestations of inconsistency and absurdity. The action with its ever changing trends brought about by the frail imagination of the hero received less attention from the author as far as the external plan is concerned than that of the "Exemplary Novels." Cervantes wished to leave the action with all the trifling inconsistencies of an improvisation quite in the Spanish manner. But that improvisation in no wise supposes lack of knowledge but rather keen, penetrating inattention which does not wish to be blunted on what is useless. Cervantes' art is not a careless one because he happens to draw liberally from popular fiction, since he knows how to carve on it facets of extraordinary poetic splendor. It is not a careless art simply to satisfy the easily planned joviality of those who say: "Let us have more quixotic stunts, let Don Quixote attack and let Sancho speak, be it what it may, for with this we are satisfied!" since he is perfectly aware of the fact that he is putting in his work a perennial human value, and "I believe," he adds, "that there is not going to be . . . a language into which it will not be translated." In the face of carelessness in a few details how much meditation is revealed in the purification of the quixotic type, what an intimate and prolonged living together of the artist with his creation!

Our point of departure is the fact that Cervantes' fancy did not conceive the type spontaneously but was in a certain fashion held in restraint by the suggestion of the "Entremés." He did not conceive his protagonist within a plan well defined from the beginning but within a somewhat confused synthetic vision. Only during the development of the work did he with slow gropings at times draw forth and call to life all that complex greatness that was latently asleep in the first conception. One can understand how easy this gradual development of an idea may be in a long novel of adventures. Far from being a wearying repetition of the initial type of the hero these adventures are a never ending revelation even for the artist himself, and therefore more surprising for the reader. The type is not perfectly declared until the very end of the novel.

Now the special madness of Don Quixote on his first sally, imagining himself at one time to be Valdovinos wounded, believing himself immediately thereafter to be Abindarráez the prisoner, and next Reinaldos indignant at Roldán, was as we have already indicated strongly prejudicial to the personality of the ingenious hidalgo. Cervantes abandoned this course completely after he had exhausted his first source of inspiration; from then on Don Quixote will be always and only Don Quixote.

His character straightway receives support. In the same seventh chapter in which these hallucinations of impersonalism come to an end Sancho appears on the scene. He, too, comes from the popular literature; a proverb ran: "There goes Sancho with his donkey," and at that moment there entered with his *rucio* the rustic, the inexhaustible sayer of proverbs, like an archaic type of squire who appeared in the fourteenth century in the oldest known book of chivalry, "El Caballero Cifar." In the first conversations between Don Quixote and his squire there is already evident a trace of that sententious cleverness which, later on, will contribute so much to the madness of the hidalgo, and which soon, in the eleventh chapter, will spread out into the eloquent discourse on the golden age. Master and squire will continue progressively to complete one another in such a manner "that the madness of the master without the stupidities of the servant would not be worth a penny," and Rubió rightly notes that when Don Quixote remains alone in the Sierra Morena and in the home of the Duke and Duchess, the only two occasions on which the genial pair are separated, we feel for Sancho that same homesick longing that the knight experiences in his own heart of gold.

Cervantes, too, as soon as he put an end to the adventure suggested by the "Entremés de los Romances," felt quite obviously that that sort of comicality obtained according to the popular art of Sacchetti or the writer of the "Entremés" through the conflict of half-witted fancy with cruel reality could not reach the perfection of humor by basing it on the heroic and national ideals of the Romancero. It is true that it and the books of chivalry are half brothers, both offsprings of the medieval epic, but the Romancero, as a legitimate child, remained in its patrimonial inheritance of the heroic world while the bastard child went in search of adventures, and lost its reason in the pursuit of them. Cervantes venerated the epic world and as soon as he saw himself free from the suggestions of the "Entremés" had Don Quixote's madness withdraw itself completely from the verses of the Romancero and take refuge, as in its own castle, in the fantastic deeds of chivalry of the books in prose. These, then, in the mind of Don Quixote rise to the level of heroic fictions; the hidalgo claims to know that in the armory of the kings of Spain beside the saddle of the Cid's Babieca stands the enormous peg, big as a wagon tongue, with which the valiant Pierres guided his wooden horse through the air, and he still places the world of the novel before the heroic world and holds the Knight of the Blazing Sword in higher esteem than the Cid Ruy Díaz. On the contrary the canon, scandalized, separates the epic heroes from the phantoms of chivalry and connects them in a general way with historic personages: he had never in the armory at Madrid seen the peg belonging to Pierres, but he believes in the saddle of Babieca (which archæological criticism has expelled from the royal collection) and he counsels Don Quixote to leave off reading the lying deeds of Felixmarte de Hircania and of the Emperors of Trebizond and to hold to those of Viriatus, Caesar, Alexander, Fernán González, and the Cid.

In fine, Cervantes realized that his Don Quixote could not continue reliving the episodes of the Romancero, of which the Spanish imagination was very fond, and he saw that coming force was to rest solely on the incompatibility of the knight-errant's non-social perfection with a life closely organized and surrounded by the powerful machinery of government. Don Quixote not only ceases forever to believe himself a personage of balladry but he also ceases to apply ballad verses to himself. He only appropriates to himself thereafter a certain famous vow of the "Marqués de Mantua" and "My armour is my only wear, my only rest the fray," as indelible memories of the first expression of his type influenced by the "Entremés." Apart from this it appears as if Cervantes wishes instinctively to remove himself as far as he possibly can from the bad road along which he first started, and in all the rest of the first part of "Don Quixote" he makes but few allusions to the ballads in spite of the fact that they were then the fashion in ordinary conversation; Don Quixote only cites as historical material the ballad of Lancelot and of the Cid excommunicated by the Pope. On the contrary in the second part of the novel written when Cervantes was free from the objectionable preoccupation of the "Entremés" the memory of ballads will occur twice as often and, as we shall see, in a much better developed form than in the first part.

And yet when Cervantes expressly avoided recalling the Romancero he had it very much in mind and made use of it for his own personal inspiration. When he wanted to enliven the first part of "Don Quixote," developing the plot with care and making the greatest effort of a novelist according to the art then in fashion, when he conceived the episodes of the Sierra Morena, there surged into his memory a ballad to imitate, although quite differently from when he was influenced by the entremés parody. That Cardenio who, rejected by his mistress, proceeds through the thickest and most secluded portion of the Sierra, leaves his mule dead and penetrates into the densest and most secret part of the mountain, mid brambles and thickets, leaping over hedge after hedge; who, surrounded and pitied by the shepherds, weeps and gives indications of madness, becomes speechless and fixes his eyes on the ground, is a figure taken bodily from that ballad by Juan del Encina which circulated along with the old ballads in Cancioneros and broadsides:

> "Por unos puertos arriba
> de montaña muy escura
> caminaba un caballero
> lastimado de tristura.
> El caballo deja muerto
> y él a pie por su ventura,
> andando de sierra en sierra,
> de camino no se cura.
> Métese de mata en mata
> por la mayor espesura;
> los ojos puestos en tierra,
> sospirando sin mesura;
> despedido por su amiga
> por su más que desventura.
>
> —¿Quién te trajo, caballero,
> por esta montaña escura?
>
> —¡Ay, pastor, que mi ventura! . . ."

("A sorrowing knight presses into the forges of a dark mountain. His steed, dead, he forsakes, and scales the cliffs alone. Deeper and deeper, from bush to bush, into the thickest of the forest he penetrates. With eyes downcast, he does not cease complaining. His beloved has scorned him, and never has he felt such pain before.

'Who hath brought thee here, Sir Knight, into this dark forest?'

'Alas, shepherd, only my misfortune!' ")

Once Cervantes corrected the connection of the hidalgo's madness with the Romancero he was easily able to conduct the hero toward his state of perfection. Don Quixote, ever since his first sally, had proposed to right wrongs and punish the proud, but in this respect he does not yet differ greatly from the grotesque Bartolo confronting the shepherd who pursued the shepherdess. Only in the above cited seventh chapter in which the suggestion of the "Entremés" ends does the hidalgo elevate his madness to a thought which is comprehensive and express the need the world had for knight-errantry to be resuscitated in him. He is thus invested with a mission and in this fleeting phrase he notes the pleasing moment when the genetic idea came to Cervantes, since the author then begins to look upon the madman's fancies as an ideal deserving of respect, then he decides to depict him big in purposes but frustrated in the execution of them. Perhaps the first mistaken blending with the Romancero aided Cervantes in fixing his attention on the heroic part that existed in the books of chivalry. They coincided with the epic, as we have noted, in the type of chivalrous perfection and Don Quixote gradually fulfills in himself both the ideal of the latter and that of the former when he becomes steadfast in his love of glory, in his tenacious struggling in the face of danger, in his loyalty which is foreign to all ingratitude, in not telling a lie even though he should be shot for it, in recognizing and judging the right correctly, in aiding every one in need, in defending the absent, in being liberal and generous, in being eloquent, and even in hearing auguries and wishing to violate those which are adverse as did the old Spanish heroes. The poems of chivalry added one more perfection to the idea of the epic: that of being in love; and Dulcinea rises up before Don Quixote because "a knight-errant without a mistress was a tree without either fruit or leaves, a body without a soul." Thus from the intricate adventures of the books/ of chivalry the confused mind of Don Quixote assumed a purer heroic ideal which descended from the same stock as that of the ancient epic.

"Poor Don Quixote!" exclaims Paulin Paris, considering the superior beauty of the French poems of chivalry from which the books of chivalry took their inspiration; "Poor Don Quixote! The novels responsible for your madness were only long colorless paraphrases. What would have become of you if you had read the French originals?" But no; if Don Quixote had read only "Tristan" and "Lancelot" with "that progress, so sweet and suave, of his amorous and brave deeds," he would have been an ordinary madman fortunate in tragic love affairs; the parody would have come to an end and exhausted itself with a few scenes verging on buffoonery in which the knight of la Mancha would win Dulcinea, the Tobosan dove, by the might of his arm, as Cervantes had in mind many times and announced with the prediction of Urganda in the introductory verses. The French poems might well have maddened Don Quixote more, but only the happy Spanish adaptation of the "Amadís" could give a superior nobility to his madness. After much racking of his brains in long meditations Don Quixote decides to imitate not the madness of Orlando Furioso but the penitence of the knight of Gaul on the Peña Pobre. "And now," he exclaims, "the famous actions of the great Amadís occur to my remembrance, and be my trusty guide to follow his example." This is the moment when his madness glimpses all the moral grandeur of which it is capable.

From then on the gradual purification of the quixotic type is certain. If before that time the fidelity and veneration which Don Quixote feels for Dulcinea possess any vacillation and any very serious irreverence (Part I, Chapters 21, 25, 26), from now on the type of faithful lover is definitely estab-

lished, especially in chapter 30 in which the knight-errant slights the princess
Micomicona. Recall the following chapter in which Sancho, telling of the
message to el Toboso, describes Dulcinea as a mannish farmer wench who is
winnowing reddish wheat and the more the squire seeks to undo all the illusions
of Don Quixote the better he reconstructs them with delicate and untiring care;
and this stubborn restoration of the beloved ideal is also treated a little earlier,
in chapter 25, but how much more infelicitously because of the vacillation and
irreverence already alluded to! And still the progression continues; the peasant
girl Aldonza who had a better hand for salting pork than any other woman in
all la Mancha, whom Sancho is acquainted with and whom Don Quixote has
looked upon occasionally in respectful silence, disappears in the second part of
the novel and is converted into an ideal lady whom her knight has never seen,
being in love with her solely from hearsay.

In like manner all the comic character which was apparent at first in a confused way gradually reaches its highest inner purification. At the end of the
first part Don Quixote can say: "since becoming a knight errant, I am brave,
courteous, bountiful, well-bred, generous, civil, bold, affable, patient, a sufferer
of hardships, imprisonments and enchantments." He has removed himself from
the tempting fascinations of that love and that force which the anarchical and
fantastic world of chivalry offered to him to accept only harsh sacrifice, "with
the goodness of Amadís, the flower and mirror of knights-errant, ever present
in his imagination"; firm in the idea that chivalry is a religion, he ennobles all
his ridiculous life with a profound mystical feeling, he ascends to the purest
founts of the heroic, and with the physical insensibility of a martyr he suffers
the greatest pains "as if he were not a man of flesh, but a statue of stone." He
is sustained by the most steadfast faith: "Get upon thy ass, good Sancho, and
follow me once more; for God's providence, that relieves every creature, will
not fail us, especially since we are about a work so much to His service; thou
seest He even provides for the little flying insects in the air, the wormlings in
the earth, and the spawnlings in the water; and in His infinite mercy, He
makes His sun shine on the righteous and on the unjust, and rains upon the
good and the bad." He always puts his hope in God even though he always
finds this hope frustrated; he wishes to "improve this depraved age of ours,"
to restore to it the purity of chivalry though the whole world be ungrateful to
him for it, and though he seek all about him in vain in order to entrust his
downtrodden honor to those who show him the most sympathy: "I have
redressed grievances, and righted the injured, chastised the insolent, vanquished
giants, and trod elves and hobgoblins under my feet! . . . My intentions are
all directed to virtuous ends and to do no man wrong, but good to all the
world. And now let your Graces judge, most excellent Duke and Duchess,

whether a person who makes it his only study to practice all this, deserves to
be upbraided for a fool." In vain; the Duke and Duchess to whom he goes
in his sadness are at that very moment playing a mean trick on him in order
to make fun of his unhealthy idealism. The most holy hopes of heaven and
earth are deluded. Is it because they are impossible? It does not matter to us.
The whole madness of the hero assumes a bitter tragicomic meaning, that madness of the hero supported by an ideal which, although never attained, is
deserving of mankind's most affectionate sympathy.

At times we let ourselves be filled with the comic aspect of the hidalgo and
we think like his niece: "that you should know so much, as to be able, if there
was occasion, to get up into a pulpit, or preach in the streets, and yet be so
strangely mistaken, so grossly blind of understanding, as to fancy a man of
your years and infirmity can be strong and valiant; that you can set everything
right, and force stubborn malice to bend, when you yourself stoop beneath the
burden of age; and, what is yet more odd, that you are a knight, when it is
well known you are none! For though some gentlemen may be knights, a poor
gentleman can hardly be so." But, after all, his ideal force transcends his lack
of reason and all the defects of reality, and being poor he amazes us with his
liberality; being weak and sickly he is a hero possessed of courage which has
never yielded in the face of misfortune; being old he moves us with his ridiculous, mad first love; being crazy his words and actions always stir vital chords
in the heart of the enthusiast.

Nine years after the publication of the first part of "Don Quixote" there
appeared an imitation which is of keen interest to us. Avellaneda seems to
have written another "Don Quixote" solely to give us a tangible measure of
Cervantes' own value. The outstanding characters and qualities of the comic
type are in Avellaneda but without all talented skillfulness. This consideration
will never be sufficiently emphasized to avoid inadequate judgments regarding
"Don Quixote": every appreciation of "Don Quixote" which can be applied
likewise to Avellaneda contains nothing specific about Cervantes.

Fixing our attention on the aspects under consideration Avellaneda, far from
understanding how much the hero was harmed by the hallucinations regarding
other people's personalities and his ravings over the ballads, dwelt on both,
tediously insisting on the commonplace madness of the "Entremés" and of
the first chapters of "Don Quixote." Avellaneda's Don Quixote, wounded and
overthrown by a melon dealer, begins to recite the ballad of King Don Sancho,
for he believes himself wounded by Vellido Dolfos and orders Sancho Panza
to call himself Diego Ordóñez and go to challenge the people of Zamora and
good old Arias Gonzalo. Again "he strings together a thousand beginnings of
old ballads without order or sequence" just like the Bartolo of the "Entremés"

and mounting upon his horse he recites the beginning of the ballad "Ya cabalga Calaínos." Upon entering Zaragoza he speaks as if he were Achilles, later on he takes himself to be Bernardo del Carpio, in Sigüenza he believes himself to be Ferdinand the Catholic, in the Prado of Madrid he imagines himself to be the Cid Rui Díaz, and later he says that he is Fernán González, filling all his discourses with irrelevant ballad verse. This fool who, teeming with vanity and boasting, appropriates his being from heroes and kings, makes us prefer the vigorous personality of Cervantes' Don Quixote from whose mouth discretion and madness alternately flow so gently. It is instructive to us to see how in the hands of Avellaneda the same popular contrast of the madman enamored of chivalry and punished by reality results in failure after Cervantes from that idea had brought an abundant vein of inspiration into flower. The endowments of narrator which actually adorn Avellaneda are not accompanied by the deepest poetic endowments of thought, and so his Don Quixote does not resemble the real one at all. In the false "Don Quixote" the greatest literary coarseness is blended in a shocking manner with agreeable form, at times solemn and labored it is true, just as moral baseness is blended with frivolous devotion to the rosary, to scourging and to hair-cloth, far removed from the mystical religiosity of the real "Don Quixote." The structure which Cervantes rears on a popular idea is so much his that even after it has been built, it cannot be copied by an Avellaneda.

But the fact is that the latter's work served as a source of inspiration to Cervantes when he wrote the second part of his novel. I believe that Cervantes had some fairly definite information of the work of his competitor before writing chapter 59 in which he alludes to it expressly and which marks the moment when it appeared in print. It certainly appears that from the envy which Avellaneda felt for Cervantes the latter wished to derive the most reasonable profit: that is, to resemble in no wise his envious rival. It would appear as if in this he saw clearer than ever the dangers of triteness and coarseness which the story contained and struggled the harder to eliminate them in writing the second part of "Don Quixote." He no longer thought of drawing those two or three crude pictures of the first part, although they were still far removed from the coarseness of his imitator. The superiority of the second part of "Don Quixote," unquestionable for me as for most people, may be attributed to Avellaneda. There are sources of inspiration *by contrast* which have as much importance as, or more than the direct sources.

The blundering way in which Avellaneda takes hold of the ballads contrasts strongly with the new use which Cervantes makes of them in the second part. Having now forgotten his aversion to the "Entremés" he begins to use the ballads again in profusion, but now of course never to impair the personality of the hero, in the form of impertinent nonsense, as did the author of the "Entremés" and Avellaneda. The ballads reappeared to render his phrases agreeable with poetic quotations which at that time were remembered by all, and which everybody used in polite conversation: the novelty now is that these poetic recollections appear not only in the mouth of Don Quixote and in those of more intelligent personages but principally in the mouth of Sancho. Sancho of the proverbs is now at times Sancho of the ballads.

This evolution is observed from the beginning of the second part of "Don Quixote" when in chapter 5 Sancho alludes to a ballad for the first time, the ballad concerning the forwardness of the Infanta doña Urraca. It is true that this chapter is accused of being apocryphal by the translator of Cide Hamete because Sancho says "things of so refined a nature, that it seems impossible he could do it." But its authenticity is assured us in the dialogue which Don Quixote holds with the squire farther on: "Truly, Sancho, thy simplicity lessens, and thy sense improves every day." "And good reason why," quoth Sancho, "some of your worship's wit must needs stick to me." Without doubt Sancho is improving and being purified, too, at the same time that Don Quixote and Dulcinea in their turn are undergoing an evolution. The Sancho of Avellaneda, gluttonous, brutal, and clownish to the point of not even understanding the proverbs which he piles up in a jumbled manner, rises up between the primitive and the new Sancho of Cervantes in order to make us esteem in all his perfection the Sancho with a poor and kind heart, with a faithful spirit which doubts all and believes all and in whom discretion in abundance shows through the hard exterior of craftiness, achieving the most geomantic popular wisdom in judgments which are comparable to those of Solomon and Peter the Cruel.

The Sancho of the second part of "Don Quixote" recalls verses from the Romancero several times in his conversation: "Aquí morirás, traidor, enemigo de doña Sancha," "Mensajero, sois amigo," "no diga la tal palabra," or he alludes to the ballad of the Conde Dirlos, to that of Calaínos, to that of the "Penitencia del rey Rodrigo," or to that of Lanzarote which, as he declares, he learned through hearing it from his master.

Moreover Cervantes utilized the Romancero not only for its phraseology but for the very invention of the novel, although in a very different manner from what he had used it in the adventure of the Toledan merchants. In this as in everything else one sees the superiority of the second part of "Don Quixote" over the first part. Savi López, an adherent to the opposite opinion, affirms that the first part is predominantly comical, while in the second part the grotesque dominates; but I believe that in reality quite the contrary occurs. Limiting ourselves to the special point which we are considering, the grotesque elements which appear in the adventure of the ballad of the "Marqués de Mantua" are totally absent from the episode which has its inspiration in the "Montesinos" ballads, an episode which excels because of its delicate comic sentiment.

Not one single adventure, as in the first part, but various adventures in the second part contain some recollection of the Romancero.

When Don Quixote enters el Toboso on that sad night, looking in the darkness for the ideal palace of his Dulcinea, he hears approaching him a muleteer who was up before daylight and on the way to his farm work singing the ballad

> "Mala la hubistes, franceses,
> en esa de Roncesvalles . . ."

> ("Ill you far'd at Roncesvalles,
> Frenchmen . . .")

His song like an evil omen startles and preoccupies the mind of the knight-errant.

Later, the recollection of another ballad, that of Don Manuel de León, who undaunted enters the lion's den to retrieve a lady's glove, is invoked for the great adventure of the lions where the audacious madness of Don Quixote borders on extremes which concern the epic more than the comic; the victory won before the lion which turns his haunches is ridiculous, but the valor of the Manchegan hero, comparable to that of Don Manuel de León, is not now solely in his imagination as on other occasions, but really stands out in the midst of the fear of all those who witness the intrepidity of the knight in the presence of the rampant beast. He rightly feels himself strong: "No, these magicians may rob me perhaps of success, but never of my invincible greatness of mind"; and he is so beside himself that he sends Sancho to gratify the lion keeper with two crowns of gold; the first time history records that Don Quixote gave a tip. Liberality, an essentially chivalrous virtue, excels only in the second part of the work, but is it not quite well known that here the comic success of the hidalgo far surpasses the repeated body-beatings into which the adventures of the first part are resolved?

Nor is there in the first part as rich a development of the frequent quixotic hallucination as there is in the second part in the adventure of the puppet show of Maese Pedro, so wisely and admirably commented upon by Ortega y Gasset. Now, only one thing is of interest for us to observe: hallucination in the presence of a theatrical performance, a common theme for popular anecdotes old and new, had already been incorporated in the quixotic fable by Avellaneda when his Don Quixote, taking for reality the performance of "El testimonio vengado" of Lope de Vega, jumped up into the midst of the actors to defend the unprotected queen of Navarre. Cervantes, as if he had seen here an excellent theme poorly developed and had wished to employ it, even giving his competitor the advantage, described the madman's exaltation not before a performance of actors but of marionettes, and not before a new and cleverly dramatized action but before the well known ballad adventure familiar to old folks and to children; a ballad which recounted how the forgetful Don Gaiferos recovered his wife Melisendra from captivity. The picturesque narrative of the boy who explains the figures on the stage is animated with such descriptive force that he creates before us an epic world of puppets; the interest increases and, when the boy's words diffuse affected emotion and anguish over the danger that the two fleeing lovers are in, the flash of enchantment rises suddenly into Don Quixote's mind and hurls him into the midst of the chivalrous adventure to destroy with his sword the stage over which the Moors of Sansueña ride at full speed in pursuit of the lovers. Soon reality takes possession of the imaginative knight and imprisons him in its powerful bonds; now Don Quixote agrees to the disillusioned appraisement of and payment for the broken paste figures, but in the presence of the most fleeting recollection of the dangerous adventure, his tenuous and inconstant imagination goes wild again and once more escapes to live as if it were reality in the world of fiction which in his and from which he sorrowfully feels himself banished.

But the perfection so often attained in the adventures of reality was not sufficient for the novel. Cervantes sought adventure which should rise out of the realm of the ordinary, "of the possible and verisimilar" in which the other adventures developed, an ideal vision which should serve as a sort of nucleus to the second part; and he prepared it in the Cave of Montesinos, the visit to which he announces with solemn anticipation, relating it afterwards to subsequent adventures until the very end of the novel. Just as in the profoundly humorous episode of the galley slaves he coupled his chivalrous hidalgo with the heroes of the picaresque novel so he wished to couple him with the true and venerated heroes of medieval fiction. These he did not seek out in any book of chivalry; once more his mind turned to the ballads, although not as we might suppose to those of Spanish subject matter, but to the Carolingian.

Among the knights of Charlemagne Don Quixote appears for a second time in action derived from the ballads by means of an extravagant illusion; but now, how much more nobly and more rationally, so to speak, than in the adventure of the Toledan merchants! The ballads had given those first chapters the appearance of a parody in caricature, now they give its happiest moment to the burlesque idealism of the second part wherein it appears that Cervantes wishes to make amends to us for having earlier allowed himself to be too greatly influenced by the "Entremés."

The Carolingian heroes, who in Italy and Spain had had a second fatherland conquered for them by the wars of Charlemagne in both countries, had multiplied in our country with new personages like Durandarte and Montesinos; La

Mancha, at the time a frontier region for the Moslems and a bulwark which the three powerful military orders defended, had made itself worthy of being inhabited by poetic figures prouder and more gallant than, though not so universally admired as that of its belated compatriot, Don Quixote. A certain ruined castle, with its fountain, which stood on a cliff in the midst of one of the lagoons of Ruidera where the river Guadiana has its source, was signalled out by Manchegan tradition as the wonderful castle of which the ballad sang:

> "al castillo llaman Roca,
> y a la fuente llaman Frida"

> ("The castle called Roca
> And the fountain called Frida")

there the silver battlements had been erected on a base of gold, as the ballad states, with sapphire stones which shone in the middle of the night like suns; there had lived the maid Rosaflorida, disdainful until she burned with love for the French Montesinos and brought him thither, strewing his path with pearls and precious stones. About the nearby cave named for the same Montesinos they told wonderful things through all that neighborhood which aroused the curiosity of Don Quixote, and this was a great, good fortune for the river Guadiana, a hapless river in which the poets of the Golden Age, who were so lavish with the Duero, the Tagus, and the Henares, could find no nymph except perchance one which had been converted into a frog in its muddy pools, like that which put Cervantes' friend, López Maldonado, out of humor. Don Quixote found in the medieval Rosaflorida the nymph which peopled those marshlands with poetry, converting them into an enchanted palace of old time chivalry, exalting them, along with the dusty roads, the burning hot oak groves, and all the monotony of the vast, disconsolate Manchegan horizon, to the dignity of a landscape that was poetical, intimate and pleasing to mankind, no less so than the sacred olive groves of Attica and the luxuriant groves of the Cephisus which are never penetrated by the summer sun nor by the winds of winter, frequented by the choruses of muses and bacchantes and by Aphrodite, guider of the golden chariot.

The exceptional quality in this adventure of the cave of Montesinos, so insistently called to the attention of his readers by Cervantes, consists in the fact that here the heroic ideal of Don Quixote does not manifest itself as heretofore in conflict with reality, but emancipated, free from annoying and painful contact with the latter. Don Quixote descends to the bottom of the cave and loosening the rope which Sancho and the guide are holding, the only bond which unites him to the outer world, he finds himself removed from it, alone in the midst of the cold, cavernous darkness. The cave is then illuminated by the light of the imagination, as noble as it is unbalanced, of the Manchegan hidalgo, and he finally finds himself among the heroes of the old ballads. He discourses amid the gloomy shades of Durandarte and Belerma, heroic-burlesque figures clothed with a misshapen idealism; he consoles his mind with the peaceful and pitiful appearance of enchanted Dulcinea; and in that mansion of ancient chivalry, where in a fantastic picture of incomparable beauty and humor the lugubrious and the comic are powerfully blended, the eager spirit of the hidalgo realizes its supreme aspiration, the consecration of his effort through the mouths of the admired masters. Montesinos himself extols the restorer of knight-errantry and entrusts to him the valiant mission of revealing to the world the mysteries of the past heroic life and that of disenchanting the ancient paladins and the new Dulcinea.

But the hero on reaching the summit of his exaltations also reaches the edge of the abyss. When Don Quixote returns to the land of mortals and relates the supreme success which he has achieved, he encounters as usual in his faithful Sancho a bold, impudent unbelief and finally he too falls into doubt. That firm soul, who always restored idealism so energetically whenever it was destroyed by the ruinous attacks of reality, in this harmless, glorious adventure does not know how to defend himself against doubt. In vain he tries to put his uncertainty at rest by questioning the soothsayers as to whether his experiences with the ballad heroes in the enchanted cave had been a dream or the truth; the ambiguous commonplaceness of the replies obtained from such oracles gradually filters into his heart; dejection gains sway over him. The hour of being reduced to commonplace thinking arrives, the hero is convinced that he will not attain the promise of Montesinos, that he will not see Dulcinea in all the days of his life, and he dies of sorrow . . . and sanity. He has recovered his reason, but lost the ideal in which he lives and breathes, so naught is left to him but to die.

In Sophocles' tragedy, Minerva, offended, sets in motion in the mind of Ajax the whirlwind of a chimera, and the hero, maddened, knifes a flock of sheep, believing that he is beheading the Atrides who wronged him. On recovering from his delirium and seeing himself surrounded by dead animals he realizes that that spilt blood is a dishonor to his invincible courage and to all his achievements, and he pierces himself with his sword. His madness is divine, θεία μανία, because it is a punishment of the divinity, while that of Don Quixote is a divine creation of his sick soul. The hero of Salamis takes his own life upon feeling himself ludicrous in the presence of the reality which he contemplates, he kills himself out of shame for himself; the Manchegan hero dies of the sadness of life on discovering that that reality is inferior to him, on seeing that the Dulcinea to whom he gave being is fading away forever into the world of impossible enchantment.

Is this novel of a madman one more book of chivalry, the last, the definitive and perfect one, as some say? Is it the ruination of chivalry and heroism, as others say?

It is not when writing "Don Quixote" that Cervantes wishes to produce a modern book of chivalry, but afterwards, on composing his last, and for him, his most esteemed work, "The Wanderings of Persiles and Sigismunda." This the good canon seems to announce when cursing the books which are the cause of the Manchegan hidalgo's madness; he finds in them however one single good thing, and this was "the subject they furnished a man of understanding with to exercise his parts, because they allow a large scope for the pen to dilate upon without any check, describing shipwrecks, storms, skirmishes and battles." All this is found in "Persiles," the real novel of adventures, not only because of the influence of the Byzantine novel but also of the novel of chivalry, which is present even in its customary motives, when Periandro at the head of the group of fishermen goes forward over the sea righting wrongs. As for "Don Quixote," we cannot help considering it simply and plainly as antagonistic to the books of chivalry which it tries to make one forget by satirizing not only their unpolished and careless composition, but also their subject, a blend of infantile marvels, incredible effort, automatic passions.

But on the other hand since these books, far from being essentially exotic to the Spanish people, are intimately saturated with that part of their spirit which is the exaltation of universal sentiments of self-denying disinterestedness and of honor, the satire of Cervantes does not seek to injure the reputation of the eternal ideal of chivalrous nobility, and when it contemplates this latter impaired through contact with real life, it does not harm the ideal as much as it does reality itself which does not turn out to be exactly as the heroic soul desires it to be. Far from wishing to destroy that world embellished with the purest moral feelings, Cervantes opens it up to our respect and sympathy, showing us its ruins, enveloped in a light of supreme hope, as a lofty refuge for the soul. Dulcinea del Toboso is the most beautiful woman in the world even when her unfortunate knight falls vanquished to earth.

In short, far from combating the spirit and fictions of heroic poetry, Cervantes received from the Romancero the first impulse to paint the ideal madness of Don Quixote, and in the Romancero he sought a great part of the inspiration and adornment of the work. Thus heroic-popular poetry attended the creation which, destroying the moulds in which the novel of chivalry was formed, taking its fictions from the world of chimera and bringing them to the world of reality, wrought the first and inimitable model, to which every modern novel is more or less subordinated.

(*Translated by* George I. Dale)

The Composition of "Don Quixote"

JOAQUÍN CASALDUERO

I

THE important consideration in the *Quixote* is not that Cervantes apologizes for writing or for having written one thing or another, but rather that he felt the need of enclosing it in precisely that whole, that he felt the rhythm of his imagination move in the direction it does with the particular air and tone he gives it.

It is Cervantes who has defined baroque composition with the most exactness: "disordered order [orden desordenada] . . . so that art, imitating nature, seems here to outdo her" (Chap. 50). Baroque art hides its strict order in a disorder that imitates nature and thus triumphs over nature itself. When confronted with a baroque work the glance is bewilderingly disconcerted by its disorder, but the sensibility and the intelligence always find that order which the artist who has mastery over his material requires and imposes in order to make it flower in confusion.

The novel appeared in 1605 divided into four parts and this division was maintained until Cervantes published his other *Quixote* in 1615. Chapters I–VIII form the first part, IX–XIV the second, the third includes Chapters XV to XXVII, and finally, the fourth is composed of Chapters XXVIII to LII. That is, the 52 chapters of 1605 are presented in groups of 8, 6, 13 and 25. It may be immediately observed that the last part alone comprises almost as many chapters as the first three together. The first eight chapters tell of Don Quixote's first sally together with the beginning of the second sally, the adventure of the windmills, and the beginning of the adventure of the Biscayan. The six chapters that follow give us the end of this adventure and the "History of Marcella and Grisóstomo." The thirteen chapters of the third part present the episode of the yanguesians, the stay of the Knight and his Squire in the inn, the adventure of the flocks, that of the dead body, that of the mill-hammers, the helmet of Mambrino, the galley slaves, the stay in Sierra Morena and the "History of Cardenio." In the last two

56

chapters of this part—26 and 27—the Curate and the Barber again appear with the intention of making Don Quixote return to his village. It should be noted at once that these two chapters are the central ones of the novel, the axis that unites the first twenty-five chapters to the last twenty-five of the fourth part, in which all the elements of the novel reach their full realization.

The mechanical axis of the *Quixote* is in the center of the novel as in all Renaissance composition. In the Renaissance, the mechanical or material axis of the composition coincides with the organic or spiritual axis. The center of the canvas is always the center of the picture. This is not so in the Baroque where the function of the mechanical axis is to emphasize the displacement of the organic axis. With the reappearance of the Curate and the Barber, in Chapters 26 and 27, there begins the conclusion of the novel. But these two characters cannot be the spiritual axis of the work which has reached its maximum tension some chapters before: Chapters 18 to 22 in which are narrated the five adventures of the modern world.

Cervantes, in keeping with his epoch, neither subjected his imagination to any certain logic nor intended to organize logically the narration and the happenings. The Renaissance disposition of material seemed to him extremely poor and rigid. The Baroque wishes to substitute light and color for clarity: it demands flexibility; violent contrasts, which make the richness of the tones more apparent; offset simplicity with exuberance. Instead of the slow and clearly scanned movement which keeps time with the step of man, a rhythm whose periodicity is measured by the stars. *The four Parts are the four steps of a cascade.* Let us remember what Cardenio says: "when the course of the stars brings disaster, as they drop from on high, hurling themselves with fury and violence, no power on earth can stop them, nor human industry prevent their fall" (Chap. 27).

The third part with its thirteen chapters counterbalances the fourteen chapters of the first two parts. And the novel establishes an equilibrium between the one half and the other, counterweighing, as I have said before, the twenty-seven chapters of the first three parts with the twenty-five of the fourth part.

The complicated workmanship of the different elements of the novel stresses the simplicity with which it is conceived. The plot is nothing more than the sally of the hidalgo from his home, his search of adventures and his return. This circular movement is repeated in the second sally. The plan of the first sally is: (1) departure from home, (2) the inn and adventures, (3) return and adventures. In the second sally the ternary movement is transformed into its corresponding quinary movement giving us this scheme: (1) sally, adventures and episodes, (2) inn, (3) adventures and episodes, (4) inn, (5) return, adventure and episode.

Cervantes used the circular form for his plot because he had to express the idea of destiny. But it was a historical destiny, the destiny of a culture which strives to keep the past alive. A past which the novelist loves, but whose love is fecund because he sees that past, although nostalgically, as irrevocably dead, and can for that reason dedicate himself without reserve to the preservation of the present. In the first sally we have the destiny of Don Quixote in its entirety and in a schematic and essential manner. In the second sally there is presented the process of this destiny. The first sally is conceived in function with the second; it gives the fundamental generating note and presents the action in its totality. This procedure is frequent in the Baroque.

The determinant of the novel is the contrast between the condition, occupation and social medium of an hidalgo of the Mancha and the "strangest idea" which could occur to him: to become a knight errant, to resuscitate the Middle Ages. This strange idea has its origin in the reading of novels of chivalry. The point of departure of the narration having been firmly established, the action is presented in a schematic, essential way, with a wisely graduated introduction of the principal characters who take part: the Housekeeper and the Niece, who open and close the novel and who are Don Quixote's iron-bound social frame; the Curate and the Barber, who carry the thread of all the literary discussion; then Dulcinea; and finally, Sancho.

One of the ways in which this contrast could be expressed was the use of parody, which complicates the action since it projects it in two different directions. On the one hand, we have always to keep in mind that Don Quixote is an hidalgo; on the other, it is essential not to forget that all his acts are an allusion. Parody, besides satisfying the baroque desires for complication, makes possible the bringing out of contrasts in sharp relief. It even reaches the point of grotesque deformation, achieves the brusque displacement of pathos for the burlesque, at times causes the jest to stem emotion, or contrives that emotion flower amidst the volutes of humor, or again, that emotion and jest spiral together.

Parody provides this double backdrop for the action. At the same time the action is charged with antithetical suggestions: society and spirit, being and appearing, idealism and realism, poetry and prose. Antitheses which do not confront each other as in the Gothic "Débat" but which are passionately interlinked in the baroque dialogue.

The catholic Cervantes, a catholic of his epoch, that is, of the Counter Reformation, does not express the struggle between the soul and the flesh, between virtue and vice. His religious consciousness adopts the modern form of a historical-cultural feeling. He sees the world as an opposition between the faith of the past and the will of the present, between the knight errant and the *caballero* of his epoch, and he succeeds in reducing the ample circles of his emotion to the limits of his own life, of his personal experience wherein Lepanto rises like a mile-post to separate the two epochs. The Renaissance, from which he has wrung the last drops, whose last rays of light have gilded his youth, and in which he not only feels himself rooted but which he remembers idealized by all the prestige of years of illusion and hope, with the primal vision of a young and poetic outlook, with all the nostalgia for the irrevocable past; and the Baroque, in which his poetic illusion has been transformed into moral experience, his youth into maturity, Spain of the Battle of Lepanto into Spain of the Armada, her heroic deeds into daily tasks. The transition from one epoch to another is made in Algiers, in captivity. At Algiers there arrives a hero; from Algiers there goes forth a tax-collector. Cervantes concentrates the rays of the ample historical-cultural confrontation of two epochs on his own life. The polarity between being and appearing, *caballero* and *bourgeois*, the idea and the real, spirit and society, is felt intensely through the medium of his own personal experience and is transformed into the stuff of poetry in the *History of the Ingenious Hidalgo Don Quixote of the Mancha.*

The principal theme is expounded with precision and clarity in the first sally. In the second, it is developed in all its frondose chiaroscuro and there appears the secondary melody: that of love, which begins as soon as the exposition of the first theme comes to a close, that is, in the second part: "History of Marcela." In the second part is stated the erotic phrase that opens with the majestic andante of the Discourse on the Golden Age, all of it with a historical-literary background; there appears briefly the theme of chivalry and immediately are heard the harmonies of love. In the third part and the beginning of the fourth, the two melodies combine; by a transposition of key they are made to go from History to the present—adventures, Cardenio and Dorotea, the Discourse on Arms and Letters, the Captive and the Judge—; then they separate—The Jealous Goatherd, Disciplinants—, and there remains once again only the main theme for the finale.

One must keep in mind besides that the main theme is intimately connected with the literary problem of the difference between History and Novel. The life of the hidalgo changes its course and flows into that of Don Quixote, not because he read books of chivalry, but because he read them as though they were history.

The content of the 1605 *Quixote* may be resumed thus: (1) principal theme: chivalresque adventures; (2) accompaniment: amorous episodes; (3) background: scrutinies of books and dialogues on literary matters. In the three themes the incessant conflict arises from the confrontation of the past and the present.

As we study the *Quixote,* the first thing we observe is the impossibility of separating the three themes of the novel, since they are coherently united; that one cannot be treated without the other two. Not only the continuity of the action but also the thematic articulation organize the parts into a unique whole.

Having soberly, energetically and briefly depicted the protagonist and his environment with the baroque will for characterization, Cervantes immediately introduces the literary theme (1) to motivate the conduct of the hidalgo: the latter believed that books of chivalry were real histories and it was for that reason that he hit upon the plan of converting himself into a knight errant; (2) to present the Curate and the Barber, whose function will always be the examination of the nature of a novel and the contrasting of this with reality; and finally, (3) to underline the imagination as the starting point both of the action and of the literary creation (with its different quality). For if Don Quixote had not made himself into a knight errant, he would have written the end to the adventures of Don Belianís and, in effect, at the end of the novel, Don Quixote imagines the adventure of the Lake. It is to be noted that the narration of this adventure coincides with the restatement of the literary problem at the end of part four. The literary theme recurs at the end of the first sally (Chap. 6 and the beginning of Chap. 7) as a scrutiny of those types of novel (books of chivalry and pastoral novels) which, having become devitalized, must give way to a new novel form that, isolated from the Gothic and the Renaissance world, might be capable of expressing the modern spirit: the conflict between the past and the present, the destiny of the individual and his opposition to the social environment.

Framed in this literary theme—the starting point of Don Quixote's destiny, the necessity for the creation of a new novelistic genre—we have the first three adventures of the hidalgo. The paladin of Dulcinea—Beauty and Virtue—comes upon an inn—Castle—and there he finds himself in the company of some prostitutes and a rascal. Immediately the adventures begin: struggle with the muleteers; on his departure from the inn, the liberation of Andrés; and finally, his encounter with the merchants. Don Quixote goes from his victory over the muleteers to his defeat through the fall of Rocinante, of which the merchants take advantage, in the interval, having experienced ideal victory in his rescue of Andrés.

The three adventures give rise to the essential conflict of Don Quixote: his clash with reality, the duality of the world—ideal, social—, and the two perspectives which that duality creates—the grotesque and the pathetic. They also mark the direction of the Knight's course, that is, from a circumstantial victory to a necessary defeat. In the first and the third adventure, the inn-keeper and the merchants are aware of Don Quixote's madness and humor him, thus making possible the grotesqueness of the incidents. This jest casts an aura of lightness about the pathos of the second adventure, that of Haldudo and Andrés, in which there is established the relationship between Justice and the means necessary for its execution. From the Romantic Period on, this adventure has been considered the first moment of full melancholy and sadness in the novel; but in baroque man it only incited laughter since the accent lies not on Andrés' misfortune but on Don Quixote's folly.

At the end of the third adventure, Don Quixote, beaten and bruised, affirms his belief in his own personality: "I know who I am . . . and know that I can be not only all those whom I have named, but also the Twelve Peers of France and, what is more, the Nine Worthies . . ." At the moment that Hamlet is doubting, when new bases to the human personality are being sought, when all is crumbling and man is capable only of feeling intimidated and disconcerted before the mystery of being, Don Quixote does not hesitate to make a declaration of will and faith. To his catholic soul the person is something clear and evident. A circle of phantoms surrounds that "I know who I am"—Valdovinos, Abindarráez, the Marquis of Mantua, Rodrigo de Narváez—; they whirl about the hidalgo and prevent him from hearing his real name. Don Quixote carries on that most dramatic of dialogues, the eternal and only dialogue: the monologue in which he convokes the legendary and poetic images.

"Thus, as our resplendent adventurer sallied on, he conversed with himself." The first sally begins with a monologue, the monologue in which Don Quixote projects himself into the distant future, "the times to come," totally giving over to history his present, his potential destiny. As he can contemplate the whole process of his life in its purposeful perfection, as he is completely sure of the direction of his impulse, he is not stirred by the form it takes, the course he has to follow, nor its development. His inner confidence makes real for him that "felicitous age and century" when his deeds will come to light and be known. Compare this with Hamlet's first monologue: "O, that this too too solid flesh would melt, Thaw, and resolve itself into a dew!" While Shakespeare introduces us to the world of perplexity and plunges us into the uncertainty of human destiny, Cervantes wishes us to smile sadly at an assurance which is no longer valid; but, without doubting for a moment, he will then substitute the Counter Reformation for Gothic faith, and all of his work from 1605 on will consist in the creation of another new inexorable world.

Don Quixote is sure of his vocation and, consequently, of the urgent need of his sally into the world. The scrutiny of the hidalgo's library ends (Chap. 7) as Don Quixote's shouts are heard. He is absorbed in another adventure (the fourth and last of the first sally), that of the Knights of the Court and the Knight Adventurers. This adventure closes the theme dealing with personality that had begun when he lay stretched out on the ground because of Rocinante's fall (Chap. 5)—the theme reappears in the fourth part. It is the only adventure which takes place while Don Quixote is asleep and should be related to the dreamed adventure of the fourth part—which occurs during the second scrutiny —because it is at the end of this last adventure of the first sally that the Niece tells him that an enchanter has made his books and the room which held them vanish. This is the moment in which Cervantes shows us the full significance of the first sally. Don Quixote says: Since this Frestón is a sage who holds a grudge against me because he knows that I am to overcome him (an allusion to the dreamed adventure which is to come later), "he therefore tries to do me all the mischief he can; *and I declare to him that little does it avail him to go against or try to avoid that which the heavens have ordained*" (Chap. 7).

Now the second sally can begin and, in fact, Sancho makes his appearance with the ass. There is no transition whatsoever. The second sally is completely united to the first. The thing which separates them is the haste with which Don Quixote and Sancho depart.

It is in this same Chapter 7 that the relationship between Sancho and Don Quixote is established. They neither form a contrast to each other nor do they complement one another. Don Quixote does not represent the ideal in opposition to a reality represented by Sancho nor the complement to any such reality. The melody of Don Quixote is the same as that of Sancho, but, in the case of the latter, in a transformed key and carried by an instrument of another tone and color. The grotesque and pathetic effect which Cervantes achieves as he deals with Don Quixote is transformed to the purely comic when he treats of Sancho. Don Quixote's grotesqueness and pathos arise when the world of the ideal and the absolute clashes with the relative world and reality. The comic result in Sancho is attained by considering the absolute and ideal world as though it were relative and real. For Don Quixote—Dulcinea, for Sancho—the Island. They are one and the same: both creations of Don Quixote, therefore both owe their existence to a single will and desire for this manner of being, they are two ideal goals. Ideal Beauty and Virtue, ideal Power. Don Quixote is fully aware of the nature of Dulcinea; but Sancho does not perceive the nature of the Island, and it is from this that all the humor is derived: he installs himself in the ideal world as though it were real.

The presence of the figure of the Squire in the first sally would have produced an element of confusion in the presentation of the destiny of Don Quixote since he is only his accompaniment. Sancho resolves the grotesque pathos of the Caballero into laughter. That is why he appears in the second sally when the quixotic destiny presents itself in all its volume and profundity; when Don Quixote can confine the burlesque merriment in a sentiment of supreme humility, of true religious spirit. Sancho is included in the first part so that his function in the novel may be left clearly established and this too is the reason for the inclusion of the adventure of the windmills. In the first sally we have seen the essential nucleus of Don Quixote's world: the transformation of reality by the individual. In the episode of the inn that metamorphosis is presented in action; and all this, in turn, is given us in compendium (the baroque summarization in series form) at the end of the second chapter. The adventure of the windmills makes us penetrate into that transformation showing us the process of the five moments of its tempo: (1) windmills-giants, (2) windmills-windmills, (3) windmills-giants, (4) windmills-windmills, (5) giants-windmills.

The beginning of the adventure of the Biscayan (this adventure has two parts: first, the Benedictine monks; second, the combat with the Biscayan) gives us the comic solution to the pathetic disaster of the windmills, because Sancho, in spite of the fact that he warns Don Quixote that they are monks and that the same thing will happen as with the windmills, on seeing that the result is different (triumph of Don Quixote) disregards his own counsel and is thrashed. Sancho cannot apprehend reality, but obedient to his ideal of Power, he interprets it according to the standards of failure or success without heed for its significance.

Knight and Squire are neither opposites nor complements to one another. They are of the same nature with a difference in proportion. The comic spirit arises from the juxtaposition of these diverse proportions which are translated plastically.

The history of Don Quixote is an actual happening (now), occupying the first plane (here) and filling it. In the second sally the action is removed to a point further away, the historical point—is the invention of Cidi Hamete Benengeli. Projected on that perspective, the parody is amplified, the figures appear smaller, their number can be augmented, the action can be complicated so as to acquire full resonance.

The change in tempo, this transfer of the action from the first plane to an intermediate one (only at the end of the novel will it retrocede to the furthest plane and into the grotesque verses which, together with those at the beginning, form the frame to the whole work) is pointed up by Cervantes in his step from the first to the second part. Here he intentionally accentuates the change by interrupting the adventure of the Biscayan, leaving both contendants, swords on high, statically posed. When the narration is taken up again, they recover their mobility. This parody of the technique of the novels of chivalry is reenforced by the fact that the novelist situates himself in reality (Alcaná de Toledo) in order to present his history as already written and to make us see his personages as figures of the imagination, showing them to us as they appear in an illustration of the manuscript.

All this is brought together with the purpose of violently displacing the narration, giving it the profundity of perspective which the theme demands. This theme is no longer the presentation of destiny in its totality, but rather its development, the process of destiny with the emphasis it gives to the confrontation of two epochs: the recent past (Gothic and Renaissance) and the present (Baroque). This confrontation of two epochs, as I have already indicated, is Cervantes' own intimate conflict, his vital experience, the fountainhead of his artistic creation, a creation which has its origin in the transfer of this experience from the personal to the extensive limits of the general.

The past is felt as such, as conclusively and irretrievably situated in the zone of the perfect; it is idealized and this feeling is expressed with the theme of the Golden Age, that felicitous age when innocence reigned, and which Cervantes contemplates from the vantage point of love in order to introduce the second melody of his novel.

In the first part, Don Quixote talks only in a general way of undoing wrongs and righting injustices. But the rascally inn-keeper (society) tells us how he himself wandered through various lands "soliciting widows and undoing damsels." The second part, as it marks the change in movement, announces ironically the theme of the Golden Age (Chap. 9) and the intent of this irony is to inculcate the poetic quality of the theme. In the same Chapter 9, the adventure of the Biscayan comes to an end: Don Quixote, victorious, restores to the captive lady her liberty.

The lady's liberator is now free to enter into the theme of his Discourse on the Golden Age, the scene is set: some goatherds, a serene night, a few acorns. In the Golden Age "damsels and honesty walked hand in hand, as I have said, wherever they would, alone and solitary, without fear that others' effrontery and lascivious desire would bring them to harm, and their perdition arose from their own choice and will. And now, in these our degenerate days, not a single maiden is safe though she were to be hidden and sequestered in another such labyrinth as that of Crete; for even there, through the crevices or borne on the air, there enters with zealous and accursed importunity the amorous pestilence and brings about their downfall in spite of all their seclusion. For their security, with the advance of time and men's malice, there was instituted the order of knights errant to defend damsels, protect widows and succor orphans and the needy." In the Golden Age, virtue was safe, the perdition of damsels arose from their "own will"; in this age, "no damsel is safe." This Discourse expounds the theory which is to be presented graphically in the "History of Marcela" and the "History of Cardenio and Dorotea." Knight-errantry was created to protect

Dorotea—the present epoch. We shall soon see the nature of this modern labyrinth; we shall soon see how not even this can free womankind from "the
zealous and accursed importunity." Marcela is sufficient unto herself, Don
Quixote is merely the spectator and onlooker in her history.

The narration of the "History of Marcela," a narration of idealized love, serves
as background and contrast to the "History of Cardenio and Dorotea." For this
reason it stands complete and alone in the second part, so that the past may be
contemplated as such and ideal love separated from reality. No sooner does Don
Quixote hear what has happened to the lover of Marcela than he assumes the
role of the enamored knight: "he spent all the rest of the night in sweet memories of his Lady Dulcinea, in imitation of Marcela's lovers."

The theme of chivalry and the literary theme are presented strongly united
and both in turn are related to the theme of love. As soon as the goatherd finishes
the narration of the pastoral episode, one of the characters points out the difference in the function of woman in a novel of chivalry. Woman in the Gothic
world is either a deified being, the star which guides the steps of man, or she
serves only to satisfy his senses: that is, she is the salvation or the perdition of
man. This Gothic antithesis disappears in Renaissance Marcela, in the woman
of the pastoral novel. Here she is man's companion, the source of a strictly
human happiness or grief. Dulcinea is not like Marcela, she is more like Gothic
woman, with the essential difference, however, that she is no longer a deified
being, but rather an idea, an idea in which "there come true all the impossible
and chimerical attributes of beauty which poets give to their mistresses" (Chap.
13). This discussion has been preceded by another in which the two ways of
Gothic life are compared—the chivalresque and the religious—as a necessary
antecedent to the Discourse on Arms and Letters.

But the literary problem becomes more complex in this second part, because,
along with the books of chivalry—a genre totally dead and whose existence aside
from its formal value only lent itself to parody—are to be found the pastoral
novels—the human relationship between man and woman, a study of the sentiments, the courtly social medium. The content of these novels still preserved a
value if they were vitalized and if given the form demanded by the current
social-urban medium to express the new human relationship. Besides, there is
the problem of style. For Cervantes, as for his epoch, medieval style was something primitive, rude and lacking in delicate artifice.

The "History of Marcela" is a pastoral novel, and its sentimental content
is manifested in the form of a "Debate on Love" ["Cuestión de amor"], clearly
announced: "her (Marcela's) affability and beauty attract the hearts of those who
would serve and love her; but her disdain and quelling of all their hopes drives
them to the point of desperation" (Chap. 12). And the whole of Marcela's dis-

course is directed toward the examination of the question: whether or not the object which is beautiful and worthy of being loved is obliged to reciprocate the love it inspires. The platonic Renaissance conclusion is the gratuity of love. The beautiful object should be loved for its beauty alone and no response should be expected.

The form, however, is completely baroque, and for that reason, the content is also baroque. The academic "debate" is transformed into a gust of passion which sweeps through the whole novel. What interests Cervantes is not a study of the sentiments but the demonstration of the suffering of a tortured heart, and the woods are filled with the shadows of lovers who convert the earth into a valley of amorous tears. Cervantes insists that the style of the pastoral life is a style of the cultural life that was born with Humanism. Grisóstomo is a student-poet of Salamanca. Marcela—an orphan under the tutelage of an uncle who is a priest interested in marrying her without forcing her will—is a rich girl. All the lovers are "rich young men." These select youths must give to their sentimental lives that idealized form of pastoral scenes and costumes. Contrasted with them, are the real shepherds, the goatherds. It is a goatherd who makes known the "debate"; but the novel is not told as a discussion of the "debate," rather as an extraordinary happening, worthy of report. The very goatherd is not permitted to unravel his story in courtly style until the difference between the popular tongue, that of the shepherds (*cris, estil, sarna*) and the elegant literary locutions has been clearly pointed out. And lastly, the curiosity of the reader is excited; this novel is filled with color and movement unlike the lineal and static clarity of the Renaissance pastoral. It is important to observe that Marcela is made to burst upon the scene, is placed, high above all those who form the funeral cortège, on a pedestal (the cliff), against a mountainous tree-covered background. From this craggy staging with its gigantic proportions, Marcela, erect, pronounces her discourse. In the Renaissance she would have spoken seated on the banks of a quiet-flowing river, on a level with her listeners, and her words would have been an invitation to dialogue. In contrast, this attitude and discourse of Marcela—who "without awaiting any reply, turned and disappeared into the innermost recesses of the mountain"—have a certain Caesarian air—the colossal air of the baroque absolute monarchy, filling all the space about with awesome admiration. In this monarchy the ruling concept is not that God has become man; it is man who sincerely believes himself to be the unique representative of God on earth, who believes himself Vice-God. Cervantes emphasizes the difference in the disposition of the scene and the colossal dimensions. Ambrosio angrily addresses Marcela: "Have you come . . . to behold your handiwork from those lofty heights, as did that other heartless Nero the conflagration of his burning Rome . . . ?" Finally, behind all that happens, we see a whole village that goes from one surprise to another, attracted by the extraordinary events which it has witnessed. The novel is no longer a discussion, a dialogue, in which all the characters in tranquil repose analyze quietly the distinguishing characteristics of a sentiment; it is an action which tensely controls the lives of some individuals and holds the attention of a whole village whose psychic and sentimental life has been stirred to its very depths by the strange occurrence. The need to express a new world imposes this new form.

Don Quixote has pronounced his discourse on the Golden Age, he has joined the chorus of lovers, he does not permit anyone to follow Marcela, and when he himself, dazzled too, would go in search of her, destiny prevents him from finding her, and directs him instead towards the real history of Cardenio and Dorotea.

Don Quixote has not engaged here in any chivalresque adventures, but just as the adventures of Puerto Lápice and the windmills of the second sally were anticipated in the first sally so here are announced previously that of Mambrino's helmet (Chap. 21) and that of the armies (Chap. 18) which are to take place in the third part. It is to be noted that now as before the adventures are alluded to in inverse order, and not in the order in which they appear, so that any symmetry of position, even in details, may be avoided.

The idealized Renaissance love of the "History of Marcela" remains isolated in the second part, but immediately its burlesque deformation is presented in the escapades of Rocinante and the galician mares, the episode with which the third part begins. Rocinante's unusual capers bring the story to the world of reality (the present), the world of nature and the instincts so aristocratically ignored in the pastoral; and they prepare the parody on chivalresque love which is to take place when Don Quixote, beaten and battered, enters the inn.

It is the inn of Palomeque, his wife and daughter, and the wench Maritornes. The wife and daughter attend the Knight. Maritornes does the same for Sancho. Cervantes disposes the amount of lighting for this scene. The faraway light of a wavering candle flame scarcely pervades the room; but, the light of the stars filters through the cracks in the roof. And all his physical pains do not prevent Don Quixote from turning to thoughts of love, touched off by the presence of a woman. While his amorous dreams raise the world of the senses to the highest plane of the ideal, at his side is the muleteer beset by desires of the flesh, and Sancho, blessedly peaceful, is sound asleep. It is not Sancho who presents the contrast to Don Quixote. The pure love of the Knight has its antithesis in the lascivious love of the muleteer. Sancho, obsessed by his idea of Power, is equally separated from both the one and the other kind of love. Maritornes is the baroque Venus of disillusionment. If, on the one hand, the Baroque revels joyfully and tragically in the senses until it reaches the very limits of exuberant sentimentality and sensibility (which will be characteristic of the Rococo), on the other hand, the Counter Reformation ideals of purity demand this bitterly grotesque vision of corporeal beauty. Following Don Quixote's moment of dreamed and pure passion, there comes a movement in crescendo, all filled with uproar and blows, which descends to pianissimo, then returns to take up again its accelerated rhythm (Chap. 17) and ends with the buffoonish effects of the balsam treatment on Sancho and his tossing in the blanket.

The parody of chivalresque love is at one and the same time separated from and united to the idealized love of the Renaissance and the real love of the baroque present which is to reach its full realization in the same inn in the fourth part: that inn which to Don Quixote in the third part of the novel was first castle and finally just an inn, and which in the fourth part he will begin by considering inn and conclude by transforming into castle.

Thematic interlinking is essential in baroque art not only in its combining function but also and principally as the source of the unity of composition and the subsequent aesthetic enjoyment. The proof, if such were needed, that thematic interlinking is a recourse in Cervantes' narrative art may be found in the introduction to Cardenio's story. Cervantes wishes to relate Cardenio's method of narration to that of Sancho thus preparing the scene of the Princess Micomicona's visit to Dulcinea. Cardenio promises to tell what has happened, but he begs them not to interrupt him because the moment that they do so, he will stop talking. Sancho had imposed a like condition when he told the story of the goats and Don Quixote points out the similarity: "These insistences of Cardenio reminded Don Quixote of the story that his squire had told, when he had not been able to ascertain the number of goats that had crossed the river, thus causing the story to remain unifinished" (Chap. 24). All of this, in addition, forewarns the reader of the danger of Cardenio's not completing his account and, in fact, that is exactly what occurs.

After the departure from the inn, we have, in a close sheaf, all the adventures of Don Quixote: adventure of the flocks (Chap. 18); of the dead body (19); of the mill-hammers (20); of the helmet (21); and finally, the adventure of the galley slaves (22). In these five adventures is shown the ideal and subjective texture of the quixotic world: from those clouds of dust that scarcely serve any other purpose than to hide the mounted hordes of the past from Sancho's eyes, to that purely verbal interplay in the adventure of the galley slaves. Reality no longer intervenes and of this there can be no doubt. The series of forms that reality assumes serve but to kindle the fancy. Dust, lights, noises, reflections, words—these are all that reality provides the senses. Sancho lives the adventure to the full until the moment of its solution because, being unable to act in a concrete immediate experience, he depends entirely on Don Quixote's interpretation of phenomena. Before Sancho sees the flocks, Don Quixote has already made numberless knights file by. Fear intimidates him until Don Quixote has disbanded the funeral cortège. He dares not move from his master's side for fear of death in the adventure of the mill-hammers. And in the adventure of the barber's basin his senses permit him to affirm only that he sees something that glitters. It is the same Sancho—Don Quixote has thrown him into such confusion—who helps to liberate the prisoners condemned to the galleys.

In the adventure of the flocks, the modern world melancholically says goodbye to the ancient medieval epic world. That medieval world seen and felt from the vantage point—Spain. The tone of evocation is what gives it the melancholy note. This adventure points to the next, that of the dead corpse—the caballero who has not perished gloriously in battle, but who died from pestilent fevers—; and this adventure prepares an atmosphere that is black with the blackness of fear, leaves the individual alone with himself to create his own world, to live, not on the reality all about him, but on his own inner longings (adventure of the mill-hammers).

In the adventure of the barber's basin, Sancho accepts the difference between being and seeming, and brings into relief the comic aspect which idealists present when they move among appearances. But immediately Sancho enters into an ideal world in which Dulcinea assumes the role of an infanta, for Don Quixote now considers her a great princess. Sancho forgets that he is married, and we behold him—who had insisted with so much dissimulation that the helmet appeared to be a barber's basin—prancing along converted into no less a personage than an earl with a *barber* in attendance, for certainly he will have more need of someone who can shave him frequently than he will of a master of the horse.

Knight and Squire always pass very cautiously from being to seeming, and end by becoming involved in the meaning of words when they come into contact with the galley slaves. The subjectivism of the world. Words, words, words, which have no meaning save that given them by the individual. These five adventures situate man in the modern world, a world of his own creation, and they involve him in the great adventure of the 1600's: the search for the essence of things.

These five adventures of the third part which are derived from mere allusions to reality—dust, lights, noises, reflections, words—are in perfect symmetry with the five of the first two parts which arise from contact with the world of forms—muleteers, Andrés, merchants, windmills and the Biscayan. The knight of the grotesque figure has been transformed into the Knight of the Woeful

Figure—an appellation bestowed by Sancho precisely at the end of the adventure of the dead body and the beginning of that of the mill-hammers. He, as is natural, sees in it no symbolic significance, and conjectures that either "the fatigue from this combat or the lack of molars and teeth" must be the cause for Don Quixote's sad aspect. But Don Quixote hastens to answer him and explains to him the meaning of his new name. These five adventures are the center of the novel in which the work reaches its maximum tension. When he introduces Don Quixote to the present world, in which the parodied adventures of chivalry come to an end—"an adventure which, without any artifice whatsoever, truly seemed to be one"—and has put him completely into touch with the 1600's—Cervantes is dedicating himself to a study of his speech and of the novel form which best suits him.

Knight and Squire go into the Sierra Morena and there reappears the harmonization of the Golden Age with the "History of Cardenio." Don Quixote, in his Discourse, had contrasted love in the real present with the idealized love of an ideal age. Cervantes contrasts the "History of Marcela" (pastoral) with the lives of Cardenio and Dorotea. These two lives are intimately related but they follow different directions. Both are members of the present world as it exists, and of a social-urban medium. The "History of Cardenio," however, is a study of novelistic atmosphere and psychological tenebrosities and is for that reason included in the third part. On the other hand, the "History of Dorotea" studies the relationship of man and woman in the present.

The goatherd of the "History of Marcela" serves as contrast to the shepherds of the pastoral and in addition recounts what has happened as an extraordinary event; the goatherd of the "History of Cardenio" has as function the facilitating of transition from one episode to another, but he does not recount what has happened to the protagonist; rather, he increases the astonishment and interest aroused by the actions whose motives he ignores. Both goatherds link the two histories to the Discourse on the Golden Age. The "History of Cardenio" is told by the protagonist himself, and the story he tells should be distinguished from the atmosphere in which Cervantes presents it to us. The atmosphere— craggy sierra, a suitcase, a mule, the ragged appearance of Cardenio, attacks of madness—translates plastically and novelistically the dramatic character of the occurrence and the state of mind of the individual. Cardenio's account acquaints us with the happenings: a series of social obstacles which give place to a purely inner action. Cardenio's history is made up of doubts, indecision and disorientation. He reveals a refined sensibility which causes him to pose problems for himself that are not of a theoretical or academic order but moral, and that constantly bring the will into play.

Cardenio takes us from one complicated situation to another that is still more complicated, entangling himself in the web which he himself spins. This perilous exploration of the inner world—alienated as much from the external action of the novel of chivalry as it is from the discursive method of the pastoral novel (although it is derived from the latter)—makes us penetrate into the modern novel. Luscinda with her moral suffering incarnates Counter Reformation woman: extremely virtuous and beautiful, she has to preserve her virtue in the world, not in an academy nor in a convent. She has to guide her enamored and chaste heart toward matrimony; submitting to parental authority, she has to marry the man destiny has chosen for her; and the Church will sanctify that union so that men may grow and multiply and sing in a world-encircling chorus, glory be to God in the highest.

The bipartite narration of Cardenio (Chap. 24 and 27) frames Don Quixote's penitence. As he, on hearing the history of Marcela, began to dream of love, so now he feels the necessity of grieving over Dulcinea's disdain. It was not possible that one of the myths most charged with baroque meaning should fail to conduct us to its hero's solitude. Don Quixote remains alone in the desert of disdain. His spiritual solitude is one of plaints and verses, tears and sighs. He addresses the sorrows of his "way-weary, suffering heart" to the mountain crags and trees. A heart tormented by an impossible love in solitary surroundings. And if Renaissance Marcela found most eloquent words with which to defend the gratuity of love, baroque Don Quixote will show all his pride and superiority in proclaiming the gratuity of pain and penitence. And immediately he makes clear the subjectivism of the world when he confesses to Sancho: "what seems to you a barber's basin, is to me Mambrino's helmet, and to another it will appear to be something else," and with this he makes us enter into all the tragic division of the modern soul. Just once, before the solitude is complete, Cervantes makes us feel the earthy quality of Dulcinea's origin, underlined especially by Sancho: "Tut, tut," said Sancho. "Did you say that the daughter of Lorenzo Corchuelo is my Lady Dulcinea of Toboso, otherwise known as Aldonza Lorenzo?" (Chap. 25). A few lines are sufficient for Cervantes to make us surmise a shy, dolorous, light, hidden history of love which is then converted into the profoundest of human sentiments, precisely because that love is all a pure creation of the mind.[1] In his epoch, the highly burlesque fact of finding the origin of the platonic idea in a proverb must have been extremely amusing.

Here Don Quixote doubly reveals the ideal contexture of Dulcinea, the necessity of creating one's own ideal in order truly to possess it; the exigency of dreams, of an inner impulse, of the outward projection of the self. The individual himself creates not only the elevated motives but also those which chain the soul to the senses. Idealistic art has the same root as realistic art. Thus, before telling us that the Phyllises are incarnations, of poets' dreams, the form that they give to their innermost aspirations, Don Quixote tells the anecdote of the widow who became enamored of the young lay-brother. That lusty fellow has exactly the same function as Dulcinea; the difference lies in the values which each satisfies. Dulcinea is the star, both guide and inspiration, she gives form to dreams and is herself a dream; she is the lode-star to which Don Quixote will never attain and at the same time, she is the very path to it. The lusty lay-brother, likewise, silences the cravings of the flesh and awakens them. They are two cleanly delimited zones, but both have their origin in the desires of the ego: desires of incessant struggle to free oneself from the material or desires to find in matter all its enjoyable density.

The literary theme runs through all this part. In Chapter 16 Cidi Hamete Benengeli's exactness is mentioned—that is, the problem is posed of the elaboration which reality—moral and sentimental experience—must suffer in order to be transformed into a work of art. The principle which rules the selection and ordering of the materials will not now be inspired in a hierarchical gradation but in the value of its significance as much from the point of view of the whole as from that of the detail, from the action as from the character, since in Chapter 20 he wants that not all that happens is worth recounting. While the classic world and classic art are based on a static arrangement of the beautiful and the non-beautiful, the noble and the ignoble, Cervantes, like all of his contemporaries, knows that the modern world and modern art—christian— seek to express the soul, the personality. Instead of creating beautiful attitudes as in the Greek statuary, or of tracing the limit of a passion as in the tragedy, modern art, from the Romanic period to the present, is the lyric revelation of a destiny whose expression is not achieved solely in beautiful or noble moments, but in moments filled with meaning, those which Don Quixote believes worthy of note. The important thing in the adventure of the dark night (mill-hammers) are not the noises but the reaction which these noises produce: they incite in the Knight's spirit desires to outdo himself, in the Squire they bring about an exclusively physiological activity. It little matters whether mill-hammers cause the noise: the essential is that each personage has projected himself as his destiny demanded. For some, Dulcinea; for others, the Island.

And finally, the literary theme is again alluded to when the Curate and the Barber make their reappearance in Chapter 26. This reminds us of the function of both characters in the first part and prepares their role in the fourth.

In the third part, then, we see that the theme of chivalry is presented framed between the parody of love in novels of chivalry and the "History of Cardenio," which, in turn, serves as frame to the exposition by Don Quixote of the gratuity of penitence.

The relationship of the second and third parts may be resumed thus: amorous theme: contrast between the Renaissance and baroque worlds; literary theme: in part two as well as in part three, given, not as a discussion, but as an embodiment of the ideal of two epochs and as an illustration of their difference— Gothic and Renaissance on the one hand and Baroque on the other. Just as, in the theme of chivalry we see how the tenebrous shadows of the baroque world are in opposition to the golden light of the Renaissance world; and just as the thirteen chapters of the third part counterweigh the fourteen of the first two parts; so the five adventures of the modern subjective world in search of essences counterbalance the five adventures of parodied chivalry in the first and second parts.

The "History of Cardenio" compared the baroque and the idealized Renaissance novelesque worlds; but the Discourse on the Golden Age studied the contrast between an ideal past age and the present one from the point of view of virginity. In the Golden Age, woman, living in full freedom, preserves her honor, and if she loses it, it is through her own will. Marcela was equally free and her viginity ran no risk of any kind. In the present age, said Don Quixote, there is no woman who can defend herself from man, although she were to withdraw into a labyrinth. Dorotea, in fact, lives enclosed in a moral labyrinth— home-loving and chaste, she had no relationship with any man—, all of which was of no avail to her for a young man succeeded in entering the room and in seducing her. Dorotea tells us of the lecture she gave Don Fernando and the one she gave herself while she was in his arms. The adventure is situated in a real medium and, what is more important, is constructed in terms of a realistic psychology. Pure love and its sudden and unexpected birth do exist; but now what interests Cervantes is the study of lust in man and how woman curbs it, conducting and transforming it into social matter. What Cervantes wishes to do is not to declare that woman is constantly besieged by man's sexual desire but rather to establish the acceptance of that desire as the basis for marriage. If that sexual attraction were not to exist, neither would matrimony. The Church has to sanctify it, making it lead man to God, making matter uphold spirit. Woman has to suffer for the desire she arouses, and she must change that suffering into a social impulse which will attract man to a purpose higher than the merely sexual one, to the social and religious aims of marriage. Woman creates man and in him the object of her grief or her happiness. For the awakening of his sexual instinct, her presence is enough, or even less—the mere idea of her existence; for the awakening of his social instinct she must actively pursue him, win him with qualities higher than those of beauty, with virtue. Dorotea tells us, with clear precision, that her fall came about through purely social motives. She could have asked for help; she did not do so, because she feared that no one would believe in her innocence; besides, she thought that it would not be the first time that beauty had bridged the gap in the unequal social status of lovers. No sooner has she yielded than she begins to feel the momentaneity of lascivious love. At once she decides to reconquer Don Fernando. Dorotea has to drop her passive role, which required no more of her than her mere presence and a defensive attitude, in order to enter actively into life with full consciousness of herself as woman, suffering woman; in order to conquer with the will and retain man whose sexual desire drifts along on the tide of woman's sexual attraction.

Dorotea's narration places the *Quixote* in a social, modern zone, but this is accomplished in accordance with the baroque technique which consists in sublimating reality, transforming it into artistic material so that its true meaning may be better perceived. In order to save Don Quixote Dorotea lends herself to the role of the Princess Micomicona. Thus (1) the theme of the Golden Age is terminated—Don Quixote intervenes as knight errant to befriend a helpless lady; (2) reality is transformed—History into Art—in preparation for the literary theme of this fourth part; (3) in Don Quixote is symbolized the moral force necessary to pass from the plane of lasciviousness to the social plane of marriage.

The literary theme, as in the first part, serves as framework to the events. The first sally *ended* with the scrutiny of the library. Now we *begin* with the scrutiny (Chap. 32). It is no longer a question of examining the literature of the past, but of reviewing the literature of the present. The material is not taken from shelves but from a suitcase. These are not printed books but manuscripts. The theme of History and Novel links this scrutiny to the earlier one. But here the theme is not dealt with indirectly. It makes evident the varied moral attitudes of the different readers; shows how art, the novel, is more real than life, than history; how the only true reality is the artistic reality or, in other words, how reality has no meaning until the poet gives it form. And to dramatize the difference in quality of these two realities, the characters of the *Quixote* begin to read a novel. The Curate ordered the burning of the books in the other scrutiny, but in this, it is he who avidly devotes himself to the reaching of a still unpublished novel: *The Curious Impertinent.*

The writers of ancient and medieval times always express the soul of the community, they incarnate their ethos; their work, as a consequence, is always understood by their public. The modern writer, having to express his individual soul which is unique, lives constantly tormented by the difficulty, which he knows to be almost insuperable, of being understood. For that reason, paradoxically, he thinks without cease of his public. This public without which his work may not live, and on whom the poet bestows an hermetical world. Therefore, the Canon, who has written more than one hundred pages of a novel, says, in Chapter 48, that he has given it to read to men who like that kind of reading and not only to the learned, but also to the ignorant; he wishes to know the opinion of all men, the melancholy and the gay, the simple and the discreet about whom Cervantes speaks in his prologue.

Cardenio has read the beginning of the manuscript and it seems good to him; the ·Curate thinks the same. It is the most critical and fearful moment of Cervantes' life, of the life of a writer. It is not enough to be sure oneself of the value of what has been written. Will it find readers? A woman—the woman to whom novels are dedicated—decides it: the enchanting Dorotea, whose spirit is not tranquil enough to induce sleep and who therefore believes it will be better "to spend the time listening to some story." All were present save Don Quixote. The Knight has retired with his dreams and will not reappear until *The Curious Impertinent* is about to be ended.

In Chapters 33, 34, 35, the modern novel is read, the novel of Faustine man, of the man who is tormented by "a desire so strange and so uncommon to others that I marvel at myself, and blame myself, and when alone, upbraid myself, and try to silence it and hide it in my own thoughts." Anselmo wishes to prove whether or not his wife is essentially good and perfect. His intent, as his friend Lotario points out to him, is a difficult thing and *new* besides, because he neither tries it for God, nor the world, nor for the two of them concerned. But Anselmo feels himself devoured by modern curiosity, by the gratuity of the act, by the desire of knowledge for knowledge's sake, by a satanic spirit which makes him live a tragic life tormenting himself when all in the world— love, friendship, social position, wealth—smiles upon him so that he may be happy. He brings misfortune down upon himself and upon those he most loves: his wife, his best friend.

In Chapter 32 the Curate alludes to the theme which is to be treated in the dialogue with the Canon (Chap. 47, 48, 49, 50) and which closes the literary theme. As all depart from the inn, and as they say their goodbyes, the *new* literature is discussed, that is, what are cited are not books of chivalry nor pastoral novels, but the exemplary novels: "El curioso impertinente" and "Rinconete." We are assured that since they are both by the same author, the latter must be good.

Now there can begin the extremely important dialogue between the Canon and the Curate. The interest in this dialogue no longer resides in the censorship of books of chivalry and in their being taken as History. (Although this aspect, which continues the thematic unity, does give rise to the invention by Don Quixote of the adventure of the Knight of the Lake in which there is to be found a unique description of baroque architecture and decorative motifs. It is here too that Don Quixote reveals the secret of baroque composition: "disordered order.") The importance of the dialogue lies in the fact that Cervantes establishes the union between the Baroque and the Gothic and examines in the latter all the formal elements which are still useful and which can and should be saved. He contrasts "the unrestricted writing in these books" to the formal Classic and Renaissance rigidity. The Baroque, by retaining the formal Gothic flexibility, can embrace the whole world in all its complex variety. The final paragraphs of Chapter 47 are the Baroque manifesto, the literary program which permits us to understand, as far as form is concerned, Cervantes' work from the *Quixote* of 1605 to the *Persiles,* with the *Novelas Ejemplares* and the *Quixote* of 1615 as the successive steps between.

The reading of "El curioso impertinente" had been interrupted by the adventure of the wine skins (Chap. 35) in which Don Quixote kills the giant of lasciviousness, in this way freeing the Princess—Dorotea; Don Fernando arrives with Luscinda and thus the modern history of Cardenio and Dorotea finds a solution. We are still in the inn—which Don Quixote transforms into a castle so that it may be a mansion worthy of the treasure of beauty it houses—witnessing the fulfillment of destiny and uncovering the secrets of human personality, when the Captive, attired in blue, arrives with his beautiful companion, Zoraida. Don Quixote pronounces the Discourse on Arms and Letters, and Cervantes indicates that it should be related to the Discourse on the Golden Age. And in the same way that he dramatized the Discourse on the Golden Age with the histories of love, he now dramatizes the new Discourse with the histories of the Captive (arms) and the Judge (letters). A dramatization which Cervantes points out, in Don Quixote's words, at the moment that the Judge and his daughter arrive at the crowded inn: Don Quixote says: "no matter what the lack of space and comfort in the world, room must be provided for arms and letters, and more so, if those same arms and letters bring beauty as their guide and leader" (Chap. 42).

Arms and letters are sisters, although between them exists that hierarchy which gives preeminence to arms. The story of the Captive is the spiritual autobiography of Cervantes. If Don Quixote is the nostalgic figure of a heroism that is past, the heroism which Cervantes dreamed, the Captive is the figure of a heroism that is present, a heroism which Cervantes lived, whose existence in the soul of the novelist allowed his nostalgia to take on an ironic form, thus keeping him from falling into a bitter pessimism. For Cervantes, the world not only longs for the times long past of Achilles, the Cid and the Gran

Capitán: he has but recently lived the last great epic, that of the Battle of Lepanto. But even this form of heroism can no longer be comprehended nor felt; however, this incomprehension will only to a slight degree cloud his spirit with a light veil of sadness because Cervantes manages to keep inviolate his faith in himself, his faith in his own will and efforts, a faith which is not destroyed but purified and made stronger by all his misfortunes and failures. The Captive says: "never did I abandon the hope of being free, and when what I planned, thought, and put into action did not meet with the success that was intended, then, without succumbing to despair, I sought and imagined another hope that would sustain me, though it were only a weak and feeble one" (Chap. 40). It would not matter if we were not to know Cervantes' biography; this confession of the Captive would always give a splendid clarity to his illustrious life. Cervantes does not undervalue modern times, nor his own epoch, and for that reason he sees the grotesqueness of a resurrected past. He needs to confront Don Quixote with the Captive; he must create the *Quixote* to free himself of nostalgia and be able to discover the new heroism of the Counter Reformation which will induce him to create the *Novelas Ejemplares,* the *Quixote* of 1615, and the *Persiles.*

Zoraida is to the Captive what Dulcinea is to Don Quixote; but if Dulcinea is Gothic woman, deified and transformed into the platonic idea, Zoraida represents the experience of captivity, the beautiful moral experience. The Catholic world, like the Protestant, is to have morality as its only basis; but while Protestants make of morality a beautiful inner experience which leads to the categorical imperative, Catholic Cervantes endows it with the splendid form of Zoraida whose beauty proclaims the dogma of the Immaculate Conception. And the blues of the Captive's raiment entone (with the resplendent coloring of Murillo and Rubens) a chant to the Virgin, the brilliant organum of "Lela Marien," which means "Our Lady, the Virgin Mary."

As the Captive has his story of love, so the Judge, too, has his in his daughter Clara. The "History of Clara" is that of an innocent love, and its function in the novel is the depuration of all human love. The love of Dorotea, of Luscinda and Zoraida carry with them too many extraneous elements. Their sorrows have distilled a drop of bitterness—the bitterness of experience—in their hearts. They have already tasted life. Clara's innocence purifies that night charged with human experience and thus, on the ample plains of the Mancha, Don Quixote can let soar his dreams to Dulcinea. Don Quixote's love in each moment —Marcela, Cardenio, Clara—takes on the tone that corresponds to the scene of which it forms a part. The action of the "semi-damsels" (the irony is in the "semi") leads the novel to the zone of the grotesque, and a series of incidents prepares the denouement, keeping it at a tumultuous crescendo which with its contrast will make more slow the slowness of the measured pace of the oxen and the Canon's dialogue. There follows a brilliant movement succeeded by a very brief quiet one, which prepares the choral finale of the village on Sunday and the last chord of Sancho and his wife (time in the present) which provides a contrast to the pastness of the deeds of Don Quixote.

When the dialogue on the novel and the theatre comes to a close, the denouement is still held off by the "History of the Jealous Goatherd" and the adventure of the Disciplinants. The literary theme acquires an immense volume in the final dialogue, a volume into which harmonizes the "History of the Goatherd" which is a *reprise*, a recapitulation of the theme of love, as is the adventure of the Disciplinants a *reprise* on the theme of chivalry.

We see, then, that the theme of love gives place to a maximum complication in which there is dramatized the fulfillment of destiny, the secret of personality, and, in addition, the modern solution of the amorous conflict which is presented in correlation with the theme of arms and letters. In turn, Clara's love provides a background to Don Quixote's pure dreaming, and while a solution is being sought to the conflict which he has implanted, a series of incidents whose turbulence and complication accord with those of love, bring forward again to the first plane Don Quixote and the theme of chivalry. The burlesque tone of its reappearance transposes the theme to the key of the first part. It thus stands in contrast to the passionate tone of the theme of love. Both themes finally unfold and come to a solution. The Baroque likes these *reprises* for their architecturally musical denouements and with them prepares the last chord of the cascading finale.

RECAPITULATION

The plan of the novel can be delineated with all clarity and its content easily summarized:

FORM: *Circular composition; composition in cascades; four parts; two sullies; two inns; two reprises.*

CONTENT: Three themes. *Theme of chivalry:* Twelve adventures, two groups of five which correspond to each other, and two dreamed adventures. *Theme of love:* Two Discourses on which hinge all of the "Histories." *Literary theme:* Related to the other two themes in the second and third parts, serving as framework in the first and fourth.

If we understand the plan of the novel, we may not only enjoy it in all its intelligent clarity, but also discover its true nucleus: the polarity (in the three themes) of the past and the present; the exact relationship of Don Quixote and Sancho who neither oppose nor complement each other, but who represent two different values of the same ideal world: Dulcinea, the Island.

II

The *Quixote* of 1615 has seventy-four chapters, which are not grouped into parts. After the first seven chapters of studied dialogue and of a constant going and coming, there takes place the third sally that fills the whole novel; at first it unfolds with marked slowness and great nuclear clarity: Toboso and the enchantment of Dulcinea, the death cart of the strolling players, the Knight of the Wood, the Caballero of the Green Coat and the lions, Camacho's wedding, the Cave of Montesinos, the braying and Maese Pedro's puppet show, the adventure of the enchanted bark. After the encounter with the Duke and Duchess, the incidents have a certain unity of place since they happen in the ducal home and its surroundings, but they take place in a more intricate pattern: colloquy of both characters with the Duke and Duchess, Merlin and the disenchanting of Dulcinea, Trifaldi, counsels, Don Quixote and Sancho separate, Altisidora, the Island, Doña Rodríguez, letters, pilgrims, the fall into the pit, the reunion of Knight and Squire, the tilt with Tosilos, the departure from the Duke's home. With the journey to Barcelona, the stay in the city and return, the events and encounters become more numerous and gain in frequency; that slowness of the beginning of the novel is accelerated into rapidity and the episodic extension replaced by a fractioning of the action.

Frequently the chapters are joined in twos or in threes and in some cases sometimes form an even larger group. Examples of the first grouping would be Chapters 1 and 2, in which we first have Don Quixote and then Sancho; or Chapters 3 and 4 both dedicated to the discussion of the 1605 novel; or 5 and 6 where we see Sancho with Teresa and Don Quixote with the House-keeper and Niece; in Chapter 13, the colloquy between the two squires; in Chapter 14, the dialogue between the two knights; in Chapter 32 Don Quixote converses with the Duke and Duchess; in 33 Sancho with the Duchess; Chapters 34 and 35 indicate how Dulcinea is to be disenchanted; 42 and 43 contain counsels and advise; 69 and 70 again take place in the home of the Duke.

The following might be examples of the articulation in threes; (8, 9, 10) the journey to Toboso; (12, 13, 14) adventure with the Knight of the Mirrors; (16, 17, 18) the encounter with Don Diego de Miranda; (19, 20, 21) Camacho's wedding; (25, 26, 27) Maese Pedro; there are other examples, but I merely wish to indicate those which are self-evident. The adventure of the Countess Trifaldi covers six chapters (36–41) and occupies the central portion of the novel.

We have noted that, from the moment of the meeting with the Duke and Duchess, the events have a certain unity of place. Moreover, part of the action hinges upon the enchantment of Dulcinea and the Cave of Montesinos; the grouping in threes also has an influence on the conformation of the episodes; Cervantes himself insists upon the grouping in twos, sometimes emphasizing it in the epigraph of the chapter: "Chapter I.—What passed between the Curate, the Barber and Don Quixote . . . Chapter II.—Which treats of the notable quarrel between the Niece, the Housekeeper and Sancho Panza . . . Chapter V.—Of the humorous and discreet conversation that took place between Sancho Panza and his wife . . . Chapter VI.—What happened to Don Quixote with his Niece and Housekeeper . . . Chapter XXXIV.—Which tells of the notice that was received of ways to disenchant . . . Chapter XXXV.— Further notice of ways to disenchant . . . Chapter XLII.—Of counsels . . . Chapter XLIII.—Second part of the advice and counsels . . . ; again, Cervantes emphasizes it in the text: "The knights were separated from the squires, the latter telling each other the story of their lives, the former, of their loves; but the novel recounts first the discourse of the squires, and then continues with that of their masters . . . " (Chap. 13); and lastly, Cervantes underlines in the text what he points up in the epigraph: "The counsels which I have thus far given you pertain to the adornment of the mind; listen now to those which serve to adorn the body" (Chap. 42). There may be too a division, within the chapter, into two or three parts.

The bimember rhythm, so characteristic of the Baroque, in all its possible combinations—alternation, parallelism, duplication, opposition—is so obviously marked because the novelist utilizes it in 1615, not to give unity to an episode as is the case in the grouping in threes, but to give movement to his work, for example, when he alternates an episode of Don Quixote with another of Sancho or to establish a rigorous order, as in the arrangement of the counsels. This parallelism acquires so much importance in the composition of the novel because it is expressing the novelist's vision of the world: two lines which depend upon one another, that run always equally separated and always with the illusion of joining one another on a horizon which is deceptively in sight.

Cervantes, precisely at the moment that he separates Don Quixote from Sancho (Chap. 44) declares how he has begun the novel of 1615 with the decision to give it a form different from that which he gave it in 1605: "They say that in the real original of this history, when Cide Hamete wrote this chapter, which his interpreter did not translate as it had been written, the Moor gave voice to his dissatisfaction with himself for having undertaken such a dry and limited history as this of Don Quixote. Because it seemed to him that he must always be talking about Don Quixote and Sancho without daring to expand into digressions and episodes of a more serious and entertaining nature; and he said that this strict adherence of the mind, the hand and the pen to the writing of just the one subject and the speaking through the mouths of only a few persons was an intolerable work whose merit did not redound to the author's credit, and that, in order to avoid this very inconvenience, he had made use in the first part of the artifice of such novels as "The Curious Impertinent" and "The Captive Captain," which are, as it were, separated from the history since all other things told therein happened to Don Quixote and could not be omitted. He also thought (as he himself tells us) that many readers, carried away by the attention which Don Quixote's deeds demand, would pay no heed to the novels and pass over them either hurriedly or annoyedly without stopping to note the choice qualities and the artifice contained in them—all of which would become very evident were they to stand by themselves and be published dissociated from the madness of Don Quixote and the follies of Sancho. And thus, in this second part, he did not wish to insert novels, either of the related or the unrelated kind, but only a few happenings of an episodic nature born of the very events which truth offers, and even these sparingly and briefly with only the words sufficient to explain them. And since he controls himself and keeps within the narrow limits of his narration, although he has ability, sufficiency and understanding great enough to treat of the whole universe, he begs that his work be not scorned and that praises be given not for what he writes, but for what he has refrained from writing."

The novelist feared that the reader would tire of the same characters, and at the same time he believed that, dominated by his interest in the main story, he would not give to the novels their deserved attention. Cervantes' problem consists in limiting himself to one subject matter, giving to its unity the greatest variety. He will have as little recourse as possible to episodes, and when he does, he will try to be brief and to relate them in a natural way to the protagonist. The story of Claudia Jerónimo (Chap. 60) and the history of Ana Félix (Chaps. 63 and 65) would probably meet Cervantes' qualifications for episodes in this novel.

I believe that the tendency we discover in 1615 as we read the second *Quixote* is, to begin with, the desire for one action; then, the necessity for the identification of action and protagonist: that there should be but one action and that the protagonist should fill it all. Reflect upon what is to be the new aesthetics of the Comedy—the so-called school of Calderón—and the political ideal of Spain, France and England up to the Peace of the Pyrenees, to that moment when inevitably there had to be proclaimed the declaration "I am the State," which has been preceded by the Conde-Duque (who incites Philip IV to be "king of Spain," not king of Castile, Leon, Aragon, etc.) Richelieu and Cromwell.

The parallel or alternating rhythm, the combination of events into groups of various chapters are nuclei which give direction to the constant flow of the novel whose chief characteristics, with reference to composition, are digression and concatenation. That predilection for the *singular,* so apparent in the Cervantes of 1605, is opposed to multiplicity, but not to dispersion, at least not when it takes the form of digression. This digression, however, does not focus our attention on a thousand different points as do the rays from a single center each of which radiate to a different point on a given circumference. The digression is a whole volley aimed at a single target or a never-ending intercalation.

Each word, each sentiment, each idea can give rise at any moment—through a natural or a surprising association—to a new word, a new sentiment, a new idea. The interest is awakened and kept awake. It is completely impossible for the reader to foretell what development the thought is to follow, and equally impossible for him to ascertain whether he has entered a gulf or whether he is navigating toward an immense sea. When the reader is caught in this agglomeration he depends entirely on the author who forces him without pity to keep time with his rhythm: slow or rapid, brief or long. Proverbs, maxims, adages, questions, anecdotes, stories, professions, types, customs—all running into an entangled mesh, and Don Quixote, indignant, exclaims: "Where are you going to end up, Sancho! Curses upon you, when you begin *to string out proverbs and stories* only Judas himself could stop you! May he damn your soul!" (Chap. 19). We do not hear Sancho's reply now but in Chapter 22: "I say of him (Don Quixote) that when he begins to thread out maxims and to give advice . . . " And already in Chapter 5 he had said: "The Lord help thee, woman, what things you have strung one to the other without head nor tail!"

To string, to thread, this is the motivating principle in the Quixote of 1615 and it applies as much to the dialogue as it does to the action. Don Quixote in his third sally has to pass away the time, precisely because he knows where he is headed: "he expected to pass away the time until the day should arrive for the jousts at Saragossa toward which his true *route* lay" (Chap. 18). (The word "derrota" [route, rout] should perhaps be read in its double meaning; it is not so much a verbal play as it is an impassioned baroque need to capture a complex in the simplest and most direct manner). Man, too, has to pass away the time of his life, because he too sets out on the road which leads him to death. The road is no longer a schematic line that traces the course of destiny's path. Instead of this all-inclusive simple scheme, there is a continual wandering about, stopping, retracing of steps, descending and ascending, entering and exiting. This rhythm of the action is a digression. There is time to arrive: "he determined to see first the banks of the river Ebro and all that vicinity before entering the city of Saragossa, for there was time enough and more to spare before the jousts" (Chap. 27). In 1605 one is constantly living the essential moment. One does not have to be on the way from one point to another; in any place whatsoever one is where one should be: in the great adventure of total Justice or total Beauty. In 1615, one explores with pleasure, promenades with delight, desires to meet people, to visit places, to satisfy that curiosity which life quickens. There is time to arrive where destiny calls; for that reason, along with the feeling that there is time, is the feeling that one has paused enough, that one must be on the way. The coexistence of these two feelings: "because it wasn't seemly that knights errant should indulge in many hours of idleness and ease, he wished to be off to fulfill the duties of his calling" (Chap. 18). One lives with that feeling of liberty of him who knows he has time, but also with the disquietude and the torture of him who has to count the days, the hours and the minutes that remain: minutes, hours and days of liberty. If in 1605 one told stories and histories and pronounced discourses, in 1615 one talks without cease; if, in the first *Quixote,* adventures and episodic actions were perfectly complete in themselves, in the second *Quixote* what most draws the attention is the interlinking of the colloquies and the actions.

Sancho in the pit thinks that at each step he takes "beneath him suddenly there will gape another pit more profound than this, which will swallow him up"; and Roque Guinart confesses: "just as one abyss leads to another, and one sin to another, so has vengeance formed a chain." The form of the novel is a stringing together, a threading and an interlinking, because social life is only an abyss which leads to another abyss; the life of man a progression from one sin to another until he arrives at death.

In 1605 Sancho had hobbled Rocinante; the Curate and the Barber had discussed the action which Dorotea carried out; the same characters, with the aid of the other guests at the inn, enchanted Don Quixote. We see, then, that they deceive[2] the Knight, and it is by means of the last deception that they succeed in getting him to return to his village. These deceptions, however, only form part of the action, they do not direct it. The hobbling of Rocinante is a trick played upon Don Quixote, at the same time that it is a sign of Sancho's fear. When Dorotea relates the story of Princess Micomicona she is really retelling the story of her own life, that of a deceived woman. Hence the name which the Curate gives to the Princess. When they enchant Don Quixote they put him into a cage and force him physically to return to the village. In 1605, the action stands out against a background of blinding sun, deep darkness, fires surrounded by night, metallic glitters, greys, dust and moonlight, oil lamps and nocturnal silence. Don Quixote and Sancho wend their way over the highways, enter the woods, stop on the craggy sierra, stay at inns, and all the tumult of humanity accompanies them. Women and more women, endowed with beauty, innocence and virtue or enslaved by vice, who make manifest all the aspects of womankind; and men, young and old, noble and ignoble, high and low officials of the secular and the ecclesiastical life, shepherds, muleteers, goatherds, all of whom present to us multiple man. Men and women, all on the highway too, in the forests, and in the inns. On every side, life—the great adventure—, everyone on the way—the destiny of man—, always in the inn—the stage of the world.

In 1605, Don Quixote left his home with no other definite purpose than that of seeking adventure; in 1615, Don Quixote wishes first, to go to Toboso, then to Saragossa, and, between one point and the other, he wishes to visit the Cave of Montesinos. He succeeds in arriving at Toboso where he immediately has to be directed and guided. He goes to Toboso looking for something definite, that is why he is lost and disoriented; he also goes to the Cave of Montesinos with a guide; when he is already near Sarogossa, he changes his mind and heads for Barcelona, where he arrives with letters of introduction. Not only does Don Quixote have someone to guide his steps; they also make him live a life of delusion. Sancho deceives him, and others go on deceiving him: the Bachelor, Maese Pedro, the Duke and Duchess, the ladies-in-waiting, Altisidora, Don Antonio Moreno and his friends. On his very deathbed they try to deceive him. This guidance and this continuous deception make of the personage and of the novel of 1615 something completely different from the work and the personage of 1605. The deception is also presented in an interlinked pattern. Not only does one deception give place to another, many of the characters are in their turn deceived. Sancho, the author of Dulcinea's enchantment, is made to believe that she is really enchanted, and also, that he is actually a governor. Doña Rodríguez is deceived and so is Tosilos; the Duke and Duchess are deceived when they plan the tilt; Don Antonio Moreno who deceives his friends with the magic head, just as Maese Pedro did the people with his monkey, is in turn deceived when the Bachelor arrives. The Bachelor is himself deceived when he believes that to challenge Don Quixote is to overcome him.

The novel has an air of play, of pleasantry, all the more amusing because there are those who are unaware of the game. These adults are playing until the last moment, until death bids them cease. And the young ones do not become shepherds, they play at being shepherds. Thus we see that the action is directed, prepared. We know that what is happening, what is going to happen, is not true. Social life is a delusion, a stage representation.

The world of 1605 was epitomized in the adventure of the dark night, of an immobility all pervaded with movement. The equivalent of this adventure of the mill-hammers is, in 1615, the adventure of Clavileño. Cervantes takes pains that we should note this. The world of dark solitude becomes a world in which men are blindfolded; the immobility is now a resting place of wood. No one laughs in the adventure of the mill-hammers until light dispels the darkness; in the adventure of Clavileño, Don Quixote and Sancho, again tightly clasped to each other, are the butt of laughter, surrounded by spectators who revel in the fun. It is not light that makes the inexistent monsters of the night disappear but firecrackers that prove the complete falseness of Sancho's fanciful lies.

In 1605, the mystery of life was presented. In 1615, life is a tangle and the novelist has to unravel it. Sancho's machinations are described; the identity of the Knight of the Mirrors is revealed; Basilio's subterfuge is explained; Maese Pedro's identity made clear; the true nature of Merlin and the Countess Trifaldi exposed; the names of those who beat Doña Rodríguez given; the workings of the enchanted head explained; the character who plays the Knight of the White Moon named. Cervantes explains why they do not go to Saragossa. Don Quixote tells us that he has been mad. Everything is explained and elucidated because everything can and should be explained. The same will be true of the Comedy. In Lope's time, the action is neither justified nor explained: it is a poetic world; in Calderón's, there will be felt the necessity of justifying and explaining it. Let us remember that in Calderón, Basilio also prepares the action for Segismundo, and that it is the literary moment when the action is to be directed and prepared by the jester. The last stage of the Baroque is being created, and from it will rise the Rococo.

In Calderón's epoch, the figure will be transformed and become a caricature; the same thing happens in the novel of 1615. I have just indicated the role played by the two characters in the adventure of Clavileño; to that might be added the incident of the cheeses, the fall of both Knight and Squire when they go to meet the Duke and Duchess, or the parade through Barcelona with the poster. The adventure is made caricature in the encounter with the lions, and other characters, Doña Rodríguez, for instance, are drawn with the same exaggerated lines. Man, that is, reason is being substituted for God. Man and life are con-templated from the point of view of reason.

In the *Novelas Ejemplares* Cervantes has recourse more than once to antithetic parallelism to conduct the action. In the second *Quixote* it is employed not only to conduct the action from beginning to end, but also to accentuate it strongly. The novel begins presenting the Knight to us in his bed, on the road to recovery and ready to sally forth once again; it ends in the same room with the moribund Knight on his deathbed. The first episode is Sancho's deception, he makes Don

Quixote believe that Dulcinea is enchanted; at the end of the novel, Sancho again deceives him making him believe that he has already flogged himself and that therefore Dulcinea is disenchanted. The same thing happens with the twice repeated challenge of the Bachelor; in the first combat he is vanquished and in the second, victorious.

In positions which are almost symmetrical—twenty-two chapters from the beginning, and twenty chapters from the end—we have Don Quixote's descent into the Cave of Montesinos and Sancho's fall into the pit. The correlation of the two descents, voluntary and involuntary, is easily established, but Cervantes, through Sancho, makes it very evident. Even the description of the pit coincides with that which Don Quixote gives of the Cave.

In the two moments of pastoral life (Chaps. 58 and 68), when Don Quixote meets the young people who represent eclogues, and on his return, defeated, when he dreams of becoming a shepherd, he is trampled, first by bulls and then by swine: the shock of reality, the end in reality toward which lead the representation and the dream.

The parallelism, whether it be antithetical or not, always transfers us from one value to another, from one measure to another, from ideal justice and beauty to earthly justice and beauty. The continual struggle between the ideal and the social, how the relative is weighed down by the absolute, how the ideal is chained, diminished and deformed by the social—we persistently have the sensation of two parallel lines, or two parallel planes, or two parallel volumes. Sancho has the ability to disenchant Dulcinea and Altisidora. In alternate chapters—Sancho on the Island, Don Quixote in the sociable solitude of his room—while the Knight is living the experience of beauty and love, the Squire is living that of justice and government.

Cervantes indicates that he has given to his novel of 1615 a form different from that of 1605. Perhaps a more profound and penetrating study would reveal other formal elements, but, for the present, we have seen how the multiple action is reduced to one, how the protagonist fills all of it; we have also noted the characteristics of this action: digression and concatenation, deception, that it is invented by other characters, and finally, the antithetic parallelism. All of these characteristics flower in the baroque art of the last period, in France and England as well as in Spain. And I have related these formal elements to the political world of the same period so that two different mediums may be compared.

In 1605 Cervantes had achieved the universal expression of his personal, inner conflict: the struggle between the past and the present. From that moment on the novelist dedicates himself to the expression of his epoch, that is, to the creation of it. He is going to give form to the society of his epoch, to the spirit of his times; he is going to create the ideal which gives meaning to man's life. The second *Quixote* stands between the *Novelas Ejemplares* and the *Persiles,* and is a novel which should be considered not as one more "part" to the 1605 *Quixote,* but as an entirely different work. The novel begins with an indication of the isolation in time from the other *Quixote*. "Cide Hamete Benengeli relates in the second part of this history, Don Quixote's third sally, that the Curate and the Barber went almost a month without seeing him"; according to baroque sense of time, this month is sufficient; the temporal separation of ten years is thus satisfactorily expressed; for the chronological sense of the XIXth Century, however, this month was completely inadequate, and one editor changed it to a year—a disrespectful alteration of the text which nevertheless complied with a spiritual necessity. In the fifth chapter Cervantes warns us that "Sancho Panza talks in a different style"; when he embarks upon the third sally he insists emphatically: "the deeds and drolleries of Don Quixote and his squire begin at this point; persuade them (the readers) to forget the past deeds of the Ingenious Hidalgo and to fix their attention on those still to come, for they begin now, on the road to Toboso, just as the others began in the fields of Montiel" (Chap. 8). If we persist in remembering those other adventures, if we read the two works as one, the rhythm of the action loses all its meaning and the composition disintegrates, leaving us in complete confusion.

With a XIXth Century training we had to believe that this advance in time represented an evolution in the character of the personages. In my opinion, this manner of thinking is foreign to the Baroque, an epoch which is very sensitive to "conversion" and to the different cycles of man's life; an epoch in which are studied either human nature or the different types into which man's way of being crystallize; an epoch in which life is impregnated with an ideal or an effort made to direct conduct. But in the Baroque one does not make history, that is, time is not entrusted with a formative function; thus, in that epoch, one does not view the course of destiny from a temporal standpoint. In the Baroque what is felt profoundly is the passage of time. From the Romantic period on, what is felt is that things come to pass in time.

This passage of time, then, is not to indicate that Don Quixote has changed; that "month" is a pause between the two works, it does not unite, it separates them. With the same figure, a new world is to be explored. For that reason, Don Quixote's death in 1605 is the last parodic note of the chivalresque medieval world, and his death in 1615 is completely different. One speaks in a different style, one dies in a different manner, not because of the novelist's carelessness, but because he causes the figure created by him to conform to the demands of the theme he is treating.

The form of the 1615 work is different from that of the 1605 and Cervantes desires that when one is read, the other should be forgotten. To capture the rhythm of the composition one must perceive, in addition to these purely formal elements, the tone of the novel and the motifs on which it is composed.

In 1605 proverbs are uttered and Don Quixote himself is first in using them, but it is only in 1615 that they are utilized in a functional way; the same is true of the states of discretion and madness. In the first novel, Don Quixote does, at times, become indignant, for example, when the wenches cannot contain their laughter; but it is only in 1615 that the Knight's irritation provides the tone for the work.

Early, in the first chapter (the prologue has already introduced us into the zone of social and personal irritation), faced with the impertinence of the Barber, Don Quixote loses his equanimity and in the course of the novel this happens repeatedly: "Don Quixote was burning with fury and rage" (Chap. 31). Cervantes shares in this irritation. Before Don Quixote angrily answers the Curate in the Duke's house, even before he has presented his character, Cervantes is annoyed at this clergyman whom he sees, not as an individual, but as the representative of a certain social type. And Sancho also gives way to annoyance. His dependence upon the Knight vexes him. This dependence is of such irritating vagueness that its growth and increase in him is not apparent, but, at the same time it makes itself felt constantly in an irritating manner, and he cannot rid himself of it. Sancho will want to leave his master, they will even come to blows; he will exclaim indignantly: what have the Panzas to do with the Quixotes! But in spite of everything, he will not be able to abandon the Knight; when nothing is left them but to separate, both weep; and they will come together again because one cannot exist without the other.

Neither Don Quixote's irritation, nor that of Sancho, nor that of the novelist results from any transcendent cause, perhaps because the transcendental world can lead to desperation or to tragedy but not to irritation. This state is motivated by social life: institutions and man. Human grossness, the mysterious social interdependence produce irritation which, like an anti-climax, resolves itself into calm when faced with the incomprehension produced by the lack of worldly experience. At times, Don Quixote tries to persuade; but what characterizes him is that he does not attempt to discuss or convince. He knows that it is useless. The novelist himself points out that calmness and also indicates its source: namely, that frequently incomprehension is rooted in affection.

Irritation, calmness and the transition from irritation to calmness. The work does not offer a violent contrast of lightness and darkness, but rather a dimming of the light. The word which Cervantes uses, as always, the exact one, is intraclarity ("entreclaridad"), an attenuated and very soft pervading clarity, diffused so that light and shadows blend into each other.

In violent contrast to this, Don Quixote could before affirm: "I know who I am, and know that I can be." In this world of intra-clarity, Don Quixote does not express the secret of personality. The Knight sees Dulcinea three times; Sancho obtains the Island. All the joy of the pursuit of the ideal has been lost. Don Quixote and Sancho have attained what they set out to achieve, and what a difference there is between reality and the dream! Unknown to anyone, alone, in the light of early dawn, Don Quixote sallies forth the first time; now he leaves late, and the Bachelor accompanies him to the outskirts of the town. Don Quixote soon comes upon that intra-clarity; immediately he becomes irritated because he does not find what he is looking for and, when he finds it in the light of day he is disheartened and saddened. Don Quixote in 1615 is the instrument through whom is expressed that sadness of finding deformed what had been sought, what had been created in self-illusion. Don Quixote expresses spiritual and physical weariness, therefore, he now affirms: "I can do no more." He expresses Baroque disillusionment.

But Cervantes who is so luminous and brilliant even in the obscurity, precisely in the obscurity; so enamored of life, of all that is vital and dynamic; so seduced by essences and the senses, emerges from the sadness of disillusionment, giving it an affirmative tone. After life there still remains death, in death the veils are torn aside, and finally, the temporal is abandoned for the eternal. Don Quixote will arrive tired, deluded until the moment of his death, in which moment he will discover the madness of his life, the madness of all life. As he enters the realm of death, when the play is over, the irritation vanishes completely and the calmness is transformed into serenity.

The three themes of the 1605 novel—the theme of chivalry, of love and the literary theme—took the form of adventures, episodes, judgments and dialogues. In 1615, the literary theme no longer consists of the discussion of the books of chivalry and the pastoral novel; that enormous literary mass is reduced to the discussion of the first *Quixote* at the beginning and, in parallel antithetical position at the end, the discussion of the false *Quixote*. The theme of history-poetry is brought to a unity in Don Quixote himself. The two characters—the Curate and the Barber—conductors of the literary theme in 1605—appear in 1615 but in reality also they become one: the Bachelor. The novelist no longer lives thinking about the work of other epochs, but concentrates on that of his epoch, that is, on his own work—the *Quixote* and the *Novelas*. For the ample historical confrontation is substituted this personal expression, an expression that is doubly personal: the authentic work and the spurious work.

In 1615 we constantly feel this personal human note: in the dialogues, in the characters, in the situations. In 1605 the literature of the past was contrasted with that of the present—the two scrutinies—, just as the heroism of the past was compared with the heroism of the Captive, or the love of the Golden Age with love in the baroque period. In 1615 the place of this historical-metaphysical confrontation is taken by the experience of social life and within that social life two dimensions are brought into play: reality and the idea and ideals which form it. Social reality is nothing more than the reflection of the ideas and ideals, both of which give shape to society and in doing so become themselves deformed, reaching in that deformation the point of caricature; art, in turn, is a reflection of society and man. Art reflects what man and society have in them of reflection; for that reason, in art, beauty is more beautiful and ugliness more ugly. The same occurs with justice, virtue, love, crime, vice and hate: in the zone of art they shine forth in their essences. In society the abstract and the concrete are to be found together, and man is a constant example of the incarnation of the eternal in temporal form and of the temporal in continuous vigil of the eternal. These two elements which constitute unity are always making themselves felt in the course of the whole novel as liberty and oppression, as two dimensions, one infinite and limitless, the other brief and petty. Don Quixote feels himself to be a prisoner, and he is made a prisoner. In 1605 they put him into a cage, but he knows himself to be completely at liberty and still intervenes in a love affair and has an adventure; in 1615 he is left at liberty but has been defeated.

The third sally begins with the enchanting of Dulcinea. A farm girl, without being aware of it, plays the role of Dulcinea. From this moment on, at the threshold of the action the stage representation begins. In this *representation,* this staging of the action, we have the first novelesque motif of 1615. Later we shall have the death cart of the strolling players, thanks to which we shall be able to contemplate the whole of humanity: death with a human face, and at her feet, love and the group led by the devil; then the combat with the Bachelor, Camacho's wedding, the puppet show of Maese Pedro and his monkey, the representations of Merlin and the Countess Trifaldi, of Altisidora, the images, the dramatization of the eclogue, the enchanted head and the staging of Altisidora's death. This motif explains the function of deceit ("engaño") in the novel and why the novel is filled with players' carts and processions. Life is no longer directed by God but by man. This limitation of horizon will be accentuated in the Rococo.

If the representation reflects the ideas and ideals which form social life, seen in society, on the other hand, the *house,* the second motif, gives us society in its aspect as reflection. The house of the Caballero of the Green Coat, the house of Basilio, the house of the Duke and Duchess, the house of Governor Sancho, the house of Don Antonio Moreno. To the highway of 1605 is opposed the house of 1615; just as the heroism of the captive Captain (in 1605, Don Quixote-Captive) is opposed to the life of the Caballero of the Green Coat (who in France will be given the name *honnête homme* and in Spain, *caballero perfecto*. In 1615, Don Quixote-Caballero of the Green Coat).

Let us compare the two meals in 1605—one with the goatherds and the other with the amorous couples in the inn—their immense medium, the two majestic discourses which rise from a historical consideration and from the contemplation of human destiny, with the after-dinner conversations of 1615—in the house of Don Diego Miranda, in that of the Duke and Duchess, and of Don Antonio Moreno—, with those "Banquets" during which poetry, platonic ideas and apochryphal things are discussed. The salon takes the place of the woods and the inn. Religious architecture, the great monumental palaces of the Baroque are to be replaced in the Rococo by domestic architecture and these houses of Cervantes with their silence or their joviality—jokes, evening parties—give us the "measure" of the new life and announce the forthcoming bourgeois house. The novel takes place in an urban medium, not so much because the events of some chapters occur in Barcelona, but because of that perspective which Doña Rodríguez uncovers in the house of the Duke; because of that nocturnal round of Sancho in which a girl creates a city and its force of attraction in her imagination. Don Quixote's pueblo takes on reality with the letters of Teresa and the life of Ricote. The *Quixote* of 1615 produces such a strong social emotion because Cervantes is isolating the social phase. The novelist or Sancho provide the link which joins one house to the other.

The players' carts give a special physiognomy to the second *Quixote*, the house and urban life complete the aspect of the novel and characterize it. In 1605 money was a burlesque element and had a magical value, hence the novelesque way in which Sancho found himself recompensed for his work—with money he encountered in the Sierra. In 1615 *money*, the third motif, has a function in the action and qualifies it. Sancho begins by asking for a salary, then, he insists on receiving a compensation and finally, Dulcinea's enchantment—the ideal in society—provides for paid thrashings. Sancho does not come upon gold, the Duke and Duchess recompense him and Roque Guinart, the bandit, gives it to him because he pities the ex-governor. Don Quixote who never once here mistakes an inn for a castle, pays for his lodgings, offers to pay for the refreshment of his fellow traveling companions, makes purchases, and solves the difficulties of his chivalresque adventures with money—the puppet show and the enchanted bark. Together with domestic coziness and comfort, which so satisfy Sancho, goes the burden of money which so worries him.

Animals, the fourth motif, from the lion to the hare, with the appearance between these of monkeys, crows, bats and other nocturnal birds; kids, cats, bulls, pigs—all give quality to the intra-clarity of the action. They serve to introduce us to society and the turbulent world of the passions, and reach a crystallization in the bronze simian and the crocodile of some unknown metal, a symbolic group which adorns the sepulcher of humanity. Christian man, enchained by his passions, is a beast. Sancho remembers this; and when, overcome with sadness after the adventure of the bark, the Knight and Squire return to their mounts, it is Cervantes who takes note: "Don Quixote and Sancho returned to their beasts, and to their state of beasthood." Man is "a compound of the animal." When the religious sense disappears he will become the *bête humaine* of positivistic naturalism, which is the last reduction of this beast of Christianity.

Don Quixote can fight only twice, and the two times have deep significance. He fights with the figures of the puppet show, he fights in Barcelona to be defeated. Don Quixote's life is translated more in words than in works. Don Quixote dialogues and dissertates, above all, he gives advice. *Advice* is the fifth motif of the 1615 novel, it is the ultimate expression of the social world. Advice on the family, on the education of children, matrimony, peace and war, etc., etc. In the advice which he gives to Sancho and to Altisidora, the motif assumes a great importance—for its extension, for its poetic form—, succeeds in giving the novel an educational character. And in the same way that the intellectual experience of politics—fall into the pit—corresponds to the spiritual experience of society—the Cave of Montesinos—, so the judgments of Sancho, the governor, the recipient of natural wisdom, serve as harmonic to the counsels of Don Quixote. Don Quixote indoctrinates until his last moment, when he discovers the best lesson, that of his death.

The feeling produced in us by the work of 1605 is one of maximum liberty. Its complicated organization competes with nature and surpasses it in the sensation of life it gives. The *Quixote* of 1615, on the contrary, constantly produces in us the feeling of being enclosed within narrow limits and this is strengthened by the contrast.

Instead of the historical-metaphysical experience of 1605, we have this political-social experience. If we penetrate the structure, tone and form of the work of 1605 and that of 1615, and give them meaning, we can capture the two experiences of such different character that serve as basis to each one of the two *Quixotes*. One novel is not superior to the other, they are different.

In 1605, Don Quixote and Sancho neither opposed nor complemented each other; the two figures were the same, what changed was their dimension, when one figure is put in relation with the other a new whole is formed. In 1615, this interplay of two different autonomous measurements forming one whole no longer exists. On the one hand, is emphasized their mutual dependence which makes more evident the different quality of the two figures; on the other, they continuously struggle to separate and there arrives a moment in which they must separate, that moment when Don Quixote believes himself, for the first time, a true knight, and Sancho, a true governor. There is being expressed with the parallelism that equal flow of two different qualities; the constantly equal separation is what constitutes the essence of its form. One is always beside the other, one is always the reflection of the other, but one is always different from the other. Don Quixote and Sancho at first live with the same aspiration: to deserve Dulcinea, to win an Island. What unites the two is that both live desiring something, although each has a different desire. But in 1615 we have the fulfillment of those two ideals, consequently their diversification. Don Quixote finds Dulcinea, Sancho receives the Island; the Knight was the champion of damsels, it is the Squire who has the power to disenchant them. First, Don Quixote creates an ideal and all humanity goes in search of that goal; then, Don Quixote reveals to men the deception. One goes from the world that creates the ideal to the world of moral lesson. Each work reflects—in composition, figures, rhythm of action, themes and motifs—one of these worlds.

(*Translated by* Esther Sylvia)

NOTES

[1] Unamuno's interpretation of the *Quixote* completely removes this moment, as it does the whole novel, from its baroque medium. However, there are few literary monuments which have been so fortunate as to be reflected in another period—the impressionist—as has been the *Quixote* in Unamuno's lyrical confession, *Life of Don Quixote and Sancho, according to Miguel de Cervantes.*

[2] Translator's Note. The word in the original is "engaño" which, in all its forms: "engaño, engañar, desengaño," encloses so much baroque meaning. It is constantly used in the following passages and, since there is no one-word equivalent for it in English, is variously translated as deceive, deception, trick, delude, delusion, disillusion, etc.

The Style of "Don Quixote"

HELMUT HATZFELD

ACCORDING to the famous French critic, Sainte-Beuve, the style of an artistic literary work is an admirable use of mediums of expression which, scarcely revealed, permeate and shine through all of the details as well as through the whole of the work. To study the style of "Don Quixote," we must inquire of the immortal Cervantes as to the artistic expression of the idea of his novel in its totality and in its details. The essence of the analysis of style, like that of anatomy, is to probe into everything; for after such a dissection, the subject becomes better known, scientifically understood, while without it, the subject is perceived through mere impression and judged only subjectively.

The idea of "Don Quixote" is very complex. The hidalgo himself has the noble intention, as Menéndez y Pelayo has said, of dedicating his energies to the service of the moral order, being urged to that end by the sublime precepts of the goodness and beauty poetically embodied in Dulcinea del Toboso. His intention, being impracticable in this world of reality, is frustrated by earthly impediments. These are represented by the person of Sancho Panza. But the simple peasant cannot escape the noble influence of his master whose madness lies only in matters of chivalry; his materialistic disposition is gradually tempered as Don Quixote slowly realizes his monomania and reconciles himself to the conditions of reality.

This broad contrast, at the same time a conciliation, is treated stylistically by Cervantes in the following manner: Don Quixote's ideal desire to accomplish a great mission through his chivalry appears in all possible forms throughout the two parts of the novel, remaining however fundamentally the same. Don Quixote has the task of righting wrongs, redressing injustices, aiding widows and orphans, protecting maidens, defending the oppressed, and so forth. The unfolding of this task represents the leit-motif of Don Quixote's chivalric mission.

In this sense, Dulcinea is a second motif. Being the cause of all his deeds, she supplies him with the force necessary for their undertaking. And so there is an abundance of expressions uniting the worth and beauty of Dulcinea to glorify femininity. In extolment, Cervantes uses the expression, "peerless" Dulcinea, happily borrowed from "Amadís de Gaula," constantly calls her "señora doña," "princess," "queen," "empress," and uses various combinations of titles for greater emphasis.

The actuations of Sancho give the counter-motifs; that of Governor, which represents his dominating desire for material wealth and power; that of the Return, his threat to desert his master and return home, which always arises when the calculating peasant sees his own person or aspirations endangered.

Commentators have appreciated the fundamental contrast between Don Quixote and Sancho, between the ideal and the real, between heaven and earth, between the spirit and the flesh, between poetry and prose. But this antithesis also represents a conciliation, the stylistic nuances of which are very interesting. The antithesis becomes mellow when Cervantes the author and observer speaks. Then, the ideological contrast is linguistically obliterated, and the severe parallelism of the elements expressing the contrast becomes attenuated.

A reflection of Reality and Ideality united harmoniously in the author's spirit is found in the union of dissimilar concepts, that is, in the linking of the concrete and abstract in one phrase. For instance: "But daylight and the hope of succeeding in their object failed them;" or "Maidens and modesty wandered at will alone and unattended;" or "accompanied by my servant and many fancies."

Cervantes understands and affirms the conditions, considerations, and realities of life in all their weaknesses. So, again and again, he points out the griefs to which lofty idealism might lead were it not muted by the diurnal, factual incidents of reality. This sweeping, twofold conception of *conditionality,* of ideals always conjoined with material obstacles, of materialistic banality always restrained by idealistic impulse, is expressed in a stereotyped form, necessarily fixed by syntax and grammar, or rather by *unreal conditionality.* How often Don Quixote's blind idealism would have led him to great disaster if it had not met with earthly realities; how often the lazy Sancho would have left everything had he not reflected upon his love and responsibility for his master. These thoughts are the sources of the following formulæ which, with many variations, fill the novel:

"If luck had not caused Rocinante to stumble and fall midway, it would have gone hard with the daring trader."

"If the sword had not turned its course, that single stroke would have sufficed to end the bitter struggle and all the adventures of our knight."

But there is more to the style of "Don Quixote" than the idea of the novel. Its literary form as a novel demands annotation on the relations between epic genre and its special individuality as found in "Don Quixote," which, according to Cervantes himself, is an epic poem in prose. There is no doubt that Cervantes aspired to an exceptional epic plasticity. His descriptions, his comparisons, his figures of speech and metaphors, his imaginative and fortunately popular inventions and findings, created mediums of plasticity essentially superior to those found in "La Celestina" and in the best picaresque novels. The author has a surprising exactitude in regard to the "tertium comparationis" and to lively characteristic portrayal in metaphorical examples, so that each time the relations between the "comparandum" and the "comparatum" must separate and thus surprise the reader. We have here Flaubert's "fatal rapport." An example: "the feet" (of the beautiful Dorothea, in the water) "seemed two pieces of white crystal born among the stones of the brook." Parallels from original similes in the writings of the Spanish mystics show the similes to have purely didactic and moral intentions, and a desire to effect visions and apparitions in a sphere of reason. The similes of Cervantes posit their poetical concepts before the eye on the epic ground of plastic and picturesque observation.

The characters, too, are portrayed clearly, visually. They appeal to the imagination, and form the very cornerstone of the work. Like creatures of flesh and bone, they leave a lasting impression in the mind, either pleasant or disagreeable. We can appreciate this incredible skill in characterization if we consider that the embossment of the most striking physical traits, always sketched in a few lines, leaves so persistent an impression that what we later learn directly from the protagonists adds nothing necessary but gives only complementary details. Who can forget Don Quixote "of hardy habit, spare, gaunt-featured, an early riser, and a lover of hunting?" Or Sancho Panza, who had "a big belly, a short body, and long shanks?"

In addition, Cervantes distinguishes his characters by language, Don Quixote always speaking in a chivalric way, Sancho Panza in a popular, roguish way, preferring to use proverbs. Secondary characters are distinguished also by language. Thus the Bachelor Samson Carrasco talks a half-learned, scholarly idiom, as in his Latin citations: "Aliquando bonus dormitat Homerus; . . . stultorum infinitus est numerus," etc. The Canon of Toledo uses the oratorical language of a chancellor: "The valor of Achilles," etc., or "Lusitania had a Viriatus, Rome a Caesar, Carthage a Hannibal," etc. The Biscayan expresses himself in his dialect, masticating Castilian: "Unless thou quittest coach, slayest thee as are here a Biscayan," etc. Marcela, the romantic shepherdess, contrives a high-flown, pastoral style; while Pedro, the realistic shepherd, like Sancho, uses simple, popular words. The galley slaves have the vocabulary of rogues and thieves, calling galleys "gurapas," speaking elliptically of punishment as by using "ciento" for cien blows, referring to him who confesses under torture as a canary, musician, singer, etc. The captive captain, returning from Algiers, sparses Arabic words through his gossip. The lovely Zoraida stammers her Spanish-Arabic, "Lela Marien." The German pilgrims who accompany the Moorish Ricote speak what might be called an Esperanto of the sixteenth century, the Frankish dialect, asking for money in their native tongue, "guelte."

The novel has an interesting and modern technical construction. Despite its richness in episodes, it causes continuous tension in the reader, unlike the chivalrous and pastoral novels, endless rudimentary works, or the biographical picaresque novel. Cervantes reflected existing literary traditions by taking for himself in a new, satiric-humoristic way the old attractive habit of interrupting narrative with humanistic digressions, by using adroitly a method of giving vague first impressions to provoke interest and anxiety in the subjects, thus inventing for his hero what Américo Castro calls "visual misunderstanding." The windmills seem giants. Again, this impressionistic method serves in the introduction of new characters, giving many amusing differences between subjective impressions and objective explanations of a situation.

Unlike the previous novels of loose, disconnected chapters, "Don Quixote" has true continuity of composition, maintaining a single thought through diverse episodes. The story of Mambrino's helmet is more than an episode. From the beginning, Don Quixote lacks an ideal knightly helmet. He ingeniously sallies forth with a provisional half-helmet, manufactured after many spirited experiments. When the helmet suffers damages in his combat with the giant Biscayan, he swears to acquire another. But he fares so badly after this oath that Sancho insinuates that perhaps the unfulfilled oath causes all the troubles. So our adventurer is feverishly longing for a helmet when, after a rain, he chances to meet with a barber on horseback with a brass basin on his head. His burning acquisitive desire lights upon the basin and sees it as Mambrino's helmet. After acquiring it, he gives it to Sancho for safe-keeping, and persistently tries to prove to him that the basin is a helmet. Later when the owner appears at the inn where Don Quixote stops, there is a heated argument over the basin, until the Curate buys it behind Don Quixote's back so that the monomaniac may keep his trophy.

The central episode of the first part of "Don Quixote," that of Cardenio, Fernando, Lucinda, and Dorothea, is another example. The author skillfully joins diverse events; he also unites the halves of the first book, Don Quixote's sallying forth to seek adventures and the search for him, with his first return by means of the Curate and the Barber. The characters in this episode, and especially Dorothea, are motivated by the Curate and the Barber.

A third example is the joining of the first and second parts of the novel by Sancho's procrastination as a messenger of love on the Toboso road, and by his prevarication as to his unrealized errand in Aldonza Lorenzo's house. This lie makes possible the beginning of the second part with the march to Toboso. But that is not all. In Sancho's famous lie are disseminated the germs of the enchantment and disenchantment of Dulcinea, protracted, laughter-causing subjects in the second part.

The rôle of a uniting medium is played in the second part by a definite character. The Bachelor, Samson Carrasco. His sharp criticism of the first part links it to the second part. Later, he throws himself into the high spirits of the course of events until the vanquishing of the audacious gentleman on the strand of Barcelona.

From a higher point of view, the magnificent, antithetical style of "Don Quixote" reflects all of Spain and the whole of the sixteenth century more than it does technical problems. Catholicism and counter-reformist Spain have their transcendental ideals, distinguishing between God and earth, soul and body, and fighting against the pagan renaissance; the ideas permeating the epoch of the Council of Trent scintillate behind typical words which occur with surprising frequency in "Don Quixote," such as "Catholic," "heretic," "sect," "conscience," "scruple," or shine behind the formulae found in the speech of certain characters, as for example, when Sancho expresses the lasting conflict between body and soul by saying, "I care more about the black of the nail of my soul than about my whole body."

The conception of the counter-reformist world could be expressed in many ways, from aesthetic negation and political apology to the love which embraces all, which always contains a certain assertion within itself. Here, Cervantes' conciliating and humorous temperament comes into play. Certain stylistic impulses permit the recognition of Cervantes as a unique humorist. In spite of his absolute and defined convictions as to faith, race, justice, and law, he does not fall into fits of bigotry, pedantry, patriotism, or any kind of spiritual petrification. Precisely because of this, he ridicules the peculiar biblio-ecclesiastical language of the hypocrite and of popular devotion, the judicial language of the courts of justice and the chancery, and the academic language of university cloisters.

This humor and comic verve appear in easily understood puns and contrasts. The humor is still more interesting when hidden in the form and context of the language, in the comical concept. Sancho says, "I'm nothing of the hypocrite; I drink when I please, and when I don't please, and when they offer it to me so as not to seem straitlaced or ill-bred." He tells his wife that "The Duchess is so unpretending and unassuming that she has been known to borrow a comb from one of her neighbors." When beating himself to disenchant Dulcinea, he says, "With three thousand three hundred lashes, less five, which I must give myself, she'll be as disenchanted as the mother that bore her."

Humor may also be hidden in the very words, in an unusual circumlocution concerning the natural and the known. So the rural guards are called "foot-pads with the license of the Holy Brotherhood," the garret of the inn with its rickety bed, a "star-lit stable." Sancho declares that he has no concern with "those born in ditches, but with those who have Christian fat four fingers deep on their souls." Witticism, the surprising, and the genial are common to all these phrases.

The whole novel as a satire on chivalric works with their situations, grimaces, perorations, and chivalric usages, is a typical work of irony. Irony gleams from the center of the Cervantian humor and style. "There is hardly a phrase in 'Don Quixote,'" says Cejador, "that does not contain a double meaning and a second intent, when it does not embrace a third one, the entire novel being ironic mockery."

Authentic humor has something jubilant, triumphant, fantastic, grand, and exaggerated. The limitations of rigid, prosaic, true, regular expression would confine it too much. Humor's objects of observation appear magnified, its sensations heightened. Therefore, its true form of expression is exaggeration, *hyperbole*. Hyperbolical expressions in Cervantes are peculiarly intense, but not out of proportion. To explain this phenomenon, it must be remembered that Cervantes resided for some time in Southern Spain where hyperboles color popular character and language: so Rodríguez Marín is right in judging some of Cervantes' exaggerations to be Andalusianisms. The hyperbole is also the traditional means of characterizing the fanfaron, the vainglorious soldier, and so, extraordinarily suitable for Don Quixote and his chivalrous extravagances. A multitude of exaggerations appear in "Don Quixote": "Don Quixote was so happy that his joy nearly burst the girths of his horse," or "The nose of the woodland squire was so large that it well nigh shaded his entire body," or "Sancho ate grapes and even pomegranate seeds with his fork."

Cervantes' style is dynamic, reflecting the rhythm of an impulsive life and the expression of a man possessing great energy of movement. Manifestations of this force must be gradually comprehended. They begin in the vivid animation shown principally in the humanizing of Rocinante and the donkey, and continue in the constant and passionate participation in the action by the author himself, either directly, or in the guise of the Arabic historian, Cide Hamete Benengeli. In the second place, they appear in language devices, in emphasis upon words, in accumulations, gradations, and repetitions, well-known figures that do not call for illustrations. Rapidity of dialogue and rapidity of narration are other forms:

" 'God go with you, señor,' said Anselmo. 'God remain with you,' the citizen answered and went his way."

" 'Then, this is the inn?' said Don Quixote. 'And a very respectable one,' the innkeeper answered."

" 'You seem clever,' said Don Quixote. 'And unfortunate,' replied Ginés, 'misfortune always persecutes wit.' 'It persecutes rogues,' said the commissary."

The animation and the rapidity of the monologues recall the famous *veni vidi vici* of Julius Caesar. Sancho in presenting himself to the Duke says, "I am a laboring man, my name is Sancho Panza, I am married, I have children, and I am serving as a squire." One of the condemned galley slaves speaking of his trial in loose terms says, "It was all proved against me, I got no favor, I had no money, I almost had my neck stretched, they sentenced me to the galleys for six years. . . . I accepted my fate, it is the punishment of my fault, I am a young man, let life only last."

The rapid, vivid narration, made up of loose members, as Clemencín says, reaches its highest peak in the description of tumults in which one feels himself a participant. In the scuffle at the inn which is caused by the agility of the wench, Maritornes, we have: "And so, as the saying goes, the cat to the rat, the rat to the rope, the rope to the stick: the carrier pounded Sancho, Sancho the wench, the wench him, and the innkeeper her."

But this popular, forceful style does not absolutely dominate the novel. Cervantes was acquainted with the Italian period of Boccaccio and with that of the pastoral novel; from them he took static elements to mix with his own style. He assimilated Boccaccian rhetorical antithesis; and imitated the magnificent epithet of the Renaissance which we see in the expressions: "the never-too-much-praised knight, Don Quixote of the Mancha," or "the strong and beyond all comparison courageous Don Quixote," etc. From the Italians, Cervantes also learned prose rhythm and rhythmical progression of narration, elements completely unknown by his Spanish predecessors like Timoneda. Who can forget the marvellous rhythm at the beginning of the novel: "En un lugar de la Mancha de cuyo nombre no quiero acordarme, no ha mucho tiempo que vivía un hidalgo. . . . ." ("In a village of La Mancha whose name I do not care to recall, there lived not long ago. . . .")?

From this union in Cervantes of the literary art of the Italian Renaissance and the pure Spanish style, there issues the remarkable synthesis of mediums of expression that has never been equaled since within or without Spain. Cervantes is and will be the flower of all the prose poets of the world.

(*Translated by* Edith Mead)

Social and Historical Background

A. MOREL-FATIO

"I USED to think in my heart," says the faithful squire, Sancho Panza, of his master, "that the only thing he knew was what pertained to his chivalry; but there is nothing he won't have a finger in." Cervantes like his hero has a finger in everything. Under his vagrant pen in a moment of inspiration, his "Don Quixote," springing from a simple idea which anticipated no great development, became little by little the great social novel of Spain at the beginning of the seventeenth century. All that characterizes that epoch—its sentiments, passions, prejudices, customs and institutions—came to find a place there. Herein lies the powerful interest of the book; aside from its value as a work of imagination and a fine treatise of practical philosophy, it possesses the added significance of fixing the state of a civilization at a given moment of its existence, and of revealing to us its inmost consciousness.

This historical and social aspect of "Don Quixote" is what I propose to examine. Much can be learned from this famous novel regarded as a faithful painting of the society to which its author belonged, and which he described in a manner possible only to a man with a wide knowledge of the world, and an artist capable of giving his material the right color and emphasis.

Religion is one of those subjects to which commentators have given free rein to their imagination. Once Cervantes was proclaimed a profound mind as well as an excellent writer, it was a simple matter to accuse him of advanced views bordering on impiety. People did not fail to do this. Know how to read between the lines, and the most orthodox of Christian novelists may quite easily become not only a pronounced enemy of fanaticism and the Inquisition, but even a *libertine* philosopher, in the seventeenth century sense of the word. But an unprejudiced examination of the text yields little support for the thesis of these over-ingenious interpreters. In this respect, it is necessary to distinguish carefully between the dogma and doctrine of the Church on the one hand, and on the other the vast host of its representatives: the priest and his acolytes, the ecclesiastical police force which in Spain bears the name Inquisition, the religious

101

orders, the pious associations, and all those who serve, protect and live on religion. These accessories of worship, especially the lower clergy, were as much despised in the Spain of Cervantes as they are in Russia today. Even during the most oppressive days of fanaticism, many a Spaniard made them the butt of an obscene joke, and spoke his mind quite freely about them, without rebuke from the police of the Holy Office. But the bounds of free speech which could not be overstepped with impunity, were marked by the whim of the judge alone. One might risk many daring remarks without punishment, and still suffer one day for a single imprudent word if directed at one of the mandarins of the privileged caste, for the personal character of the insult greatly increased its seriousness.

Cervantes was no more daring in these matters than many others. Even if he had been, there is no reason to question his orthodoxy, or to attribute to him exceptional freedom of thought. He was a fervent Catholic, with a faith strengthened by contact with the infidel, at the place where the struggle between the two faiths was at its worst. Like all Spaniards of his time, with rare exceptions, he was respectfully submissive to the doctrine of the Church, and unconcerned both by temperament and training with the subtleties of theology. What could a man so constituted have written that smacked of heresy?

Regarding the clergy Cervantes shows himself quite non-committal. This reserve, however, does not spring from caution or excessive benevolence, for there is plenty of evidence that the ecclesiastical garb does not frighten him. Cervantes treats very well the village rector, who plays an important rôle in his book as adviser and defender of the poor crazy hidalgo, humble representative of the great hierarchy though he was. He makes him balanced and affable, with sound judgment and correct speech. There never appears in the words of the Licenciate Pero Perez the heavy pedantry and lack of taste so common in country priests. Without a doubt, the novelist liked this type rather well. On the other hand, he has little esteem for the ecclesiastic who does not live in his benefice among his flock, but is found again and again in ante-chambers and on the highways; for in those days the clothes of the priest were a protection and insured him a host of prerogatives. In the adventure of the corpse escorted by priests, whom Don Quixote mistakes for ghosts, and whom Sancho Panza conscientiously deprives of their food, there is a short phrase thrown in casually referring to "those clerical gentlemen . . . who seldom put themselves on short allowance." Its significance should not be exaggerated, but it proves, at least, that Cervantes was man enough to discern the basic egoism and sensuality that a cassock could cover. He knew, moreover, that the vow of chastity was not always observed with due rigor, in that milieu. He has Don Quixote tell without hesitation, the story of a certain sophisticated widow who might very well have chosen a lover from among the learned theologians around her, but she preferred instead a rather plump lay brother, whom she considered as learned as Aristotle for all she cared.

There is a kind of ecclesiastic that Cervantes did not spare, and went so far as to lash with great gusto. This is the long-gowned parasite, the confessor and factotum of the aristocratic household, the priest-intruder who pretends to rule the grandee and to teach him his business, measuring the liberality of his master by the narrowness of his own soul, and making him miserly by trying to restrain his expenditure. "What do these people want of us," he exclaims, "who have been brought up in the straitness of some seminary, and who have never seen more of the world than lies within twenty or thirty leagues? They think that they have only to get a footing in the house of the wealthy, to pass judgment on everything!" In this remark the soldier crops out. Cervantes, like the majority of the writers of that time, had been forced to seek help from the mighty, and to get shelter under their shade. He cannot restrain his anger when he sees these presumptuous and pedantic theological students who are totally unsuited both, by training and ignorance of life to the rôles assigned to them. Why should such positions be entrusted to these people, when they might so easily be granted to laymen who had acquired experience of things and long rubbed shoulders with their kind, and who had seen foreign countries and fought and suffered? In short such men as Cervantes himself. Such men would be capable of advising the grandee in the just administration of his power and wealth, and of bringing him in closer touch with the downtrodden and the humble. This stinging reprimand may have been evoked by personal resentment, aimed possibly at some ecclesiastic who had done Cervantes an ill turn with one of his protectors. But even if this were true, it would take away none of the significance of the words which strike at the species beyond the individual.

Of certain religious orders widely denounced in Spain, because of the vices which they practiced or were accused of practicing, Cervantes says nothing in his novel. But he does not neglect the hermit, a type of religious exploiter very common in his time. The hermit was a kind of highwayman with a long venerable beard and a sanctimonious face, whose shameful practices and cynical way of life so many authors have criticized. "For those hermits we see now-a-days," observes Don Quixote, "are not like the hermits of the Egyptian deserts who were clad in palm-leaves and lived on the roots of the earth." Though he glosses over his criticism, maintaining that a hypocrite masked in virtue is preferable to a sinner parading his unworthiness, Cervantes does not delude us as to his actual feelings. Nothing can have been so repugnant to his straightforward and brave nature as the vicious idleness of that low class of false worshippers.

Thus there is not the slightest evidence for charges of impiety and free thinking in anything that Cervantes wrote concerning the Christian doctrine. More-over on the occasions when he reproved some shortcomings of the clergy or their exploitations of religion, no one can accuse him of exceptionally vitriolic criti-cism. There are various incidents in the last years of his life that confirm the sincerity of his convictions, and his respect for certain devout practices in usage then among the wordly. His affiliation in 1609 with the brotherhood located on Olivos Street, which brought him the title of "slave of the Most Holy Sacra-ment," and his entrance four years later into the third order of Saint Francis, give significant evidence. To be sure, there were many who entered these brotherhoods not so much for the purpose of performing acts of repentance as to give themselves an air of importance and to parade their showy paraphernalia when great ceremonies afforded the members an opportunity to march in pro-cession through the streets of the capital. In seventeenth century Spain a brother-hood took the place of the club of today. The people of a certain class belonged to such and such a *cofradía,* and they announced their social position by adding to their names that of the pious group that had admitted them. This afforded them not only a certain prestige, but a protection against untoward suspicions and sometimes against actual misfortune. The brethren were somehow jointly and separately liable, obliged through their pledged word to help each other. A well organized *cofradía* must have been something like our mutual aid societies. That explains why so many men of letters solicited the honor of being received as members of the congregations of the Caballero de Gracia or of Olivos Street, the two best known in the Madrid of Philip III. Cervantes did as Lope, as Quevedo, as Calderón, and so many others did. Old, tired, and poor, he sought a place under the folds of a pious flag where he might find protection, associate with influential people, and spread his relations. The interests which motivated this decision made late in life are immaterial. The very act of affiliation, the fact that he made application and was accepted, indicates clearly that those who had it in their power to admit or reject him, and who were jealous of their rights and disinclined to show indulgence, did not ask him to account for a few daring remarks in his "Don Quixote," and did not hesitate to give him the diploma which made him a brother of the most orthodox.

What does Cervantes think of that powerful governing machine both administrative and judiciary, constructed with so much trouble by the Catholic Sovereigns, strengthened by the ministers of Charles V, and enlarged and com-plicated by that meticulous scribbler, Philip II? How does he appraise it? We have no right to demand of him more than rough estimates and personal impressions about certain parts of the machine he knew from intimate contact. It is unlikely that a man who was present at many scenes of the great political drama of the sixteenth century, and whom fate initiated into some of its worst parts, should have nothing to reveal about the functioning of the apparatus, its intricacies, and the defects of more than one of its cogs.

Imbedded in Cervantes, as in the majority of his compatriots, was the conviction that the governor and the magistrate are the born enemies of the downtrodden and the poor; that they belong body and soul to the first comer who bribes them; that their acts have no other motivation than personal interest; the conviction that jobs are given only through favoritism or for money; that one enters an office solely to fatten therein, and leave sit only when gorged with gain. An honest judge, a disinterested administrator, exist only as exceptions. The rule is venality, corruption, and also incompetence, for after all what is the good of merit, since everything can be obtained without it? "We know by ample experience," says Don Quixote, "that it does not require much cleverness or much learning to be a governor, for there are a hundred round about us that scarcely know how to read, and govern like gerfalcons." Cervantes is so tranquilly convinced that public functions can only be exercised to the injury of private virtues, and that you must leave at the threshold as you enter all that makes you an upright man and earns for you the esteem of your fellow men, that there is no bitterness in his judgment of the various royal agents. That is the way things are. He is even ready to add, no doubt—that is the way they always were and we are no worse than our forefathers. Consequently, he never seriously pits the past against the present, the virtues of a Golden Age against the ways of his own period. He would rather believe that his times were a little better than the others, for he served under Philip II and he could not have been indifferent to certain strict measures taken by this monarch to redress many wrongs. This was the virtue of Philip II's governmental policy, that he took the welfare of his subjects greatly to heart, and he did not hesitate to use the scalpel when he located the source of the malady. With an ease which is praiseworthy, he would sacrifice the highest dignitaries when they failed in their duty, while he surrounded with esteem the holders of modest offices from the "Bizcayan secretaries" down to the corregidors of the smallest town. Whenever injustice was revealed, exemplary punishments and prompt executions followed, with absolutely no consideration for the offender's person. Catholic Isabella would not have disclaimed these feats. But the administration of the immense empire was rather like the broken cistern of the Danaïdes. In vain Philip II read all that his agents wrote to him from all parts of the world, blackening reams of paper and annotating with his own hand piles of reports. In vain, like a bookkeeper overloaded with work, he enlisted the help of the queen and the infantas, his daughters, to sand the letters and carry the documents to the faithful Santayo who sent them on to the secretaries. Most of the time this prodigious activity as administrator and scribe, which has no other

example in history, came to naught. The more orders the Chancellery des-
patched, the more enquiries, petitions, and complaints it received; the papers
continued to pile up on the tables of the clerks who could not keep up with the
frightful task. The master, belatedly informed, did not decide at the opportune
moment, and, by nature timorous and hesitating, his decrees missed their mark
and went up in smoke. The empire was too big and the work too far beyond
human strength, and moreover, the evil was too deep-rooted and too difficult
to be extirpated.

People have claimed that the description of Sancho Panza's government of
the Isle of Barataria is a satire on the administrative system of Spain at the time
of Cervantes. According to them, it was in this chapter that the author of "Don
Quixote" expressed his ideas on the management of public affairs with the
greatest frankness. I do not contradict this entirely. Just the same, I do not find
there anything that is distinctly characteristic of the government of Philip II
or of his immediate successors. The moral of the experiment attempted by the
Duke on behalf of Don Quixote's squire is conceived in very general terms and
yields only the summary that there is no science of politics. Ordinary common
sense suffices to settle the most delicate questions, and any peasant with his
natural wit knows more about them than the jurist gowned in Salamanca. The
will of the governor and his desire to put useful reforms into effect, gives way
before the bureaucracy and the hostility of the people surrounding him, steeped
as they are in tradition and traditional abuses. Disinterestedness, in itself a
praiseworthy virtue, brings you neither esteem nor gratitude; when the governor
comes out rich, people say he is a thief, but on the contrary, when he comes
out poor, he is called a silly fool. Such aphorisms are applicable to all times, to
those that preceded the appearance of "Don Quixote" as well as those that
followed it. None of the modifications of the preceding régime brought about
by Philip II, and none of the measures that marked the advent of Philip III and
the rule of the favorites, are aimed at here. Furthermore, there is no cry of
indignation, no virulent touch, no aspiration to any ideal whatever, no Utopia
half seen in one's dream, pictured here. Cervantes does not believe in the
principle of social and political innovations, and he is ready to treat as Utopian
any one who seeks evil in institutions instead of seeking it where it is, in men
themselves.

All reformers affect him somewhat like that idealist of one of his short stories
who, to meet the deficit of the royal finances, proposed to the king that he force
his subjects to feed themselves once a month on bread and water, and to pay
into his treasury the amount they would have used that day for luxuries.
Doubtless an ingenious remedy, but, says Berganza the dog, "Haven't you
noticed that those who extol similar panaceas all go to die in the poorhouse?"

One of the serious problems of seventeenth century Spain was how to treat the population of Mussulman origin. These people had been partially assimilated by the Christian régime for a long time, but there still remained groups, especially in the regions of Aragón and Valencia, who resisted the fiery propaganda of the priests and administrators, and adhered to the traditions and customs of their own race and religion, thus speckling the heart of the chosen people, the Catholic Nation. Another question, closely allied to the first, was what attitude to adopt towards the States of Barbary of North Africa, sworn enemies of the Spanish monarchy? Their corsairs were a perpetual peril to her, hindering her relations with Italy, laying waste the coast of the Peninsula, and attempting to establish contact with their old co-religionists who had remained in Spain. The Duke of Lerma, supported by the clergy but opposed by the aristocracy who had many Moorish vassals, settled the first difficulty by expelling all the Mussulmans from Spain, but he let the second problem remain. Spain deprived herself in a few years of a decent, hard working population, whom she exported to her enemies and was never able to replace with native elements. Neither did she succeed in insuring the safety of her coasts, nor in putting a stop to the advance of the pirates from Barbary. In our times, Lerma's conduct is considered a serious economic mistake, and the abandonment of any policy of expansion in Africa whatsoever is even a greater one, for the Spaniards have had frequent cause to regret that they did not firmly establish their dominion on the other side of the straits when they had the opportunity.

As regards this struggle between the Cross and the Crescent, Cervantes considered himself competent. He knew the infidel, he had met him with gun in hand at Lepanto, he had gone under his yoke at Algiers. Back in Spain, fresh from his martial achievements and the painful incidents of his captivity, he kept more intensely alive in the depths of his heart the holy hatred for the unbeliever, that credo of Old Spain, than did many others who had not been forced to undergo the same trials. The Turk is the danger on the outside, the Moor is the scourge within. Let us fight the first and uproot the second. In the epistle to Mateo Vasquez, the minister of Philip II, written when he was still in chains in the bagnio, he announces his intention as soon as he is ransomed, to throw himself at the feet of the king and to speak to him in these terms: Powerful monarch, who have subjugated a thousand barbaric peoples, who received tribute even from the Negroes of India, how do you suffer a miserable little hovel to resist you? Its defenders are many but weak and badly equipped, and its walls are crumbling. Why do you wait? You hold in your hand the key which opens the dark prisons wherein more than twenty thousand Christians groan in pain and torture. Listen to them; they beseech you on their knees.

Oh, that you might finish what was begun by your valorous sire! Show your-self, and the mere announcement of your intervention will fill these butchers, who tremble while waiting for their punishment, with amazement and fright. This eloquent appeal was not heeded. Philip II had other cares. At the time Cervantes invoked him, he was preparing for the annexation of Portugal, seeking to "resew the piece once torn from the robe of illustrious Castile." Later he formed still more ambitious plans, in the project of a kind of universal Catholic monarchy, the vision of which vanished in the loss of the Armada. The last years of his reign passed in gloom and were vexed by many internal difficulties. He died without even the hope that his weak successor could cope with the enemies from within and without, or could succeed in keeping intact the immense inheritance. The Crusade so much yearned for by Cervantes never occurred, and the bagnios resounded for a long time more with cries of suffer-ing from the captives, and the ransoming priests began again their pitiful peregrination.

Cervantes spoke several times of Moors in "Don Quixote," in the "Exemplary Novels" and in "Persiles," and he always did so in a tone of hatred and scorn. No mercy for this Moorish rabble which is our vermin! Look at them: they are sober and beget many children, for soberness increases the causes of births; they work, and as they work they make money, and take all our coined money; their girls do not enter any convent and do not remain sterile like ours; their sons do not go off to war and do not return like ours, crippled and diseased; they do not study, for what else is there for them to learn but the art of robbing us, and this art is inborn with them! Blessed be the heroic resolution of our holy king Philip who in his wisdom has taken on his shoulders the task of uprooting this poisonous plant, of purging Spain of this accursed pest! A Dominican father could have said it no better. Poor Cervantes! What he right-fully pleaded for against the Mussulmans of Africa received no response and was never accomplished; but what he advised and approved, scorning justice and good sense, against the Mussulmans of Spain, was only too thoroughly done, to the great misfortune of the very people who hoped to benefit by it.

It is striking to notice that this pitiless enemy of the infidel is at times com-pelled in all fairness to admit the superiority of certain institutions of the fol-lowers of Mohammed. He mocked the practices of justice in his own country, its formalism, its delays, its hocus pocus, its heavy costs, the guilty collusion between lawyers on both sides, not to mention the venality of the judges, of whom he delighted to say that, "You must know how to grease their palm if you don't want to hear them squeak like an ox-cart." And he is the same man who confesses that such things do not obtain among the Moors! "For them there are no indictments nor remands as with us . . . . The Cadi is a supreme judge and rules in the capacity of an upright man, reducing lawsuits to a minimum and judging them in a flash, without ever having recourse to the repeal of his judgments." Here is an admission that he too readily forgot on other occasions and that should at least have tempered somewhat his fierce intolerance.

Cervantes possessed a resigned scepticism, as I have mentioned before, whereby he realized that government, administrative affairs, and justice were institutions which men of all epochs abuse and which it would be childish, therefore, to pretend to reform. Because of this, he had no real reason for a presentiment that this great monarchy was bound toward its decline and that the rottenness of certain limbs, not amputated in time, would attack the whole body. He had seen the climax of the system and he loved to live on his memories. The Spanish military power always appeared to him in the splendid setting of Lepanto, where the god Mars himself shone in the features of the fiery and dapper Don Juan of Austria. The *tercios* were still holding fast when he died, and the drums had not sounded a parley. The Great Empire with its infinite dependencies seemed to be standing upright, the galleons continued to bring gold from the Indies to Seville, the viceroys were still ruling at Naples and in Sicily, the Portuguese had not taken their revenge, and art and literature shone with splendor. How could he have seen the inescapable and impending decadence? To do so, he would have needed an uneasiness of mind and at the same time an unusual perspicacity which were not in his nature. He died convinced of the grandeur of his nation, and it must have been a supreme consolation in his last hours to be able to say to himself that he was departing as a citizen of the first empire of the world.

Now let us see how, according to the testimony of our author, a society lives and struggles within the framework that history has traced for it, and at the very moment of the greatest territorial expansion of the State seems to shrink and wither under the pressure of religious fanaticism and outworn prejudices.

At the top, stands a titled nobility of several grades, from the grandees down to those enobled by the king. It is a class without any political significance, and it exists only by virtue of the prestige acquired, the wealth accumulated, or the favors that it still knows how to obtain for any kind of service. This nobility cannot boast that it belongs to a superior race, and there does not flow in its veins a purer strain than in the masses of the people. Here there are none of those distinctions, none of those antagonisms, existing elsewhere between Franks and Latins, between Normans and Saxons. Everybody is a Goth, or thinks he is.

The outstanding characteristic of this noble class is shown clearly by the name *ricohombre,* which its members at first gave themselves. It signifies wealth, possession of land, a fief, and the enjoyment of royal favors. One is recognized as a nobleman and one can remain a nobleman only on condition that he is rich. That is the general opinion and in particular that of Don Quixote's niece. "How," she answers her uncle, "how call yourself a knight when you are not one; though gentle-folk may be so, poor men are nothing of the kind."

This first nobility of Castile, which included certain bastards of the royal household, exercised more or less influence in the State according to the time. It had moments of splendor such as that in the fifteen century when its turbulent chiefs counterbalanced the royal power and undermined it. Restrained and held under leash by those stubborn restorers of royalism, the Catholic Sovereigns, it regains importance under Philip of Austria and Charles V. Again it loses much under Philip II, who humbles it as much as he can, gags it, and sacrifices it to the lawyers with whom he fills his council and his administrative offices. Philip III gives back to it a part of its prestige and power, and the seventeenth century becomes the reign of the favorites of the great families. It is then, even more than in the Middle Ages, that the term *rich man* exactly defines the class. All the high dignities, all the profitable posts, all the fat viceroyships in Italy and the Indies, fall to its lot.

Cervantes witnessed the return to favor of the titled nobility and the enormous spoils which marked the advent of Lerma as prime minister. It may seem astonishing that he should not have sketched some silhouettes of these grandees, cynically proud of their plunder and bloated with arrogance by their positions snatched from weak monarchs. But he, like all men of letters in that epoch, had need of them. He was their servant and had to use a portion of his talent to solicit their good will. The poor author would have been ruined by drawing too faithful portraits in which one of them might have recognized himself. So, when he decided to paint a nobleman, he took good care to take him out of his environment. This is illustrated by the instance of the Duke and the Duchess who take in Don Quixote and amuse themselves at his expense to beguile the boredom of a long sojourn in the country. These types of the Spanish aristocracy are presented in an agreeable light and flattered in the delicate terms so common in the current literature of the day. Some stinging remarks here and there, however, attest that the author has not parted with his independence and frankness. The backbiting prattle of the Duenna, who reveals to Don Quixote the secret of the lily and rose complexion of the Duchess, is only a minor drollery. Another confidence of the same respectable gossip is more pointed. Her daughter, seduced by the son of a rich peasant, cannot persuade the Duke to intervene on her behalf in forcing the seducer to make amends. The master closes his eyes and lends a deaf ear. It is due, says the Duenna, to the fact that the peasant's father, rolling in wealth, lends money to the Duke and often pulls him out of embarrassing situations by serving as security for him. Most of the households of the grandee class were in that condition. The money gained by embezzlement was carelessly handled and vanished in extravagances of pleasure, display, countless servants, and faithless administrators. Then it became necessary to have recourse to money lenders, to live by shift, to alienate one's rights to inferior agents who took advantage of the scheme to pillage the land, squeeze the vassals, and exercise a veritable local tyranny. That improvised government of Sancho Panza in the isle of Barataria which, as I have said, has been taken as an attack aimed at the internal political régime of Spain, seems to me to be rather a parody and a criticism of the seignorial régime. The Duke enters with ease into the scheme of fun devised by the Duchess, and finds it very droll to appoint the squire of a madman as governor of a portion of his estates. This one would do as well as any, he seems to say. The comical incidents of Sancho's rule, from the grievances of the vassals to the wiles of the courtiers in circumventing their master, lulling him to sleep in peaceful security, and either preventing him from seeing or showing him the inevitable necessity of such abuses—these and other touches skilfully arranged form a perfect caricature of the feudal administration as it flourished in Spain in the sixteenth century and fully justify the popular Castilian remark. "Do not make your nest in the land of a lord."

Every one would like to be noble, that is Spain's great malady. People want to be in the nobleman's class in order to live as nobles: to avoid paying the personal tax, which falls with all its weight upon the lowest, who having some original stigma, such as Jewish or Moorish ancestors, dare not claim a place among the chosen ones. There are even some provinces in which people have ennobled themselves on their own authority, where everybody is born noble, the Basque provinces, the Asturias, the cradle of the restored Christian monarchy: "A gentleman like the king himself, for he came of a mountain stock," says the duenna, Doña Rodríguez, about her husband. In Castile people do not go so far, and consequently all the towns, villages, and hamlets are encumbered with law-suits. When the candidate is rich, the enquiry is speeded up. Carefully recruited and duly bribed witnesses declare all that is desired of them and the trick is done. After court proceedings, the hidalgo receives his warrant, a thick piece of parchment embellished with his coat of arms, and setting forth the proofs of his nobility in fine legal style. The poor man is less lucky; his petition drags on, and since he cannot pay his witnesses, they tell the truth. Family skeletons are dragged from their closets, and shocking scandals revealed. The victim rebels and to get revenge in turn besmirches those who, armed with their warrant, believed themselves noblemen. Thence terrible grudges arise, family hatreds are handed down from father to son, and hostile factions watch each other and fight when they meet, to the great detriment of the commonweal.

At court and in the big cities the hidalgo almost succeeds in maintaining his rank. These are callings which do not entail loss of nobility and yet feed their followers, for example, domesticity in the homes of the grandees, the position of squire and protector, and for women, that of duenna. But in the country there is nothing at all. The hidalgo lives parsimoniously on a bit of land, idly and proudly. Proudly, because it is pleasant to feel oneself a nobleman; idly, because it is degrading to work. And this haughty sloth results necessarily in deplorable poverty. Cervantes, who had often experienced it but had manfully fought against it, thanks to his fearless energy, remarks, "Goodbye, cutting hunger of the hidalgo, rather than fall dead at your threshold, I prefer to get out of my country and myself." Cervantes was bound by the very subject of his book to make illusions to this subject many times. There is the ragged and torn hidalgo who shines his shoes with soot, darns his black stockings with green silk, and picks his teeth to make people think he has eaten when his stomach is as empty as a drum: the hidalgo, "insipid through being destitute." This specimen of the poor relation of the Castilian aristocracy appears the more frequently in Cervantes because he is, on the whole, something of a portrait of his hero.

It cannot have been by mere chance that he made Don Quixote a country hidalgo. It was quite necessary for the Knight of La Mancha to belong to that social class. The special kind of folly that the author wanted to describe for us could arise and develop only in that environment. The essential factors of the terrible mania of chivalry could be fed only by an absolute want of occupation, and poverty in an out-of-the-way hamlet of the most desolate province of Spain joined to the state of mind of a petty nobleman who believes himself moulded out of finer clay, and who sits all day long admiring himself in the brevet which he has hung on the wall of his room, sinking into fantastic day dreams to escape painful reality. Cervantes has made clear the cause of Don Quixote's malady without exaggerating his lines or dragging his hero down to the level of the coarse parodies of the popular farce. Don Quixote is poor but not wretched, he takes care of his person and dresses properly. When Sancho tells him of the remarks which the village aims at him for putting on airs too lofty for a threadbare hidalgo, he cries out, "These criticisms do not touch me, for I always go well-dressed and never patched." A gripping sadness gets hold of him when at the home of the Duke he discovers one night on going to bed that his stockings have holes. What would he not have given to have a skein of green silk or the money to buy it with! Thus by preserving him from the defilements of the hidalgo fallen into sordid want, and by raising him morally high above the people of his circumstances, Cervantes makes him seem truer and compels us to love him in spite of his ridiculous antics. In fact, these country lordlings in their destitute solitude and boredom ran the risk of acquiring manias, when, like Don Quixote, they had besides their self-respect and correct bearing a sublime soul, delicate sentiments and noble aspirations. It is easy to conceive that the habit of reading novels filled with marvels is quite enough to derange forever those narrow minds, naïvely in love with an unattainable ideal of virtue and honor. It is only by reflecting on the condition of Don Quixote and by placing him exactly in his world that we can unravel what, I think, is the principal intention of the book. It is a criticism of *hidalguism*, that sore of Spanish society whose depths Cervantes knew how to measure better than many others. His criticism is the stronger because he did not formally state it anywhere, and even concealed it by clothing his hero with fine qualities of heart and charming traits of character. Cervantes assumed the task of killing *hidalguism* by making us laugh gently at the most attractive of hidalgos.

Corresponding to the squire-hidalgo in the other sex is the duenna, who has been popularized in the theatre outside of Spain, where she has become a stock character. An old maid, or a nobleman's widow who watches over the women of the household, supervising the female servants, and giving decorum by her presence and her hairdress to the drawing room of the lady of the house, the duenna has again and again run the gauntlet of the most malicious criticism. But never yet had she served as the butt of such pitiless and jocose mockery as that which creates the charm of many chapters in "Don Quixote." Here Cervantes has outdone himself and has squandered the treasure of his astonishing imagination. We can never forget his Doña Rodríguez de Grijalba. She is an immortal caricature, as perfect in her kind as the portraits of Don Quixote and Sancho. Her pretensions to nobility, for she descends, you may be sure, from an eminent Asturian family of Oviedo; the tale she tells in a low tone of her needy youth; the weaknesses and errors which she tries to lessen with all sorts of genteel precautions; her old-maidish simpers and her affectations of shocked modesty when she finds Don Quixote solemnly seated on his bed and asks him in an ineffable tone, "Am I safe?"; the petty perfidies which little by little slip into her disclosures, drops of gall, discharged from her embittered and spite-swollen heart; her backbiting, at first hesitant, then bolder, implacable to her victim; and the whole crowned by that memorable "mauling" inflicted by her mistress, whose slaps still seem to resound in the silence of the night: what a gathering of subtle nuances and how masterfully superposed!

Still other ridiculous things peculiar to this itching for nobility which devours the nation, have been pointed out by Cervantes. The mania for example of using the "Don." Strictly speaking, an hidalgo had no right to that honorary title. The "Don" which Mr. Alonzo Quijano bestowed upon himself did not entirely please the bigwigs of the village, especially the other hidalgos, who thought they saw in it an intention to get ahead of them. "I don't know, I'm sure, who affixed the 'Don' to him, which neither his father nor his grandfather ever had," says Teresa Panza to her husband, Sancho. And Don Quixote might have retorted that he only "don-i-fied" himself in chivalry and to conform to the established usages of the illustrious knights-errant whom he professed to follow to the last precept. Moreover, he cared little for the clamoring of the jealous scandal-mongers; his grand spirit soared above such trifles. Sancho shows himself more discreet. He knows what it costs to bedeck yourself in too high-sounding titles, even when a turn of Fortune's wheel has lifted you above your rank. Distrustfully he fears the guffaws of his neighbors. " 'And whom do they call Don Sancho Panza,' he asks the majordomo of the island who greeted him respectfully with that title, 'Well, then, let me tell you brother, I haven't got the Don nor has anyone of my family ever had it; my name is plain Sancho Panza, and Sancho was my grandfather's and they were all Panzas, without any Dons and Doñas tucked on. I suspect that on this island there are more Dons than stones; but never mind, God knows what I mean, and maybe if my government lasts four days, I'll weed out these Dons.' " In this fashion the shrewd honest sense of the peasant treated this childish tic as it deserved. His opinion was not heeded at that time and the donification habit continued to flourish and wax prosperous. But the Spaniard finally decided in favor of Sancho. In extending to everybody as he did this title, which became in the long run a simple form of courtesy, he at the same time took away all its pre-tentiousness. When everyone is a Don, there is no cause for envy.

Hidalguism, however did not invade everything. They may be few, but there are some Spaniards who work industriously with hand and brain. Not even all the impoverished noblemen wallowed in the wretched idleness of rural life or embellished the antechambers of the great.

To the hidalgos is open the career of arms, the noble calling par excellence, which Cervantes, more from circumstance than choice, embraced in his youth. Finding himself in Italy, where he had followed Cardinal Acquaviva as chamberlain, he was carried away by the tinsel of soldiery and enlisted under Don Juan, taking part in the memorable campaigns of the Holy League. We should not decide what Cervantes thinks of the military profession merely from his famous parallel between arms and letters, which concludes that the former is absolutely superior to the latter. This parallel was only one of those exhibition pieces with which Cervantes loved to show his powers as a great writer by rising to general ideas. No doubt he avowed for the army the esteem which service under such glorious chiefs as Don Juan and Alvaro de Bazán and Lope de Figueroa, had given him. He always considered the episode of Lepanto the glory of his life. On various occasions he nobly boasted of his wound, and silenced with righteous indignation anyone who had the audacity to treat it lightly. But at the same time he had no illusions about the disappointments of the trade, and the injustice and foulness which caused the soldier of fortune so much suffering in his day. Even in that parallel there are bitter reflections on the precarious lot of the soldier compared to the leisurely life of the magistrate governing the world from his comfortable armchair. Cervantes could not speak about himself there, but we feel sure that he is thinking of his own disappointments. He recalls the labors of his campaign years, and sadly observes how little he profited from taking part as a conqueror in the most famous day of modern times. We feel that he is on the verge of exclaiming like the soldier of the song: "I do not complain of having lost everything for my king, for the law and Madam Isabel, but I do complain of returning home old, poor, crippled, to die by the hand of secretaries." The good days of the army are past; those of red tape are beginning. The great emperor is not there any more to defend and reward his companions in arms. Philip II, unfortunately, did not inherit his father's war-like virtues; he used the soldiers but he did not love them. As for Philip III, a kind of crowned monk, he never even understood that it is a king's duty to make at least some pretense of military spirit. Under his reign, only the titled nobleman and the younger son of famous households could hope to have careers in the army. They alone could obtain promotion, and after some campaign receive as remuneration a uniform of the order of Saint James. It is the time when the highways are infested with soldiers on furlough or discharged, crawling along in rags, exhibiting real or make-believe wounds for alms, or brutally extorting them by force. It is a time also when the offices of the ministries are besieged with troops of battered soldiers, showing beseechingly their "honorable discharge papers" to impassive secretaries. Cervantes had been a witness to many of these ignominies. He had often passed the steps of the Church of Saint Philip in Madrid, which is the meeting place of these victims of bureaucracy, and heard them excite one another with their clamorings, and enumerate to the amazed civilians feats which the Gran Capitán himself would have had difficulty in accomplishing. He recalled such scenes as he wrote, and that is why the soldier appears most often in his works as a rowdy or a tattered and miserable old man. Look at Vicente de la Roca: on his return home he parades in his gaudy uniform, twists his mustache, tells how he has killed more Moors than have ever been born in Algiers and Tunis, displays scratches as the wounds of battle, addresses the men familiarly and seduces the girls. Observe at the door of the hospital of the Resurrection the standard-bearer

Campuzano, leaning on his sword which serves him as a stick. He pays dearly for his swaggering gait, his soldierly trappings and the feathers in his hat, when a sharp hussy, pretending to fall in love with him, gives him the slip and leaves him without a red cent. Look at the beggarly soldier of *La Guarda cuidadosa:* this fellow curses and swears, exhibits twenty-two certificates from twenty-two generals under whose flags he has served, writes to his girl on the back of a granted petition which would bring him four or five reales if he presented it to the chief-almoner (a noteworthy sacrifice!), pursues his love affair like a Captain Fracasse, and finally runs foul of a sacristan as beggarly as himself but luckier, who elopes with the damsel. Such sketches, though less sombre, remind us of Callot's "Miseries of War." They testify certainly to a great disillusionment about this career of arms which Cervantes found at first so brilliant, and later so unjust.

Besides the military nobility there is the nobility of the long robe. Letters also give rank, but one must enter through certain prescribed gates. Students must first pass the required tests of the famous secondary schools, and then secure a degree from the universities, for a scholar with a degree is a kind of nobleman, or at least a privileged being. Everyone knows that Cervantes pursued no university studies; he did not bathe, as the Spanish say, in the learned waters of the Tormes or the Henares. He studied at the municipal secondary school, and learned the little Latin that he knew under the rod of a teacher maintained by the City of Madrid. Some of his contemporaries criticized his too secular culture, and excluded him as one of the uninitiate from the sacred ranks of the "sabios." Through a natural turn of events, the Cervantists, from the end of the eighteenth century on, rebelled against the disdain of these university graduates, and delighted in hurling sarcasm at these pedantic hair-splitters whose pretensions seemed so ridiculous. Assuredly, none of those who criticized Cervantes, with all their degrees, could have written a single chapter of "Don Quixote." Genius has prerogatives which no studies can replace, much less those of the Spanish scholastic system. What there is of genius in the work of Cervantes, could have been learned no better at the universities than it was through his initiation into good literature at Madrid. The very doctors and licenciates who felt themselves so superior to Cervantes were, almost without exception, guilty of the very faults they attributed to those unlearned in the classics. But however undeserved these attacks of his contemporaries, there are indeed obvious gaps in Cervantes' literary training. Such a richly endowed mind would not have been hurt by a stronger hold on the humanities, a thorough knowledge of Latin, Greek, which was scarcely taught in Spain then, and more extensive reading in the classics. These studies would have polished and refined his art, and forearmed it against certain mistakes of taste and style.

Ariosto lost none of his charming fantasy because he knew how to write fine Latin verse. Had he been better educated, Cervantes would have reasoned better and written better in certain situations, I believe. Since he possessed exactly what his detractors lacked, genius, an ampler literary culture would have given him that indisputable superiority in everything and over everyone, which we cannot unreservedly bestow upon him with justice.

"Lego" in the world in which he lived could be taken as an insult. He evidently felt its smart and did not forget to pay it back. The university folk, noisy and obstructive, furnished many a pretext for his criticism and he put several specimens of them in the path of his hidalgo. There were the graduates of small provincial universities, whose diplomas people never took very seriously. Such is the priest of Don Quixote's village, "a learned man, a graduate of Siguenza," and also the inmate of the Seville madhouse, "graduate in canon law of the University of Osuna," who, Cervantes says, "though he had been of Salamanca, as many think, he could not have helped being mad." Still another is the doctor of the Island of Barataria, a doctor of Osuna, who prescribes for Sancho that famous diet which so distressed the good governor. These words: a graduate of Siguenza, a licenciate or doctor of Osuna, never failed in their aim, and in his time, brought forth smiles on everybody's lips. There are also certain practices relating to the getting of degrees which Cervantes underscores with witticism: "I advise you," says Don Quixote, to a young poet who intends to take part in a poetical tournament, "to contrive to carry off the second prize. For the first always goes by favor or personal standing, and the second by simple justice: *in the same way as licenciate degrees are conferred at the universities."* Neither does Cervantes neglect the petty frauds that university folk practiced in conferring upon themselves degrees to which they had no right. The custom was so widespread that the authorized powers decided to sanction it, and the Council of Castile, for a financial consideration, issued licenses permitting a bachelor of arts to sign himself as a licenciate. Apparently, poor Alonso López, one of the priests of the escort for the dead man, had forgotten to furnish himself with a license of that sort. For when he is thrown from his horse, and feels Don Quixote's lance pushing into his belly, he cries out that he was very wrong to call himself a licenciate when he was in fact only a simple bachelor.

After the plays of the popular theatre, there is little to say about the hunger-stricken student, who puts learning to shame with his poverty and filth, his expedients and swindles. This quarrelsome scoundrel is one of the stock characters of the entremés and sainete; like the village mayor, the doctor, the court clerk, the Basque and the blind man. Cervantes merely touches upon him, in the parallel between arms and letters which he puts into the mouth of Don

Quixote. There he speaks of the sufferings of these poor wretches, soup-imbibers, whom he compares to the lowest class of ragamuffins. But he does not take them in hand for their depravity and vices, because misfortune, whatever its nature, hushes his criticism. The poor student, who to live honestly must serve some privileged younger son as valet, a wan and wasted servant in his threadbare cassock, is the only one of all the representatives of the university career for whom Cervantes entertains any sympathy. He willingly forgives the poor creature his hunger and scabs, and prefers him still to the doctor, enjoying his big income and fatuously fond of his degree, or even to the conceited academic pedant.

The university prepares for many careers, but it trains doctors and lawyers especially. Cervantes hauled the doctors over the coals only once, but that once is all-sufficient. His mockery is as good as Molière's, and because it is more concentrated, it produces an even greater effect. Doctor Pedro Recio de Agüero, a native of Tirteafuera (which means "Get Out"), is physician to his Excellency, Don Sancho Panza, Governor of the Island of Barataria. His services consist of being present at his master's meals, and prescribing for him the right diet for his constitution. He takes himself very seriously. Everything that is brought to the table is sent back without any mercy: fruits because the aqueous substance is indigestible; highly seasoned dishes because spices provoke thirst and too much drinking destroys the humid radical which is the source of life; roasted partridges, fried rabbits, stewed veal, everything is put on the list. Take it away! Take it away! cries the learned man at the entrance of each new dish. Sancho, convinced that the governor's function is to eat his fill, would like to retain some of the dishes, whose very smell delights him, but he dares not do so in face of the terrible aphorisms which fall on him like hail, and completely silence him. But when the *olla* appears, the genuine *olla podrida,* stuffed with all the ingredients which make it a dish wholly divine, and when the graduate of Osuna, resuming his monotonous tune, explains that the Spanish stew, besides being unworthy of the table of a governor, is a very dangerous food, because of its exceedingly complicated nature, he throws himself back in his chair and fires at the doctor this ringing volley: "Doctor Pedro Recio of Evil-Augury, native of Tirteafuera, a place that is on the right hand side as we go from Caracuel to Almodobar del Campo, graduate of Osuna, get out of my presence at once; or I swear by the sun, I'll take a cudgel and by the force of blows, beginning with you, I'll not leave a doctor in the whole island; at least none of those whom I know are ignorant. . . . Once more I say Pedro Recio, get out of here, or I'll take the chair I am sitting on and crush it over your head. And if they call me to account for it, I'll clear myself by saying I served God in killing a bad doctor—a general executioner. And now give me something to eat, or else take your government; for a trade that does not feed its master is not worth two beans." After this tirade, it may well be supposed that Cervantes was not at all pleased with the diagnoses and care he himself had received from the clever doctors of his country. Nor was he impressed by their unselfishness and scrupulousness, judging from his remarks in "Persiles" about the unscrupulous surgeons who get paid twice for a single consultation.

We have already seen what Cervantes thinks of jurists in the capacity of magistrates, the "lettered men," as they said in Castile, invested with some important judicial office. But there is in the lower ranks of the profession a humble limb of the law that could not escape the lense focussed by Cervantes on the society of the time. This limb, a step above the crier of the court and the bailiff's assistant, is the notary. A true scapegoat for the hatred and scorn which the law inspires in all Spaniards, the poor "escribano" is vilified as no one else. He has certainly received as many drubbings on the stage as the alguazil, and the jokes concerning his tricks and intrigues have become by constant repetition, insipid commonplaces. Cervantes has also abused "this satrap of the pen," as he calls him, but less in "Don Quixote" than in one of his short novels, "The Colloquy of the Dogs." Here, after allowing the worst possible things to be said about him, he pretends that he is going to take up his defense, a procedure which amounts to giving him his death-blow. "Yes, there are many notaries, I tell you, who are honest, conscientious, and loyal, ready to be agreeable without doing harm to their neighbors. Yes, all of them do not drag out lawsuits; do not put the two parties wise, do not spy and dog the lives of people for the purpose of finding evidence to use against them. All of them do not enter into collusion with the judge: reach me the rhubarb, and I'll pass you the senna." This careful enumeration of the vicious actions of which certain of the notaries were not guilty, is no more than a skilful way of denouncing with cruel precision the misdeeds which all the others practiced.

Let us descend now, in the manner of Dante, from the upper regions of society, composed either of Spaniards of high birth or honorable profession, down to the bottom ranks of the wretched. "Don Quixote" is not a critical review in the style, say, of the "Visions" of Quevedo. We cannot expect to see in the works of Cervantes, a procession of all the social types, filing by like penitents, under the lense of the professional moralist's dissection. "Don Quixote" is a fanciful trip through Spanish society which we take under the whimsical guidance of the author's imagination. We go only to those places where his hero walks. Moreover, since the knight's adventures take place in the open fields, and even in the most barren parts of the country, it follows that many types, such as the city dwellers, do not figure in the book. We shall see for the most part the people you come across on the highways, when you follow them, like Don

Quixote and Sancho, in short day's journeys, and when you delight as they did in questioning passers-by. We shall see inn-keepers, muleteers, prostitutes, pages in search of a master to serve, rural police, bandits, strolling players, owners of puppet shows, pilgrims, tramps, and even galley slaves.

Let us examine more closely some of these nomad inhabitants of the road.

First the inn-keeper, lord of his inn, as the knight once was of his castle. The road is his fief, and no one passes by who does not pay his tithe, and stop, willy-nilly, at his dwelling. The inn-keeper of Spain is also something of a rural constable, and he who has a heavy conscience and too light a purse to buy his silence, feels himself under surveillance. There he stands at his door, flanked by his Maritornes: the two certainly make a pair. He, stocky and surly, and noisily expensive when he has succeeded in thoroughly fleecing travelers of quality; she, the typical Galician woman, rolling in fat and as broad as she is tall, dirty, dishevelled, her little eyes opened wide and her mouth stretched from ear to ear, streaming with sweat from her heavy labors, and in other respects, compassionate and with accommodating morals, not at all displeasing to the wagoners. Look at them, and at the muleteers, slowly crossing the deserts of Castile, under a burning sun which makes a man irascible, brutal, and savage. They arrive at the "venta," with a wrench picked up at the last halt. The inn resounds with their cries and curses. Then comes supper and gambling which inevitably ends in a wild fight, silenced only when the host throws them onto the pack saddles of their mules, where they fall into a drunken sleep.

Next we encounter the players of the itinerant troop of Angulo the Wicked, piled into a cart, on their way to the neighboring town to give the *auto* of the the "Assizes of Death." To save time they have put on the costumes of their parts. The coachman is clad as the Devil; behind him are crowded together Death, with an over-joyous face which belies his rôle, an angel, whose long wings are seen sticking up, then a crowned emperor. In the background stands a little Cupid, who has taken off his fillet, but he still holds in his arms his bow, with his quiver and arrows. What figures, and what dark and frightful things they will suggest to the constantly simmering mind of Don Quixote! Yet he accepts their explanations, takes them for what they are, and does not kill them outright. But let us leave this adventure which, as it happens, ends badly.

Let us pass on to the mountebank, the impresario of the Punch and Judy show. Him we already know. He is the old convict Ginés de Pasamonte, by whose cunning Sancho was so long separated from his beloved donkey. According to Cervantes, he is one of those "hawkers" frequently seen in Spain, who appears to live by his avowed trade, but in reality merely uses it to cover all kinds of rascalities, by which he lives royally in his gay company. It may seem that Ginés had a bad hunch when he chose from his repertory the adventures of

the beautiful Melisendra to present before Don Quixote. Such names as Don
Gaiferos, Marsilio, Charlemagne, and Paris, all allusions to the great Carolingian epic, must inevitably have awakened his madness in the old knight.
They did indeed arouse him to the extent of seizing his sword. The result was
the massacre of many fine marionettes: a beheaded king Marsilio, a Charlemagne split from head to foot, a Melisendra one eye the poorer. All these
mishaps had to be made good in cash to the great sorrow of Sancho, but not to
the detriment of the sly Ginés who knew how to profit from such untimely rage.

Finally, the social scum, the army of vice and crime, summarized in the
account of the chained convicts, whom Don Quixote frees with the assurance
of a man who knows he has done a generous and just deed. This episode has a
beautiful swing, and never did Cervantes handle his irony with more daring
and charm. Don Quixote sees the chain, escorted by its guards, coming from
afar. These men are chained and certainly not by their own volition, he says to
himself, and sees in it only another act of injustice. This fixed idea absorbs him,
despite the reproaches of Sancho and the curt protests of the guards. He
approaches them and asks each convict the reason for his sentence. The answers
of the men are varied: some funny and boasting, seasoned with thieves' slang
which Don Quixote has to have explained to him, and others sadly embarrassed,
wrung with difficulty from their shame and despair. The replies and his interpretation of them convinces him that these men if not innocent are at least
unjustly persecuted; this one doubtless lacked the money with which to corrupt
the judge, the other the protection to placate him. The majority of them are
certainly victims of the arbitrariness of an unjust magistrate, and all this determines his will and puts his weapon in his hand. He pounces upon the guards
and frees the galley slaves, who pay him as we know. The chief varieties of
infamy in general and of vices more particularly Spanish have been put together
skilfully by Cervantes in this chain. First comes the simple thief who, cross-
examined, had the artlessness to confess his guilt; then the hardened criminal,
the bandit whose famous misdeeds are sung in ballads and who is admired and
respected as a master by his followers, and finally the old pimp, whose confession
suggests to Don Quixote that strange paradox on the virtue and utility of the
procurer's trade. Despite this unfurling of irony and jesting cynicism which is
somewhat disconcerting, we easily perceive that Cervantes was, at heart, of the
same opinion as Don Quixote. He was by no means convinced that those who
were dragged to the galleys were the most guilty, and to his mind the crimi-
nality of an act did not depend at all on the judgment pronounced by those
judges he had seen at work so many times. This gives us a new and last con-
firmation of his very decided ideas about penal justice.

Cervantes has described very few provincial types: a few Basques of clumsy speech and limited judgment, a few Andalusian muleteers, some Galician scullery-maids, to say nothing of the peasant of La Mancha, with his unforgettable model Sancho. In short he gives us no outstanding descriptions of these different kinds of men, nor any design indicating by details of features, dress, and customs, the distinctive types of Spaniards of different sections of the land. It is true that Cervantes did not take his knight into that province that he knew best after his own, Andalusia, where he had gone up and down to collect taxes, and rummage for stories which he has told with consummate art in several of his "Exemplary Novels." Perhaps through his desire to please his public and avoid repeating himself, he preferred to travel in less familiar regions, unfrequented by the Spaniards of the centre. But why did he not depict their inhabitants as he had the Andalusians, especially the Sevillians? When Don Quixote leaves Castile and enters Aragón and Catalonia, there seems to be no change of scene. Nowhere are the men of those provinces stamped with the seal of their land and race. In Catalonia, the knight meets only highwaymen, a product of that soil indeed, whom he describes quite aptly. Moreover, this banditry of chivalrous bent, these robbers of the open road, ticklish about points of honor and with the manners of gentlemen, were the type to please the historian of Don Quixote. But that is all. At Barcelona, a city he knew and loved especially, which he has named "flower of the beautiful towns of the world," he pictures only the surface of things, the galleys in the harbor, the crowded streets, and the wealth of the inhabitants. How was it he did not seek to initiate us a little into the busy life of these active, hard-working Catalans, so different from the monotonous existence of the Castilian? How was it that he did not select a few significant types from the crowds of the big industrial city, to contrast in mirthful scenes with the two heroes of the book? To tell the truth, this stay of Don Quixote at Barcelona leaves indeed a painful impression. The ridiculous aspect of his mania becomes too obvious in contrast with the civilized life of a city. His ramblings, so delightful under the sky of Castile and on the steppes of La Mancha, become grotesque here. His journeys and his lance thrusts have a carnival air, which only amuse the street urchins running to see that sad masquerader pass. It seems that Cervantes could have corrected this grievous impression which such a degradation of his hero makes on us, by submerging in a way the person of the noble knight, and emphasizing the descriptive details and local color. We should thereby have come off the richer by a few priceless scenes of Catalan customs.

There remains still to be described a group which has no fixed place in the social hierarchy,—the men of letters. Literature which is neither theology nor science, the literature of pleasure, is not a career. Then the poet or the novelist, the dramatist or the essayist, even the historian, when he does not fill the position of official historiographer, can only devote himself to his art occasionally. He must at the same time exercise some lucrative calling, or be protected and supported by some grandee. For literature does not feed anyone, at the most it only helps one to exist. In addition to this, the man of letters in Spain has not the opportunity offered in free countries of writing on political subjects, or hiring out his pen to the factions which alternately direct the affairs of the state and hold the keys of the treasury. Absolute power is hardly pleased with this class of literature, and one who has the audacity to verify its acts or to criticize them, is requested to find a home in Holland or elsewhere. If any political pamphlet circulates, for restrictions have their limits and cannot reach everything, it is only under cover. Such means of publicity have never brought anything but drubbings, a sentence in a swampy penal colony, or prolonged exercise at the oars of the king's galleys. Only one of all the literary genres cultivated in Spain approached being a profession. This was the drama, at the time of the greatest vogue of the *comedia,* and included a very few who exercised a veritable priesthood, such as Calderón, who possessed for a long time an exclusive monopoly over the *autos* of Corpus Christi at Madrid, and such as Lope de Vega, whose dramatic factory supplied ample material for the theatrical managers of all Spain. Yet both of them must have made greater profits from their prebends and the generosity of their patrons than they did from their royalties.

Cervantes was no more favored than many others; his "Exemplary Novels," his "Don Quixote," and his plays were never enough to provide for his needs. From his early youth, when he left Spain to follow a cardinal to Italy, to his last moments, he had to be a servant or toil at some task. He was in turn a cardinal's servant, a soldier, a collector of royal taxes, an agent for private enterprises. He took up the story-teller's pen only at odd moments, and sacrificed to the Muses only after finishing the commonplace job that provided bread for his family. Never having had much occasion to be grateful for the bounty of the aristocrats he was not at all backward in telling them what he thought of their duties toward men of letters. To him, there is something like a tacit contract between the author who dedicates his work to a prince and the prince who benefits from the incense burned in his honor. Tit for tat: a dedication is worth a pension, and the lauded grandee who does not repay praise breaks a contract.

After all, the prestige which the patron derives from the work of his protégé, when it is successful, is an appreciable value whose price may be fixed by bargaining. He goes further: since literature subsists only in proportion to the favor bestowed upon it, the aristocrats are, to a certain extent, responsible for the fate of the works. They create reputations and direct the taste of the public which is inclined to rely on the judgment of its betters. It is therefore the duty of the aristocrat to choose well, to welcome the homage of people of worth, and to reject inferior writers and wretched poets. Thus, this kind of parasitism, which the necessities of life in those days imposed upon so many literary men, might very well be unaccompanied by degrading and servile forms. It might even be so compatible as to reconcile us to those customs which nowadays appear so galling.

Literary criticism, as might be expected, occupies a rather large place in "Don Quixote." Cervantes takes advantage of the coming and going of the characters in his novel, their encounters and conversations, to set forth certain cherished literary theories and to speak his mind about some of his contemporaries. However, it is not literary criticism as we understand it, since it has become an art and a science; but rather a type of criticism a little too dogmatic and summary, but certainly not devoid of interest. In the time of Cervantes, the arbiters of taste, the donors of precepts, the dispensers of palms to the most deserving, followed one of three paths. Either they commented upon Aristotle, diluting for the most part the Italian commentators of the master; or else they composed Arts of Poetry, patterned after that of Horace; or finally, they wrote panegyrics, Temples of Memory. The last kind is in vogue. One praised the other, to be praised in turn by him. You took care of your own reputation by extolling your neighbor's. Cervantes had a hand in this game, in the "Song to Calliope" of the "Galatea." Nothing is more insipid than this fulsome flattery scattered right and left, in a shower of laudatory epithets, so promiscuous that they have no meaning at all. There are no subtle shades in the praise which falls indiscriminately upon all; the mediocre and the deserving alike are admirable, excellent, divine. What do we learn in those stanzas or in the endless rhapsody of Lope de Vega, entitled "Laurel of Apollo," about the characteristic qualities of the poets of those days, about the workmanship of their style, or the rhythm of their verse? Very little indeed. The "Journey to Parnassus" is more valuable; here the burlesque tone and the satirical tendency authorized Cervantes to mix criticism with his eulogies, to conceal a few snakes beneath the flowers, and to sharpen his arrows against the persons of the poets. But personalities in criticism is another peril. Too often a literary dispute degenerates into a diatribe in which the adversary alone is aimed at; it is no longer the faults of the writer but the shortcomings of the man that are denounced and ridiculed. Even today a foreigner is surprised at the considerable importance that personal questions and tiffs among writers of antagonistic political or religious parties assume in literary discussion in Spain.

The various pieces of criticism inserted into "Don Quixote" are unequal in value. Such and such a romance of chivalry praised or depreciated, or such and such a pastoral novel or epic poem, whose merits or weaknesses Cervantes explains, do not interest us. No one will ever read those faded works any more;

therefore whatever our author thinks of them matters infinitely little to us. The judgments of Cervantes which have kept their interest have to do with the theatre, but before examining them, it is fitting that we consider his doctrine. Cervantes is, before everything, a disciple of Italy, an enthusiastic pupil of him whom he calls the divine Ariosto. The master taught him, along with certain tricks of style, the technique which became his strength and his glory, and which gives life to "Don Quixote": an amiable, playful, almost indulgent irony, diametrically opposed to that cold, cruel, crushing irony of the Spanish writers of picaresque novels. Cervantes is entirely imbued with Italy, the quotations of great Italian writers rush to his pen, and Italian oozes out of him through every pore. He poked fun, in one passage in "Don Quixote," at the translators of his day who closely imitated the Tuscan books instead of transposing them; but he himself is not free from Italianisms, as his commentators have already noted. Italy not only transmitted to Cervantes all the honey of her best prose-writers and poets, but she opened up for him antiquity. The only works of the ancient writers that he really knows are those which passed into circulation, thanks chiefly to the numerous Italian *popularizers* who were extensively patronized in Spain.

Regarding the theatre, he espouses naturally the opinions of those who, in Italy, interpret the "Poetics" of Aristotle and convert it into formulas for the use of poets unacquainted with learned literature. He respectfully submits, like Lope, to Minturno, to Castelvetro, to Robortello d'Udina; and he believes in the dogma of the unities almost as much as Corneille. This was in theory, but his practice flagrantly gives the lie to his beautiful speculations.

Cervantes wrote for the theatre on two occasions, once at the age of thirty-five or forty—and the plays he composed then were, he says, produced with success— and a second time, during the last years of his life. The latter appeared long after Lope, who as the recognized sovereign master of the theatre had put all the actors of Spain under his jurisdiction. Of the dramas of the first epoch, we have only the "Numantia," a beautiful patriotic declamation in dialogue; and the "Life at Algiers," a curious picture of captivity and the bagnios, at times rather eloquent. Both of these are chamber tragedies of a sort, interesting to read but difficult to stage. The real dramatic work of Cervantes, therefore, consists essentially of the eight *comedias,* and the eight interludes of the second period which were published in 1615. Since these plays, and I am referring here exclusively to the eight *comedias,* are worthy of inclusion among the most extravagant productions of the Spanish Thalia, as well as among those most opposed to the rules which Cervantes accepts and recommends in his writings, it has been asked how he came to compose them first, and then print them, guaranteeing them to be good or at least tolerable. Anxious to solve the problem, a fanciful writer of the eighteenth century, Blas de Nasarre, maintains that Cervantes behaved toward the theatre of his country in the same way as he did toward books of knight-errantry. He intended to kill it with ridicule, by parodying it. This is a freakish idea that no one has taken seriously. A parody must be amusing, like "Don Quixote": but where is the parody in eight deadly boring plays which contain not a single remark to inform us that it is all a joke and that we are being laughed at! No, the truth of the matter is that Cervantes wrote these plays just as they are, without caring a snap more for the rules of Aristotle than for the rules of good taste and sense. He did it because he did not have the necessary leisure to write them differently, and he sold them to a publisher because he needed the money. We cannot expect very much logic from an artist who has a family to feed and debts to pay. Moreover, the famous Lope had already set the example of a contradiction even more shocking, for he was the inventor of the new *comedia*—when he condemned without mercy in his "Poetics" in the name of the principles of his school, all his own dramatic works with the exception of six plays which are composed *according to a theory of art*. Cervantes makes a few judicious remarks about the childishly exact copying of historical details and local color and about the feats of ingenuity which authors must perform to fit their subject to the unchangeable frame of the *comedia* and its obligatory stock characters. But with these exceptions, the dramatic criticism set forth in Chapter XLVIII of the first part of "Don Quixote," with the addition of some passages in the "Exemplary Novels," "Persiles," and the "Journey to Parnassus," is exceptionally narrow and limited. Cervantes has not discerned the real causes of the weaknesses of the Spanish classical theatre. He believed that its weaknesses resulted from the disregard of rules, whereas they flow essentially from weak psychology, from a too summary study of character and passion, and from a too hasty and careless composition. On the other hand, he did not feel the strength and the grandeur of that theatre, nor did he realize that it represents the most powerful manifestations of national feeling which Spanish literature has known since the great epoch of the *romances*.

Such are the principal vistas which Cervantes has opened up for us on his age and country. Assuredly, he does not show us everything, and he does not take us everywhere. He nibbles right and left, chooses among men and facts those fitting into his fiction; the rest he overlooks. But what he does depict stands out in such relief, with such life, that we willingly supply what he leaves in shadow, and we retain from the reading of his novel, a picture of sixteenth and seventeenth century Spain, whose accuracy cannot be questioned. By itself, "Don Quixote" is worth many books of moralists and historians who have pretended to judge or describe the Spain of that time. It has been said, without too much exaggeration, that if of all Castilian literature of the great period, "Don

Quixote" alone remained, this peerless book would sufficiently instruct us about the things we most care to know of that vanished world.

The historical value of a work of imagination does not always become apparent at the first reading. We let ourselves be carried away by the romantic elements as we follow with keen interest the incidents of the fable, and we think only of the hero himself and his adventures. But return to it, and you will then understand the interest afforded by the accessory elements, the very real historical background, against which the fiction stands out. "Don Quixote" is then a novel that you must reread often if you wish to enjoy to the full all that constitutes its high literary, moral, and social value.

(*Translated by* Mary Campbell Brill)

PART TWO

The Spirit of Castile

MIGUEL DE UNAMUNO

FROM whatever point you penetrate into the Spanish peninsula, you will find yourself confronted almost at once by a region of hills; you will then enter into a labyrinth of valleys, gorges and ravines; and finally, after a longer or shorter ascent, you will emerge upon the central tableland, barred by the naked sierras whose wide and deep valleys form the mighty cradles of mighty rivers. Across this tableland stretches Castile, the land of castles.

Like all great expanses of earth, this tableland receives and irradiates heat more quickly than the sea and the coast-lands which the sea refreshes and tempers. Hence, when the sun scorches it, an extreme of heat, and as soon as the sun forsakes it, an extreme of cold; burning days of summer followed by cool fresh nights during which the lungs gratefully inhale the breeze from the land; freezing winter nights following hard upon days which the bright cold sun in its brief diurnal course has failed to warm. Winters long and hard and summers short and fiery have given birth to the saying, *"nueve meses de invierno y tres de infierno"*—nine months of winter and three months of hell. In the autumn, however, there is a serene and placid breathing-space. The sierras, shutting out the winds from the sea, help to make the winter colder and the summer hotter; but while they impede the passage of the gentle low-trailing clouds they form no barrier to the violent cyclones which burst among their valleys. Thus long droughts are succeeded by torrential deluges.

In this severe climate of opposing extremes, in which the transition from heat to cold and from drought to flood is so violent, man has invented the cloak with which to isolate himself from his environment, a personal ambience, constant in the midst of external changes, a defence at once against both heat and cold.

The great storms of rain and snow bursting upon these sierras and drained thence by the swollen rivers have in the course of centuries scoured the soil of the tableland, and the succeeding droughts have prevented the retention of the rain-washed soil in a network of fresh and robust vegetation. Thus it is that the view presents a wide and desolate expanse of burning country, without foliage

131

and without water, a country in which a deluge of light throws dense shadows upon a dazzling surface, extinguishing all intermediate tones. The landscape is seen cut out in hard outline, almost without atmosphere, through a thin and transparent air.

You may sometimes range over leagues and leagues of desert country without descrying anything save the illimitable plain with its patches of green corn or yellow stubble, here a sparsely extended array of oaks, marching in solemn and monotonous procession, clothed in their austere and perennial green, there a group of mournful pines, holding aloft their uniform crests. Now and again, fringing a bright river or half-dry stream, a few poplars, seeming intensely and vividly alive in the midst of the infinite solitude. As a rule these poplars announce the presence of man: yonder on the plain lies some village, scorched by the sun, blasted by the frost, built of sun-baked bricks very often, its belfry silhouetted against the blue of the sky. Often the spinal ridge of the sierra can be seen in the distance, but if you approach it you must not look to find rounded bossy mountains, fresh with verdure and clothed with woods, with the yellow of the gorse and the carmine of the heather flecking the bracken. Here is nothing but a framework of bony fleshless rock, bristling with crags, sharp-cut hummocks nakedly displaying drought-cracked strata, covered at most with a scanty scrub, where flourish only the hardy thistle and the naked scented broom, the poor *genestra contenta dei deserti* of Leopardi's poem. Down in the plain the highway with its festoon of trees loses itself in the greyness of the earth, which kindles into an intense warm red when the sun sinks to rest.

The setting of the sun in these immense solitudes is full of beauty. The sun dilates as it touches the horizon as if greedy to enjoy still more of the earth and in sinking it sheds its light upon it like blood and fills the sky with a dust of gold. The infinite dome of the sky grows paler and paler, then swiftly darkens, and the fleeting twilight is followed by the profundity of a night tremulous with stars. Here are no northern twilights, long, soft and languorous.

Broad is Castile! And beautiful with a sad quiet beauty this sea of stone beneath its expanse of sky. It is a landscape uniform and monotonous in its contrasts of light and shade, in its sharply juxtaposed and unmodulated colours. It presents the appearance of an immense floor of mosaic, without variety of design, above which is spread out a sky of intensest blue. It is lacking in gentle transitions and its only harmonic continuity is that of the immense plain and the massed blue which overspreads and illumines it.

It is a landscape that awakens no voluptuous sensations of *joie de vivre,* that inspires no longings for ease and idleness. Here are no lush green meadows inviting indolent repose, no dells that beckon like nests.

Its contemplation does not call forth the sleeping animal in us, the animal

that delights to drowse in a leafy paradise, brooding over the remembered satis-
factions of those appetites which have been kneaded into the flesh since the
earliest dawn of life.

Nature does not here recreate the spirit. Rather it detaches us from the low
earth and enfolds us in the pure naked unvarying sky. Here there is no com-
munion with nature, no absorption in her exuberant splendours. This infinite
landscape is, if it may be so said, monotheistic rather than pantheistic. Man is
not lost in it so much as diminished by it, and in its immense drought he is
made aware of the aridity of his own soul.

The population of the Castilian country-side is concentrated for the most part
in hamlets, villages or towns, in groups of clustered dwelling-houses, separated
from one another by immense and naked solitudes. The villages are compact and
sharply delimited, not melting away into the plain in a surrounding fringe of
isolated homesteads, the intervening country being entirely unpopulated. The
houses seem to crowd together round the church as if for warmth or for defence
against the rigour of nature, as if the inhabitants sought a second cloak in which
to isolate themselves from the cruelty of the climate and the melancholy of the
landscape. Thus it is that very often the villagers have to journey considerable
distances on mule-back in order to reach the fields where they work, one here,
another there, in isolation, and it is already dark before they return to their
homes to stretch themselves on the hard kitchen settles and sleep the comforting
sleep of toil. A notable sight it is to see them at nightfall, mounted on their
mules, their figures silhouetted against the pale sky, their sad, slow, monotonous
songs dying away on the sharp night air into the infinity of the furrowed plain.

While the men labour in the sweat of their brow on the hard land, the
womenfolk perform their tasks at home, filling the sunny arcades in front of
the houses with a murmur of voices. In the long winter evenings it is usual for
masters and serving-folk to assemble together, while the latter dance to the
accompaniment of the sharp dry tap of the tambourine or sometimes to an old
ballard measure.

Go into one of these villages or drowsing cities of the plain, where life flows
slowly and calmly in a monotonous procession of hours, and there you will find
the living souls beneath whose transitory existence lies the eternal essence out
of which is woven the inner history of Castile.

Within these towns and villages lives a breed of men of a dry, hard and
sinewy constitution, burned by the sun and inured by the cold, a sober, frugal
breed, the product of a long process of natural selection by searching winter
frosts and intermittent periods of scarcity, tempered to withstand the inclemency
of the skies and the asperities of penury. The peasant who gave you a grave

"Good day" as he passed by on his mule, huddled in his cloak, will receive you without overmuch courtesy, with a kind of restrained sobriety. He is collected in his movements, circumspect and deliberate in his conversation, with a gravity which gives him the air of a dethroned king. Such at any rate he appears when he is not cunningly ironical. This sly biting irony—*socarronería*, a racy word full of racy character—is the classical form of Castilian humour, a quiet and circumspect humour, sententious and phlegmatic, the humour of Sanson Carrasco in *Don Quixote* and of Quevedo, he who wrote the discourses of Marcus Brutus.

His slowness is matched by his tenacity, qualities that have an intimate association. His reaction-interval, as the psycho-physiologists would express it, is long; it takes him a considerable time to realize an impression or an idea, but once he has grasped it he does not readily relinquish it, does not in fact relinquish it until another has impinged upon it and driven it out. The slowness and tenacity of his impressions would appear to be due to the lack of an environing and unifying nimbus, blending them into a conjunctive whole; they do not merge into one another by subtle gradations, but each one disappears completely before the next takes its place. They seem to follow one another like the succession of uniform and monotonous tones in the landscape of his country, sharp edge against sharp edge.

Go with him into his house. On the front wall the violent contrast of strident blue paint against a snow-white background exposed to the full blaze of the sun is almost painful to the eye. Sit down to table with him and partake of his simple dinner, prepared without much culinary art, accompanied only by keen and fiery condiments, a meal that is at once both frugal and violent, providing the palate with sharp-edged sensations. After the dinner, if the day chances to be a holiday, you will witness a dance, a dance slow and uniform, danced to the monotonous beat of drum or tambourine, a series of stabbing sounds that strike upon the ear like blows. And you will hear songs, wailing and monotonous, full of long-drawn-out notes, songs of the steppes, with the rhythm of the dragging labour of the plough in them. They testify to an ear that is incapable of appreciating the finer gradations of cadences and semi-tones.

If you are in a town and there are any pictures there of the old traditional school of Castile, go to see them—for in the great days of its expansion this race created a school of realistic painting, of a rude, vigorous, simplified realism, very limited in range of tone, which has the effect of a violent douche upon the vision. Perhaps you will come across some canvas of Ribera or Zurbarán—your eye is held by the bony form of some austere hermit, whose sinewy muscles are presented in high light against strong shadows, a canvas meagre in tones and gradations, in which every object stands out sharp-edged. Not infrequently the figures fail to form a single whole with the background, which is a mere accessory of insignificant decorative value. Velázquez, who of all Castilian painters possesses most of the racial character, was a painter of men, of whole men, men all of one piece, rude and emphatic, men who fill the whole canvas.

You will find no landscape-painters, you will discover no sense of tone, of suave transition, no unifying, enveloping atmosphere, which blends everything into a single harmonious whole. The unity springs from the more or less architectonic disposition of the several parts.

In this country of climatic extremes, without any softness or mildness, of a landscape uniform in its contrasts, the spirit likewise is dry and sharp-edged, with but a meagre ambience of ideas. It generalises upon raw facts, seen in a discrete series, as in a kaleidoscope, not upon a synthesis or analysis of facts seen in a continuous series, in a living stream; it sees them sharp-edged like figures in the Castilian landscape and it takes them as they appear, in their own dress, without reconstructing them. And it has given birth to a harsh popular realism and to a dry formal idealism, marching alongside one another, in an association like that of Don Quixote and Sancho Panza, but never combining. The Castilian spirit is either ironic or tragic, sometimes both at once, but it never arrives at a fusion of the irony and the austere tragedy of the human drama.

Incarnation in "Don Quixote"

AMÉRICO CASTRO

THE supreme novelty of *Don Quixote* and the basic reason for its enduring merit do not lie essentially in its wealth of episodic invention nor in the vivid realization of certain ideals, which are, in effect, very characteristic of Renaissance neo-stoicism (for example, the substantiation of character in the energetic will to maintain it.[1] Nor would Don Quixote's unselfish purpose to combat or uproot evil in the wicked suffice to explain the sustained interest of so singular a work throughout the vicissitudes of human preferences. The moralists of that epoch (Montaigne, Justus Lipsius) offer keener, more original ideas than does Cervantes regarding human behavior. Consequently, we should not attribute the excellence of *Don Quixote* exclusively to its imaginative richness, its moral exemplariness, the art with which it infuses fresh life into new and old cultural themes, the pleasant, cleverly contrived arrangement of its episodes, the variety of its forms and literary genres, the expressive movement of its unique style, and its vivid spectacle of Spanish life. All this and much more is found in *Don Quixote,* but it does not reveal the ultimate and essential source from which stems this surprising form of fiction.

We have here a work unfailing in its captivating charm, one which provokes alternate merriment, profound meditation, subtle amusement, unrestrained laughter, or deep melancholy, as has been said thousands of times. These factors contribute to the delightful effects of the book, but none of them brings us nearer to the irreducible literary essence of *Don Quixote,* nor permits us to understand the sensation of life which is engendered by almost all of it.

It is obvious that Cervantes did not intend to write just another imaginative book, following the line of narrative works at that time so familiar to Spaniards and Italians, and sustained by a millenary past. The artistic value of all of them —including the fictional tales in the Oriental mode—consisted in the ingenious manner of combining the eternal stimuli of human life[2]: love, hate, the struggle to overcome obstacles interposed between intent and achievement of goal, and abandonment to the delightful play of fantasy, all poured into molds or frames

136

which kept the tale at a remove from the real, immediate experience of both author and readers.

Cervantes rejected equally the idea of composing an ideological treatise upon the norms which should guide man to the attainment of virtue, fame, or eternal happiness. Nor would he accede to giving us an acrimonious, detailed diatribe, in picaresque style, against a society oppressive and hostile to him, a society whose shortcomings and miseries he had experienced more acutely than had Mateo Alemán or Don Francisco de Quevedo. These and many other plans must have clashed in the author's mind during the span of twenty years from the composition of the pastoral *La Galatea* to that of *Don Quixote*. Fortunately, his moralizing or rancorous feelings, as far as he experienced them, did not affect the decisive project of his life.[3]

Shunning abstract moralizing, cultivation of a religious theme, or the amusing game of traditional ventures into fantasy, Cervantes chose to immerse himself in the concrete intimacy of certain individuals who undergo the strange phenomenon of performing actions of very different natures (noble, base, imaginary, beautiful, ugly, ridiculous, grandiose, or mad) as the result of the expansion of their own lives—lives *not* founded on a predetermined character,[4] nor constructed entirely within themselves, without any relation to the outside world, and as a hermetic development of reflection upon their own consciousness (as *La Princesse de Clèves* of Mme. de Lafayette). The lives of the major characters created by Cervantes may be described as the vertex where an incitement, outwardly initiated, and the actions provoked by that incitement, converge.

The characters appear to us at the outset as typical cases, enclosed in a generic frame and lacking a perspective that would serve as living background: a small-town "hidalgo," a coarse peasant, a beautiful girl of a well-to-do family, a student who returns to his village full of wisdom, or a bachelor of arts with university-inspired pedantry, etc. Such figures in themselves are inert and have little chance of capturing our interest, since none of them, alone, shapes for himself an original manner of living, which would depart freely from the situation in which he finds himself. The intimate depths of their souls are not illuminated through meditation or introspection, as occurs in Hamlet, and before him, in Oedipus. Nor are the most fully developed characters in *Don Quixote* molded step by step under the pressure of a social environment, the spirit of the epoch, or inevitable fate. The transition from a confused, static existence to a dynamic, fiery (personalized) life has its origin in an outside incitement, which suddenly transforms the type into an individual animated by the most unexpected motives and challenges. An animating "form" is projected upon the generic "matter," creating, recreating it, and infusing into it a new meaning. Such a transition is not gradual or psychological, but vital; it comprises the total existence of the person. Both his goals and his conduct change completely in this unforeseen crisis, and thus there looms before our eyes the dual perspective of what the individual was and what he is and will continue to be.

A dynamic tension emerges from outward circumstances, from a transcendent incitement, and thenceforth, the life of the character is identified with the contexture of his previous existence and the incitement it met with. We might say then that the process of life, as conceived by Cervantes, is a dialogue between a life-giving, formative "logos" and an inert passivity ready to receive it.

Such a new conception of life expressed in art led to the liberation of fiction, centuries later, from the narrowness in which it had lain fettered since antiquity. Before Cervantes, it had not been possible organically to harmonize the expression of the imaginary or fictitious and the concrete, contemporary experience of the character or the author, without falling into moralizations or grotesque farce. The unreal time of the narration and the contemporary time of the writer were irreconcilable. Roland could not leave his mythical abode and penetrate into the historical atmosphere of the 15th century in any other form than the burlesque (Luigi Pulci: *Morgante Maggiore*). In other cases, the author intervenes in fiction to wrap it in moralization (Mateo Alemán: *Guzmán de Alfarache*). In this way, literary production became a hybrid narrative-didactic work, incapable of procreation. The very fact that one had to resort to intellectualist criticism, reduction to the comic, or moralizing sententiousness in order to bring to the immediate, contemporary level events transpiring in the world of fiction proclaimed the incompatibility of the two.

The new manner of fictional creation came upon the reader as a *fait accompli*, just as a delicious but unknown delicacy is savored without need of knowing its composition. But when the learned gentlemen who were not artists attempted to explain the structure of *Don Quixote,* they had to do so with the canons of an inadequate philosophy: the Aristotelian precepts of the Renaissance, or the intellectualism of the 17th and 18th centuries. This is the reason for *Don Quixote's* having been viewed as a satire, a farce, or even as a moral lesson. Of course, there were those, more artists than critics, who perceived other values (the splendid essays of Turgenev and Ortega y Gasset, for example); but even today we find, as the logical fruit of a long tradition of rationalism, judgments hardly in accord with the creative intent of Cervantes.

Don Quixote shows us that the reality of existence consists in receiving the impact of all that can affect man from without, and in transforming these influences into outwardly manifest life processes. The illusion of a dream, devotion to a belief—in short, the ardently yearned in any form becomes infused in the existence of him who dreams, believes, or longs, and thus, what was before transcendency without bearing on the process of living becomes embodied into life. This is the functional idea of *Don Quixote*—the idea integrally incorporated in it, though not expressed theoretically. The fascination of this work does not stem, then, from the prodigious inventiveness of the author, but from this primary idea which permeates the richness of imagination, with incalculable significance. Unconsciously, we lose ourselves in the charm of these unique pages, for in effect, such is the essential process of all human life—that of self creation and expression in contexture with all possible circumstances.

The major theme of *Don Quixote* is the interdependence, the "interrealization" of what lies beyond man's experience and the process of incorporating that into his existence. The fantastic books of chivalry become an integral part of the life of Don Quixote; ethereal pastoral tales induce the beautiful Marcela to wander through the real-irreality of a forest; the inflexible knight errantry of Don Quixote threatens seriously to abbreviate the sojourn on earth of the argumentative Sansón Carrasco. Life, in view of all this, would be rather similar to the fecundity of the earth, moistened by beneficent rain, and revitalized by opportune winds. But it also happens that warm, wet lands give off vapors which cloak them in a dense cloud risen from its soil, and that man *emits* imaginative sparkles and beliefs (just as he can be incited by them). The inseparable solidarity of both phenomena is evident in Cervantes' simultaneous preference for those who seek nourishment in the manna of an incitement, and for those who project outward illusions without meaning for others. The madman from Seville, who thought he was Neptune, and the Cordoban who inflated little dogs may be regarded as an inverted perspective of those who incorporate into their lives the beneficial or adverse rain of a vitalizing "logos." The difference lies in the orientation of perspective: whether illusion is seen as pendent from a vital process, or the latter as pendent from illusion.

This is the significance of Cervantes' strange predilection for the unbalanced (for the "incited") of all types[5] and his open disesteem for the Knight of the Green Greatcoat, or for the Duke's private priest, insulated against any untoward draft that might ruffle their paralytic, generic existences. Contrast those limited lives with the inner richness of Don Quixote, in whom is incarnated the dual process of achieving the plenitude of his existence, incited by an illusion, and of being himself the creator of Dulcinea. Passing from illusion to illusion, his is an existence which finds justification and completeness in itself.

Let us clarify here a point of utmost importance. Although life consists essentially in reflecting, refracting, and transmuting the incitements coming from any point of the compass rose, life itself is channelized into forms of highly varied structure, and in accord with certain courses and outlines traced by history. Within the "kingdom" of life there are types and species comparable metaphorically to those which exist in the kingdoms of nature.

We noted previously that the lives in *Don Quixote*, (especially that of the protagonist) reach fulfillment and consummation in the realization of their own values, without objectivization in thought (as occurs in Milton or in Goethe), or in pragmatic results (as in *Robinson Crusoe*). On the other hand, *Don Quixote's* philosophical or doctrinal contributions, valid in themselves, are indeed insignificant. The reason for this is that Cervantes' work has given us the supreme instances of Spanish life—which is independent of the novel's being intelligible and enjoyable to all types of people—just as the peerless Andes give of their beauty to whosoever wishes to contemplate them. But it is no less certain that the very extraordinary lives created and expressed in *Don Quixote* are conceivable only within the Spanish tradition. To live, for Cervantes, is not to know, nor to make distinctions between this and that; nor is it a search for the ultimate truth behind the fleeting, uncertain appearance of all that surrounds us—"All Is Deception," as he entitled one of his lost plays. Nor does life consist of an effort to forge a new or better world through the discovery of firm principles founded upon physical or moral experience. Cervantes and his characters pay scant heed to the progress or retrogression of the world of men; nor does the author, unlike Shakespeare, lead us to explore the shadow-darkened abysses of consciences flogged by their own destiny. Instead, Cervantes makes us see simply how the flow of life emanates from the fascinating interplay of illusions, beliefs, and hopes with the consciousness of the individual existence, and with the urge to objectify this interior-exterior interaction in human behavior. We observe the characters from within as well as from without, in a double perspective, which I have termed for many years simultaneous introspection and "extraspection." Don Quixote bears within him, quite transparently, the form of Alonso Quijana, and at the same time projects himself into the Knight of the Rueful Countenance. Thanks to such a new conception, the author-poet succeeds in creating characters of multiple dimensions, each of which is related to the others in widely varying forms and combinations. Dorotea appears initially as a static character drawn from a pastoral novel; we encounter her first "bathing her feet in the brook that flowed past"; her feet "were so fair that they looked like two pieces of shining crystal." "This," says the Curate, "is no human being, but a divine creature." Such an abstract figure begins to take on living, personal form as we hear of the havoc wrought upon her by the illusion that Don Fernando could raise her from her humble condition to the state of a great lady: "I shall not be the first who has risen through marriage from a lowly to a lofty station." She surrenders to that gentleman, who, upon departing from her chamber, leaves her in uncertainty: "He then took his departure, and I was left I know not whether sorrowful or happy; all I can say is, I was left agitated and troubled in mind and almost bewildered by what had taken place . . . " (I, 28).

With introspection, the abstract type becomes personalized, and no longer can be described as hitherto, in the indirect style of the third person; she herself must tell what occurs in the depths of her soul. The hermetic seal of her generic life now broken, Dorotea can reveal the powers of her intelligence and the versatility of her talents in performing the difficult rôle of Princess Micomicona: " . . . the curate observed to Dorotea that she had shown great cleverness, as well in the story itself as in its conciseness, and the resemblance it bore to those of the books of chivalry." "She said that she had many times amused herself reading them; but that did not know the situation of the provinces or seaports, and so she had said at haphazard that she had landed at Osuna" (I, 30), certainly not a seaport! Dorotea, lovely daughter of Andalusia, ignorant of geographical complications, receives and emits at the same time the reflections of pastoral and chivalric novels. But she herself is now something apart from all that: she is a human being, animated by keen intelligence, whom the chance of an impulse propelled, like a diminutive, glowing star, across the vast spaces of *Don Quixote.*

The characters are placed immediately upon a double plane: first, we find them still and tranquil, then caught in the whirlpool of action unleashed by this new manner of living. The country gentleman that was Alonso Quijana is transformed into the Knight of the Rueful Countenance; Camila, the honorable wife, changes before our eyes into an adulteress; etc. The same process can also be seen as only a conceived possibility. In the proposed case of writing a chivalric novel in the mode of Cervantes, the author could "show himself to be an astronomer, or a skilled cosmographer . . . and sometimes he will have a chance of coming forward as a magician, if he likes" (I, 47), that is to say, to pass to another mode of existing, new and unheralded. The previous form of existence limits its mission to serving merely as pedestal to another, occasioned by adventitious circumstances which have happened to the person. It is not a matter, therefore, of one more episode, but of a renascence. The impression of unpredictable surprise is consubstantial with the art of *Don Quixote,* not because of unexpected prodigies outside the individual (as is normal in novels of chivalry) [6] but because certain potent stimuli are incarnated in him. Nothing happens without repercussions; everything happens *to someone.*[7] The adventures are chosen and woven into the narration, less for their comic element than in order to put Don Quixote and all those who surround him to the test. Just as Montaigne deliberately sought ideological pretexts to "try out" the mettle of his discursive faculty, so Cervantes accumulates adventures and occasions of all types to continue the process initiated by the chivalric novels on Alonso Quijana. In other words, the episodes are selected so that the personages and even inanimate things may reveal their latent possibilities, becoming radiant with future promise, and poetized with the incarnation of the incitement that has pervaded them. The chivalric novel, now an inherent part of the life of the protagonist, makes him feel himself Don Quixote; the new knight then projects his special views of the world upon the windmills, thus turning them into giants; or he kindles a spark in the long-smothered village curate, Pero Pérez, embroiling him in the arduous task of "de-Quixotizing" the man he calls his mad parishioner; or he makes of Sancho a dreamer of unknown "isles." And thus the incitement goes on indefinitely in a continuous brilliance of dawns and sunsets.

The lyric poet had limited himself to duplicating everyday reality by projecting it into its metaphorical equivalent. The firmament at dawn is viewed by Góngora as a field of sapphires peopled with stars, where the Sun-God Apollo grazes each morning as he appeases his divine hunger: "through sapphire fields to feast on stellar corn": a very beautiful image which, like its many analogues, remains floating in the magic and inaccessible air of a transcendency unrelated to our lives and as remote from us as the atemporal material of the epic.[8] The lofty lyric and epic always allude to a lost, longed-for paradise, and are real only as symbols of the eagerness for infinitude and eternity consubstantial with the life of man.

Cervantes' inspired departure, however, permitted both the objectivized poetry of the lyric or of the epic to penetrate into the process of our lives; the windmills are not only giants, but also the content of the experience of one who lives them as such, and of those who continue to see them as windmills. The metaphor ceases to be that of the lyric poet and actually becomes a metaphorical existence, since the windmills are giants to the same degree that Alonso Quijana is Don Quixote—a figure so truly alive that we call "quixotic" those who resemble him. This new mode of fiction includes, then, not only the metaphor, but the poet who creates it.[9]

Since then, an individual's life can well serve as a literary theme, if it manifests a creative will that involves the totality of its being, and a projection within it of án inciting stimulus capable of expanding it in turn into a *poetic* projection, that is, one formed and created from within the person's vital experience. The possibilities of expansion for the projection of that life can be reasonable or chimerical, worthwhile or ridiculous; and there are examples of all of these in *Don Quixote*. But the essential point is that in this work the abyss that separated the life of the poet from the unattainable world in which he objectified his creation is bridged; the artistic theme is now the poet who wields his metaphors and figures, and the characters of which they are the projection—a difficult and hazardous task which it took thousands of years to realize. It is for this reason that magnificent outbursts of lyricism are more abundant than excellent novels, which represent perhaps the most difficult literary genre, that which requires the most profound understanding of man and of his possible worlds.

We understand now why there are in *Don Quixote* no other "extrapersonal" realities than those associated in one way or another with the immediate existence of the characters. The brief descriptions of nature are erratic fragments of certain literary genres (the pastoral novel), the function of which within the work will be treated later. In general, no person or thing plays a passive or ornamental rôle. If it rains once (I, 21), in a form neither metaphorical nor imagined, it is so that the barber may cover his head with his basin, thus making possible the great adventure of the helmet of Mambrino. Objective phenomena are used to provoke dynamic effects in the characters, and actually, an essential characteristic of Don Quixote consists precisely in his inspired impertinence. One of various opinions that Sancho has heard of his master is that he is "courteous, but meddling" (II, 2).[10]

The Hispanic world to which Cervantes belonged never dreamed of changing the structure of reality by the adoption of new ideas; the "scientific" nature of things remained that bequeathed by inert tradition, modified here and there only under pressure from imported scientific knowledge. On the other hand, what enormous wealth lay in life itself as the target for every impetus coming from without! The Spaniard never ascertained the scientific reality of the earth and its inhabitants, but he incorporated into his very life the most remote, the most inaccessible lands, and men of every appearance, all of whom finally fused biologically with him, by speaking and believing as he does. *Don Quixote* is the supreme document of a form of life which strives to realize itself in personal existence, the "biocentric" life. The most elementary realities, as well as cultural phenomena, affect prodigiously here the interior and exterior behavior of man.

Ever since the Middle Ages, the Spaniard felt that his beliefs, and all that which transcended him spiritually, formed an inviolable whole; in the realm of belief (*not* of thought) dwelt the abstractions, the moral principles, the values, and everything we would generally term today psychic and ideal objects.[11] To the Spaniard, the supernatural and the natural, the religious and the profane, the spiritual and the physical, the abstract and the concrete, coexisted in one and the same unit of consciousness. There was not the least critical discrimination between actual experience and that which transcends the witness of the senses, as is shown by the curious fact that the medieval Spaniard never saw the need for any theological proof of the existence of God, which was never regarded as problematical. A belief could wane or disappear, but not because it had been supplanted by a rational truth. For example, when faith in the patronage of Saint James dwindled in the 17th century, it was replaced "officially" and effectively by the patronage of Saint Teresa, and the *Cortes* of Cadiz were still concerned with the question in 1812.

I believe that this is the explanation of the linguistic-literary phenomenon of linking in a single expressive unit the mention of a physical and of a psychic or ideal object: "I abandoned *home* and *patience;* to break *lances* and facilitate *difficulties*," (I, 29; I, 46)—and any number of other instances.[12]

This phenomenon, which occurs as early as the Middle Ages, is noteworthy less as a peculiarity of Cervantes than as the epitome of the conception of man upon which *Don Quixote* is based,[13] for language, aside from its character as a grammatical skeleton bequeathed by tradition, is at the same time a living body expressive of a people's form of life.

The fact that both categories of objects (material and immaterial) are integrated so frequently in expressions well harmonized in their duality reveals that, unlike *La Celestina, Don Quixote* was not conceived on the principle that "omnia secundum litem fiunt,"—"all things are created in the manner of a conflict."[14] Don Quixote and Sancho blend in their very opposition, just as the novels of chivalry become infused in their readers, and Rocinante and Sancho's Dapple are entwined in their vital medium.

It is inaccurate to think that *Don Quixote* consists in the conflict between the ideal and the real, if that implies a thesis or theoretical principle, objectified in preferences and evaluations: Sancho is artistically as valuable as his master, and Maritornes, as Dulcinea. *Don Quixote* is not a manual of moral exempla designed to show man the path toward the "good life," nor to prove that immoderate aspirations or beliefs should be tempered to the exigencies of "common sense." The eccentricities of *Don Quixote* are often unjustifiable, but on occasion they are also justified, since the author took the precaution to classify him as "a madman in streaks, full of lucid intervals" (II, 18). The actions, attitudes, or opinions of each character do not appear as good or bad, clever or stupid, judged from without; rather, they are "presented" as originating in someone and as coming into contact with those of another individual in a continuous "departing from" and "going to." The scene of so prodigious a spectacle is the workshop in which the life of each one is forged, and is not a didactic or logical transcendency superimposed on the process of living. This is why Cervantes did not create a social medium (ignoring the question of whether or not he was capable of doing so), except to the minimum extent necessary to sustain the figures evoked by his imagination. Their life is not a sojourn within themselves, but a peregrination through the hills and valleys of the human; and from this come forth the inns, the country dwellings, the streams, the mountains, the limitless forests—like a physical duplicate of the longings of those beings, emergent, descended from some fount of life, or ascending impelled by the urge of reaching it. Some live in a constant crisis of assault and attack (Don Quixote and those who attempt to force him down from the summits of his peaks to the flatness of their valleys), while others flee harassed by overwhelming circumstances (Marcela, Cardenio, Dorotea, the liberated galley-slaves, Roque Guinart and his fellow bandits, etc.). Those idle witnesses of so much activity, who remain passive and with a purely sermonizing attitude (e.g., the Knight of the Green Greatcoat and the ecclesiastic attached to the ducal palace) are attacked "ad hominem" by *Don Quixote*, and reveal thus the fragility of their position.

In the characterization of Don Diego de Miranda (II, 16), Cervantes injects all the traits requisite to a life withdrawn from all heroism; that gentleman, symbolic of the idle nobility of the reigns of Philip II and Philip III, indulges, for example, in a paralytic type of hunting: "I keep neither hawks nor greyhounds, nothing but a tame partridge or a bold ferret or two." The pacific gentleman delegates all daring to his ferret; it is not surprising, then, that he is interested in "making peace between those whom I know to be at variance; I am the devoted servant of Our Lady, and my trust is ever in the infinite mercy of God our Lord." Such is the man whom Cervantes, with inspired perversity, places beside Don Quixote in the adventure of the lions, creating thus a dialogue between peak and abyss: " . . . for valor that trenches upon temerity savors rather of madness than of courage. . . ." "Gentle sir," replied Don Quixote, "you go and mind your tame partridge and your bold ferret. . . ." (II, 17).

The ecclesiastic comfortably installed in the ducal palace also reveals the poetic sympathies of the author, who was not interested in presenting an opposition between the "real" and the "ideal," but rather, in confronting those incited by any goading stimulus with others similarly incited and with those refractory individuals impervious to uneasiness of soul and to the pricks of fantasy. The ecclesiastic essays to keep the lives of others from exceeding the humble level of his own, submerged in the inert quietude of the generic.[15] He is one of "those who rule noblemen's houses; one of those who, not being born magnates themselves, never know how to teach those who are how to behave as such; one of those who would have the greatness of great folk measured by their own narrowness of mind; one of those who, when they try to introduce economy into the household they rule, lead it into meanness. One of those, I say, must have been the grave churchman who came out with the Duke and Duchess to receive *Don Quixote*" (II, 31). The repetition five times of "one of those" proclaims the author's rhetorical emphasis and aggressive spirit. The diminutive drama in which the hero and his prosaic opponent clash consists of three episodes: (1) the utterly derogatory characterization of the ecclesiastic; (2) the face-to-face dispute between the two: addressing the Duke, he said angrily to him: "Señor, your excellence will have to give an account to God for what this good man does. This Don Quixote, or Don Simpleton, or whatever his name is, etc." To which replies the heroic knight, trembling from head to foot like a man dosed with mercury; in a hurried, agitated voice he compares his insolent reproacher to an irresponsible woman: " . . . a gownsman's weapon is the same as a woman's, the tongue . . . " (II, 32). (3) The retrospective allusion to the ecclesiastic, as previously to Don Diego's tame partridge and bold ferret: "I wish, señor Duke," replied Don Quixote, "that blessed ecclesiastic, who at table the other day showed such ill-will and bitter spite against knights-errant, were here . . . " (II, 36). Neither Cervantes nor Don Quixote had forgot the incident.

The violence employed in this case is even more striking when we recall the sympathetic treatment accorded previously to that mundane, open-hearted prebendary, better versed "in chivalric books than in Villalpando's elements of logic . . . " (I, 47), and in whose mouth the author placed an intelligent criticism of the books of chivalry, and even the project of writing one: "I myself . . . was once tempted to write a book of chivalry in which all the points I have mentioned were observed; and if I must own the truth I have more than a hundred sheets written. . . ." (I, 48). Such an "incited" figure attracts the poetic sympathy of Cervantes; he does not abuse the priest Pero Pérez—"so jovial and fond of enjoying himself" (II, 67)—and who is so preoccupied with "de-quixotizing" Don Quixote, even though it mean fighting on the latter's own grounds. From the radiant aureola of Don Quixote emanates the only light that lends visibility to the sparkless existence of the rural town priest.

Let us discard, then, the inveterate habit of calling Don Quixote an "idealist" and Sancho a "realist," since both master and squire share both characteristics, as we shall see. These romantic-positivistic concepts proceed from the tendency to seek types and prototypes in every literary form, and from the confusion between the creations of art and those of thought—in short, they are the result of contemplating literature from *without*. These concepts are inadequate for the full comprehension and evaluation of the structure of *Don Quixote,* which is founded upon active forms of life which define themselves as they develop before our eyes, like a constant flow, propelled by external and internal incitements, oriented in descending and ascending directions, now consonant and parallel, now dissonant and clashing. Perhaps the supreme innovation of this work lies in its making perceptible, through full, vital existences, the articulation of the most varied incitements coming from without and the will to life inherent in each authentic existence. Cervantes, Christian and stoic, is permeated with a multisecular Oriental tradition; his art consists in blending the conception of life as a purely phenomenistic succession of "withins" and "withouts" (like a linear, open, bodiless arabesque), with the stoic, Judaic, Christian idea of man's rising upon the rock of his will and on the consciousness of his personal liberty. Full awareness of the "self" is attained at the cost of an uninterrupted effort to sustain one's self, without pausing to consider outward circumstances: "There are just as many letters in 'nay' as in 'yea.'"[16]

Don Quixote and his squire stand resolutely upon their firm consciousness of the desire to live as individuals: "I know who I am," replied Don Quixote (I, 15), "each of us is the maker of his own fortune" (II, 66);[17] which is not didacticism superimposed upon the work, but rather an aspect of its very structure. Sancho repeats at every step: " . . . naked was I born, naked I find myself, I neither lose nor gain" (I, 25); " . . . I'd rather lie in summer under the shade of an oak, and in winter wrap myself in a double sheep-skin jacket *in freedom,*[18] than go to bed between holland sheets . . . , and tell my lord the duke that 'naked was I born, naked I find myself, I neither lose nor gain;'" (II, 53) " . . . so I can say *with a safe conscience—that that's no small matter* 'naked was I born, naked I find myself, neither do I lose nor gain'" (II, 57). Aside from his rôle as hog-herder, squire, governor, good story-teller, citer of proverbs, or what will you, Sancho is a person acutely conscious of his individuality: " . . . there's not so much difference between me and my master that he should be washed with angels' water and I with devil's lye" (II, 32).

If Cervantes had limited himself to conceiving his personages as characters plunging into themselves, he would have presented to us a collection of illustrious, vigorous men, capable of replacing the uncertain vacillation of their feelings with the sparkle of eternity that gleams in their minds. Such characterization would have produced, at best, a psychological *roman,* peopled with half-lives, individuals afraid of living to the fullest, never ceasing to observe themselves as a reality already terminated, objectified—lunar, superficial beings, who reveal only the unchanging face of their reasoning. But man is not a demigod, master of himself, and consequently, absolute stoicism is an unreal abstraction, which resolves difficulties without developing them authentically and without duly challenging them. The vaunted inner calm of stoicism does not make it possible to express the totality of human existence, and thus it is surprising indeed that many have centered the most salient traits of the Spanish character in Senecan philosophy (a doctrine, imported from Italy). The theme of Spanish literature, and that of *Don Quixote,* may be summarized as the *difficulty* of living, when it tries to integrate body, soul, and mind—which is different from giving preference to the latter at the expense of the other two.[19]

The consciousness of themselves serves Cervantes' characters as the hunters' starting point serves the hunters, a point from which they set out and to which they return; but actually, hunting wild boar is something more than the indispensable decision to go in search of them. Life weighs heavily on "naked"

Sancho when the sparkle of the incitement gleams before his eyes; for the second time, he "takes upon himself" the dangerous office of Squire, "decoyed and beguiled by a purse with a hundred ducats that I found one day in the heart of the Sierra Morena; and the devil is always putting a bag full of doubloons before my eyes, *here, there, not here, perhaps over there,* until *I fancy at every step that I am putting my hands on it,* and hugging it, and carrying it home with me, and making investments, and getting interest, and living like a prince; and so long as I think of this I make light of all the hardships I endure with this master of mine, who, I well know, is more of a madman than a knight" (II, 13).

The frenzied search and anxiety that possess Sancho, body and soul ("here, there, not here, perhaps over there"), are painted clearly in this passage of rare plasticity and vital force. Desire and illusion are integrated in the perspective of the longed-for reality, just as the Knight also sees and touches with his hand the achievement of his glory, like a Messianic promise: " . . . it is requisite to roam the world, as it were on probation, seeking adventures, in order that, by achieving some, name and fame may be acquired, such that when he betakes himself to the court of some great monarch the knight may be already known by his deeds, and that the boys, the instant they see him enter the gate of the city, may all follow him and surround him, crying: 'This is the Knight of the Sun' . . . " (I, 21).[20]

Doubt and misgiving are combined with the frenzy of illusion: "By the living God . . . I cannot endure or bear with patience some of the things that your worship says . . . ; [what you tell me] must all be made up of wind and lies, and all pigments or figments, or whatever we may call them" (I, 25). The character, thus, has a part of his life engrossed in the height of the incitement, and the rest of it, quiescent in his static reasoning—so that actual experience is poeticized and the hitherto unreachable poetry of books is vitalized into an integral reality, as in hawking, wherein the falcon takes wing from the fist of its master, only to return to him. If the falcons in captivity could express themselves, their literary genre would be the Cervantian novel.

Once we have perceived this keystone of the architecture of *Don Quixote,* Sancho appears as somewhat different from the comic character who is brought down amid guffaws after each ludicrous act (the "gracioso" in Lope de Vega, for example). The Squire does more than put into relief certain follies of his master, since he maintains his own existence and fulfills efficiently and worthily several difficult tasks. Sancho is the antithesis of the spectral, cold-hearted "pícaro" in Mateo Alemán and Quevedo—a product of circumstances less real than are the dreams lived by the farm laborer of La Mancha, who is capable of merciful sympathy, and is naturally clear-sighted and wise, though ignorant and uncouth.[21] From this level, then, he rises, enticed by the various induce-ments offered him: an "island," gold coins, donkeys, the title of "countess" for his daughter, the pastoral life, etc. The desire awakened in him by the enchanted ascent on the back of Clavileño stands out among so many illusory perspectives because of its delicate spirituality: "Ever since I came down from heaven, and from the top of it beheld the earth, and saw how little it is, the great desire I had to be a governor has been partly cooled in me; for what is there grand in being ruler on a grain of mustard seed, or what dignity or authority in governing half a dozen men about as big as hazel nuts; for, so far as I could see, there were no more on the whole earth? If your lordship would be so good as to give me ever so small a bit of heaven, were it no more than half a league, I'd rather have it than the best island in the world" (II, 42).

Sancho expresses himself here like a Lucianesque character, and the sky of which he speaks is the firmament, a coveted goal for disillusioned souls or sceptics since the *Dialogues* of Lucian were made accessible by the Renaissance humanists. Menipo says: "As I saw it, all Greece could span some four inches . . . And thus I realized how small is the base upon which rests the pride of our rich." A segment of the Peloponnesus seemed to be "no longer than a lentil." "A brief inspection of life has convinced me of the absurdity, misery, and inse-curity of all human things—wealth, position, power. I felt disdain for it all, thinking that preoccupying myself with such trifling cares was making me abandon the truly worthwhile; and thus I decided not to debase myself again and to fix my glance on the great *Whole*."[22]

The literary figure of the Squire achieves the utmost of elasticity because it was not conceived as a materialistic "type," but as a life conditioned by the varied perspectives which rose before him: an "island," gold, comfort—or the firma-ment towards which Clavileño carried him. Sancho pursues the paths of many divers incitements, and thus can incarnate the essence of a good judge, or feel the yearning to place himself in the heavens to contemplate from there the insignificant preoccupations of earth-dwellers. Everything depends upon what is being offered him.[23]

The contrast between Sancho and Don Quixote stems from the fact that the latter creates and invents the course of his life, overcoming or ignoring adverse circumstances—blows, gibes, enchanters, and disillusionments. Upon finding himself obliged to suspend his chivalric functions, as a result of his defeat by the Knight of the White Moon, Don Quixote hits upon a pastoral existence: " . . . if so be thou dost approve of it, Sancho, I would have ourselves turn shepherds, at any rate for the time I have to live in retirement" (II, 67). Don Quixote continues to live from the lofty incitements which are contained in the paradigmatic works of his time. To call this insanity, or to suppose that the author wished to present us a "case of abnormal mentality" in the naturalistic vein, would be a complete absurdity. The madness of Don Quixote is merely a vehicle for a certain way of living, as Cervantes understood it, because he was a Spaniard of the Renaissance, imbued with the neo-Platonic spirit and the possessor of literary ideas, as I have pointed out in other works. In contrast to his master, Sancho, prompted by the world he confronts, to which the author relates him through temporal, concrete links, incarnates the idea of conditioned living.[24] Hunger makes him eat with both cheeks; pain draws forth bitter complaints from him; Clavileño incites him to yearn for a supraterrestrial peace; his governorship, to become a perfect governor; his master's pastoral vision, to become an illusory shepherd. The contents of life change because the character is a living person, who artistically does not grow old or lose interest. His *raison d'être* is not exhausted in what he does, no matter how varied and pleasing that may be, solely because it rests on the richness of the creative fount of his existence—a vital category highly distinct from the logical-moral concept injected in the literary type (the patience of Griselda; the sadism of her husband, the Marquis of Saluzio; the valor of Amadís; the treachery of Ganelón, etc.). We have a "Sanchoesque" mode of life and *not* a character type.

Consequently, it is not a question of the opposition of idealism and materialism, but rather, of the projective will of Don Quixote and the receptive will of Sancho. The former prefers whatever fits into his program; he drives his world over the routes that he has previously traced and forges Dulcinea from the depths of his creative capacity (the development of which we shall discuss later), just as he concocts the balm of Fierabras really to check his suffering. Sancho, on the other hand, adjusts his receptive mode of life to the exigencies which he encounters, be they material or ideal; he lets himself be affected, we would say today, by the "objectified" spirit,[25] whereas *Don Quixote* is the "objectifying" spirit, and everything about him becomes "quixotized." The one invents hazards; the other suffers them, or avoids them if he can. Don Quixote attempts to force his Squire to receive the lashes necessary for the disenchantment of Dulcinea; "Seeing [which] Sancho got up, and grappling with his master, he gripped him with all his might in his arms, and giving him a trip with the heel stretched him on the ground on his back, and pressing his right knee on his chest held his hands in his own so that he could neither move nor breathe." And Sancho, whose personality is no less strong than that of his master, replies to the indignant protests of the unhappy Knight: "I neither put down king nor set up king; . . . I only stand up for myself who am my own lord" (II, 60). The fundamental difference between the two is that Don Quixote's great incitement was what led him to become the Knight of the Rueful Countenance, and this lies therefore in his "prehistory"; whereas Sancho's incitement is "historic" and carries him through entirely different paths. "Señor, . . . travelling on foot is not such a pleasant thing that it makes me feel disposed or tempted to make long marches" (II, 66).

The two immortal characters lead parallel existences, although they go in opposite directions; but both possess the supreme human gift of being able to accept and reject what life offers them; it is upon their lives that the "novelistic" forms of the future will be built. The literary figure appears here destroying the frame of a millenial form of literature. The epic-chivalric hero could not question the meaning of his heroic life, as does Don Quixote. " . . . and I, so far, know not what I have won by dint of my sufferings . . . " (II, 58). The character of a tale, from Achilles to Gargantua, could not discuss seriously, and from his authentic conscience, the meaning and goal of his existence; the character was not aware of being a person, for he was placed there, solidly, to be a noble or grotesque figure. With the definitive rupture of the generic profile, the use of the literary form was made possible (which one day was to become a genre in turn), capable of allowing the character to live the novel of his own life from its beginning to assert or complicate his own existence. Because of complex historical reasons, this phenomenon was produced in Spain.

THE ACTION AND EFFECT OF THE WRITTEN WORD

A great deal has been said of the literary sources of *Don Quixote,* but very little about the presence and function of books in the creative process of the work. Reading or having read, writing or being in the process of writing, are states and activities which occupy many of the characters who people the pages of *Don Quixote,* states and activities without which some of these characters would not exist. The written word suggests and sustains the life process or serves as the expression of life; it does not fulfill a decorative or illustrative function, but appears articulated with the very existence of the individuals involved. We might say, in view of this, that *Don Quixote* is a book forged and derived from the active elements of other books. Part I issues essentially from the books read by Don Quixote; Part II, in turn, is the issue of Part I, since it does not limit itself to a continued narration of new events, but incorporates into the life of the character the consciousness of having already been the subject of a book. The Don Quixote of Part II continues himself and the literary interpretation of Cide Hamet; among those who meet him now the Knight appears as a person of flesh and blood, and also as a human-literary figure: "Tell me, brother squire . . . this master of yours, is he not one of whom there is a history extant in print, called '*The Ingenious Gentleman, Don Quixote de la Mancha,*' who has for the lady of his heart a certain Dulcinea del Toboso?" (II, 30). To the Duchess, who speaks these words, the Knight is an old acquaintance, a literary character, and also a person who really is alive, just as Don Quixote was already in the first part an "Hidalgo" of La Mancha and a literary projection of the books of chivalry. The traditional themes of literature are now fused with the living experience of those themes; the book then becomes not only a book, but it also becomes the reader who has incorporated its poetic material into his very life. *Don Quixote* is, among other things, the amalgamation of the words of the author, Cervantes, and those of the other "author," Cide Hamet Benengeli.

The characters are presented from a double perspective, from that of the successive acts which they carry out (the bare content) and that of the form of their personality (the container). The latter appears as a volatile substance, emanating from the life-giving matter of certain books, or passing through the interpretations of other persons, or of other written words. Ginés de Pasamonte (I, 22) is Ginesillo de Parapilla to the other galley slaves, even though he does not accept this version of his person; the "truth" of what Ginés really is will be found, he says, in his own life story, written by him, in a manuscript which he left "in the prison in pawn for 200 reals" and so good is it that "a fig for *Lazarillo de Tormes,* and all that kind that have been written, or shall be written, compared with it. . . ." "And is it finished?" asked Don Quixote. "How can it be finished," said the other, "when my life is not yet finished?" (I, 22). The characters live here, consequently, from, in, and through books. The container of life (its form and consciousness) and the content (its actions) are blended harmoniously, like a melody and its accompaniment.

Such fluid aspects of reality cannot be enclosed in rational categories, nor are they rendered fully in the abstractions that we may attempt to impose on them. We have already seen how erroneous is the effort to explain Don Quixote under the heading of "idealism" and Sancho, under that of "materialism," because both figures elude imprisonment in such classifications. Unamuno interpreted Don Quixote in the form of life most dear to himself—the search for the eternal without consideration of the insignificance of the concrete and conventional; but he must have derived the impression that *Don Quixote* is a work which narrates and creates itself, and in which not everything happens in accordance with his conception of the Knight from La Mancha; and the result of this impression was the strange notion that Cervantes is inferior to his book, since "he showed in his other works the feebleness of his creative faculty and ordinarily how far he was below the prerequisites for relating the deeds of the Ingenious Gentleman, and even his own narration of them."[26]

Unamuno was not alone in dissociating *Don Quixote* from its author, who is treated at times as a poor ignoramus ("a lay talent") incapable of perceiving the greatness of his own creation.[27] The reason for such a flagrant error is easily seen: an intellectualistic criterion is applied to the book, and a "vital" criterion

to the author. It is taken for granted that Cervantes oscillated between the opposite poles of grandeur and penury, but still one assumes that he should conceive
his protagonist in accord with our stenciled, petrified canons. When we observe
that, seen in this way, the character escapes us, then we consider the author
incompetent for not having given us a Don Quixote more consonant with our
fancies. Such a naïve simplification requires less energy than resorting to vital
categories more appropriate for the object we want to understand.

We should widen our view of *Don Quixote* in such a way that the whole
and the details form a whole integrally united. This problem really requires
analysis and development in a full-length book. However, I shall attempt to set
down here everything necessary to make plain the function of the written word
in the structure of the major work of Cervantes.

His contemporaries frequently exploited the theme of an escape from this
world—an abode as unhappy as it is empty of actual reality, and which is very
frequently compared with wind, smoke, crystal, or with dreams. The only sure
and truly desirable goal was the future after death. Cervantes was perhaps the
only great figure who, though feeling the need of escaping from the disagreeable
pressure of the immediately given, achieved freedom from it without departing
from the terrain of the strictly human. *Don Quixote* avoided the religious solution as carefully as it did the generic and lyrical flight to the impersonal world
dear to the "beatus ille" of Horace.

The author definitely preferred figures removed from urban life, voluntarily
or through necessity (Don Quixote, the galley-slaves, despairing lovers, bandits,
etc.), and has them roam through the open spaces of the country, or tarry briefly
at inns, as at a point of momentary repose for their restless, incitement-ridden
lives. A domestic, sedentary atmosphere, and static, immovable realities are carefully avoided, except for an occasional appearance in the form of a light background curtain (forests, wooded fields, meadows) upon which to project the
continuous movement of life.[28]

Don Quixote was conceived as an obscure and indistinct emptiness, as a con-
tour brightly illuminated both at its highest and at its lowest points. We may
perceive in this empty, tacit reality what makes it rise to a "summum," or sink
to the depths of insignificance. The laborer from El Toboso, mentioned in the
preceding note, appears in the poetic flight of his song and in the harsh noise
of his plow as it drags along the ground. This ascent and descent both emanate
from a single idealizing intent, which branches out in opposite directions to
realize their respective values. The beauty of Dulcinea is as "ideal" as is the
monstrous ugliness of Maritornes; the one is far above, the other far below, the
middle zone (the static, "non-incited" zone) in which we customarily live, and
which here is, as it were, spirited away. All that is essential in *Don Quixote*

exists in so far as it is attracted and compelled by extremes; and in this dynamic process incitement, course, and goal are harmonized.

The fecund emptiness from which this great human light emerges did not originate in the personal disillusionment of the author, for that alone would never have engendered a work of such multiple, vast dimensions. Nor is it sufficient to seek its explanation in the vacuum in mundane matters created by the negations of the corrosive ascetic literature, or by the religious anguish consequent on the Council of Trent. The roots of the greatest secular work that Spain has produced are sunk deep in human motives. *Don Quixote* reflects the twilight of heroic Spain, which had risen upon its firm belief in valor, a belief identical with the inviolable consciousness of the self-willing personality. Faith in God and in the king was identified with faith in the person, completely enclosed in his purely personal life, and unconnected with the objective world or with thoughts. Don Quixote curses (as Ariosto does) the advent of firearms with all the fury of which he is capable, since they minimize the efficacy of the strong man, and place on a par the valiant and the coward. In this sunset of heroic Spain the crimson glow of incitement still alternates with the faded beauty of the evanascent grays: "I was born, Sancho, to live dying . . . " " . . . and I, so far, know not what I have won by dint of my sufferings; . . . " " . . . in last year's nests there are no birds this year" (II, 59, 58, 74).

Cervantes gave personal and universal meaning to the theme of the anguished void of Spanish life, a theme which he had not invented, since it already existed in many souls and had been finding expression ever since that moment after the capture of Granada in which the nation was unified. During Philip II's reign of almost half a century (d. 1598), the country was submerged in a feeling of disquietude, and groped despairingly for an outlet for its only possible activities. In a poem written by Cervantes upon the death of the King, called "The Prudent" (a title that hardly suggests incitement), the poverty of the treasury is not surprising since: "they say that you hid your treasure in heaven."

As early as 1580, Father Pedro de Rivadeneira, biographer of Ignacio de Loyola, had written confidentially to Cardinal Gaspar de Quiroga, advisor to the King and Grand Inquisitor, that the soldiers had lost their combative spirit, as a result of their dislike of the King, and that it was dangerous, therefore, to send them to fight against the Portuguese: "I see their hearts very changed from the love, devotion, and desire for the glory and honor of their king that they used to feel"; towns, grandees, gentlemen, prelates, clergymen, priests, all "are bitter, angered, and stirred up against His Majesty."

Years later the royal preacher Alonso de Cabrera said in one of his sermons: "Our grandfathers, gentlemen, lamented Granada's having been taken from the Moors, because on that day horses were lamed, cuirass and lance were laid to rust, and shields were let rot, and there came to an end the illustrious chivalry of Andalusia, and youth was maimed, and thus its gentilities so valorous and well famed."

This is not the place to quote more texts. One feels in them the decline of the heroic spirit, a sentiment which still surges up as a distant yet resplendent horizon for the chief personages of *Don Quixote*. The immortal "Hidalgo," in one of his lucid intervals, expresses the noble, ardent thesis of the eloquent discourse on Arms and Letters: "Don Quixote delivered his discourse in such a manner and in such correct language, that for the time being he made it impossible for any of his hearers to consider him a madman; on the contrary, as they were mostly gentlemen, to whom arms are an appurtenance by birth, they listened to him with great pleasure. . . ." The living word of the Rueful Knight now irradiates enthusiasm among the company: "I am almost tempted to say that in my heart I repent of having adopted this profession of knight-errant *in so detestable an age as we live in now;* for though no peril can make me fear, still it gives me some uneasiness to think that powder and lead may rob me of the opportunity of making myself famous . . . " Attesting to the profound wisdom of Don Quixote's remarks, "The curate told him he was quite right in all he had said in favor of arms, and that he himself, *though a man of letters and a university graduate,* was of the same opinion" (I, 37, 38).[29]

Both knights and humanists, in well-harmonized cadence, join in rendering homage to the supreme majesty of martial heroism, as in the previously cited case of " 'nay' has no more letters in it than 'yea.' " In these instances the style of *Don Quixote* makes evident to us the basic elements of its art and its humanity.

A style built thus upon distant perspectives and upon elusion must of necessity be extreme, dashing, in key with the fugue—the flight from the immediate—from which it takes inspiration. The author flees the inert, the prosaic, all that does not affect, or is not affected by the incitement; the middle ground is abandoned and the extreme is eagerly sought. The gentleman-knight begins his major peregrinations along the highways of the world (I, 2); for a whole day he travels over indeterminate spaces, "without anything remarkable happening to him"— elusive style—; he looks about him "to see if he could discover any *castle* or shepherd's *hut"*—the style of extremes. Why is it that a town, or any settlement at all (a farmhouse or its outbuildings for example) is not sought, but rather a manorial castle (supreme limit) or a shepherd's hut (the humblest abode)? The inn that comes into view strikes the knight as "a star [distant perspective] guiding him to the *portals* [the manger of Bethlehem], if not the *palaces,* of his redemption . . . " The creative intent of the artist widens its scope toward a maximum, and traces thus the lines that determine the makeup of *Don Quixote:*

the evasion of all neutral reality and the anxious search for the ultimate frontiers of human experience—from the apex of the noblest madness to the realm of negative values—inertia, vice, or ugliness; or the zone in which one encounters extra—or pre-social existences (a group of bandits, or a hut of solitary shepherds).

This stylistic form persists throughout the entire span of *Don Quixote*. The galleys in the port of Barcelona "displayed themselves decked with streamers and pennons that *trembled in the breeze and kissed and swept the water* . . ." (II, 61). Don Quixote, the apex figure, is dubbed knight by the roguish inn-keeper, Juan Palomeque el Zurdo, and by two whores. The knight later meets (II, 58) two beautiful maidens, disposed to perform eclogues of Garcilaso and Camões, and dressed "in fine brocade" and in "rich farthingales of gold-embroidered tabby." But immediately following that sublime lyric adventure, a herd of wild bulls and tame bullocks tramples over "Don Quixote and over Sancho, Rocinante and Dapple, hurling them all *to the earth* and rolling them over on the ground." They do not dare then "to go back to bid farewell to the mock or imitation Arcadia . . . "

Innumerable other examples confirm that such is the stylistic nature of the work; within that frame the major figures of the Knight and the Squire are expressed, which appear unrelated to the medieval types of "the" knight and "the" squire. The sharp relief of the extremist style is fused with the blank spaces created by the elusive style (superficial allusions or conscious omissions).[30] The author does not recall the name of the town in La Mancha where the "hidalgo" lived, nor even the hero's exact name, because it "is of but little importance to our tale." (I, 1). Neither is the home of Diego de Miranda accorded detailed description (II, 18): " . . . the translator of the history thought it best to pass over these and other details of the same sort in silence, as they are not in harmony with the main purpose of the story . . . " For the same reason, the town of El Toboso remains similarly immersed in shadow, and the great city of Barcelona, in empty clarity. The author requests that "credit be given him, not for what he writes, but for what he has refrained from writing" (II, 44). It is indeed rare to find a work of art that expresses with such firmness just what its author wished and did not wish to do.

Beyond a shadow of a doubt, Cervantes was a good Catholic, for Hispanicity and faith were indissolubly united. At times, he devotes himself with exceptional insistence and with a meticulous, sometimes comical, care which we do not find in other writers, to the task of conforming thoroughly to the orthodoxy of his time.[31] Cervantes probably feared that his irrepressible tendency to divide all life into the sublime and the low might lead him to upset religion (at least, the visible and ecclesiastical aspects of it) in an inadmissible and dangerous way.

Spanish literature was always extremely free in its censure of friars and nuns, and in its treatment of divine things, merely because they were considered highly familiar and personal. But, as far as we know, no one took the liberty that Cervantes assumed in the first edition of *Don Quixote*—in which he had the hero pray a million "Ave Marias," using for a rosary "a great strip off the tail of his shirt" (I, 26), which, we can imagine, probably was not very clean. This sarcastic jibe was corrected in the second edition of 1605. When we peruse the original rough drafts of Cervantes' works, we find (as occurs with two of his "exemplary novels") that the printed text is full of numerous emendations of ecclesiastical or moral character. This means that Cervantes articulated religious themes as well as profane themes on two extreme planes of opposing values. In his encounter with the statues of St. George, St. Martin, St. James, and St. Paul, he treats ironically, or humorously of the first three, but reserves for the last a tone of sober, profound emotion: "a knight-errant in life, a steadfast saint in death, an untiring laborer in the Lord's vineyard, a teacher of the Gentiles, whose school was heaven, and whose instructor and master was Jesus Christ himself" (II, 58). St. Paul was all spirit, whereas the other saints on horseback meddled excessively in the affairs of this world. St. George "was called Don Saint George, and he was moreover a defender of maidens." St. Martin appears "dividing his cloak with the beggar and giving him half of it; no doubt it was winter at that time, for otherwise he would have given him the whole of it, so charitable was he." In the battles against the Moors, St. James has been seen "many a time . . . beating down, trampling under foot, destroying and slaughtering the Hagarene squadrons in the sight of all . . . " These three saints represent the "lower strata" of which St. Paul is the "upper." The "million Ave Marias" are—stylistically speaking—in the same position of inferiority compared with the chivalric sublimity of the gentleman from La Mancha. I could offer yet other examples to prove that religious material was utilized by Cervantes, just as was the secular, to serve the stylistic ends of the author, and in a manner that defies analogy in the literature of Spain. It is likely then that in order to compensate for such irrepressible audacity, Cervantes, consciously or unconsciously studded many parts of his book with pious notes and qualifications.

But the religious theme is also treated with the same elusive technique in a way which is foreign to other writers. Don Quixote says in his discourse upon Arms and Letters that he does not speak "of divine letters, the aim of which is to raise and direct the soul to Heaven, for with an end so infinite no other can be compared" (I, 37); here, perhaps without Cervantes' even intending it, he coincides with Montaigne, who is interested solely in worldly affairs within the scope of human experience: "La doctrine divine tient mieux son rang *à part*

comme reine et dominatrice . . . Les raisons divines se considèrent plus vénéra-
blement et révéramment seules et en leur style qu'appariées aux discours
humains" (*Essais*, I, 56).[32]

The comic version of the deliberate withdrawal from religious themes appears
in Sancho's persistent fear lest his master decide to become a knight "of the
divine school": "What will become of me if my master takes a fancy to be an
archbishop . . . ?" (I, 26). " . . . but I was trembling all the time lest he
should take a fancy to go into the Church, not finding myself fit to hold office
in it"; (II, 13). As for his comportment in face of religion, Cervantes shows
some personal nuances.

The art of *Don Quixote* consists in a well-organized system of flights to the
supreme and descents to the depths, and of evasions and reticence in regard to
all common-place, inert reality which is unsuitable for this very special form of
poetry.[33] The frenzied march toward the highest and toward the lowest is not
an artificial process of "poetic art," which is superimposed upon the work, but
a disposition vitally incarnate in life itself, the birth and progress of which we
contemplate at every step. By virtue of incitements oriented in one direction or
another, individuals rise to new heights or simply fall down. Although space
does not permit mention here of all the vital incitements present in *Don Quixote*,
it is evident that the written or spoken word and the love of human beauty stand
out as the most potent ones.

It is surprising that Unamuno, who casts such excellent light upon certain
aspects of Don Quixote, did not realize the function fulfilled by books in the
work.[34] Don Quixote visits a printing establishment because "he was curious
to know what it was like" (II, 62). Don Quixote and Don Diego possess good
libraries; judgments are passed upon the merit of books and of their translations;
books are found in forgotten valises; there appear those who write books, who
are in the process of writing them or intend to do so, seriously as well as in burlesque form. *Don Quixote* is a contexture of chivalric, pastoral, and historical
works; and even cultured poetry, the traditional "Romancero," religious works
savoring of the influence of Erasmus (such as *Luz del Alma* by Felipe de
Meneses), and numerous Biblical quotations figure prominently throughout the
book. Allusion is made to the theatre of Lope de Vega, concerning which the
author takes personal exception. Nothing in it is haphazard or decorative or
redundant. Cervantes, obsessed with the written word in poetry, erudition, or
religion, injects the serum of his incitement into lives which otherwise would
never have emerged from their inert insignificance. Further, this is unrelated to
the question of "literary sources" or to what Cervantes may or may not have
read personally.

Don Quixote owes its existence as much to a tradition of literary forms and genres as to the tradition of literature as "lived" by its readers—a point of view indispensable to our full understanding of Cervantes. The gentleman from La Mancha is extremely affected by reading books, but it is no less certain that other characters are affected by the same experience. Books appear here, not as coldly objectified realities, with certain ideas or tales to present, but as being read, as a personal experiencing of values in which a person reveals his individuality while incarnating the living substance of the book into his own life. According to the Curate, the volumes absorbed by Alonso Quijana "had turned his brain" (I, 32); but the Innkeeper feels otherwise, because in *him* they produce other effects: " . . . for when it is harvest-time reapers flock here on holidays, and there is always one among them who can read and who takes up one of these books, and we gather round him, thirty or more of us, and stay listening to him with a delight that makes our gray hairs grow young again. At least *I can say for myself* that when I hear of what furious and terrible blows the knights deliver, I am seized with the longing to do the same, and I would like to be hearing about them night and day." Each one speaks of the books according to his own experience and impressions; and so the book becomes identified with the vital experience of the individual. The Innkeeper's wife would like to see the reading prolonged, but for other motives: " . . . I never have a quiet moment in my house except when you are listening to someone reading; for then you are so taken up that for the time being you forget to scold." Maritornes reduces the entire book to the scene in which "they describe some lady or another in the arms of her knight under the orange trees," which, it strikes her, is "as good as honey." (II, 32). The Innkeeper's daughter, a modest young maiden, whose sensibility probably has suffered the infiltration of several pastoral novels, *does not like "the blows that my father likes,* but the laments the knights utter when they are separated from their ladies; and indeed they sometimes make me weep with the compassion I feel for them."

Books are, therefore, what each reader makes of them by living through them. Literature becomes personalized and individual living reveals its latent poetic dimension; this is the source of the undying beauty of *Don Quixote*. The Innkeeper opposes the burning of his books; in fact, to such an extent does he believe in their truth that Dorotea whispers into the ear of Cardenio: "Our landlord is almost fit to play a second part to Don Quixote." Books, people, or things lack a rationally determinable essential reality. In *Don Quixote* (as generally in all Spanish life), the rational is not the real, but rather, only that is real which lives in contexture with the individual's "livingness" (*Erlebnis*). Truth and falsity are fluid transcendencies eddied in the personal experience that serves them in each case as contents or warranty. Judgments of value, not logical judgments, lead to and build reality. Right is, or is not, within the person, and not in the objectified reality of thought.

Books figure here prominently because they are an inexhaustible arsenal of rich and possible "livingness." When "livingness" is re-lived by other lives there appears before our fascinated eyes the infinite gamut of humanity: amusing, melancholy, impassioned, demented, judicious, or problematical lives. The content of the book is multiplied by the experience of those affected by it, or it rebounds upon the experience. The essential foundation of so strange a phenomenon is that the written word is felt as an animate, vital reality, and not as a mere expression of imagination or knowledge far removed from the reader. Here books play such an important rôle because of their "contagious vitality," and not because they are "repositories of culture." In short, the ultimate reality of *Don Quixote* cannot be understood if we keep it enclosed within the strict orbit of Western history.

To the European fully articulated with the Greco-Occidental tradition, a book is a book and man, a man; therefore it cannot occur to him to create the "centauric" existence of the "humanized book" or the "book-shaped man," as a normal phenomenon, without any touch of magic or allegory. Rabelais (who certainly was not lacking in imagination) piles up on the table of the voracious Gargantua the most learned works of Greece and Rome: Aristotle, Polybius, Galen, Heliodorus, Pliny, etc., so that the young pupil may know and learn "la vertu, propriété, efficace et *nature* de tout ce qui était servi à table." With this purpose, "faisaient souvent, *pour plus être assurés,* apporter les livres susdits à table" (I, 18). Montaigne, also an Occidental of the highest category, withdrawn into the solitude of his library, says: *"Je ne cherche aux livres* qu'a m'y donner du plaisir par un honneste amusement; ou, si j'estudie. *Je n'y cherche que la science* qui traicte de la connaissance de moi mesmes" (II, 10). To the European a book is the objectified end of his thought or emotion, and not a lover or enemy that lives with him in a relationship of love or hatred.

The chivalric or pastoral novel becomes infused into certain lives in *Don Quixote,* and in this new incarnation it arouses harmonic accord or polemic dispute, according to the disposition of the other persons by whom it is reflected further. This phenomenon occurs with the object, the barber's basin (I, 25), transformed into the helmet of Mambrino or into a basin-helmet, depending upon the life in which it happens to figure. No one appears to assert gravely, according to logic and good sense, that serious dispute and the chaotic confusion that it unleashes are completely absurd. In accord with the same vital ontology, Don Quixote is alternately insane, rational, simpleton, clown, "beast," magnificent orator, firm or vacillating in the consciousness of himself, etc., according to the vital situation in which he finds himself immersed. The author took care to state clearly at the very outset that he is the stepfather and not the father of Don Quixote. The evaluational criterion of each individual can therefore be the only possible means for determining the "truth" of the facts involved.[35] To the boys in the street, Don Quixote is an amusing, absurd spectacle; to the dull ecclesiastic, he is a simpleton; yet to those capable of feeling such profound emotion, he is the paradigm of the most noble and desperate anguish. Sansón Carrasco believes that "his chance of recovery lies in quiet . . ." (II, 65) and in ceasing to be Don Quixote; Don Antonio Moreno, disagrees with the bachelor of arts: "Do you not see, señor, that the gain by Don Quixote's sanity can never equal the enjoyment his mental antics give?" (II, 65). In the supreme repertory of axiological themes that is *Don Quixote* is presented the problem of which of the two is preferable—the pain of the hare or the pleasure of the wolf that eats it.

To feel books as a living, animate, communicable and inciting reality is a human phenomenon belonging to Oriental tradition, and is related to the belief that the word is content and transmitter of a revelation. The idea of religion revealed through sacred books is Oriental, and not Occidental. From the conjunction of Hebrew concepts with neo-Platonic thought in Philo Judaeus sprang forth the belief in the logos-word as a divinely emanative and creative spirit: "And the Word [*logos*] was made flesh and dwelt among us." Condensing into a few succinct statements what would require more extensive development, let us limit ourselves to recalling the rôle of the book, as a humanized entity, in Arabian literature.

There is a story in *A Thousand and One Nights* entitled "The Magic Book." The caliph, Harun al-Raschid feels depressed and troubled, and Giafar says to him: "When our souls are not gladdened by the beauty of the skies, nor by gardens, nor by the sweetness of the breeze, nor by the sight of flowers, there remains no other recourse than a book, for the most beautiful garden is a bookcase filled with books." The monarch began to read one of them, and "suddenly he was possessed with such a fit of laughter that he fell to the ground. He continued reading and began to shed such tears that his beard became soaked, and through it, so became the book that he had in his lap."[36] The foregoing is not an anecdote here, but something that acquires meaning only in connection with the form of life in which Arabian literature is articulated: the "interior" of life would be then a correlation of external circumstances integrated into vital experience. Masudi, a writer of the first half of the 10th century, states: "Man's best and most sure friend is a book. As you desire it, its manifestations enchant you, its new observations amuse you; it gives you, *as you wish,* fortifying precepts, and marvelous aids. It offers you at the same time, beginning and end, little or much;

it brings what is distant close to you, past and present . . . It is a corpse that speaks to you in the name of the dead, and that brings you the voice of the living. It is an intimate friend who rejoices in your happiness, who sleeps in your sleep, and who speaks to you *only of what pleases you* . . . Fortify your heart, uphold your spirit, and increase your knowledge . . . God has said: 'Read in the name of the generous Lord.' It is He who has taught Man the use of the *qalim* [pen, writing] and all that of which he was ignorant [Coran, XCVI, 3–5]. In those words, which He has taught us through the *qalim,* as He reveals to us, we are told that generosity is one of the divine attributes."[37]

The theme of the book as the friend of man appears in the poetry of the Castilian Jew Sem Tob (middle of the 14th century), although here without reference to the divine origin of the written word. But this word, filled with effective stimuli transmissible to the life of each one, is, in the last analysis, a reflection of the divine logos. To Philo Judaeus (a contemporary of Christ), "the sacred and divine Logos is the inner, revealed word that the pious hear in the secret depths of their soul, and which integrates the teaching of divine things —that is, worship and philosophy. Philo uses the same word as both the force that impels the world (the logos in the stoic sense) and the revealed word of God; surprising as it may seem, this double meaning is what forms the essence of his notion of Logos."[38] "The intermediary powers, analogous to the Logos, participate with God in the creation of man, a mixture of good and of evil."[39] "The intermediary powers, analogous to the Logos, participate with God at the creation of man, who is a mixture of good and of evil."[40]

The oriental Spanish tradition made possible the existence in Spain of the theme of the reading of books as a source of both good and evil, and the presence of this theme in the pages of *Don Quixote,* in a form that we do not find in the literature of the rest of Europe,[41] except for occasional rare instances. Whenever we find in Western literature the incarnation in a life of the incitement coming from a book, we perceive in it an echo of the Oriental conception of the world. It is not mere chance that in Arabic the one word "kálam, kállam" means "to wound" and "to converse with someone," and that "kálima" means "verb," "divine logos." Reading the book about Lancelot and the Queen Guinevere occasions the fateful kiss that Paolo bestows upon Francesca in the *Divine Comedy:* "Galeotto fu il libro e chi lo scrisse" (V, 137), since Galeotto serves in that work as go-between; his words act upon the lives of the two lovers and cause them to appear in a strikingly poetic perspective.[42]

The preoccupation with noting the effects of reading upon the vital processes of readers is characteristically Spanish. Don Galaor "was *moved by a* great desire to become a knight" through having read "in some ancient books . . . of the former deeds that knights in arms performed" (*Amadís*, I, 5). Scarcely had *La Celestina* been published (it appeared in 1499) when it began to impress its readers to such an extent that the author was to reflect their desires in subsequent editions of the tragi-comedy: "This present work has been a source of dispute or conflict to its readers, placing them at odds, with one another, each one passing judgment upon it *in accordance with his own tastes*." Fernando de Rojas states how his work has been lived, and how varied were the interpretations and evaluations placed on it: "some wanted the period of time in which the lovers enjoyed their passion to be prolonged, which became very annoying, and so I agreed, against my will, to set my hand for the second time to a labor so strange, and alien to my own field." There is, then, no clearly drawn line between the existence of the work and the living experience of those who read it; the readers intervene in the "rewording" of *La Celestina*, which is not very inferior to *Don Quixote* artistically, just as the readers of the first part of the Cervantian novel later injected their living experience into the second.

The effect of books (religious or profane) upon the life of the reader is an ever-present theme in the letters of the 16th century. The youth of Ignatius of Loyola was spent very much in tune with the novels of chivalry, which "he was very curious and fond of reading." But chance placed in his hands a life of Christ and a *Flos Sanctorum*. "Not only did he begin to find enjoyment, but his heart also began to change, and he was filled with the desire to imitate and put into action what he read."[43] While still undecided between earthly and heavenly values, he sheltered within him both the person that he had been and the one that that great incited man aspired to be: "Then there followed a sovereign light and wisdom, that Our Lord *infused* into his mind."[44]

The *Confessions* of St. Augustine, the great Roman-Semite, immediately come to mind, but I do not have sufficient space in which to analyze the similarities and differences between his case and those with which we are directly concerned now; for the logos came to him through the word of his mother, as well as from books. But in sixteenth-century Spain books were already living beings, animated by a good or bad spirit. Ignatius read the *De Imitatione Christi*, "the spirit of which *enraptured him and adhered to his soul*. Consequently (as a servant of God once told me) the life of Ignatius was merely a highly perfect outline of all that book contains" (p. 30). But the spirit of a book may be repellent, productive of a negative reaction, as were the books of chivalry to Don Diego de Miranda. Ignatius reads the *De milite christiano* of Erasmus and experiences "a very new and marvelous thing, and that is, that upon picking up this book of Erasmus and reading in it, his fervor verily began to wane and his religious devotion, to grow cold. So that it seemed to him that *he was not the same person* after the reading as he was before it" (p. 30). How could such a phenomenon and its expression have been possible without 800 years of Islamic tradition in Spain?

The great influence of reading upon the mystic formation of Teresa of Jesus is well known; "I never dared to indulge in prayer [mystical meditation] without a book; for my soul so feared to be without it in prayer as if I were going to fight with many people" (*Life,* Chap. IV). The subject of the written word surged about the saint like an obsession; one sister of the order told her that "she had come to be a nun only because she had read what the Evangel says: 'many are called and few are chosen'" (Chap. III).

Books held to be pernicious because of the doctrines or ideas they contained were suppressed everywhere; but the peculiarity of sixteenth-century Spain was the attention accorded to the vital effect of the printed word upon its readers; the communicative power of the word was stressed above even errors and literary defects of the books themselves. The immorality or perniciousness ascribed to a work was an index of its power of infiltrating into other existences. The books of chivalry *"move* weak-willed women to fall into licentious errors"; with them "the devil deceives and *enchants* and entertains the foolish" (Gonzalo Fernández de Oviedo). The chivalric tale *"haunts* the soul of young maidens"; it makes them *"leap* from their quietude as fire does to gunpowder" (Alejo Vanegas). The young-lady reader desires *"to be another Oriana* as there [in the book] and to be served by another Amadís." Young men "afire with natural desire, contemplate only how to dishonor maidens and to affront married women" (Francisco Cervantes de Salazar). "And what effect on a mediocre intelligence is a nonentity composed at the fireside in wintertime by the brain of some one who dreamed of it?" Some object that "in them *one learns daring and valor* in arms, good breeding and courtesy towards ladies, fidelity and truthfulness in one's dealings" (Fray Pedro Malón de Chaide). "Their doctrine *incites* sensuality to sin, and diverts the spirit from the good life" (Antonio de Guevara). The Cortes of Valladolid asked the king in 1555 to prohibit chivalric novels, since "young men and maidens . . . lose their senses and take special fancy to the cases that they read." In 1531, the shipment of *Amadís* and analagous works to the Spanish Indies was forbidden, "because this is a bad example for the Indians," and in truth, because it was feared that their combative, exalted impetus might be transmitted to the colonies.[45]

It would be unnecessary to cite many other texts in order to show that the written word possesses a vital essence capable of informing other lives, and that its reality consists in its very flowing into other existences. The stream of the sinful is counteracted by that of sanctity (the chivalric tale; *Flos Sanctorum*).[46] Behind the moral doctrines which were taken for granted, surges forward the person who lives or does not live in conformity with said doctrines, and consequently, moral books turn into sermons. With the substitution of the interest in moral experience for that in moral theory, a vast horizon is opened to every possible creator of literary personalities as well as of human experiences, in which the impulses emanating from a logos and the sympathy or resistance of the one who receives it, meet. Contrary to what we have been wont to believe, the didactic sermonizing of Spanish letters served as a vehicle for the marvelous vitalized and personalized art of Cervantes, Calderón, or El Greco. To resolve the sententious, didactic style only into proverbs, preachments, etc., does not embrace the totality of the problem. Moral experience is the living ground where outside appeals meet with personal possibilities. The person then directs his living towards a longed-for and dreamed-of future and at the same time is repressed by the demands of his previous existence.[47] Such a conception of life became fecund for art when keen, daring observers decided to contemplate, to "live with," the intussusception of an impelling logos, from within the life of the subject who suffers or experiences it, and not from without, as does the moralists. The account of a life thus becomes a description charged with biographical and lyrical sentiment, and what was hitherto purely generic assumes concrete form in a specific, individualized experience. The generic reader of chivalric books, one felt as "generically" stimulated, turns, then, into an Alonso Quijana, who lives in a certain town of La Mancha.[48] The first and very crude utilization of such possibilities appears in the anonymous *Entremés de los romances* in which a comic character, Bartolo,

> From reading the book of ballardry
> Has hit upon wedding knights errantry
> To resemble the heroes of song;
> And I dare say that 'ere long
> His mind will be turned to insanity.

The innovation of this literary situation is not that reading changes merely the course of a life, but rather that in the same work there appear living together the "incited" individual and those who observe him from the normal plane of their existence. But I shall have to leave for another time the study of the significance of the now famous farce, and the question of whether or not it could have been written by Cervantes.

THE ORIENTATION OF STYLE

The basic theme of *Don Quixote* is life as a process creative of itself—the onrush of incitements (the written or spoken word, love, wealth, possibilities of amusement, etc.) into the river bed of the life of each individual. The previously given—immutable, objectified realities confronted with the rushing current of life—does not play an essential rôle in the most important literary work of Spain. The *Entremés de los romances* and the traditional disturbances occasioned by the reading of chivalric novels enter here only to serve that fundamental theme. The style of *Don Quixote* rests on the assumption that all reality is something transitory, "transient," something that is inundated by effluvia emanating from some individual life, or that is already stylized in literature. The consciousness of feeling oneself living is the foundation upon which this oscillating world of constant flux finds stability. Don Quixote feels himself Don Quixote, and later, Alonso Quijano ("I was Don Quixote, and I am now Alonso Quijano the Good" (II, 74).). Sancho is conscious of being an irreducible, naked person, a firm channel for the most varied fluid currents.

Years ago I attempted to interpret *Don Quixote* with excessively Occidental norms, and I believed that Cervantes was interested on occasion in determining the nature of the reality that lies behind the fluctuation of appearance. But the problem of logical truth or error does not preoccupy the author; it is rather a question of showing that reality is always an aspect of the experience of the person who is living it. As I pointed out in *El pensamiento de Cervantes,* Cervantes undoubtedly was familiar with the question often debated in Renaissance poetics as to the difference between poetic (universal) truth and historical (particular) truth. But the innovation of *Don Quixote* consists in its establishing as true what is authentically interlaced with a vital experience, and not what is determined by a cognitive process. Consequently, all that is implicit in the effective life of someone (a literary character or an actual person), and all that is connected with the creative, well-articulated intention of the poet-novelist is true.[49]

When the author begins to give life, in elusive style, to the fluid figure of Don Quixote, he says that ascertaining whether his name was Quijada, Quesada, or Quejana "is of but little importance to our tale; it will be enough not to stray a hair's breadth from the truth in the telling of it" (I, 1)—from the truth, or rather from the proper fluidity of the artistic process, which has become real as a "value," and not as an objectified entity or an extraliterary reality. It is for this reason that Sancho's wife is called in different ways, and that at the end of the book, the gentleman from La Mancha is called Quijano, and not any of the three names mentioned at the beginning. Such minor discrepancies are not oversights or careless slips, but the result of the fact that what seems to exist here does not matter very much. This technique may be conceived as the antithesis of the naturalism of the nineteenth-century novelist. In one of the cases brought before Sancho during his governorship, the law says that if someone "swears truly, he shall be allowed to pass, but if falsely, he shall . . . be put to death for it by hanging on the gallows . . . " (II, 51). Truth here means veracity—truthfulness.

Don Quixote asks the enchanted head " . . . was that which . . . happened to me in the cave of Montesinos the truth or a dream?" and the answer is: " . . . there is much to be said; there is something of both in it" (II, 62). In that adventure we are given, in effect, the truth about dreams, and also about him who lives the episode and about those who relive it in their own manner upon hearing it recounted. Such disparate phenomena are articulated in the vital experience of time, which is here an index of the extreme limits within which, as with a shuttle, the style of this novel is being woven. The atemporal time of the poetic illusion (*Amadís,* etc.) would then be in the same relation to time felt as an actual factor as is the supreme limit of ascending aspiration (Dulcinea), to the most abject extremes of that which is poetically scorned (Maritornes).[50]

The adventure of the cave of Montesinos (II, 22, 23) is fitted into precise terms of space and time: "They had let down the hundred fathoms of rope," till they could not give Don Quixote any more; " . . . they waited about half an hour, at the end of which time they began to gather in the rope again with great ease and without feeling any weight, which made them fancy Don Quixote was remaining below; . . . Sancho wept bitterly, and hauled away in great haste in order to settle the question. When, however, they had come, as it seemed, to rather more than eighty fathoms, they felt a weight . . . " They pull out the Knight, who eats heartily with Sancho and the Cousin, and then the author begins his tale: "It was about four in the afternoon when the sun, veiled in clouds, with subdued light and tempered beams, enabled Don Quixote to relate, without heat or inconvenience, what he had seen in the cave of Montesinos to his two illustrious hearers . . . " Aside from the heat, which could have been avoided by any of the conventional devices so frequent in *Don Quixote,* it is just to think that a soft light would be more suitable than the dazzling sun of La Mancha for the story of what has been lived between the sunrays of imaginative poetry and the twilight of implacable criticism ever prone to attack it. Montesinos and the Knight converse about the events narrated in the ballad or "romance"; Montesinos took out the heart of his friend Durandarte to take it to the Lady Belerma, not with a dagger, but with "a burnished poniard sharper than an awl" (II, 23). The epic figure steps out of his nebulous poetic context and reveals himself to us as living his own story, and thus he can enter into the lives of those who are outside the sphere of illusion. Sancho observes immediately (now that Montesinos is made accessible to him) that "that poniard must have been made by Ramón de Hoces the Sevillan." And Don Quixote replies—with half of him outside the realm of his fantasy"—that "it could not have been by that poniard maker . . . because Ramón de Hoces *was a man of yesterday,* and the affair of Roncesvalles, where this mishap (*desgracia*—a word of *today* and vulgar) occurred, *was long ago."* Montesinos marvels that "though I know it to be as sure as day that Durandarte ended his life in my arms . . . how comes it that he now moans and sighs from time to time, as if he were still alive?" Durandarte thus passes from the eternal present of his poetic existence into the "now" in which we are living. It would not suffice to think that this is merely an attempt to achieve a comic or grotesque effect, because our laughter or smile upon reading these pages is not like that which bursts forth upon reading the strophes of Boiardo, Pulci, or Ariosto, in which we feel the rational criticism of those excellent poets. Cervantes creates his unique scene by making the living experience of atemporal time flow into that of actual time, just as Don Quixote enters into Sancho, and Sancho into Don Quixote, in the integration of their reciprocal fluid lives. Literary creation is here a closed, absolute world, wholly self-sufficient, and into which the reasoning of the author is not heterogeneously injected.[51]

Montesinos lives his own enchantment: " . . . the sage Merlin has been keeping us enchanted here these many years; and although more than five hundred have gone by, not one of us has died . . . " Upon passing into the *time of "now,"* the character finds himself at the beginning of the seventeenth century, and calculates the date on which he changed from a "person" to a "personage"—in the eleventh century—the epoch of the Cid and of Alphonse VI, which was the limit of the epic-historic horizon of the Spaniard of those days. The accuracy of such a belief is not what concerns us; the essential fact is that Montesinos feels himself a man encased between a *yesterday* and a *today,* and an eternal atemporal entity, all at the same time. The eternal Montesinos is integrated into the temporalized Montesinos, just as is the Knight of the Rueful Countenance into the person invited by Sancho to satisfy his most elemental needs; in the same way the poetic dagger of the ballad becomes the poniard of Ramón de Hoces; the song of the farm laborer of El Toboso merges with the discordant noise of his plow as it drags along the ground; and the Dulcinea of quixotic dreams takes form in the cave of Montesinos as a Dulcinea who sends one of her companions to ask her lover to lend her "half a dozen reals . . . on this *new* dimity petticoat that I have here" (II, 23). And this is Don Quixote, and not Sancho, who tells it.[52]

The living experience of time, in consequence, is organically articulated with the total structure of *Don Quixote:* "I can not understand, Señor Don Quixote," remarked the Cousin here, "how it is that your worship, in such a short space of time as you have been below there, could have seen so many things, and said and answered so much." "How long is it since I went down?" asked Don Quixote. "Little better than an hour," replied Sancho. "That can not be," returned Don Quixote, "because night overtook me while I was there, and day

came, and it was night again three times; so that, *by my reckoning,* I have been
three days in those remote regions beyond our ken." Sancho thinks that "as
everything that has happened to him is by enchantment, maybe what *seems to
us an hour would seem three days and nights there."*

The difference in the estimation of time, expressed in terms of "what seems
to be," is founded upon the same vital criterion that permits the object that
shines on the barber's head to be at one time the helmet of Mambrino, and again,
an ordinary shaving basin. One might say then that all this is pure, arbitrary
relativism or capricious fantasmagoria; but if that were so, *Don Quixote* would
not be the immortal work that it is. The vacillation of this dance of semblances
acquires solidity, not as a logical reality, but as an existential value that impresses
itself on us. The reality of the style of *Don Quixote* lies in a vital articulation of
its values; beliefs, be they what they may, are made acceptable to us to the
degree that they are held and lived, by those who interweave them with their
existence. Instead of being logically arbitrary, they become vitally valid, and we
accept them, not as a farce or an amusement, but as one accepts all that appears
authentic. Our esteem, our artistic enjoyment, and lastly, our conviction proceed
from the self-assurance, from the integrity of all those who speak and live in
these pages. The fundament for the "truth" of the three days spent by Don
Quixote in the cave, and the hour of waiting spent by Sancho, is embedded in
the total, well-integrated structure of human existence, which Cervantes imposes
as a necessity, and not as an arbitrary caprice. *Don Quixote* is a beautiful piece
of architecture, a well-harmonized symphony of meaningful manifestations of
life the value and existence of which are mutually interdependent. The literary
character is split into a person who "lives" his literary existence, and those who
approach him, live, in their turn, in this double dimension. From this stems
the incalculable influence of *Don Quixote* upon the modern novel, which arose
during the Romantic period, and in which the central characters are not only
what they portend to be but also a poetic projection of themselves (good Père
Goriot of Balzac is a manufacturer of vermicelli and a reincarnation of the
imprudent and despairing King Lear; Julien Sorel of Stendhal's *Le rouge et le
noir,* is the boy from the lumber sawmill, and also a projection of the hero of
the *Mémorial de Sainte Hélène;* etc.).

These living experiences of values do not postulate any objective conclusion
(such as Calderón's "man's greatest crime is having been born . . . For all of
life is a dream, and dreams are but dreams"). Instead we find ourselves before a
polarity which is integrated into the forms of life: flight toward the supreme
and descent toward the depths. This way of living manifests itself and finds
"realization" in such a polar existence upon being projected into inexhaustible
perspectives. Cervantes did not confront the epic world with the purpose of

objectifying it in comedy, gay diversion, or morality. For the epic and all the other forms serve here as incitements aimed at nurturing the polarized current that flows between the creative "eros" and the absence of "eros." *Don Quixote* was neither written against books of chivalry nor was it *not* written against them. In formulating the question this way, we are focusing upon the work from a logical, rational category that does not fit it at all. Don Quixote's *raison d'être* is found exclusively in his will for heroism, his noble courtesy, and in his infinite goodness, all of which are evident in the very process of his existence. Don Quixote is bolstered by his faith in the values that man creates, sustains, and diffuses with his very life. The book is a great repertory, as I have already said, of axiological themes, always lived with maximal tension—and from this arises its fascinating beauty.

The foregoing discussion could be illustrated with a brief examination of the subject that I would entitle "jests turn to earnest." When Knight and Squire begin their wanderings along the byroads of the world, they act as an incitement upon all who observe them or deal with them; thus they become the object of jest, respect, pity, anger, or of an indifferent, vague curiosity. Sancho is very variously reflected as he affects the lives of his master, his wife, and his daughter, of Tome Cecial, Ricote, the Duke and Duchess, the duenna Rodríguez, the ecclesiastic, etc.—just as Don Quixote, the island, Clavileño, Dorotea, etc., produce many varied reactions and opinions in Sancho. The same phenomenon occurs with regard to the amusing or cruel jokes so frequent in this work, especially in Part II, wherein the author forgets his vacillations of the First. These episodes owe a great deal to the burlesque tradition of Italian literature, which was so familiar to Cervantes. But the Italian themes of farce and skepticism were generally one-dimensional, their character was not modified by the moralizing glosses that were at times superimposed upon them. The situations in *Don Quixote* are different. There is nothing more "farcical" than the episodes that occur during the ephemeral governorship of Sancho. One night he is taken on a patrol of the island, for the purpose of finding more comic material with which to fill the idle vacuum in the existence of his Lordship, the Duke. But note that while the night patrol invents fictitious tasks, there is one among them that is different; a beautiful young girl has escaped from her home in company with her brother, in order to break the monotony of their secluded existence; they come upon the night patrol, which is not at all a laughing matter to them, but a very serious predicament. The lovely maiden confesses her mischief: "I longed to see the world, or at least the town where I was born." She had received word of an outside world unknown to her: "When I heard them talking of bull-fights taking place, and of jousts, and of the acting of plays, I asked my brother, who is a year younger than myself, to tell me what sort of things these were, and many more that I had never seen; he explained them to me as well as he could, but the only effect was to *kindle in me a still stronger desire to see them"* (II, 49). This beautiful and bold victim of boredom bears within her the germ of a Madame Bovary. But this is not what interests us now. The governor's chief waiter and taster—an opaque figure in the droll comedy of the night watch—remains as if enchanted upon observing the beauty of this girl: "The maiden's beauty had made a deep impression on the head-carver's heart, and again he raised his lantern for another look at her." The "incited" now incites. The following night was a sleepless one for the poor head-carver: " . . . so full were his thoughts of the face and air and beauty of the disguised damsel" (II, 51). Mocking? Serious? In the last analysis, the idea that hordes of enchanters wander about spying on our slightest movements is not really so absurd.

Let us recall the colossal battle between Don Quixote and the lackey Tosilos (II, 56) in which the latter renounces the combat in order really to marry the ruined daughter of the duenna Rodríguez. The Duke "was amazed and extremely angry at it" (which is not in jest either), while the girl declares her preference for being "the lawful wife of a lackey rather than the cheated mistress of a gentleman." Let us mention as the ultimate example (among the various that could be employed here) the episode of the enchanted head in the home of Don Antonio Moreno (II, 62), who had to put an end to a game that provided him with so much amusement, *for fear* "it might come to the ears of the watchful sentinels of the faith . . . " that is, the Holy Office of the Inquisition. " . . . the inquisitors . . . commanded him to destroy it up and have done with it." Jokes, pranks, and farce are included within the polarity that governs this style, and they rise up and topple down just as do islands, castles, shepherd's huts; Dulcinea, the coarse farm girl, and Don Quixote and Alonso Quijano the Good!

The length of this essay obliges me to leave the analysis of other questions related to the major work of Cervantes for more extensive future consideration.

(*Translated by* Zenia Sacks Da Silva)

NOTES

[1] The galley slaves "ill-treat, and snub and jeer and despise" one of their companions in chains "for confessing and not having spirit enough to say nay; for, say they, 'nay' has no more letters in it than 'yea,' and a culprit is well off when life or death with him depends on his own tongue and not on that of witnesses or evidence; and to my thinking they are not very far out. 'And I think so too,' answered Don Quixote." Galley slaves, guards, and knight-errant coincide here in a magnificent accord of stoic morality, thus harmonizing the differences among the three types of men. Don Quixote and Sancho base their individuality on the solid rock of their volition, but their lives as a whole bear distinct relation to ulterior problems.

[2] The word "life" is used here in a special sense, which may be worth defining. "Life" means that underlying activity which is itself grounded on the rationally unknowable infinity on which man depends. The reality of human, as distinguished from physical or animal, existence involves three main aspects: (1) the inescapable acceptance or rejection of the possibilities it always faces; (2) the faculty of planning even against instinctive or physical urges; (3) the incorporation of the effects of all this living activity with the very course of its progress. If we could integrate into a single idea-intuition a ship, its engine, its rudder, its skipper, the shipyard, the port which it sails, and the course of the ship as determined by the ship's seaworthiness and the weather conditions, then we might have an approximate notion of what we are trying to convey—a notion not to be grasped solely by logical reason. Consequently, the word "vital" as we use it does not mean "important." It is used merely as an adjective formed from "life." Kindred words such as "to live," "living," "alive," should be understood within the same frame of reference.

[3] Cervantes appears personally in his work, expressing himself almost as would Don Quixote in establishing a correlation between his objective and the totality of the world: "And as he confines himself and restricts himself to the narrow limits of the narrative, though he has ability, and brains enough to deal with the whole universe, he requests that his labors may not be despised, and that credit be given him, not for what he writes, but for what he has refrained from writing." (II, 44). Although these words are attributed humorously to Cide Hamete Benengeli, it is nevertheless certain that they confirm what we already knew even without them, namely, that *Don Quixote* was the result of a careful selection among various possible departures.

[4] Boccaccio's characters appear already molded into "types," and conform to what they must be: Griselda, the patient wife, stonily virtuous; Calandrino, the congenital idiot; Iancofiore, the courtesan who so aptly despoils unwary businessmen of their possessions, etc.

[5] Outside of *Don Quixote* we find cases of mental disequilibrium caused by physical disorders (*El licenciado vidriera*). If Cervantes had adhered to those "materialized" motivations, he would never have composed a work like *Don Quixote*.

[6] In the *Knight Cifar,* some jugglers "climbed on the rays of the sun to the windows of the palaces, which were very high" (p. 231, Wagner edition); but this has no effect on the conduct of the knight, who continues nevertheless exactly the same as ever.

[7] The author censures himself in the second part for the novelettes intercalated in Part One, claiming that they are external to the action of the personages, who are reduced here to the passive state of mere auditors. And that, despite the fact that in the Captive's Tale, he converts the protagonist into the brother of one of the travelers present in the inn. I suppose that in the last analysis this is the greatest objection to the short novels from the point of view of the author.

[8] The Castilian epic constitutes an exception, because its historicity and personalism bear the germs of what was later to be *Don Quixote* and the modern novel. Cf. my *España en su historia,* Chap. VI. (Buenos Aires: Losada, 1947.)

[9] I have already indicated this, with less precision, in my essay, "The Prefaces to *Don Quixote,*" which appeared in the *Philological Quarterly,* 1942, xxi, pp. 65–96. I should like to point out there that the pastoral novel is an essential ingredient of *Don Quixote,* since it "has incorporated into its action both the lyric and its author."

[10] II, 2. "It grieves me greatly, Sancho, that thou shouldst have said, and sayest, that I took thee out of thy cottage, when thou knowest I did not remain in my house."

[11] In my book *España en su historia,* I attempt to show how it happened that *belief* came to constitute the axis of the form of Hispanic life.

[12] Other examples may be found in the excellent study of H. Hatzfeld: *Don Quixote als Kuntswortwerk,* 1927, pp. 30ff.

[13] We have already in the *Knight Cifar:* "It is a coffer [filled with] pouches of envy; what the eye sees, the heart desires; rather would I have one silver coin than craftiness" (Wagner edition, pp. 112, 115, 135). Many other authors use this form of expression; Lope de Vega wrote of his mistress, Marta de Nevares, that "if she dances, it seems that *with her air she draws all eyes after her,* and that with her clogs she *treads* on *desires*" (dedication to the play *La viuda valenciana*). I should like to utilize this opportunity to point out that the tendency to unite the actualities of experience and the "halo" that transcends them explains the curious phenomenon of linking a pronoun, not precisely with a previously expressed

word, but with another felt as the development or expansion of it. In the furious battle against the Biscayan, Don Quixote determined to "[ad]venture all in *that* of a single blow" (I, 8), that is to say, in "the venture"—a noun that would be as a projection emanating from the verb "to adventure." Saint Teresa says: "Even though [the Lord] may wish to adorn himself with a soul and to regale it, there is no way; for he wants it unhampered and clean and with the desire to receive *them*," in which "them" refers to unexpressed gifts; "regalos" (*Vida*, Chap. VIII). More examples may be seen in F. Rodríguez Marín's edition of *Don Quixote*, 1927, III, 227.

14 Fernando de Rojas—a despairing genius—defines love as "a hidden fire, a pleasant ulcer, a savory poison, a sweet bitterness, a delightful ailment, a happy torment, a gentle and ferocious wound, a bland death" (Act X), in the tradition of the *Roman de la Rose* and even more remote sources. "Oh, woe to me," exclaims Melibea, "for if what you say is true, doubtful is my future wellbeing." The idea of a universal struggle, upon which *La Celestina* is founded, proceeds from Petrarch and Heraclitus, and reveals that Rojas attempted to objectify what was to him the insoluble conflict of life, *La Celestina*, rather than the work of Cervantes, indicates the departure characteristic of seventeenth century literature (man's worst crime is having been born), which was then contemplated as a phenomenon exterior to the individual man, and utterly incapable of being integrated into the process of his own existence. Only thus can we understand why the new, audacious form of Cervantes could not have any continuators in seventeenth century Spain, nor, for yet other reasons, in the rest of Europe, until the moment of Romanticism, when *Don Quixote* wielded a strong influence on Flaubert, Stendhal, and others.

15 The generic is unavoidable here, for such is the existence of those who are incapable of shattering the binding frame that encloses their lives, as routine and paralytic as aggressive. (The "common man" of Ortega y Gasset.) Although an "hidalgo," Don Diego de Miranda is a "man of the masses," satisfied with not gossiping, with his methodical regularity, with his carefully chosen books (some in Latin, some in Spanish, some devotional, some literary), and with his "entertainments neat and well served, without stint of anything."

16 The Jews accused of having assassinated ritually the "La Guardia" child took heart before going to the rack by singing the following verse:

"Cling fast to the branch, girl, and
    mind thine eye,
Cling fast to the branch, girl, and
    thou shalt not die.
Castle of my heart, hold me near
And death no longer shall I fear."

According to a record written in 1544, *apud Boletín de la Academia de la Historia*, Madrid, 1887, XI, 144. The "inner abode" was an impregnable "castle" before torture or death, because it was sustained by faith in God: "My flesh and my heart faileth; *But* God is the strength of my heart and my portion forever" (Psalm LXXIII, 26). "The Lord is my rock, in him will I trust, My shield, and the horn of my salvation, my high tower" (XVIII, 2). "Be thou my strong rock, for an house of defence to save me" (XXXI, 2). "Therefore will we not fear, though the earth do change, and the mountain shake with the swelling thereof" (XLVI, 2): The doctrine and sentiment of the liberty and immovable firmness of the inner self did not proceed, consequently, only from the stoic-Christian tradition. In the conviction expressed by very divergent characters in *Don Quixote* concerning "nay" and "yea," there appears in a secularized form a doctrine that did not spring from the philosophy, but from the religious belief of the Jews, the Christian martyrs, or even the Moslems. When the books of the Cordoban Ibn Hazm (994–1063) were burned in Seville, the Arab scholar wrote: "Although you burn the paper, you will not burn what the paper contains; rather, on the contrary, it will remain in my heart, it will go with me wherever my feet carry me, and will stop where I stop and will be buried in my tomb" (*Aben Hazam de Cordoba*, by M. Asín Palacios, I, 235).

17 See *El Pensamiento de Cervantes*, pp. 337, 342.

18 Areusa says in Act IX of *La Celestina*: "Ladies' chief sport is shouting, their glory is quarrelling; the best deed brings forth least contentment. For this reason, mother, I have

preferred to live in my humble house, unhampered and mistress of it all, than to live in their rich palaces, subjugated and captive." The author of this singular work, of course, was the Spanish Jew Fernando de Rojas.

[19] The subject of hunger injects an anguished note into a great part of Spanish literature; "By means of this sophistry Sancho was made to endure hunger, and hunger so keen that in his heart he cursed the government, and even him who had given it to him; however, with his hunger and his conserve [and "four sups of cold water"] he undertook to deliver judgments that day. . . ." (II, 51). Cervantes is not attracted to asceticism or poverty: " . . . he must have a great deal of godliness [that is to say, of the "superman," of the "inhuman"] who can find any satisfaction in being poor." (II, 44).

[20] Cervantes, the incited *par excellence,* and the great victim of illusion, speaks of himself in a style which later was to reach sublimation in the unparalleled florescence of *Don Quixote.* Witness the terms with which he addresses King Philip II, in 1590: "[Your servant] humbly asks and begs Your Majesty with all his heart please to see fit to give him one of the three or four posts that are now vacant in the Indies, one being the auditorship of the New Kingdom of Granada, or the governorship of the province of Soconusco in Guatimala, or purser in the galleys of Cartagena, or mayor of the city of La Paz; for with any of these offices that Your Majesty would so kindly deign to give him, you will be satisfied, because he is an able man, and competent and indeed worthy of Your Majesty's favor." Those four possibilities of power and wealth probably danced before Cervantes' eyes like the "here, there, not here, perhaps over there" of Sancho, and like Don Quixote's dreams of fame; recognizing the abyss that intervenes between actual life and artistic creation, we note that the vivid tension in the most personal, spontaneous document that we possess of the author is expressed in a style analogous to that which later was to appear in *Don Quixote.* Both are derived from the same "incited" life.

[21] He hastens to the rescue of the boy Andrés with "a piece of bread and another of cheese," saying to him: "Here, take this, brother Andrés, for we have all of us a share in your misfortune" (I, 31). And he says of Don Quixote: " . . . he has no thought of doing harm to anyone, only good to all, nor has he any malice whatever in him; a child might persuade him that it is night at noonday; and for this simplicity I love him as the core of my heart, and I can't bring myself to leave him, let him do ever such foolish things." (II, 13).

[22] Similarly from this stems the ode "Noche Serena" of Fray Luis de León. After the quotation cited above, Lucian continues: "Here I found the primary problem of what scholars call the universe; I could not tell how it came into existence, who made it, what was its beginning, or what its end. After examining the details, I remained even more perplexed. I found the stars scattered through the sky very haphazardly, and I could not figure out what the sun was. The phenomena of the moon, especially, seemed to me most extraordinary and were beyond my comprehension . . . Nor could I find greater certainty about the travel of lightning, the rôle of thunder, the fall of rain, of snow, and of hail." Luis de León says

> ¿Es más que un breve punto
> el bajo y torpe suelo comparado
> con este gran trasunto
> do vive mejorado
> lo que es, lo que será, lo que ha pasado?
> Quien mira el gran concierto
> de aquestos resplandores eternales,
> su movimiento cierto,
> sus pasos desiguales
> y en proporción concorde tan iguales:
> la luna como mueve
> la plateada rueda, y va en pos de ella
> la luz do el saber llueve, etc.

The same theme returns in the ode:

> ¿Cuándo será que pueda
> libre de esta prisión volar al cielo . . . ?

Entonces veré cómo
el divino poder echó el cimiento
tan a nivel y plomo,
do estable eterno asiento
posee el pesadísimo elemento . . .
Porqué tiembla la tierra . .
do los tesoros tiene
de nieve Dios, y el trueno dónde viene, etc.

For different reasons and to satisfy different longings, Luis de León and Sancho Panza yearn to flee from this world and to contemplate it from the heavens, under the expert guidance of Lucian, although polishing the latter's rationalistic asperities, of which Luis de León and Cervantes were probably not unaware. In any case the coincidence of Sancho and the sweet poetry of the Augustinian cannot fail to be amusing.

[23] "God has not been pleased to provide another valise for me with another hundred crowns, like the one the other day; but never mind, my Teresa, the bellringer is in safe quarters." (II, 36).

[24] Sancho says: "I thought your worship, mentioned *Hilo* [thread] in it." "I said only *Fili*," replied Don Quixote (I, 23). Sancho still pronounced the aspirate "h," perceiving thus the connection between "hilo" and "filo" (rustic pronunciation of "hilo"), a play on words which the contemporaries of Cervantes would understand easily.

[25] "All who knew Sancho were astonished to hear him speak so elegantly, and did not know what to attribute it to unless it were that office and grave responsibility either *smarten* or stupefy men's wits" (II, 49). Sancho is one of those whom objective responsibility "smartens."

[26] *Vida de don Quijote y Sancho* (*Life of Don Quixote and Sancho*), last chapter.

[27] F. Rodríguez Marín, the erudite commentator of *Don Quixote*, is carried away in the vertigo of Cervantian style, and unconsciously yields to the idea of separating the book from its author: "Don Quixote, to its author . . . was merely a person of good ability who had gone ridiculously astray because of a madness that possessed him; the best, the most spiritual part of the hero, the delicate virtues of his soul, *were in the book*, of course; but *its own creator* did not even see them . . . It is we the readers who have discovered the full extent of the treasure of the great work" (*Nueva edición crítica*, 1928, VI, 443).

[28] It is well known that Don Quixote was brought to Barcelona as the result of the external influence of the apocryphal *Don Quixote* of Avellaneda (another living influence of books) and even then, the picture of the city is purely abstract. The visit to El Toboso takes place at night (II, 9), and is described merely in a marvelous symphony of nocturnal noises, or in the indistinct profile of a few buildings: "Now and then an ass brayed, pigs grunted, cats mewed . . . that great dark mass that one sees from here should be Dulcinea's palace." The person of the early-rising farmhand is revealed solely in "the noise the plough made as it dragged along the ground . . ." and in the ballad verse that he is singing: "Ill did ye fare, ye men of France,
In Roncesvalles chase"—

[29] The "vital" significance of the theme, and the manner in which it is integrated here into the life of the people involved, relegates to a very secondary plane the point that the debate between Arms and Letters is medieval humanistic, Renaissance, or of any other epoch.

[30] Flaubert, referring to *Don Quixote*, says: "Comme on voit ces routes d'Espagne qui ne sont nulle part ·décrites" (quoted by J. Ortega y Gasset).

[31] While making preparations for the battle between Don Quixote and the lackey Tosilos, the Duke ordered the heads to be removed from the Lances, since "Christian charity, on which he plumed himself, could not suffer the battle to be fought with so much risk and danger to life . . ."; he limits himself to giving them a "battlefield on his territory (though that was against the decree of the holy council, which prohibits all challenges of the sort) . . ." (II, 56) (Ormsby, II, p. 285).

[32] The desire to maintain the divine and human neatly apart is manifest in the texts of other works of Cervantes. El Licenciado Vidriera "told a thousand bad things about

puppeteers: he said that they were vagabonds and that they treated indecently of divine things, because the figures that they showed in their performances *turned piety into a laughing matter,* and that he was amazed that those who were able to do so did not impose permanent silence upon their shows, or exile them from the kingdom." (*El Licenciado Vidriera*). This feeling that religious art is an exclusive appurtenance of the Church, and should not leave it, was in direct opposition to the customs and the very essence of traditional Spanish life, which is founded upon the indistincton between heaven and earth. This belief and the idea that serves as its base, reveal the Erasmian, intellectual, Renaissance (or whatever it be called) aspect of Cervantes.

[33] Several Aragonese gentlemen who come to know Don Quixote personally, as well as through the narration of his history, "On the one hand . . . regarded him as a man of wit and sense, and on the other hand, he seemed to them a maundering blockhead, and they could not make up their minds *whereabouts between wisdom and folly they ought to place him.*" (II, 59). Of course, discretion and madness may be divided into maximum and minimum values, although with such distinctions, we proceed indefinitely within the same evaluational system.

[34] In his commentary upon *The Life of Don Quixote and Sancho,* the chapter that deals with the scrutiny of the hidalgo's library is skipped: "It deals with books and not with life. Let us pass over it."

[35] Let us say in passing that only through this criterion of personalized vitalizations can we analyze the question of whether or not *Don Quixote* was written as an attack against chivalry novels. The sentence in which the author expresses his desire to write against those books exists within *Don Quixote,* just as does the rest of the book, and in reality depends upon the vital situation in which it is incarnated. The curate would like to burn them all, but someone feels that *Amadís* "is the best of all the books of this kind that have been written, and so, as something singular in its line, it ought to be pardoned." "True," said the curate. . . ." (I, 6). The same bitter enemy of chivalric literature says of *Palmerín de Inglaterra:* " . . . let that palm of England be kept and preserved as a thing that stands alone, and let such another case be made for it as that which Alexander found among the spoils of Darius and set aside for the safe keeping of the words of the poet Homer." (I, 6). Thus, even if we knew that the author's purpose sometimes has validity as a logic-moral judgment, the truth is that the moment it penetrates into the avalanche-like movement of the work, it submits to the existential system of the rest. The books in question are good, in the opinion of some, and bad, to others; they appear as highly worthy or as contemptible to the curate and to the canon; in short, they vary as do the living momenta of their readers. When Don Quixote declares: ". . . odious to me now are all the profane stories of knight-errantry; . . ." (II, 74), it means that he is really dying, for his soul ceases to emit reflections. " . . . one of the signs by which they came to the conclusion that he was dying was this so sudden and complete return to his senses . . . ," since absolute sanity or insanity means non-existence. This is the basic meaning of *Don Quixote.* Those who are inclined to treat vital matters logically will question this; but the issue is analogous to attempting to determine the particular town in which was born and died this supreme protagonist of life; "whose village Cide Hamet would not indicate precisely, in order to *leave all the towns and villages of La Mancha* to contend among themselves for the right to adopt him and claim him as a son . . ." (II, 74).

[36] The Morisco who reads the manuscript of Cide Hamet for the first time, "after reading a little in it began to laugh." (I, 9).

[37] Masudi, *Les prairies d'or.* Text and translation by C. Barbier de Meynard, Paris, 1864, vol. III, pp. 136–138.

[38] E. Bréhier, *Les idées philosophiques at religieuses de Philon d'Alexandrie,* p. 101.

[39] *Ibid.,* p. 98.

[40] *Ibid.,* p. 99.

[41] When the medieval philosophers called nature "the book of God," they were employing a metaphor with Oriental overtones; but this idea, naturally, did not become personalized in the vital experience of the philosopher.

[42] Since Italian commentators of Dante are loath to confess that Dante was influenced

at times by the Arabs, this and other phenomena have not been noted, nor surely will they be in the future.

[43] See his *Life,* by Pedro de Rivadeneira, in "Biblioteca de Autores Españoles," LX, 14.

[44] Ignatius proceeds to a certain degree as does Don Quixote later: he imitates the saints as the Hidalgo does Amadís (p. 17); he has his Dulcinea in divine fashion (p. 17); he stands watch over his arms (p. 18); he sets out as does Don Quixote (p. 18). Ignatius was motivated by the double incitement of arms and religious devotion; whereas Don Quixote contemplates secular glory exclusively. As we have said previously, he flees from the world without leaving it.

[45] Bibliographical references for these texts may be found in M. Menéndez y Pelayo, *Orígenes de la novela,* I, CCLX ff. Until now we have paid scant attention to the vital phenomenon reflected in those critical remarks, which are generally quoted by all of us if they were merely the echo of rationalistic Erasmian tendencies, or destined only to "shackle the cultivation of purely mundane sensibility and fantasy." (Cf. my *Pensamiento de Cervantes,* p. 26.) What is especially interesting here is to show that those who spoke so of the chivalric novels had passed, or could pass, through the same type of experience that they censured: "The devil, satiated with flesh, becomes a friar." Let us recall that the curate did not venture to burn either *Amadís* or *Palmerín,* and that he knew both very well.

[46] Spanish literature does not really possess anything that may be considered a moral system, objectified in principles and comparable to Guillaume De Vair's *Exhortation à la vie civile,* Pierre Charron's *De la sagesse,* etc.

[47] The most important and original theme of Spanish literature is perhaps life as a living experience of itself. Such a theme already integrates the outstanding stylistic features of *La Celestina* (1499).

[48] The epoch was laden with possibilities, awaiting only the genius who could develop them. "The Sevillan Alonso de Fuentes in his *Summa de philosophia natural* (1547) sketches the semblance of a 'patient,' a precursor of the gentleman from La Mancha, who knew by heart the entire *Palmerín de Oliva,* and never was without a copy of it although he knew it through and through." In 1600, a student at Salamanca "instead of reading his lessons was reading a chivalric novel; and when he found in it that one of those famous knights was hard pressed by some villains, he got up from where he was, and seizing a broadsword, began to flourish it throughout the room and to fence in the air; and when his companions heard this, they rushed over to find out what the matter was, and he replied: 'Leave me to my own, good sirs, for I was reading this and that, and I am now defending this knight. What a pity! How those ruffians had him cornered!'" Adolfo de Castro: *Varias obras inéditas de Cervantes,* p. 130. See Adolfo de Castro: *Ibid,* p. 144. Also, R. Menéndez Pidal, *Un aspecto en la elaboración del Quijote* in "De Cervantes y Lope de Vega," 1940, an excellent and penetrating study, which approaches our problem from other points of view.

[49] This point is well illustrated already in *La Galatea,* Cervantes' first work (1585): "Your true reason and unfeigned words" (Book I). The shepherd Lenio, a bitter enemy of love—one who has given up love—says that his adverse opinion of Cupid is based on "verified *science,* which . . . because it bears the truth with it, obliged me to sustain it." But such unloving person ends by surrendering completely to love, and he weeps and despairs just as do so many other shepherds and shepherdesses. The truth of his life contradicts the pseudo-truth of his reasoning.

[50] A similar thing occurs in *La Galatea* regarding the concept of space. The lyrical style of pastoral loves ("things dreamed and well written," Cervantes called them) could not permit the mention of Seville or Alcalá de Henares as actual realities, and therefore, they appear in elusive expressions such as "on the banks of the Betis" or "on the shores of the famous Henares" (Book I). But already in this work there is manifest the intent to offer a lower stratum in opposition to the supreme of the poetic, both of which are removed from the prose of everyday life. It is for this reason that the meeting places of the shepherds, situated on the periphery of urban society, which is always eluded and evaded, bear names not at all metaphorical: "Brook of the Palms, Village Common, Fountain of the Slate Shales" (Book I), contrasting thus with "the famous Complutus" (Alcalá) and "Mantua Carpetana" (Madrid) in Book II. The contemporary geography, on the other hand, emerges

with clearly defined precision, when themes of struggle and passion lived by the author or by other Spaniards are treated: Jerez, Milan, Naples, Perpignan, Catalonia, the viceroy of Barcelona (Book II); La Goletta, Gaeta, and the islands between Africa and Italy (Book V). The living experience of geographical places is expressed in one form or another according to the artistic intent: evasive with respect to the cities, and exact when referring to the freedom of the open fields; or yet it may be engrained within the individual consciousness of the author: the heroic or mournful theme of sea voyages or of the piracy by the Turks. To these incitements do we owe several of the most rhythmically beautiful pages of *La Galatea:* "The beautiful shore of Genoa, covered with lavishly embellished gardens, white houses, and resplendent spires, which, when struck by the rays of the sun, reflected such flaming rays that one could hardly look at them. All these things that were visible from the ship *could* inspire contentment, as it did to *all those on the ship, except me,* to whom it caused even greater sorrow." (The beauty of Genoa is reflected in one way in the lives of some, and in another way, in those of others—just as the books of chivalry and all the other things of this world are lived.) "One night I remember—and I remember well, for in it began the dawn of my day—the sea being calm, the winds still, the sails fastened to the masts, and the sailors, without a care, stretched out in various parts of the ship, and the helmsman almost asleep because of the fair weather we were having and the favorable aspect of the sky, in the midst of this silence, and in the midst of my imaginations . . . seated aft on the castle, I took up my lute and began to sing . . . " (Book V).

[51] Ariosto relates that Angelica, the

> "fior virginal cosi avea salvo,
> Come se lo portò del materno alvo."

And the poet adds:

> "Forse era ver, *ma non peró credible*
> A chi del senso suo fosse signore." (I, 55, 56)

There we peer into the abyss that separates Cervantes from his Italian "sources," and we feel notably the distance between Graeco-European Italy and Christian-Islamic Spain. In my book *España en su historia* I have explained the meaning of this.

[52] Already in the poem of the *Cid* (1140), when the cousin of the Cid's daughters finds them tied to a tree, lashed by their husbands, and dying of thirst, he brings them water in the only receptacle he has—a new hat, which had just been bought in Valencia.

The "Simpatía" of Don Quixote

BENEDETTO CROCE

IT is often said of *Don Quixote* that it is a work which is "alive" from beginning to end. This word represents a metaphor of recognized poetic beauty, but it does not suffice to satisfy the critical mind, which, not content with metaphors, and knowing that poetry is not merely life but intense awareness heightened into fantasy, therefore inquires as to what precisely is the feeling depicted in the person and the vicissitudes of Don Quixote.

So vividly expressed is this motivating force that all can grasp and define it, because all discover in it the reflection of what is in their own hearts. It is the feeling of "simpatía," that is (as it is defined in the old Italian dictionaries), the sense of "reciprocal affinity or similarity of temperament, of desire, and of affection." It implies recognition of something which is identified with what we ourselves honor and cherish. Whoever is lacking in love and a sense of the ideal is correspondingly devoid of or meagerly endowed with "simpatía." Nor does "simpatía," in spite of etymological relationship, have anything to do with the "compassion," which is directed toward the sorrows and trials of humanity, whatever be the worthiness or unworthiness of the sufferer. Indeed, no one has ever thought or would ever think of offending Don Quixote by saying that in his folly, in his mishaps, his tumbles, bruises, and wounds, he arouses compassion, because what he does always arouse is "simpatía."

Don Quixote receives constant testimonials of this feeling from the people among whom he moves; and if at times he falls among those who do not understand him, or who scorn or mistreat him through thoughtless rudeness or malicious intent, the good ones among them all like him. And most of all is he loved by that rogue from his own home town, whom he has called to his side, in whom the lust for wealth and power is transcended by his love and veneration for his master. Sancho is even smitten by a sense of honor, an honor of which he would soon weary, were he to break that bond. Thus, when, having hesitated to follow him a second time, he sees Don Quixote resigned to seek a new squire, suddenly he relents and, his eyes filled with tears, places himself at his disposal,

179

protesting that he is incapable of ingratitude and of desertion, and that he does not want—this between pity and comedy—to sully the reputation of his family, "for all the world knows, but particularly my own town, who the Panzas were, from whom I am descended" (II, 7).

Moreover, when Don Quixote reproves him, he feels quite stricken with remorse and confesses that he is a complete ass, that all he lacks is a tail, and he wants his master to fix one on him and he will serve him as an ass all the remaining days of his life (II, 28). Still more in agreement in this matter than his fellow characters in the novel, are and have been his readers, who have loved Don Quixote since he first appeared on the literary scene, and have hailed him as most charming and ingenious; and, later, with the romantics of the 19th century, have lavished upon him words trembling with affection, as Byron did in some of the stanzas of *Don Juan*.

In these famous stanzas, the author's affection for Don Quixote reaches a point of fury over the smiles of which he has been the object; whereas the real evidence of the "simpatia" which Don Quixote arouses is at once a smile and a feeling of tender understanding, so perfectly intermingled that the smile never detracts from the admiration for his nobility of character and rightness of judgment, which remain intact and stand out the more vividly among the flashes of comic effect.

The fact is that this synthesis of seriousness and laughter, of dismay and imaginative fervor, of rejecting and accepting, is common to the collective soul of humanity which cannot wish and act except by hoping, and cannot hope without believing in the reality of the things hoped for. Every man, no matter how wise he may be or think himself to be, is always wholly enveloped in illusions: having attained his goal, and having realized its illusoriness, then, in order to go on working and living, he must delude himself again and invent new, yet similar illusions. Byron, in the verses which we have recalled, said that Socrates too was a Don Quixote, the Don Quixote of wisdom; but we are all, in some fashion, Don Quixotes of something or other, deceived like him, and like him, partly mad. From time to time we all suffer the sorrow of having dreamed and trusted, only to face cruel awakening and disillusionment. This is the price paid for life by even the most noble and expert, the most austere and wary. The man who is moved by pure and abstract reason is a lifeless puppet created by pedants—who, too, in their own way, are Don Quixotes. What then is to be done? The deception, the disillusionment, and the grief must be swallowed; but, in the hour of serene contemplation, stirred and smiling, one can regard the human tragicomedy in a portrayal like *Don Quixote,* and be philosophically aware of the logical process whereby all this is proved necessary.

Don Quixote, too, requires illusion, without which his life would be meaningless and empty. He desires it as obstinately as he desires the most trying experiences, the most obvious proofs. Sancho's words of good sense, which are constantly ringing in his ear, disturb him, and the will to be deluded keeps suggesting to him new rationalizations. At some moments it seems to overtake him almost to the point where he consciously deceives himself. For example, testing the firmness of the helmet he has made himself, Don Quixote breaks it to pieces at the first slash of his sword-blow; but he makes it over again with new zeal, only he is careful this time not to put it to the test, and considers it adequate without further ado (I, 1). The voluntary quality of the illusion discloses something of its transient extremity; we ourselves are deceived by pretending not to see. But, beyond appearances, there is in the midst of illusion true reality, the reality of the ideal which makes us live and work, the ideal for which we suffer and die. Here, at times, one is at the point of despair, here one rises to sublime reaches of grief and heroic will power, as happens to Don Quixote when, hurled to the earth by the Knight-of-the-White Moon, and vanquished as he is, having been enjoined to admit that his lady is not the most beautiful in the world:

> bruised and stupefied, without raising his visor, said in a feeble voice as if he were speaking out of a tomb: "Dulcinea del Toboso is the fairest woman in the world, and I the most unfortunate knight on earth; it is not fitting that this truth should suffer by my feebleness; drive your lance home, sir knight, and take my life, since you have taken away my honor."

At this point in the novel, the smile has been withdrawn and hidden from our view. More often it attempts to take flight without interfering with the words and deeds of Don Quixote, as, for example, in that most delightful scene of the meeting with the goatherds (I, 11), who invite the good knight to their rude table, offering him an overturned trough as a seat, and, after the meal, as he takes up a handful of acorns and meditates over them, he is reminded of all the trite sayings which he has read in the books of romances and of poetry, about acorns and about the Golden Age, and he goes on declaiming and recalling to mind:

> "Happy the age, happy the time, to which the ancients gave the name of golden, not because in that fortunate age the gold so coveted in this our iron one was gained without toil, but because they that lived in it knew not the two words *mine* and *thine!* In that blessed age all things were in common; to win the daily food, no labor was required of any save to stretch forth his hand and gather it from the sturdy oaks that stood generously inviting him with their sweet ripe fruit. The clear streams and running brooks yielded their savory limpid waters in noble abundance . . ."

All these platitudes he recounts with full conviction and pious fervor, with the tone of one who knows and can instruct and admonish others, going on with the story of the bees, which in the hollow trees set up their communities and offered freely of their sweetest honey to whoever held out his hands; describing the cork trees, which offered roofing for the huts; and the earth, which produced of itself without the plow's piercing its tender bowels; and peace, and concord, and harmony which reigned among all men; and young shepherdesses who roamed about innocently, barely covered where modesty requires, and decked only in leaves of green dock and ivy; and thoughts of love expressed in simple words, fraud and malice, deceit and violence, being unknown; and justice undisturbed by the efforts of favor and of interest. Whereupon, he turns to explain how that Golden Age was lost by the world, and how the knights-errant went forth to defend maidens, protect widows, and succor the orphaned and the needy; and how he is, himself, one of these champions:

> "To this order I belong, brother goatherds, to whom I return thanks for the hospitality and kindly welcome ye offer me and my squire; for though by natural law all living are bound to show favor to knights-errant, yet, seeing that without knowing this obligation ye have welcomed and feasted me, it is right that with all the good-will in my power I should thank you for yours."

To this long harangue, the conclusion and peroration of which is addressed more personally to them, the goatherds, "listened, gaping in amazement without saying a word in reply." At that moment, they, his "brothers," were lending form to Don Quixote's illusion; but the reality lies in that holy zeal which was burning in his bosom and which from that illusion was deriving its sustenance.

To be sure, not all of *Don Quixote* has this purity of portrayal and of poetry, for Cervantes was a man of letters who wanted to compose a work of entertainment value. He introduced, for ornamentation and variety, many extraneous elements and followed the first part with a second which, no matter how many very fine passages it may have, has also, in some instances the defect of forcing the narrative to the point of farce. This did not escape Gœthe who, in one of his customary solid and meaty opinions, conversing with Chancellor Müller in 1819, made the observation that "as long as the hero creates illusions, he is romantic, but when he is merely railed at and made fun of, the interest declines."[1] Cervantes, the genius,—and therein, moreover, lies his charm—was not fully aware of his own genius, of the poetic world he was creating; and, instead of presenting it in compact unity, as a more disingenuous artist of a more disingenuous age might have done, he blended it with more or less felicitous themes of entertaining literature.

(*Translated by* Frederick F. Fales)

---

[1] *Unterhaltungen mit dem Kanzler Friedrich von Müller,* hg. von C. A. H. Burckhardt (2nd ed., Stuttgart, 1898), p. 34.

The Career of the Hero

WALDO FRANK

DON QUIXOTE is but the final name of the ingenious knight of La Mancha. In Chapter One of his book, it is set forth that he was known as Quijada, Quesada or Quejana. Four chapters later a worker in the neighboring fields addresses him as Quijana, and as Quijano he made his will at the end of his last journey. His Christian name was Alonso. Quixote (Quijote in modern Castilian) was the choice of the old man himself. And as Cervantes gives him birth, he is old—old for his fifty years in a frustrate Manchegan village. He is noble but poor. He is an eater of cheap meats. He is a cadaverous, lantern-jawed, brittle-boned, deep-eyed fellow. His house, one room of which is stocked with the chivalric books that have drawn his substance and addled his brains, is cared for by an old Nurse and a niece. There is as well a boy servant who disappears from the tale after the first chapter. Doubtless Cervantes meant to employ him as Don Quixote's squire: but when the independent knight after his first sally made choice of Sancho Panza, there was naught left for the poor *mozo*. Of course, in the stable stands a splay-hoof nag. After four days of meditation on such names as Bucephalus and Babieca (the stallion of the Cid), Quixote christens his jade Rocinante. *Rocín* means hack horse: wherefore Don Quixote meant that his mount was *before* all the other hacks of the world.

This detail, appearing in the first chapter of the Book, might give the canny reader pause. "Why," he might ask, "if the deluded eyes—as we are told—of Don Quixote saw his hack as a mount equal to the steeds of Amadís or Alexander, as he was soon to be equal in renown, did he christen him with a name so comical and so revealing?" The reader will be aware of a curious shift in this Don Quixote's "madness": a note shivering in at once of self-conscious irony.

However, the madman to whom Cervantes introduces us seems on the whole at first to be consistent. A poverty-struck Manchegan, finding his treeless world too empty for his senses, let them roam in a realm of knight-errants, ogres, fairies, virgins, Magic. Until his senses are strayed. Whereupon, deeming himself a Roland or an Amadís, he buckles on his rusty sword, takes his nag from the stall and sallies forth into a Spain sordidly realistic, sick of heroes, to perform adventures. He cuts a ridiculous figure. And his fate is what a sane man might expect. He is unhorsed, drubbed, pounded. He loses teeth as his molested countrymen lose tempers. The ladies he meets are foul-breathed wenches; the lord of the Castle in which he takes his rest wants his pay, being the keeper of an inn. His battles are with goats, sheep, windmills and Biscayan servants. It is clear that some day his madness will discomfit him entire. At which time he will be forced back to his house where the good Nurse and the niece will staunch his wounds, bathe the dust from his mad eyes and put him to bed. Meantime, there is the tale to tell—with much laughter—of his absurd adventures. Cervantes wishes to laugh at this medieval scarecrow, jousting with the Modern. His fellow Spaniards, sick like himself of gestures and heroics, will roar along—will pay *reales* for the book—will put money in the purse of a scribbler.

Such a Quixote is the child of Cervantes, and is the subject of the early chapters. And now a fundamental difference sets in, marking off this character from others. Most literary creations remain their maker's. As he willed, modeled, developed them, so they live—or die. This is true in great books. The evolution of the hero is explicit in the poet's mind or at least in the action's threshold. But for the analogue to Don Quixote we must go to biology, rather than to art. The mother forms the baby in her womb. It is organically hers, and so for a brief time it will remain. But she has endowed it with a principle which will make her child recede ever more from being her creation. This inner life, seeking substance in the world of sense and of impression, becomes itself. The mother has created a babe—only to lose it. Similar is the fate of Quixote with Cervantes. From the womb of his will and bitter fancy comes the child. But Don Quixote is no sooner set on earth, than he proceeds by an organic evolution, by a series of accretions, assimilations, responses, to change wholly from the intent of his author—to turn indeed against him. He does not lose organic contact with his source, even as the man is child of his own childhood and of his parents in a way deeper than the parents' conscious will or than biologic pattern. But above all, the child becomes himself. He has transcended vastly the amorphous thing lodged in his mother's womb. So Don Quixote is transfigured beyond the sprightly scheme of his maker.

He was conceived and formed, as a broken writer's bitter turning against his heroic soul and his heroic age; he becomes the Body of sublime acceptance—the symbol of what his misfortunes were to mock. Cervantes' conscious will has no firm hold on Don Quixote. And this is plain almost from the outset in the fact that the Manchegan knight, despite his author's assurance, *is not mad*. We had an inkling of this already in the too conscious, too ironic naming of Rocinante. Soon the proofs multiply; for the clown-blows that continue to rain upon Don

Quixote in Part One cannot hold him from his organic growth. With Part Two, written ten years later, the blows and buffets are less frequent. Cervantes has had time to catch up with and humbly to accept his son.

In the matter of the selecting of a Lady (that needed spur of every true knight-errant) it is clear that Don Quixote knows the facts about Aldonza Lorenzo, wench daughter of Lorenzo Cochuelo of El Toboso. Quite consciously, he turns her into the divine Dulcinea whom henceforth he will worship. Her he makes his "truth"; there is no evidence that the *fact* of the girl is ever hidden from him. He needs a helmet, indeed he needs Mambrino's magic helmet. A barber comes, riding an ass and on his head (for it is raining) a copper bleeding-dish. This shall be the golden helmet of Mambrino; and as such Don Quixote takes it. But in the parley before and after with Sancho Panza, it is plain that the knight accepts Sancho's *fact* about the dish: he merely turns the fact, for his own purpose, into "truth."

In the Sierra Morena, Don Quixote resolves to follow a tradition. He and Sancho have reached the mountains that bar the smooth plains of La Mancha from the fluid meads of Andalusia southward: mountains of rock flung to sky, titanic gestures of rock, pourings of cosmic might into the waste of rock. The Sierra, sudden beneath La Mancha, suggests delirious excess. So here, Don Quixote will have his knightly spell of madness, in anguish of his absent lady love. How does he set about it? He debates the merits of two schools of madness. There was the furious way of Roland after his Angelica had slept with the Moor Medoro. And there was the quiet melancholy way of Amadís. Don Quixote is fifty: he elects the quieter madness. He takes Sancho to witness of his straits, ere he sends him off to beseech mercy of Dulcinea. Nor is he fooled by Sancho's meeting with the lady. The fact that Sancho has left behind him the very letter which he describes as giving to Dulcinea does not disturb Don Quixote. He is not dwelling with facts, but with truths of his own conscious making. And he tells his squire, speaking in elegiac temper of himself: "That if he did not achieve great matters, he died to achieve them; and if I am indeed not disowned and disdained by Dulcinea del Toboso, it sufficeth me . . . to be absent from her." Later he meets the swine girl whom he has transfigured into princess. And since he speaks of the magic making her appear as the facts (and Sancho) would have it—a coarse and silly female with a breath of garlic—it is plain that the facts are in his mind. He is not fooled. Nor is he lying when he speaks of magic. Magic is the deep inner change of attitude. This is the secret of the fakirs of the East. This is *true* magic. Don Quixote's attitude changes the fact of the swine girl into his truth of a princess.

The fooled is Sancho. For Sancho does not understand that fact and truth may be foes. He takes one for the other. He believes that Dulcinea's enchantment, the Cave of Montesino, the Island which he is sent to govern, the Empress whom his master is to wed are facts. As the tale grows, poor Sancho is more and more enmired in confusion. He is in danger of madness, losing his distinction between the world of shapes and this world of ideas in which Don Quixote rides.

The old knight's progress is willful. There is, for instance, the wondrous ride on Clavileño, the wooden horse in the garden of the Duke, upon which the pair are wafted through heaven and hell. Sancho claims to have stolen a glimpse and to have seen them soaring through the firmaments of fire. And Don Quixote answers:

> "If you desire me to believe you in what you have just seen in the sky, I desire that you should believe me in what I saw within the Cave of Montesino. No need for me to say more. . . ."

He is proposing to Sancho what is neither more nor less than a deal; he will accept his squire's lies, if Sancho accepts his own distinction between a glorious truth and a drab world of facts. But Sancho's mind has no such athleticism. He is not Ramón Lull! He has never heard of León Hebreo. He is forever mixing two insoluble realms.

At last Don Quixote meets his fate. In Barcelona, having been acclaimed by crowds with mingled laughter and devotion which they can never understand, he is challenged to combat by the Knight of the White Moon. He is worsted, of course: and this is his end. For the *caballero de la luna blanca* is none other than the bachelor Sansón Carrasco. The goodly Don Antonio cannot understand this medieval nonsense in his busy modern seaport. Carrasco explains:

> "My lord, know that I, the bachelor Sansón Carrasco, am of the same place as Don Quixote de la Mancha, whose simplicity and madness have moved to tears all of us who know him: and among these none has wept more than I: and believing that there lay his health and peace, in that he should reside in his own land and house, I determined to return him thither; and so three months since I went upon the road as a knight-errant, calling myself *el caballero de los espejos,* meaning to fight him, vanquish him without hurt, and having put as the condition of our encounter that the vanquished remain in the discretion of the victor: and what I thought to demand of him (for I judged him beforehand already vanquished) was that he should return to his home, and sally not forth from it for a whole year; in which time he might be cured; but fate ordered otherwise, for I was the defeated. I was hurled from my horse, and hence my purpose could not take effect; he went his way, and I returned, beaten, bruised, mashed by my fall which to be sure was dangerous enough; but for this I did not give up my meaning which was to seek him out once more and defeat him, as you have seen me do this day. And since he is so punctilious in all that pertains to the knight-errant,

without doubt soever he will obey the order I have given him, in honor of his word. This, my lord, is what has passed, without my need to say another thing; I beseech you, do not discover me nor to say to Don Quixote who I am, in order that these my good intentions may have effect, and that there may return to reason a man so excellent in reason, when he is left alone by the unreasons of chivalry. . . ."

Carrasco reveals that his deep instinct against Don Quixote is buttressed by a shallow understanding. When the old knight saw the familiar face of his friend within the vizor of the defeated *caballero de los espejos,* he was not troubled: he knew that magic had turned the truth of the defeated warrior into the face of his neighbor, the bachelor Sansón Carrasco. Had he now been told that the Knight of the White Moon appeared to others as this same bachelor, he would have found a similar solution—and obeyed the knight, though his heart broke.

So now, stripped of his harness, Don Quixote makes his ashen way homeward from Barcelona. He does not yet know that he is vanquished for good. His word binds him for a year: thereafter, can he not sally forth again? Meantime, he need not stay idle in a gross world of facts. "If it seem well to thee," he tells his squire, "I should like that we turn pastors even for the time I am caught up." He makes his plans. "I shall buy a few sheep and all other things needed for the pastoral life." His friends will share this new transfiguration which has the advantage of being more sociable than the life of the knight-errant. He will become the pastor *Quixotiz;* Sancho will become *Pancino.* Sancho's wife Teresa will be *Teresona.* The bachelor Carrasco will be known as *Sansonino* or *Carrascón:* being a learned man, he shall take his choice. The priest (*el cura*) he might call, not knowing his true name, *el pastor Curiambro.*

These persons, being facts, must change their names ere they can enter his truthful pastoral Eden. Dulcinea remains Dulcinea: for already *she* is of the world of his truth. With this last lucid statement of his mind, the old man comes upon his home where soon he is to die. No more may he be a knight, dispensing Justice in a real world inhabited by such true concepts as ogres, virgins, sorcerers. Even the little interlude of pastor is denied him. He languishes; and with his strength, his creative will expires.

The child returneth to the mother. Don Alonso Quijano el Bueno lies upon a death-bed and renounces Don Quixote. Again Cervantes' child shrinks to the arms of his parent. He abjures the careers of all knights-errant:

"Ya soy enemigo de Amadís de Gaula y de toda la infinita caterva de su linaje; ya me son odiosas todas las historias profanas de la andante caballería; ya conozco mi necedad y el peligro en que me pusieron haber-las leído; ya por misericordia de Dios, escarmentando en cabeza propia, las abomino. . . ."

Don Quixote, as he emerges unscathed from the mind of his author, is a man possessed: not a madman. He is a man possessed as were the Hebrew prophets, or Jesus, or Vardhamana, or Boehme or Plotinus, or any poet. . . . The difference is subtle but is clear beyond the logical distinctions of man's reason. No atheist would call Amos mad, but a man possessed. To Jesus saying: "When ye have lifted up the Son of God, then shall ye know that I am he, and that I do nothing of myself, but as my Father hath taught me" no Jew would ascribe madness, but possession. Quixote is possessed of an Ideal. And since this ideal was mothered of the world struggling toward light, and since now it mothers him entire, becoming his truth and his world, Don Quixote takes his place among the broken and triumphant prophets. Even the alienist durst not call him mad, for in the drama which he enacts he knows his part: and the more fully senses what he calls the truth, knowing its bodily difference from the facts about him.

Reality for the medieval soul was neo-platonic. The conceptual was real: all else was merely fact. The bitter apartness of Jew and Arab from medieval Europe was due to the failure of the Semite, despite Philo and Al Gazali, to assimilate neo-platonism deeply. Plotinus, Porphyry, Augustine, Iamblicus created the psychology of a thousand years of Europe. The real is not this world. We are snared and mired in a viscous web of seeming. All congeries of sense is this. And knowledge tends, not to a translating of this factual film into the real but to the piercing it, the abandoning it altogether. This attitude is far from the naturalistic mysticism of the Hebrew, from the intellectual mysticism of Plato; from the profound nihilism of the Hindu who recognized the unity of the ideal and the factual, interpreting one always in terms of the other. Medievalism is a child—and a childish offshoot—of all these. It declares: There is a real world, and it is not this one. Man can reach the real world, by various means. He must crucify the fact, he must worship the saints, he must lose his body in order to save his soul.

Don Quixote moves through a world neo-platonically real. He is as aware as Sancho of sheep, windmills, inns, country wenches. He chooses to disregard these lies of fact. He erects a systematic symbol whereby his senses vault the phenomena about him, and deliver him the truth. Thereby, the windmill serves him as a giant; the sheep as enchanted armies; the empty cave of Montesino as the scene of Glory, and Maritornes the whore as the virgin lady languishing in love. He has elected to do Justice upon earth. These giants, armies and disasters serve him as means to that end.

By a similar process, the medieval mind made all history into parallel and symbol. The medieval mind is subjectivism carried to the intense conclusion made possible by the barbarous Germanic will. Philo's allegories of the Scriptûre, the Book of Zohar, the way of Egypt and India with all written words, treating them as intricate and recondite symbols, obsessed the mind of medieval Europe. No act is simple, no name is simply a name. The world becomes a dramatic Mystery, with every scene bearing upon the central Plot: the soul's salvation. For a thousand years, literature and art, to be serious, had to be allegory.

The mood of medieval symbolism, while it was fathered by Plato and the Jews, is neither Greek nor Jewish. With these two adult peoples, symbolism held its place: it remained a relative and ancillary life within the mastering testimony of the world. Already in Plotinus and Saint Augustine, the balance is lost. When we are deep in the Middle Ages, we are deep in an allegoric jungle: the paths of fact are gone; there comes no daylight of reason in this tangle of monster foliage and whelming branches.

Don Quixote's world is medievally real. It is a hypertrophy of such births as Chivalry, Romance and Sainthood. In its character of wholeness, or deliberate disregard for fact, it springs from the fountainhead of neo-platonic thought.

But if this transfiguring of the world to his own will is a medieval act, Don Quixote's impulse is not medieval, is not even Christian. The medieval will, myriad in its flowerings, was childishly simple in its seed: the soul's salvation. Nothing else counted: or rather, everything had its sole significance, indeed its reality, as it bore on this monomaniac problem of each soul: to be saved. That a man's soul might be saved, all acts since Adam had been apportioned. For this, the Hebrews lived, the Prophets preached, Christ died: for this, Peter builded his Church and the Jews remained outside in perpetual testimony of damnation. For this, men went on Crusades, conquered heathens, gave birth to children in holy wedlock. For this there was love and justice: for this there was life and death. But Don Quixote is no more centrally concerned with his soul's salvation than if he had been a Jew. He believes in his soul; he hopes it shall be saved. But his acts are motived by a will far less personal: the enacting of Justice.

Don Quixote looks upon himself as the instrument of Justice. He is the embodied and moving will of Justice. The neo-platonic Christian lived justly, that he might pierce better the Phenomenal Lie and win salvation. The Arab warrior spread justice with his sword because the Prophet was just, and he must serve the Prophet to be saved. The knight of the Round Table of King Arthur performed deeds of justice—rescuing the virgin, slaying the bad giant—because it was good sport and because it was a way to his salvation. But Don Quixote wills Justice upon earth, because he hungers after Justice, because there is naught else true save Justice. If, by the sheer testimony of his words and deeds, we analyze this passion of Don Quixote, we learn that for him instinctively Justice meant Unity. The world must become One: and the means thereto is Justice.

The symbols with which he works are medieval Christian; his mental mechanism is neo-platonic: his knightly attitude is more Moorish than Teutonic (as contrasted with the Germanic tenor of the freebooting Cid). But this heart of his will is Hebrew. The parabolic line of its enactment in his life links Don Quixote with the Prophets.

The words God and Christ are surprisingly seldom on the old knight's lips. He cites Roland and Amadís more often than the Saints. They, indeed, are his saints. But his God is Justice. And so impersonal, so monotheistic is He, that He wants more than a body; almost He lacks a name. Or rather His body is the world: His name is Justice.

The eidolon-making Greeks said in wonder of the Jews: "They are a people who see God everywhere and localize him nowhere." So Don Quixote created for himself a world that should consist solely of opportunities for Justice. To this end he rejects, selects and builds in the world which meets his eyes. His mind works like the instinct of an artist. But he is a peculiar sort of artist. His ethical purpose, the intensity with which he imbues every action with his vision and turns the social fact into a spiritual Word, recalls the Prophets. Amos, too, looked out on a world made wholly the matrix for the vision of God: and moved in Israel as a flame within the burning wood. To Hosea, even the wife of his bed was a symbol of the intention of the Lord. Every detail of the Prophet's life— even the silence and the dark, even the failure and the sin—is caught in the unity of his vision and becomes a Word to express it. Thus Don Quixote sets forth to perform Justice. He must perform it constantly. The world must become material—a continuum of material—for his performance. But like every artist and like every prophet Don Quixote must translate his vision into the accepted formulæ of his mind. In his case, these formulæ are the shoddy regalia of decadent knighthood. Justice is to be performed by rescuing virgins, unseating ogres, slaying giants, despiting necromancers. Don Quixote rides through Spain. Along these highways graze sheep, trudge merchants: there are inns but no castles. Don Quixote does not see the enactment of Justice in such terms as these. So he transforms them.

His Justice is an attempt at unity. But it is very simple. The real world of Don Quixote is no intricate entexture of hierarchic values. It is not like the mazed affluence of life which the Hindu fused into One. It has none of the deep involument of souls and states fused by Hebrew and Hellene into God. It is a simple pyramid. At the base are knights and villains, virgins and married ladies, angels, enchanters, demons, ogres. And at the pyramid's peak is the ideal of all this homogeneous matter: freedom and liberty. This ideal is uncorrupted by any political or sectarian dogma. It is never more clear than in the adventure with the convicts. With clinking chains, this squad of scoundrels is led south by the soldiers of the King, to meet the galley in which they must serve their terms.

Here are men in chains: Don Quixote's ideal of Justice demands that chains be stricken off. The soldiers protest that these chains are virtuous and lawful: it avails not. The freed rascals repay their liberator with a shower of stones and make off with Sancho's ass: this avails nothing. Don Quixote will not be swerved from his immaculate conception of Justice.

In such episodes as this, we touch the core of the miracle of Don Quixote. His nature is ridiculously funny, and is Christlike. The freeing of legally judged robbers, the letting of lions out of cages, is farce: and yet illumes a justice above laws whose vision is Christlike and whose enactment brings upon the knight a Christlike fate. In laughing at Don Quixote, we crucify him. Mockery and buffets create the knight of the Sorrowful Figure: our own roars of glee at his well-earned mishaps hail the ridiculous Christ.

And here we come back into the medieval. The Jesus of the Synoptic Gospels i⸱ a dominant unbroken man. The Passion on the Cross is a mystic interlude— probably an interpolation—which rends the Temple far more than it does Jesus. His cry, about the ninth hour; "Eli, Eli, lama sabachthani" is a shredding weakness against the serenity and might of the historic Man. Jesus in his true character is almost wholly Hebrew Prophet. With the Lord in his mouth, he is impervious, even overbearing. The Hebrew spirit is as adverse from ill-health— from martyrdom as an end-in-itself—as the Greek. But with the infantilization of the West, with the upshowing of the childish spirit within the iron carapace of Rome, Jesus becomes pitiful. Medieval art makes him lean and ugly; asceticism borrowed from the Hindus and Egyptians mangles his body. Within the splendor of the Gothic church there comes to live a shrunken Christ. And as medievalism stumbled southward, the process gathered. The baroque churches of Seville are fantasmagoria of tropic wealth, writhed like a forest about the Sensitive Plant: Christ, milkpale, blood-spotted.

So at the end, Don Quixote. He is laughter-spotted, blood-spotted. Reason bespatters him and makes him comic. But since in the minds of men this reason is profane, and his mad impulse holy, he is a Christ—a medieval, an unjewish Christ.

His deeds get him into trouble. Part One abounds in buffets that unhorse him, knock out his teeth, bathe him in blood and muddy him all over. Part Two has a less rollicking mood. Cervantes has been affected by Don Quixote. But there is worse: Don Quixote, enacting Justice, brings trouble to others—and to the best of them. There is the boy whom he frees from a flogging master, and who is flogged the worse, in payment for the humiliation the master has suffered from Don Quixote. There is the freeing of the convicts—a menace to every household in the land. There is the freeing of the lion, to the probable disgrace

of the poor keeper. Don Quixote wrecks funerals: he maims an innocent Peni-
tent for life. He unhinges Sancho's peace: brings the anarchy of ambition into
the breast of this sweet clod of the earth. He visits destruction upon the unfortunate inns which he takes for castles. He robs a barber of his copper dish. He
drubs innocent servants. He smashes the sole fortune of Maese Pedro—his set
of puppets. He commits sacrilege even: plunging full-tilt upon a pilgrimage of
disciplinants, breaking legs and wresting from the outraged hand of a priest
an image of the Virgin.

Though he offends many and amuses more, he convinces no one. That a
prophet should inspire jeers and hatred is natural: but that he should have not
one disciple? and that at the end of his mission, he should recant, and call his
mission folly? How can such win the love of the world?

The strong whom he encounters laugh at him. The weak flee from him. The
Nurse and his niece do not laugh: they weep and tear their hair for his unseemly
conduct. In the bachelor Carrasco he inspires a nagging irritation. This man is
common sense incarnate: he is ill-at-ease before the irreducible vision of the
artist. He goes out of his way to down him: dons the armor of folly in order to
bring home the fool. This must not be construed as altruism. Carrasco pays
tribute to Don Quixote, in despite of himself. It is his own peace he is after. He
is aware, albeit far too rational ever to admit it to himself, that this utter idealist
stalking La Mancha robs his small reality of ease. Common sense—the sense of
approximation and of compromise—is fragile and is nervous. It must sequester
the poet-prophet in his home town.

Perhaps the ugliest episode in the book treats of the knight's entertainment
in the castle of the Duke and Duchess. They are the worldly-wise, the worldly-
cultured, even as Carrasco is the pragmatist. They take Don Quixote in; and
make him a show for their own genteel delectation. They are the perpetual
patron of the artist. They feed him, flatter him, serve him: everything but
believe him. Their minds hold him safe from their hearts. And nowhere does
the knight of the Sorrowful Figure appear so pathetic, so ridiculous, so disarmed,
as under this ducal roof where he is lionized and where whole pageantries are
enacted to pander to his need of enacting Justice.

Quixote survives the sophistical salon of the Duchess and of her lecherous
ladies. But while he is among them, he is shrunken. He goes forth at last, aware
of the subtle poison of their praise, to seek the adventure of Justice—to be laid
low by the bachelor Carrasco.

But there is his squire? are there not moments at least in which the squire
is a true disciple? Sancho Panza seems to have come latterly to Cervantes.
Indeed, this loamy son of the Manchegan desert is less immediate altogether to
the world illumined by Don Quixote. That treeless, sapless plain whose horizons

are beyond eye, whose winters are blasts of ice, whose summers are fire, whose indeterminate panorama of details—dust, men, towns, roads—is chaos, is the true mother of Don Quixote. La Mancha is a defeated desert: neither waste nor garden, it imposes the way of gardens upon the mood of the desert. Don Quixote transfigures its inns and sordid villages, its hard-fist peasants and its heavy girls into a ruthless psychic unity; much as the son of the true desert drew its vast horizons and its breastlike slopes into the body of God. But how in this world was Sancho Panza born? For not Falstaff of verdant England is more robustly gay, not Panurge of luxuriant France more subtly sensual.

Sancho is wholly the creation of Cervantes. Don Quixote, born of his author, outgrew him. Sancho, too, grows organically. Contact with his master determines this. But none the less he lies ever full within Cervantes' will: he is the sheer miraculous birth of gayety from the frustrate desert of Cervantes' life.

To Sancho, the "phenomenal" world, the world of facts is everything. Since he conceives no other, and since his master continuously lives within another of his own conceiving, Sancho is held busy translating into factual terms the entire adventure which he rides with Don Quixote.

A vertiginous effort it is, and it ends by making Sancho more nearly mad than his knight. He believes factually in his Island. He believes himself its governor, though he has crossed no water to attain it. The maid who is to wed Don Quixote after he has gone to Africa to slay her foe is factually to him the Princess Micomicona. This enchantment must be a fact, like the one which befell Dulcinea, turning her into the wench Aldonza. Sancho vacillates forever between the credulity and the skepticism of the literal mind: ignorance is so clearly the matrix of his sanity that the delusions of his master become wise by contrast. There are no dimensions to his thinking. Don Quixote is mad—or he is a true knight-errant: the adventure is wild,—or there will be a veritable island.

His dominant impulse, either way, is greed. Greed makes him doubt: greed makes him trust his master. Yet underneath, there works subtly upon Sancho a sweeter influence: his indefeasible respect for Don Quixote. Howsoever he argue, howsoever clear he see, howsoever he sicken from constant thumpings and sparse earnings, howsoever wry are the pleasures of his Island, Sancho cannot altogether free himself from the dominion of an idealizing will which he can never understand. In a directer way (since he is no intellectual) than that of Sansón Carrasco, he is held and haunted by Don Quixote. When he is absent from his master he is lost. When, in a scene more touching than the pathos of two quarreling lovers, Don Quixote gives him leave to depart homeward, promising him reward for his past service, Sancho bursts into tears and vows that he cannot forsake him.

He loves his master. Not greed alone, or if so, the greed of devotion to an ungrasped grandeur, holds him astride his dappled ass to follow Don Quixote to the sea. And yet, he despises him; and he betrays him. He judges him, and he exploits him. He makes sure of his reward in Don Quixote's will, and he gives up the comfort of his wife to follow him through ridiculous dangers. He is this sensual, lusty, greedy oaf of the soil. And yet in the love that masters him he is Cervantes, himself: Cervantes who created Don Quixote to laugh and to mock—and who remained to worship.

For this is the crux of the matter. Cervantes needed Sancho to keep Don Quixote in the perspective for laughter. "Common-sense" rides along with the "madman," and constantly shows him up. But here is Sancho, shown up himself! Here is Cervantes, shown up! For Cervantes accepts Don Quixote. And that is why we accept him. Cervantes builds up these countless reasons for rejecting him: the havoc wrought by his acts, the shoddy stuff of his dream, the addled way of his brain. It avails naught. Cervantes ends with love. And we—the more humbly in that we have mocked and roared—avow our veneration.

Of such stuff is made the holiness of Don Quixote: mildewed notions, slap-stick downfalls. We laugh at his unfitness to impose his dream upon a stubborn world: we see well enough that Rocinante is a nag and the knight himself, helmeted with a dish, a mangy addled fellow. And we accept, in order that he may live this nonsense, the disruption of inns, the discomfiture of pilgrims, the routing of funerals, the breaking of bones!

Cervantes strives hard to snuff out the aspiring hunger of his soul. For this, Don Quixote is bemuddled and deformed. But Don Quixote lives: and his chief enemy—Cervantes—gives him blood and his passion, in order that he may triumph.

Critical Realism

MARIO CASELLA

1. ASPECTS OF THE TRADITIONAL CRITICISM

IN treating several particular aspects of Cervantes' masterpiece, Ortega y Gasset, in his *Meditaciones del Quijote,* yielded to that initial fright which takes hold of us—unless we possess frivolous souls or vain mentalities—in the presence of the closed and enigmatic individuality of a great work of art: "¡Cervantes—un paciente hidalgo que escribió un libro—, se halla sentado en los elíseos prados hace.tres siglos, y aguarda, repartiendo en derredor melancólicas miradas, a que le nazca un nieto capaz de entenderle!"

Ortega y Gasset was voicing what could be called the inmost thought of an age-old criticism. Every time that it has added up its labors in a sum total or has attempted to harmonize in a synthesis the results obtained, it has had to fuse together a complex mass of unequal, unorganized, divergent, and contradictory notes. But the first duty of Ortega y Gasset, in his noble endeavor to reveal "los secretos últimos del *Quijote,*" should have been to abandon Blondel's system without further ado and not seek to apply it at any cost, that is, more or less with the same quiet dialectic elegance with which the philosopher of action tends to place on a new foundation the essential realism of the knowledge which he possesses.

The *Meditaciones* of Ortega y Gasset remain what they are: an ingenious theory to interpret the content of lyric and epic poetry and to explain the rise of the modern novel. And they are the beautiful and keen reflections of an academic university professor, who borrows a system of thought from a professional philosopher and applies it to a work of art with the illusion that this system, which does not really belong to him, must instead belong to Cervantes. This illusion, which doubtlessly belongs to all young men—or to all those who manage to keep young even after the age of fifty—is made to belong by Cervantes to two university students: Sansón Carrasco, who holds a bachelor's degree from Salamanca, and Lorenzo de Miranda, who is still at the elementary stage of his theological studies. One applies Aristotle's *Poetics* to the masterpiece,

195

and the other brings to bear on it the rigor of his dialectic or sophistic logic. And, naturally, pure poetry escapes both one and the other, "and slips through their fingers like an eel."

The history of Cervantes criticism has repeated itself from century to century with the same characteristics that it had from the very beginning when the first part of the *Quixote* appeared. Cervantes tells us about it. The work was immediately received with universal acclaim. Its editions were multiplied in prodigious numbers and translations of it in the principal languages of Europe began to appear. Even at that time, in the lecture halls of universities, the learned professors who were expounding the *Poetics* as a beautiful novelty just come from Italy, hastened to evaluate the work that had aroused such admiration. They felt it incumbent upon them to place it within the sphere of their understanding. Upon the Christian realism which profoundly animates it and which justifies it in each of its parts and gives it unity, they superimposed the abstract idealism of the Greeks and thereby failed utterly to understand it. The pedants and rhetoricians of the time became lost in queer and inconclusive minutiae. They noted, to their own satisfaction, a few factual inconsistencies and put forward a few would-be formal emendations of their own. The moralists, with that typical lack of comprehension which characterizes them in the face of a work of art, vainly sought in it their sacred and sacrosanct precepts expressed in didactic form. The erudites, who turn poetry into a document and the poetic act into a historical fact, and lean on metaphors in their opaque materialism, stopped short before a work that afforded such keen pleasure. They did not grasp the essential motif of the novel. If they had, they would not have opened their mouths. Don Quixote had, like them, mistaken pure poetry for history.

Cervantes answered all of these with serene indulgence and, in the way of laying the groundwork for a clear theory of art and of the criticism of a work of art, he wrote the second part of the *Quijote,* which is certainly the more living, more human, more profound, and more fertile of the two. It is the interpretation and the illustration of the thought which is poured into the first part. Here, with the objectivity of a historian who is interpreting, he had brought into contrast the formal reasons (*rationes formales*) according to which we must group and consider the articulations of the real in the pure poetic irrational and in the pure instinctive irrational. By means of intercalated anecdotes and stories he had given the reader to understand that the reason of one and the other irrational is similar, by analogy, to that infinite reason which urges man on from the innermost depths of his consciousness and directs and illuminates him in his practical and constructive activity at every moment of his life.

In the second part Cervantes started out from the principles of identity, or *raison d'être,* and of finality—this last in its two aspects: one being the consecration of potentiality to actuality and the other, from the point of view that every action implies some perfection and some communication of being and actuality —and he established rationally the intrinsic and constituent characteristics of Don Quixote and Sancho. Cervantes demonstrated that his two heroes are two complete individualities that must be interpreted in their subjective and ineffable truth, for what they long to become, in relation to the idea which each of them aspires to realize.

The knight declares himself freely, through knowledge and will, for the unconditional beauty of virtue and honesty. He is determined to perfect himself in his own vital spontaneity and in his analogical knowledge of God in the trinity of His attributes: goodness, mercy, and justice. The squire necessarily declares himself, through the blind impetus of his appetite, for the unconditional beauty of utilitarianism. He is determined to perfect himself in that particular good which is rendered desirable to him by virtue of its resemblance to the supreme God. Don Quixote and Sancho are therefore, figuratively speaking, two universal tendencies. They express a whole order of relations, at whose base is to be found a fundamental connection of analogy, which gives meaning to each of the relations that can be established in a Christian universe between the creature and his creator. The poetic reason for Don Quixote and Sancho is that which is imminent in the natural love of oneself: as an innate inclination to love one's own being, which is therefore an analogue of God. This reason cannot be understood by the Aristotelian rational golden mean. It is a reason that is lived in a vital act and, therefore, escapes from the argumentations of logic, the rigorous restrictions of dialectics, and pure intellectual knowledge.

Don Quixote has chosen knight-errantry as a means of realizing, in the actuality of his contemporary Spanish history, the imminent reason of his own life: the pure poetry of a love which becomes perfectly intelligible to itself in the mental symbol in which it recognizes itself. But the romances of chivalry are the pure poetry of the subject that loves itself exclusively in the world of things with which it enters in relation: the poetic irrational, individuated nature which is incapable of perfecting itself with the art of love. In the images of chivalry Don Quixote grasps only the vibrant actuality of his love, and there he understands himself as thought. He is always intelligible to himself on the basis of a metaphysical certainty that remains his individual and ineffable poetic truth, as the assertion of the purest subjectivity. But this is precisely the truth of pure poetry. It loves itself and understands itself in its own spiritual images, in which lyrically and ideally it rejoices in its own intimate life as truth, goodness, and beauty.

With the coherence of a thought which makes itself known by objectifying itself in concrete images, and each one intelligible in itself, Cervantes clearly noted the errors into which the critics of a work of poetry can fall. He posited, as a prime and indispensable necessity of any value judgment, that of interpreting the work and reliving in oneself its spiritual content in its singularity and particularity, for what it actually is in the uncommunicable individuality of the poetic act which is posited as an absolute in its original and creative impetus. Not until you have made internal that which is external in a work of poetry, not until you have divested the word or the image of its material characteristics by bringing it back to the living spontaneity of the act which is expressed within it, which is recognized in it, and which is loved with infinite love, not until you have unconsciously subjected the work of art to the pure subjectivity of your particular sentiment or of your abstract intelligence, will you ever understand the individual secret of a mind that acts like a creative spirit. And you will never penetrate into the profound intention (*intentio*) that has presided at the composition of a masterpiece and harmonized from within the various parts into an organic unity. And you will never grasp that autonomous truth which unfolds itself within it and takes form and becomes manifest in a continual process of becoming like an infinite in which everybody can participate according to the capacity of his mind and his personal experience of life.

Cervantes demonstrates it to us in the second part of his masterpiece. When the criticism of a work of art, which is the expression of the living humanity of the poet, has not attained in its intellectual habits the point where it does not sacrifice anything, either its own object to itself or itself to its own object, that criticism will resolve itself into its own ideal illusions. We shall then have a poetry which flourishes on real poetry with a sort of pleasant hedonism. We shall have the lyrical effusions of what we experience through it without, however, being able to distinguish it from what it is not and from what we put into it of our own. We shall have the assertive dogmatism of one who asserts himself with the generic and subjective content of his theoretical or practical preoccupations and seeks in it that which is not there and might have been or should have been there in order to satisfy him.

Among the men of his time, in the specific historical reality of that Spanish world which is contemporary to Cervantes, these are the adventures of Don Quixote at the close of his third and last sally. He travels about the world with the burden of glory which the publication of the first part of his chivalrous exploits has laid on his shoulders. The empiricism of his readers, who are incapable of divesting the metaphorical expression of his language of its material characteristics and therefore, incapable of grasping, in their innermost being, the truth of the act which has lived that expression and has felt it to be completely in keeping with its own being, obtains various results that are all intrinsically contradictory. Don Quixote is sometimes considered a crazy man and sometimes a wise man, sometimes a man who pretends to be crazy and sometimes a perfect simpleton. Nobody succeeds in recognizing in him that universal poetry which is the lyricism of a nature providentially orientated toward the good: a lyricism which is the vibrant life of an act that is always identical to itself in the infinite variety of the explicit historical forms that it has taken. Everybody has grasped the body of pure poetry tightly. Nobody has been able to relive it and recognize it in itself in order to distinguish it then and recognize it in Don Quixote as a universal tendency.

If the first part of the novel is dedicated entirely to the glory of Don Quixote, the second part is the comic epic of Sancho. He has identified the poetic image of Dulcinea with a coarse peasant girl of Toboso; and he deludes himself into believing that he has deceived Don Quixote, and considers himself superior to him. It is the unspeakable glory of Sancho; and it is the comic epic of that empiricism which repeats itself continually through the centuries in all classes of persons, the educated and the uneducated, in men of broad experience and in children who dream with their eyes open. This empiricism seizes hold of the sensible image—which lives lyrically in the spirit of the poet who reads himself into it—and contemplates it from an ideal point of view and transforms it into a real being without becoming aware that it is transforming the poetic act into a fact which, as such, is susceptible to a thousand different interpretations, and all intrinsically subjective. This same irrational empiricism attempts to imprison pure poetry in the fantastic molds in which it has taken historical form with the intention of leading it back to the sources of its inspiration. Violating in this way its nature and depriving it of its ideal independence in relation to all things, empiricism kills pure poetry. The pure poetic irrational cannot be conquered with the weapons of reason. The death of Don Quixote is only the dissolution of a poetic illusion, which is living and real in the mind of Alonso Quijano the Good. It is brought about by the grief which has been caused inadvertently in him by a dear young friend of his, whose mind had been led astray by the aesthetic theories he had learned in the university lecture halls. Sansón Carrasco, the self-confident asserter of Aristotle's *Poetics,* which he took to be a sort of breviary of literary criticism, thought that the true reality of Don Quixote—the reality of pure poetry—was in the chivalric images in which, ideally speaking, it became intelligible to itself. With these same images he succeeds in subduing it. Sansón Carrasco defeats Don Quixote in a chivalrous duel and forces him to return to his village.

But historical life is entirely and solely in its ideal images. When they fade away the poetic irrational sinks into its own certainty and there it attains its own inner truth. Don Quixote dies, and Alonso Quijano the Good is born anew. Thus the triumph of Aristotle's *Poetics* marked the end of the last true medieval novel of chivalry and love.

Now this is the supreme art of a great poet. What Cervantes has universalized in smiling images has repeated itself from century to century. The ideal illusion never fades away on its own empiricism. It has been constantly born anew and will continue to be born anew under new aspects the more criticism loves itself and its own theories rather than serve the truth of the work of art. The *Quixote* has been the touchstone of all systems and all methods of literary analysis. Every reader has made it subservient to his own taste, his own particular sentiment, and his own conception of life and history. He has made it subservient to himself, unconsciously, and has deluded himself into thinking that he knows it to the extent of being able to cast a value judgment on it. In France the gallant seventeenth century dismembered it in order to enjoy its isolated stories. Rationalism, which was applied to art as a poetic ideal, saw no unity in it and interpreted it in a farcical manner. In England the rancor which was directed at Catholic Spain led to the identification of Don Quixote with St. Ignatius Loyola so as to ridicule both one and the other at the same time. Voltairian illuminism discovered in it reason's criticism of ideal values. Rousseauian naturalism wept over the hero, who personifies the good man that is derided by a society that cannot understand him. German romanticism from the Schlegels to Heine romanticized its content and derived logical symbols from it. Documentary historicism, from Herder up to his last followers, broke it up anew in order to derive from it the biographical details of Cervantes' life and the representation of the society that was contemporary to him in the warm atmosphere of southern characters. Erudite positivism poured into it and contemplated its own blithe illusion of an artist without thought who gathers together only empty fantastic molds. Pure aestheticism, which ingenuously puts its trust in the false transparency of images, asserted its own hedonistic subjectivism and made a theory out of it in the name of the unconscious poet who creates without knowing what he is creating. Learned commentators have boasted that it is they who have discovered the great and sublime soul of Don Quixote and have assured his immortality with their for the most part impertinent annotations. Pure erudites have suspected that, in order to identify the hero of the poetic irrational, laborious researches should be inaugurated, not only on historical and literary documents and the criticism of sources, but also and especially on private correspondences and the archives of Esquivias.

We have confined this true history of ideal delusion, which some learned man calls the *fortleben* of a masterpiece, within the space that it deserves: in the notes, specifying from time to time its initial moments and disregarding its echoes. We have not thought it expedient to suppress it altogether, as we had intended, in order not to take away a joy from those who seek and find their prime and vital interest in books only in the notes. They are fortunate in being able to satisfy thus their own meager curiosity. But if we do not penetrate into the vital essence of a work of art and grasp its concrete unity and the poetic reason which gives meaning to everything—to the work of art itself as well as to the person of the poet who has translated into images in it the content of his moral experience— the ideal delusion may be a pretext for interesting theses and monographs, but which are useless as interpretations and explanations of poetry.

Likewise we have relegated to the notes and attacked there the incoherent, disorganic, and punctual interpretations which have become fashionable in recent years particularly in Spain and in France. We find in them a borrowed terminology taken from recent philosophical systems, but devoid of their original value and lacking in speculative interest. If we see the profound transformation that the concepts of mimesis and verisimilitude undergo when Scaliger or Pinciano and then Cervantes are interpreted with the ideas of Aristotle's *Poetics* and not with the Platonic-Augustinian aesthetics which is proper to them, we shall be able to know what Kierkegaard's existential truth, Bergson's *élan vital,* Blondel's *intussusception,* or Gentile's actual idealism can become in the hands of literary men. All of these intellectual positions have been assumed in a frag-mentary way, in good faith, of course, as a foundation for a new and original exegesis of the *Quixote.* But to them has been added the claim of proving by documents that Cervantes did not understand the profound significance of his masterpiece; or, vice versa, a need has been felt to demonstrate his recondite knowledge in order to present a writer who was not devoid of thought, as the positivistic school of criticism had characterized him.

Ideal illusions. They might make us lean toward that exegetic pessimism of which Anatole France once made himself the spokesman in a famous passage. "Si la race future gardait quelque mémoire de notre nom ou de nos écrits, nous pouvons prévoir qu'elle ne goûterait notre pensée que par ce travail ingénieux de faux sens et de contressens, qui seul perpétue les ouvrages du génie à travers les âges. La longue durée des chefs-d'oeuvre n'est assurée qu'au prix d'aventures intellectuelles tout à fait pitoyables, où le coq-à-l'âne des cuistres prête la main au calembour ingénieux des âmes artistes. Je ne crains pas de dire qu'à l'heure qu'il est, nous n'entendons pas un seul vers de l'*Iliade* ou de la *Divine Comédie* dans le sens qui y était attaché primitivement."

The quotation is not inopportune. It serves to present an aspect of a problem that Cervantes poses in an Augustinian manner in the *Quixote.* Here, as we shall see, the exchange of ideas is reduced to an exchange of words, where each one listens only to his own inner voice. Dialogues are always reduced to a series of parallel monologues.

2. CRITICISM AND INTERPRETATION

The *Quixote* has remained an enigma, just as all the literature of the chivalrous and courtly Middle Ages in France has remained an enigma. The latter, also, has always been considered as pure literature. In the uniformity of a content, which was defined as a conventional game, a strict adherence to the ontological articulations of love considered as a metaphysical reality has never been followed. Thus they have also lost sight of the personal variety of the poetic expression as an ideal coherence of images specifying a sentiment that has really been lived and historically conditioned.

The medieval concept of poetry, which was also that of Cervantes and of the authors who wrote in the pastoral genre—and in general, we may add, of the sixteenth-century theorists of poetry—has been explained and illustrated by us in the first volume devoted to the interpretation of the *Galatea* and the *Novelas ejemplares,* which are fragments of the masterpiece. And we refer to it whoever may wish to form an idea which will enable him to penetrate into the inmost meaning of the *Quixote*. It is there that anyone may learn what is this superabundance of love, which finds its imaginative expression in the exploits of the hero. It tells of the spontaneous generosity of the being that gives itself wholly to itself, and perfects itself with its own immanent activity, and loves itself in its own dear images in which it recognizes itself with joy by virtue of ideal principles that are common to all creatures.

This theory of love, justified in itself, and pure poetry that gushes and flows from the depths of the being in the face of the beauty that delights it in its essence, is expounded by Cervantes within the rational fabric of the images out of which his first novel is woven; and he explains it in a didactically clear manner that does not admit any arbitrary interpretations. That theory animates and gives form to his entire production from the *Galatea* to the *Persiles,* from the Comedies to the *Entremeses,* and constitutes the fundamental basis of that Christian realism which, for the great wounded veteran of Lepanto, was a profoundly experienced truth with the sure promises of a sincere faith.

All that was necessary was to recognize this Christian realism of Cervantes and not confuse it with Platonism or Neoplatonism—but for *Quixote* scholars conceptual distinctions have been a bit like the fluttering about of empty words —and the gates of the masterpiece would have opened wide for us. Except that Cervantes does not stop there. The romances of chivalry, like the picaresque novel moreover, were for the most part considered exclusively in their objective content by the masses, both learned and ignorant, by the classical rhetoricians, and by the frowning moralists. But that content was rather their body. It was a body no longer alive in its real life; a body, however, that could once more become spirit for whoever *had lived it and known it* in the very act in which it lived it.

At that time was initiated that material and erudite study of poetry which transformed it into little intellectual curiosities and insignificant things or minutiae. And in the universities, together with the triumph of classicism and the commentaries on Aristotle's *Poetics,* was beginning to take root the method of studying the poetic expression with extrinsically formal or objectively stylistic research. That is the method which will later be transported bodily from classical philology into the field of romance philology with the consequences that Cervantes brings to light in his masterpiece. Because when romance philology, abandoning its own useful and scientifically indispensable work, begins to judge the poetry of the Middle Ages, it falls into empiricism. By adhering strictly to the material images, the metaphors, the pure and simple literary expression, and the empty imaginative molds that have become the terminal object of knowledge, philology cannot understand, through the study of sources sought in Ovid or in Virgil, the rise and progress of a love that enters into the order of divine causality, and whose conception is distinctly Christian.

In the Middle Ages pure love and pure poetry flow from the same source of life. They are the internal superabundance of the being that receives the Sacrament. They are the pure poetic irrational or, in other words, Don Quixote. In the hands of a philologist who is ignorant of the thought of the Middle Ages and preoccupied solely in documenting his own doctrine with a wealth of literary parallels and with the research of extrinsically formal derivations, it is easy to imagine what can become of poetry experienced as goodness, truth, and beauty, as the inmost joy of life and the eternal youth of the spirit. And it is still easier to imagine how dark and opaque becomes the imaginative expression that translates the ineffableness of the poetic act when this act is no longer considered metaphysically and explained morally as an individual relation to God.

For the system of interpretation that, as an essential activity of the spirit, leads back the crystallized word to the intimacy of the poetic act—and grasps the individual history of each poet and the way in which he has lived this history and realized it artistically so as to be able to relive its beauty once again—there have been substituted, on the one hand, the analysis of a content devoid of spirit and, therefore, without any reality whatever, and, on the other, the comparison of literary forms as the object of aesthetics considered as the science of that which has been accomplished, according to ideal and rigidly defined schemes.

By adhering to the temporal and contingent forms of pure sentiment which has historicized itself in the poetic expression according to the vital experience and literary culture of the poet, it is no longer possible to grasp the original activity of a spirit that creates itself by creating a world correlative to itself: the imaginative world of a dream actually lived. Pure poetry immanent in the act of its true infinity—the immanent universal of nature which belongs to all men and to all times, always equal to itself in the variety of its expressions—immediately disappears as soon as its language is accepted as a fact to be explained historically. Read the adventure of Basilio's erudite cousin. He is good man who has written learned monographs and measures himself according to the number of his printed pages; but he is very ingenuous when he materializes a poetic expression, a simple image, and makes of it a historical document. The prologue of the *Quixote,* where with subtle irony Cervantes laments the fact that he cannot enrich his book with dusty marginal citations, finds its best commentary there.

The poetry of the chivalrous Middle Ages (of the troubadours) is solely preoccupied with tracing, by means of images describing individual sentiment, the immanent rationality of love. It introduces us to the articulations of the real, whose ideal articulations are only a means of knowledge and not the end of knowledge. By accepting these last articulations as reality, one falls into empiricism, as Cervantes makes clear, and creates a history understood in the Aristotelian manner. Don Quixote causes us to smile because he mistakes poems of chivalry for history and wishes to make them come true in his experience. But he reënacts the vital act of the poems of chivalry, (that act) which is recognized in its own spiritual images. He relives that same innate love of self, which characterizes its content, as will which has its own specific object: a natural desire to know God and to reintegrate in himself an image of God.

Don Quixote is in the truth that is immanent to his particular life; he is in the truth that is immanent to the perennial process of becoming of human history. He decidedly does not commit the error of abstract historicism: the error of Léon Gautier, who offered his own volumes on romantic chivalry as a historical vision of the Middle Ages, dedicating them to Cervantes, the glorious soldier of Lepanto, and not to Cervantes the author of the *Quixote.* And nevertheless, our hero from La Mancha was more consistent than the learned romance scholar. The latter shed romantic tears over the beautiful age that had set for ever. Don Quixote, instead, wanted to relive it. And through the faith that he had put in the bewitching images of chivalry, which was, moreover, nothing other than the irrational faith that he put in his own sentiment, he lived it with so much constancy and so much ardor that everybody laughed at his insanity.

But if we wish to understand the thought of Cervantes, we must be very careful. All those people were laughing at empty forms, which were seen from without and judged objectively and empirically, without the poetic life of that act with which at one time they had seen them and recognized them as true.

They laughed without returning to that act by means of which they would have known Don Quixote and themselves by distinguishing themselves from him: a pure nature, that is not ennobled by art, which is the generating reason and perfection of love. This reason, which Don Quixote lacks, is lacked also by the empiricism of all those who laugh at him.

Fools! They laughed at Don Quixote without knowing him. And yet he was a creature who lived along with them and who formed part of that infinite reality toward which they should have had a feeling of solidarity. They laughed at mere images, in which they read what they put in of their own, indirectly experiencing through them their own individual sentiment: their own poetic irrational. And they did not know themselves! If they had really loved Don Quixote, they would have understood what that irrational is which belongs to all and none, because all find it within themselves, in their own intimacy, as a life anterior to their life, as an infinite which operates in them even before making itself known for what it is. The irrational of pure poetry which lives in us is that irrational that we must love, in order to know it from within, in us and outside us, in the things which confront us. And only thus does the irrational, as an infinite reason that nestles in the deepest roots of our being, reveal its intelligible mystery.

The fate of the *Quixote* through the centuries is that same history that is adumbrated in the second part of the masterpiece. It is the history of an empirical criticism that has constantly limited itself to the tangible appearances of the artistic representation. For the processes of the real or moral logic immanent in it, it has substituted the processes of abstract logic. The *Quixote*, like all of Medieval literature, like the *Divine Comedy* itself, was taken out of the sphere of reality. The individuality of the hero was no longer considered according to what it is in itself and to what it wants to be in order to realize itself within that historical world, contemporary to Cervantes, which conditions it. It was considered logically under the formal aspect of the order of concepts grasped within the spirit in its march toward the truth.

And here we must understand ourselves.

The aesthetics to which Cervantes adheres we already know from the *Galatea* and the *Novelas ejemplares;* but, having just returned to it in our examination of the *Quixote,* we have fathomed its aspects because we have grasped them under a different color in a new atmosphere. It is the Platonic, Augustinian, and scholastic aesthetics which prevails throughout the Middle Ages up to the late Renaissance. It continues in the first commentators of Aristotle's *Poetics*—if recent scholars have not found it there, it is their fault and due to insufficient preparation—and not until the seventeenth century does it die. This aesthetics calls for the rational immanent in single representations as a truth which evolves and organizes itself autonomously around its own core within the internally woven fabric of the images. Art, according to Pinciano's expression, which Cervantes makes his own, came thus to be *llegado a razón,* adhering to reason, without ever falling into history, which would have been empiricism, and without ever falling into sophistic dialects, which would have been abstract logic. Its basis was metaphysical, but it went beyond metaphysics, because through imagination, *in via inventionis,* it was extended even to what is not.

The reason of which Pinciano and Scaligero speak is not Plato's or Aristotle's ideal or idealizing reason, which stops subjectively at abstract forms, considered in themselves, statically isolated and subtracted from all the positive and qualitative determinations of the sensible. It is reason considered as a distinct faculty, with its own specifying object, capable of drawing upon the real through the screen of abstraction and speech on the basis of a certainty valid for things themselves. By means of interpretation, it grasps them from within, in the vital act from which they emanate and in the intention which keeps them united with one another, and thus succeeding in discovering their organic and concrete unity.

What has happened to the *Quixote* is that which in part has happened and is still happening to the *Divina Commedia.* Every commentator, with his own dialectic ability, feels he has the right to establish symbols, starting from an intuition, to be sure, but also putting aside any rational analysis which would make them manifest and necessary. For a real content they have substituted, without wishing to and in perfect good faith, a logical content that can exist only in the mind of the commentator, who reasons it out and defends it with stubborn sophistry. And the confusion—the reader should recall our quotation from Anatole France—has been disastrous; so much so that a few serious Dantists, in deference to the aesthetics of Benedetto Croce, have declared themselves ready to throw out all symbolism. Precisely what a learned Cervantes scholar, who was however a university professor of metaphysics, had said concerning the *Quixote.* And he certainly must have been well acquainted with metaphysics.

Now the history of Don Quixote, interpreted by leading the external to the internal, is the history of the rational immanent in real love; immanent in all the creations of that pure poetry that lives and subsists in man. And it is a rational that man can succeed in knowing when he is able to realize it in himself through action and in knowing it again in others also with that art which is proper to him: with the art of a reason which finds in itself its own absolute criterion of judgment.

Therefore, the interpretation which we present proposes to demonstrate no particular or subjective thesis; it does not pretend in any way to document any new and original discovery; it does not even attempt to convince anybody in the remotest way. It simply wishes to enable any reader to understand a masterpiece and to relive in himself the thought that Cervantes has concretized in imaginative form. Our interpretation rests completely on the rational fabric of a series of representations, each one of which is intelligible in itself according to a truth that belongs to everybody because it is the truth of an absolute reason. And anyone can make it his own precisely, as Cervantes declared, according to his capacity of the moment, according to the clarity of his intelligence accustomed to the habit of reason, according to the joy of a moral experience not theorized in abstract, not ideally enjoyed, but actually lived and, therefore, known through action, and loved and willed.

3. THE OCCASIONAL THEME OF THE "QUIXOTE"

In its remotest and occasional conception Cervantes' masterpiece is derived from the first skirmishes which occurred in Spain in the latter part of the sixteenth century between the followers of the Platonic, Augustinian, and scholastic aesthetics and the fervent and intransigent commentators of Aristotle's *Poetics*. Actually the disputes between the innovators and the traditionalists had begun in the field of lyric poetry when the works of Garcilaso and Boscán first appeared; but at the time of Cervantes they had been stirred up again through the very effective aid of a text that transformed them into a struggle of ideas. The old literary production was passed in review by these innovators with that intellectual haughtiness which leads to scoffing and irony, to abstract dogmatism and the poison of severe and bitter criticism.

The *Quixote* is a work of living and urgent actuality. The cultural background, in which it must be placed in order to be understood in its varied and complex humanity, reveals it to us not as the idle pastime of an artist nor as the romantic dream of a poet who goes into voluntary exile from history. At the very outset, and even before we are aware of it, Cervantes plunges us into that movement of thought which was an energetic defense of the national literature, in that which was most characteristic and most deeply rooted in the Spanish soul and, we may say it without hesitation, most typically medieval.

The publication of the *Quixote* (1605) is posterior to the *Filosofía antigua poética* (1595) of Alonso López el Pinciano and precedes the *Exemplar poética* (1606) of Juan de la Cueva and *El arte nuevo de hacer comedias* (1609) of Lope de Vega. But Cervantes goes much beyond all of these. In their aesthetics they indirectly theorized their own literary production and justified it, defending themselves to a certain extent. Cervantes does indeed confirm the direction to which he had adhered in his previous work in the theatre and the novel, but he rises to a general vision of reality, to a religious sense of concrete life, and to an organic and universal interpretation of history.

The disputes which had at that time arisen in Spain were the same ones that were already raging in Italy, and which from there had spread to France and England. Extreme traditionalism and extreme innovation. Immutability or mobility. A rigidifying of theoretic positions with a corresponding losing sight of the sense of the relative, which, in the final analysis, is the sense of the absolute which lives in us and with us in order to lead us more and more beyond ourselves and raise us more and more above ourselves.

Those disputes, in which certain people persisted in doggedly attacking others, were becoming increasingly bitter and violent. From the heights of his thought Cervantes contemplated them and resolved them in the world of contingent things. They were fruits of every season because they ripen continually on the same tree of human history. Things that belong to all times and to all countries, even before the rise of these deluded souls who were then banding together in secret societies and forming themselves into Academies. Even before the appearance of poisonous pamphlets and vain logomachies, and reviews with fixed programs, and the methods journals which campaign only for the method which they set up. But all of them, always and without a single exception, are poetically animated by the love of truth and by the desire of dominating the fluid reality of history and of impressing upon it a new and original seal.

As a consummate artist who grasps the universal in the particular, Cervantes concretizes in the fable of Don Quixote a literary and philosophical dispute which presented itself as being pregnant with consequences. Cervantes intuited them clearly. They hid themselves in the Aristotelian distinction between poetic universal and historical particular. Through this distinction was obscured little by little that sense of the irreversible becoming of history, of the movement and the development of the world in the sense of time which had until then been the most beautiful and fertile heritage of Augustinian thought. Through it the Middle Ages appeared to be estranged from the modern age, becoming the open field of all the dusty and minute looting expeditions of seventeenth-century erudition. Because of it that real and concrete poetic universal, which was common to all of medieval poetry, came to be sacrificed, even though it did not succeed in idealizing it in the contingent and historically determined forms of classical poetry, which the Renaissance had exalted to the position of unsurpassed and unsurpassable model.

At bottom, as Cervantes brilliantly understood and emphasized (*Quixote*, II, 3; RM., IV, p. 79 *et seq.*), the commentators of Aristotle's *Poetics* exerted themselves in discussing the ideal truth of art, neglecting to illuminate the term which is correlative to it: history. They spoke of the illustrious and very illustrious character, the lord of history; but they forgot that this character is such precisely because he lives in history, and is so deeply rooted in it that he appropriates for his own its tendencies and aspirations. The poetic universal defended by the infatuated Aristotelians as an individual and ideal expression, as an adequate representation of life and of its eternal essence, is an abstract universal. It is something absolute and definitive which, like *Don Quixote,* does not owe anything to anybody and everything only to itself. It is something that is superimposed on history, as an ideal truth, which is only to be thought statically and to be contemplated, like a refulgent light that is projected on the scattered and accidental plurality of things, on which man must also live in so far as he is immersed in the current of history. And Don Quixote, in order to live and really know this ideal truth, arms himself as knight-errant and advances on the stage of history.

Cervantes transports us thus, immediately, into the realm of that symbolic art which carries, locked in its own breast, the sense of real life. At the extreme confines of Cervantes' inspiration, there where the poet speaks only with himself, are the lights which irradiate the imaginative forest of his novel. On the basis of a keen aesthetic emotion, these lights lead us to everything which is beyond pure images. The fable of Don Quixote is only a means, just as the fable of Dante the pilgrim in the realms of the dead is only a means. The nimble imagination of the child who finds delight in beautiful representations can be estranged from the true reality which renders them intelligible in themselves made to pursue vain appearances. The abstract intelligence of the commentator, armed with a learning which is dear to him, can transcend the sensible representation and organize in his own brain some logical symbols. Truth is neither the former nor the latter. The fable of Don Quixote, devoid as it is of any general and idealological formula, is only a means to lead us into that moral reality that we are and wish to be, into a world that historically conditions our life and our existence.

The occasional theme of the *History of Don Quixote*—which is none other than the historical and contingent aspect under which the problem of life presents itself to a "hidalgo ingenioso" of La Mancha contemporary to Cervantes —is more or less that same theme that was debated in Italy on the subject of Ariosto's poem, and which had been stirred up in a desperate manner, in the concreteness of a particular case, on the subject of Tasso's *Gerusalemme Liberata.* The aesthetics which was being elaborated, especially in the great university centers, posited its rigid distinctions, its fixed and immutable precepts, and its conventional categorical imperatives. Ideal poetic beauty was set up in opposition to documentary truth, the universal of art to the particular of history; and in art was sought either pure aesthetic pleasure or moral interest.

It is well to bear in mind that in the *Quixote* the priest, who stands for the particular truth of history is a graduate of Siguenza, the bachelor Sansón Carrasco, who demands the ideal truth of art, has a diploma from Salamanca, that Lorenzo de Miranda, who wants to adhere closely to dialectic logic, is a student of theology. Furthermore, it must be noted that the chaplain of the Dukes derives morality from the romances of chivalry, the erudite cousin of Basilio takes poetic images as historical documents, several noble lords of high society taste their delightful aestheticism by transforming the eclogues of Garcilaso and Camoëns into pastoral adventure, and Sancho insistently demands from pure poetry that material truth which is to satisfy the impulses of his appetite.

Art, therefore, according to the new aesthetics, was an idealization of empirical reality intelligently purified and withdrawn from the mobile flux of things. History, on the other hand, was documentary truth painfully verified with the criticism of all sources in order to put it back into the realm of pure contingency. But then, in which of the two categories was to be and could be placed the romance of chivalry, of which Aristotle does not speak (*Quixote*, Prólogo; RM., I, p. 42)? The new rhetoricians observe that it is not art because it was abstracted from that empirical reality that had to be idealized. But neither was it history, because it was a work of pure imagination. And yet, the romance of chivalry lived within history, since everybody read it, especially the uncultured classes, which constitute the living universality of history.

The critical realism of Cervantes is all here: always ready to justify not only the ideation of the novel, but also the constant search for an analogy between the inner life of the two protagonists and that of the other characters who live, along with them, in the history of the Spanish sixteenth century. Cervantes must by no means be confused with the contemporary Italian or French rhetoricians; a thing which attracted a few superficial and easily satisfied scholars. His realism does not in the least depart from the intelligible necessities that regulate the historical development of thought and art. The romance of chivalry really existed, observed the rhetoricians; it did indeed exist, but it was the hybrid monster of a defunct age. It was a late shoot of that medieval barbarism that was to be definitively eliminated from history in the name of the ideal beauty of art.

This is a typically idealistic position. It started out from the thought rather than from the thing. In the place of an incontestable reality it substituted abstract idols, which were its counterfeit coin. Cervantes gives us its subject in the person of the Canon of Toledo, who discourses magnificently on art and poetry, but refuses to write what should be, according to him, the model romance of chivalry. That is the basic difficulty or weakness of idealism, which does not know how to pass from criticism to positive construction. Those who review other peoples' books all belong to this league, always feeling secure from the ideal heights of their journals.

The rhetoric of the dramatic unities and of the *simplex et unum* of the poem was rising together with this idealistic and pseudo-Aristotelian criticism. The rhetoric of styles according to the literary *genres* and the rigorous distinction between prose and poetry was rising. Criticism, according to preconceived molds, was being brought to bear exclusively on the work of art as an object to be judged, disregarding that more lively and intimate reality that is the humanity of the artist. They disregarded precisely the person who, following his own natural inspiration and dominating it intellectually, had conferred upon it an autonomous existence. He alone had loved himself in his own creature and had made of it an individuality harmonious in itself and enclosed within itself: spiritual life of his deepest life which had manifested itself by organizing itself spontaneously on itself: intelligible truth and splendor of being within a sensible fulguration of beauty.

Criticism was orientating itself toward those forms of individualistic absolutism which leads to dogmatic contrasts of ideas, to mutual incomprehension, and to intolerant judgments. And in the meantime were beginning those academic lectures in which everybody felt himself to be the repository of truth; and everybody sought to impose that truth, born from a closed concentration within oneself, either with the prestige of a long gown of some sort or with the summary conclusions of absolution or condemnation. The polemics of that time, always harsh, violent, and malicious, document it openly; and not only in Spain.

The human subject matter of the *Quixote* is already all here, presented objectively and in foreshortening. Cervantes, therefore, seizes the idea of writing a perfect romance of chivalry (*Quixote,* I, 52; RM., III, p. 476 *seq.*), in which will be observed the rule of mimesis (*Quixote,* Prólogo; RM., I, p. 43), as the imitation, by means of expression, of a form in the metaphysical sense of the word. He adheres completely to the norms of medieval aesthetics, actualized in the poems of Chrétien de Troyes and in the prose compilations of *Lancelot of the Lake* and the *Queste del Saint Graal.* This perfect romance of chivalry which Cervantes composes is the poetic dream, but which is actually lived, within the society of the Spanish sixteenth century, by an "ingenioso hidalgo," whom everybody judges to be an insane man.

Actually Cervantes becomes the historian and poet of a contemporary of his: Alonso Quijano the Good. The latter feels an urge to satisfy an inner desire for happiness. And he dubs himself Don Quixote, and he acts with the weapons of ancient knight-errantry in the living reality of history. The secret of Don Quixote, that which constitutes in him the presence of an intelligible and operating mystery, is the real and dialectic inspiration of a love which, as a universal of metaphysical nature, vibrates in an ineffably personal way in the heart of every man. The secret of Don Quixote is an anxious, unexhausted, and inexhaustible longing for transcendental knowledge: immanent action of thought and love: actuality and perfection of his own being as truth, goodness, and beauty.

Thus the History of Don Quixote reduces itself to the history of an individual whose intimate life is relived by Cervantes by following the real articulations of that love which inspires him. The line of these internal formal determinations is ideally reflected in the images in which Don Quixote recognizes himself from time to time. And these individuate the activity of the hero in the bosom of that universal reality which conditions his existence and within the particular history in which, as will, he asserts himself and develops.

But then, the history in its secret principle and its profound truth reduces itself to the history of that poetic irrational which is spiritually always identical to itself in the variety of the thousand individual expressions, and all historically determined, in which it is actualized. And the truth of the history is precisely that which has no history, but which becomes history only in so far as it is the continuous poetic creation of every individual with that art of which he is capable.

The true history is the life that each individual realizes. It is that life which can belong to a man who lived a thousand or two thousand years ago: a life that can always become our own personal life if we succeed in transferring ourselves spiritually into it and recognizing its inner beauty. And all of history in its irreversible course transforms itself into history of art: into the history of the infinite and individual realizations of beauty whose historical and contingent dress is only its external aspect. The stuffed Aristotelianism of the new rhetoricians and the sapient commentators of the *Poetics* is thus routed decisively with the benevolent irony of a smile.

On the subject of the romance of chivalry that Alonso Quijano, under the name of Don Quixote, writes with his own actions in the last years of the sixteenth century, all are laboring to prove what it is not or what, according to them, it should be in order to become a perfect novel. All would like Don Quixote not to be Don Quixote, but that other individual that everybody dreams he should be in order to satisfy in every way the individual exigencies of one's own poetic irrational. And they do not perceive that they no longer desire the romance of chivalry as it stands before them in its closed individuality, but another romance, which might satisfy, so far as subject matter is concerned, a new historical sensitivity. Since what varies in time is not the poetry which subsists in man. This is always equal to itself in the multiple plurality of the expressions in which it actualizes itself historically. The only thing that varies is the technique of art. And this does not have fixed rules and clearly labeled molds. It is born from every single experience, progresses with this same experience in order to become an operative habit in the vital and spiritual state. The same poetic reason that creates history is that which creates the work of art. And it also creates the criticism of a work of art without there being an absolute method. Truth belongs to all those who know how to live it from within and make it their own spiritual life. Actually it does not belong to anybody.

Every work of art is an individual and original creation of beauty which is truth. And to wish to judge it independently of the poetic reason which informs it is to be lacking in meaning. This poetic reason was immanent in the love of that particular beauty that inspired the artist, guiding him and supporting him *cum delectatione,* with disinterested contemplation, in every moment of its construction. To wish it to be different from what it actually is by failing to take into account the person who has created it as the life of his own sentiment and of his own intelligence, to judge it according to what it should or could have been, in order to satisfy our theoretic and practical preoccupations, is pure illusion. The concrete in criticism is love and intelligence of the individual that has been realized in sensible form as love and as intelligence. Outside of this concreteness, criticism is reduced to empty verbal formulas or to that pure subjectivity that contemplates and loves only itself in the object.

The art of the romance of chivalry, of which the history of Don Quixote is only an example perfect in itself, rests entirely on the pure poetic irrational; in the same way as the adventures and misfortunes of Sancho are patterned on the art of the picaresque novel, which is based on the instinctive irrational. The commentators of Aristotle's *Poetics,* with their theory of art idealizing reality according to fixed rules and conventional preconceptions, would have claimed the right to eliminate the two irrationals of nature from history. But both one and the other were alive in them in the very act which denied them. And all the more alive, the more they labored to deny the reality of an art whose original beauty they were incapable of reliving from within.

Looked at from this vantage point, which carries into the foreground the problems of nature, skill and art, the problems of history and poetry, the problems of poetic reason, in the order of acting as well as in the order of doing, and the problems of literary criticism and interpretative analysis, the content of the *Quixote* gives us the measure of Cervantes' mind and helps us to distinguish him from his great contemporary Lope de Vega.

A lyrical, passionate, and violent temperament in the face of the exigencies, the criticisms, and the vain claims of the rhetoricians and innovators, Lope claimed to be indifferent to all the rules when he wrote under the goad of his inspiration. The artist vindicated his full liberty when he created. And he made a personal issue out of it. Cervantes, on the other hand, transforms a contingent fact into a symbol, and it becomes the theme of illusion and reality. With the proud and clear intuition of a great artist, tested and tried by misfortunes and edified by a long experience, Cervantes grasps and represents in its vital elements that which was a sterile struggle of academic pedants or blind traditionalists—both frozen in their theoretic positions. He counter-balances Greek abstract idealism with Christian concrete realism.

Cervantes knows that the art, the criticism, and the aesthetics which we really know are only the art, the criticism, and the aesthetics which we practice. For him the notorious problems of critical method did not yet exist. If a work of beauty is conditioned by the artificer who has spontaneously placed it in the world of existence, it is not possible to judge its art except by means of the poetic reason which is immanent in it. True criticism is that alone which rests on interpretation. And in fact, only then, through aesthetic feeling, does the critic succeed in identifying himself with the object he knows and in reliving its poetic reason in order then to come back to *otherness* and distinction, without which it is not possible to give a value judgment. Where there is the individual there is no other way out. And one must travel on this road to the very end.

But Cervantes also knows that beauty belongs to the transcendental and metaphysical order, and that its value is analogical, since it can be grasped under different aspects which some discover and others do not. The only thing which he cared about in writing the history of Don Quixote was that his work should turn out to be beautiful. He left it to each reader, boy or young man, business man or one already advanced in years, to read in it what he knows and is in a position to read in it according to his capacity of the moment, according to the maturity of his intelligence or of his judgment, or according to his personal experience of life and of art.

(Translated by Joseph De Simone)

PART THREE

PART THREE

"Don Quixote" and "Moby Dick"

HARRY LEVIN

THE profoundest tribute to Cervantes is that which other writers have paid him by imitation and emulation. It goes too deep to be altogether reducible to terms of conscious literary influence; it springs from the almost Homeric circumstances that made him the first to master a *genre* which —through that very process of mastery—has come to predominate in modern literature. *Don Quixote* is thus an archetype as well as an example, the exemplary novel of all time. Not only has its characterization invited an endless round of sequels, from Avellaneda to Kafka, but its conception has enabled later novelists to unfix a whole series of preconceived ideas, with consequences that range from *Candide* to *War and Peace*. Each of the major European cultures, it may be said, has provided characteristic variations on the theme of Quixotry, *mutatis mutandis* adapting itself to the uses of French realism, British humor, German metaphysics, or even the exploration of the Russian soul. Scholars and critics have traced this chronicle of adaptation in fascinating detail. We must not infer, from the fact that Don Quixote's adventures in North America are still untraced, that Cervantes was unimitated or unemulated here.

That story would begin, if we sought to recount it, when the translations of Jervas, Smollett, and others were imported along with the eighteenth-century English novel. The most significant early product of this cross-fertilization would be H. H. Brackenridge's *Modern Chivalry,* which first appeared in 1792. Not feudal but democratic institutions are there subjected to a genial criticism which, in some respects, anticipates Tocqueville. The chivalrous figure of Captain Farrago, a whimsical observer of human nature, is gradually eclipsed by the political career of his servant, the Irish bog-trotter, Teague O'Regan. Perhaps it would be self-explanatory to mention—along with the name of the author, Tabitha Tenney—the title of her book: *Female Quixotism, Exhibited in the Romantic Opinions and Extravagant Adventures of Dorcasina Sheldon.* This cautionary tale of an incorrigibly susceptible spinster, written in 1800, lacks the animation of its English forerunner, *The Female Quixote* by Charlotte Lennox, who coincidentally had been born in this country. With Washington Irving's

Knickerbocker History of New York, we should come much closer to the main-stream of American letters. Irving, like his Peter Stuyvesant, "had studied for years in the chivalric library of Don Quixote."[1] Among his later projects, for which he gathered documents, was a life of Cervantes. His interest in everything Spanish would be matched on more academic levels by the work of Ticknor, Prescott, and Longfellow.

At first glance it might seem that a culture which prided itself upon being so matter-of-fact and getting so close to nature would spontaneously express itself in realism and naturalism. Yet our greatest writers functioned in the atmosphere of romanticism. The enchantments of the Gothic, rather than the disenchant-ments of the picaresque, enlisted the genius of Poe. Hawthorne, who had encouraged his sister to translate Cervantes' *Exemplary Novels,* eschewed the contemporary form of the novel for his own particular version of the romance—for a tradition of fiction, half didactic and half poetic, which he had derived from the religious allegory and the philosophical tale. In weighing the claims of the present against those of the past, *The House of the Seven Gables,* like many of his stories, gives a New England inflection to the argument of Cervantes' anti-romance. But the resolution of *The Marble Faun* is predicated upon a nostalgic return to the storied ruins of the old world. Following Haw-thorne's footsteps, and writing his biography, Henry James lamented the numer-ous ivy-covered items of high civilization that were so conspicuous by their absence from the American scene. Though James's passionate pilgrims seem Quixotic rather than Cervantesque, it is the intrusion of mundane realities upon their personal idealisms that constitutes the drama of their lives.

The opposite point of view, the new world's critique of Europe, is bumptiously personified by Mark Twain's *Innocents Abroad.* His tirade on "Castles and Culture" in *Life on the Mississippi* attacked the nineteenth-century revival of medieval architecture, and deplored the debilitating influence of Sir Walter Scott upon the South. His *Connecticut Yankee in King Arthur's Court,* designed as a stream-lined revision of *Don Quixote,* today appears more dated than its model.[2] It is noteworthy, however, that when a school of American naturalists finally arose, their leader turned out to be a lifelong admirer of Cervantes. W. D. Howells has left a memorable description of how, as a boy on a farm in Ohio, he was originally affected by the narrative of the ingenious *hidalgo.* "I believe that its free and simple design, where event follows event without the fettering control of intrigue, but where all grows naturally out of character and conditions, is the supreme form of fiction," Howells adds, "and I cannot help thinking that if we ever have a great American novel, it must be built upon such large and noble lines."[3] A recent critic and novelist, Edward Dahlberg, has reaffirmed this belief; but it is precisely the effort to transcend a photographic naturalism, to visualize an enchanted helmet in a barber's basin, that he calls upon his contemporaries to make.[4]

It is not so much the letter as the spirit of Cervantes that the critical realists of our own period call to mind. If the mock-heroine of Sinclair Lewis' *Main Street* recoils before the drabness of Gopher Prairie, she has a more immediate exemplar in Flaubert's female Quixote, Emma Bovary, dreaming at Yonville-l'Abbaye. James Farrell's anti-hero, Studs Lonigan, may not be a studious admirer of Amadís de Gaula; but the movies and tabloids have colored his fantasies to the point where all experience is a grim disillusionment. The mood of *desengaño* has seldom been probed more desperately than in the train of novels that followed the first World War: Ernest Hemingway's embittered account of the retreat from Caporetto, for example, ends by questioning all such abstract words as "glory" and "honor," and by accepting only place-names and concrete numbers. Nowhere is there a greater disparity than in America, Jean-Paul Sartre has recently observed, "between men and myths, real life and the collective representation of it."[5] Hence the formula that Cervantes discovered is peculiarly applicable. In a broader sense, the arid region of La Mancha is timeless and placeless. It bears a striking resemblance to that expatriate wasteland which T. S. Eliot invokes, ever awaiting its wounded hero whose quest is the promise of ultimate fertility.

No American author, however, can more fitly be compared with Cervantes than Herman Melville. The harsh schools in which the two men educated themselves were immeasurably far apart: a whaling ship, Melville boasted, was both Yale and Harvard to him. Yet a sailor in the South Sea islands may learn, even as a soldier in Algerian captivity, to make life itself a commentary on book-learning. Melville's sea-faring bookishness possessed the measurable advantage of also including *Don Quixote* within its ken. He has not registered for us, as Howells did, the actual impact of discovery; but *White Jacket,* published in 1850, describes a Quixotic shipmate who read the book and only became more confirmed in his native Quixotism.[6] The autobiographical hero of *Redburn,* published in 1849, runs truer to type; the young American's expectations of Europe, nourished upon a quaint old guide-book, are undeceived by the slums of Liverpool. In the same year Melville bought a copy of *Guzmán de Alfarache;* again, the following year, he borrowed *Lazarillo de Tormes;* he had previously demonstrated his acquaintance with Smollett and other English masters of the picaresque.[7]

At London, in December, 1849, while arranging for the publication of *White Jacket,* he picked up the Second Folio of Beaumont and Fletcher. According to the flyleaf, he spent New Year's Day, 1850, at sea; his homeward journey was lightened by reading these plays, several of which draw their plots or characters from Cervantes. To judge from his markings, he was particularly interested in *The Knight of the Burning Pestle,* which closely parallels the situation of *Don Quixote.* "A hit at Shakespeare in Hotspur" he notes in the margin, where the grocer's apprentice parodies the famous speech on honor, thereby bracketing two Elizabethan plays in which the chivalric way of life conflicts with more bourgeois standards of comfort and common sense.[8] It is worth the trouble of gathering up these stray indications, because Melville was to spend the next year in the composition of *Moby-Dick;* and though his masterpiece—as we shall find —attests his profound admiration for Cervantes explicitly as well as implicitly, the *Don Quixote* that survived in Melville's library was not actually printed until two years after *Moby-Dick.* "H. Melville, Sep. 18. '55" is pencilled in his own hand on the *verso* of the flyleaf to the first volume.[9] Pencillings throughout the two volumes seem to indicate that Melville, having purchased this new edition, gave the novel a careful rereading shortly thereafter.

A comprehensive study of Melville's reading would reveal much about his writing, and even more about his thinking, especially during that later period when he seldom put his thoughts into his own words. He used his books as journals, choosing minds that reflected his own, and bringing out—by a sequence of annotations, underscorings, and checks—the latently Melvillian aspect of whatever he read. Such marks, in his *Don Quixote,* are frequent and consistent. Some of them seem to be merely guideposts: notable chapters checked against the table of contents. Again, the backleaf of the second volume contains a list of references to the Cid Hamet; the man that spoke through Ishmael evidently had a special interest in Cervantes' Arabic narrator. But he was more interested, as marginal lines make clear, in discussions of knight-errantry. Agreeing with the humanitarian school of commentators, he emphatically approves of a sentence in Louis Viardot's introductory memoir: "Don Quixote is but the case of a man of diseased brain; his monomania is that of a good man who revolts at injustice, and who would exalt virtue."[10] The object and inspiration of his quest, the fair Dulcinea, is often signalized by Melville's pencil. Her knight's defense of courtly love prompts Melville to append his most revealing note: " 'I have already often said it, and now repeat it, that a knight-errant without a mistress is like a tree without leaves, a building without cement, a shadow without a body that causes it.' "*

> *or as Confucius said 'a dog without a master,'
> or, to drop both Cervantes & Confucius para-
> bles—a god-like mind without a God.[11]

Thus the significance of Cervantes' absent heroine is momentarily transposed into Melville's key; she is the symbol of an elusive faith. And if she incarnates— or rather etherealizes—womanhood for Don Quixote, his relationship with his fellow men is symbolized in the person of Sancho Panza. From the initial pun on *hombre de bien,* which Jervas translates "an honest man (if such an epithet may be given to one that is poor)," Melville gives the squire his most serious regard.[12] The social theme, even more than the philosophical, is the *leitmotif* he seems most anxious to score. Though he stresses democratic implications more heavily than his text may warrant, it must be admitted that Cervantes has furnished him with congenial passages on the dangers of authority and the blessings of liberty.[13] With Don Quixote himself, Melville justifies the liberation of the convicts bound for the galleys, and sympathizes with the impoverished suitor at Camacho's wedding.[14] He is impressed by the Spanish proverb, if not by Sancho's application: "'There are but two families in the world, as my grandmother used to say, the *haves* and the *have nots,* and she stuck to the former.'"[15] To this the sadder and wiser Sancho of the Second Part, on attaining his governorship, supplies a retort which Melville has also checked: "'. . . while we are asleep, the great and the small, the poor and the rich, are all equal.'"[16] Equality and love—the two themes blend in the meal with the goatherds that evokes Don Quixote's vision of the Golden Age. A double line marks Melville's enthusiasm for the knight's invitation to the squire:

> "That you may see, Sancho, the intrinsic worth of knight-erranty [*sic*], and how fair a prospect its meanest retainers have of speedily gaining the respect and esteem of the world, I will that you sit here by my side, in company with these good folks, and that you be one and the same thing with me, who am your master and natural lord; that you eat from off my plate, and drink of the same cup in which I drink; for the same may be said of knight-erranty, which is said of love, that it makes all things equal."[17]

The light in which Melville must have reread Cervantes is caught in the introductory sketch of *The Piazza Tales,* where the enchantments of the Berkshire landscape remind him of "Don Quixote, that sagest sage that ever lived."[18] By the end of that year, 1856, he had embarked upon a Mediterranean voyage, which was to stimulate further reminiscences: "At noon, off Algiers. In the vicinity beautiful residence among the hills. White house among gardens. Reminded one of passages in Don Quixotte [*sic*], 'Story of the Morisco.'"[19] This episode—with the one that comes closest to Cervantes' own adventures, "The Captive's Story"—must have furnished more than a hint for Melville's powerful tale of a Spanish captain and a slave mutiny, *Benito Cereno,* with its atmospheric tension of mingled races and its sense of grim realities smouldering beneath romantic surfaces. But the greatest fiction is never an escape; it is a means of apprehending "more reality than real life itself can show," as Melville argued in the last novel he published, *The Confidence Man,* which had just appeared when he returned to America in 1857.[20] The truly original characters of literature, for him, are as rare and impressive as revolutionary philosophers or religious prophets. They illuminate everything around them "so that, in certain minds, there follows upon the adequate conception of such a character, an effect, in its way, akin to that which in Genesis attends upon the beginnings of things."[21] Each of the three examples that Melville mentions—Hamlet, Don Quixote, and Milton's Satan—had such an effect, a creative impact, upon his own conceptions.

Melville's comments on *Don Quixote,* then, display a set of attitudes which he himself had crystallized five years before in *Moby-Dick*: a questioning of the nature of reality and an affirmation of the brotherhood of man. Nor can it be doubted that previous acquaintance with Cervantes' seminal work had suggested some of the technical features of his own. In its picaresque structure he found that free and simple design which—according to Howells—would characterize the great American novel. The course set by the Pequod, sailing across the high seas, continues and enlarges the pilgrimage of Rocinante, ambling along the highroads of La Mancha. The large, loose plot is integrated again by a single character: a monomaniac protagonist who, by dominating all that surrounds him, fulfills Melville's definition of literary originality. And though his style shows a temperamental affinity, rather than any specific indebtedness, to the prose of the Castilian master, yet each achieves a richness of texture unique in its respective language by ranging freely from salty colloquialism to empurpled rhetoric. A comparison between Américo Castro's *Pensamiento de Cervantes* and the chapters on Melville in F. O. Matthiessen's *American Renaissance* would find further analogies in the eclectic and independent use to which both novelists put the body of tradition that lay behind them.

No two novels would satisfy, better than *Don Quixote* and *Moby-Dick,* the Canon of Toledo's criteria for an epic in prose. Yet *Don Quixote* is a mock-epic, as well as an anti-romance: its Homeric catalogue introduces an army of sheep. Whereas the purpose of *Moby-Dick* is to cast a romantic and heroic glow over its subject: not to exorcise demons but to conjure them up, to speak of the Captain's mess as if it were Belshazzar's feast. For the later book, as for the earlier one, the point of departure is a library; a host of quotations on cetology, compiled by a sub-sub-librarian, replaces the authorities on chivalry; and whales are classified bibliographically in terms of folios, octavos, and duodecimos. On behalf of "the honor and glory of whaling" Melville stands ever ready to break a lance, split a helmet, and unhorse the gentle reader; he even undertakes to prove that whalemen liberated South America "from the yoke of old Spain."[22] The doubloon nailed to the mast, "so Spanishly poetic," is transmogrified like the Helmet of Mambrino, while the Whiteness of the Whale signifies all things to all men.[23] Where Cervantes undermines romance with realism, Melville lures us from a literal to a symbolic plane, turning nautical yarns into metaphysical flights and offering us "the Phaedon instead of Bowditch."[24] His savage and sordid crew, under the influence of their phantom quarry, come to show "a certain generous knight-errantism," not unlike the Crusaders of old.[25]

> If, then to meanest mariners, and renegades and castaways, I shall hereafter ascribe high qualities, though dark; wave round them tragic graces; if even the most mournful, perchance the most abased, among them all, shall at times lift himself to the exalted mounts; if I shall touch that workman's arm with some ethereal light; if I shall spread a rainbow over his disastrous set of sun; then against all mortal critics bear me out in it, thou just Spirit of Equality, which hast spread one royal mantle of humanity over all my kind! Bear me out in it, thou great democratic God! who didst not refuse to the swart convict, Bunyan, the pale, poetic pearl; Thou who didst clothe with doubly hammered leaves of finest gold, the stumped and paupered arm of old Cervantes; Thou who didst pick up Andrew Jackson from the pebbles; who didst hurl him upon a war-horse; who didst thunder him higher than a throne! Thou who, in all Thy mighty, earthly marchings, ever cullest Thy selectest champions from the kingly commons; bear me out in it, O God![26]

The credo here enunciated is Melville's religious belief in democracy itself, in the dignity of labor and the potentialities of every man to be president, genius, or hero. Hereupon the outcast narrator, Ishmael, proceeds from his "knights" to his "squires," from the mates to the harpooneers and finally the common seamen. Most of them, he tells us, are islanders, "each Isolato living on a separate continent of his own," and yet their individualistic energies are harnessed by the Pequod, "federated along one keel."[27] The plight of the drowning castaway, described in Father Mapple's sermon on Jonah, conveys a terrifying sense of isolation. The same object-lesson was preached, in benignly classical rather than sternly biblical terms, with Don Quixote's apostrophe to the Golden Age: that primitive community where men lived happily together without owning property or waging war. When Sancho Panza became Governor of Barataria, he attempted to practice his master's preaching, and adumbrated the tragi-comic pattern of democratic action. It is not without significance that his so-called island was actually a part of the mainland. His Melvillian counterpart is the harpooneer Queequeg, whose companionship resolves Ishmael's dilemma between society and solitude. Queequeg, a "George Washington cannibalistically developed," embodies the human condition as Melville had glimpsed it in *Typee* and *Omoo*: the peace and joy of "one insular Tahiti" which lies in the soul of man.[28] That Queequeg's canoe, designed as a coffin, should be Ishmael's life-buoy when the others meet death by water, is Melville's final paradox on life-in-death.

Cervantes, the realist, dissolved Don Quixotes' fantasies in the bright light of the comic spirit; only the ambiguous Cavern of Montesinos left any room for illusion. For Melville, the idealist, visible objects are "pasteboard masks," and the tragedy is that man—in striking through them—fails to apprehend the mysteries they prefigure.[29] For Captain Ahab, the White Whale is "the mono-maniac incarnation of all those malicious agencies which some deep men feel eating in them," all too tangibly evil in contradistinction to the evanescent good-ness of Dulcinea.[30] His mania fills him with a Quixotic consciousness of his mission: "I am the Fates' lieutenant. I act under orders."[31] But if he can say, "my means are sane, my motive and object mad," the exact opposite may be said of Don Quixote, whose motives are admirable.[32] Neither is destined, like Bunyan's pilgrim, to attain his object: one, unhorsed, is trundled away in a cage, while the other, "dismasted," rages in a straitjacket. The fatal pride, the "irre-sistible dictatorship," the sinister hints thrown out—"that deadly scrimmage with the Spaniard afore the altar at Santa"—these tragic faults could be summed up in a Cervantesque epithet, *el curioso impertinente*.[33] To make Don Quixote the butt of their jests, the others were always play-acting; to consecrate his ill-fated harpoon, Ahab stages a solemn drama; he enacts the rôle of Shakespeare's king, in whose madness Melville detected the voice of truth.[34] The sphinx-like heads of whales are Platonic and Kantian; the waves are Cartesian, the elements Spinozistic; but none of these natural philosophers will satisfy Ahab's doubts. To the end he is "a grand, ungodly, godlike man"—and afterwards his author will observe that a knight without a mistress resembles "a god-like mind without a god."[35]

The relation of *Moby-Dick* to *Don Quixote* is neither close nor similar; it is complementary and dialectical. One proposes worldly wisdom as the touchstone for an outworn set of ideals; the other, abandoning economic values, goes questing after a transcendental faith. Where Cervantes, whose skepticism was less fundamental, objectively jested at social inequalities, the failure of Melville's subjective idealism threw him back upon the only God he perceived—that Spirit of Equality which ends by levelling Ahab and confounding his quest in a shipwreck. The allegory and satire of *Mardi* had not clarified man's position in the cosmos; they had merely implied that he was both the pursuer and the pursued. With *Pierre*, immediately after *Moby-Dick*, Melville dramatized the problem more explicitly; he might have been referring to Ahab or Don Quixote when he registered the doctrine "that in things terrestrial . . . a man must not be governed by ideas celestial."[36] When he wrote *The Confidence Man*, around the time he was rereading *Don Quixote*, he seems to have exchanged his

Quixotry for misanthropy. The theme is not illusion but delusion; the protagonist is not a dupe but a quack; and the moral is succinctly expressed in the barber's sign: "No Trust." Even so, the author laments, in one of his many excursions on the art of fiction: "After poring over the best novels professing to portray human nature, the studious youth will still run risk of being too often at fault upon actually entering the world."[37] Perhaps the eternally Quixotic mind should live out of this world. At all events, after fifteen or twenty years of virtual retirement, we find Melville taking up his *Don Quixote* again and identifying himself with its knightly misadventures:

> *The Rusty Man*
> (By a timid one)
>
> In La Mancha he mopeth
>   With beard thin and dusty;
> He doteth and mopeth
>   In library fusty—
> 'Mong his old folios gropeth:
>   Cites obsolete saws
>   Of chivalry's laws—
> *Be the wronged one's knight:*
>   Die, but do right.
> So he rusts and musts,
> While each grocer green
> Thriveth apace with fulsome face
> Of a fool serene.[38]

NOTES

[1] S. T. Williams, *The Life of Washington Irving* (New York, 1935), I, 114, 357.

[2] O. H. Moore, "Mark Twain and *Don Quixote*," *Publications of the Modern Language Association* (June, 1922), XXXVII, 2, p. 324.

[3] *My Literary Passions* (New York, 1895), p. 26.

[4] *Do These Bones Live?* (New York, 1941), p. 92.

[5] "U.S.A.: Présentation," *Les Temps Modernes* (August–September, 1946) I, 11–12, p. 196.

[6] *White Jacket* (London, 1922), p. 284. A further allusion occurs on page 63.

[7] *Herman Melville,* ed. Willard Thorp (New York, 1938), p. xxviii.

[8] Francis Beaumont and John Fletcher, *Fifty Comedies and Tragedies* (London, 1679), II, 47. Permission has kindly been granted by the Committee on Higher Degrees in American Civilization, Harvard University, to utilize this and other unpublished material from the collection of Melville's books and manuscripts in the Houghton Library.

[9] *Don Quixote de la Mancha, Translated from the Spanish of Miguel de Cervantes Saavedra by Charles Jarvis, Esq. Carefully revised and corrected. With numerous illustrations by Tony Johannot. Philadelphia: Blanchard and Lea. 1853.* 2 volumes. Unlisted in the Cervantes bibliography of Ford and Lansing, it may be a reprint of an edition they list for 1848. A label indicates that Melville's copy was bought at Sprague's bookshop in Albany.

[10] *Ibid.,* I, lii.

[11] *Ibid.*, II, 216.

[12] *Ibid.*, I, 106.

[13] *Ibid.*, II, 362.

[14] *Ibid.*, I, 280.

[15] *Ibid.*, II, 144.

[16] *Ibid.*, II, 276.

[17] *Ibid.*, I, 126.

[18] *The Piazza Tales* (London, 1923), p. 9.

[19] *Journal Up the Straits,* ed. Raymond Weaver (New York, 1935), p. 7.

[20] *The Confidence Man* (London, 1923), p. 244.

[21] *Ibid.*, p. 318.

[22] *Moby-Dick* (London, 1922), I, 157.

[23] *Ibid.*, II, 189.

[24] *Ibid.*, II, 159.

[25] *Ibid.*, I, 267.

[26] *Ibid.*, I, 144.

[27] *Ibid.*, I, 149.

[28] *Ibid.*, I, 349.

[29] *Ibid.*, I, 204.

[30] *Ibid.*, I, 229.

[31] *Ibid.*, II, 352.

[32] *Ibid.*, I, 232.

[33] *Ibid.*, II, 182; I, 116.

[34] Charles Olson, *"Lear* and *Moby-Dick," Twice a Year* (Fall–Winter, 1938), I, p. 165.

[35] *Moby-Dick,* I, 99.

[36] *Pierre* (London, 1923), p. 298.

[37] *The Confidence Man,* p. 91.

[38] This poem is transcribed from the Jack Gentian MS. in the Houghton Library. It varies in several readings from the only published transcription, in Raymond Weaver's edition of Melville's *Poems* (London, 1924), p. 412, where the sixth line reads "Cities' obsolete laws," the twelfth line gives "thrives" for "thriveth," and the subtitle gives "soured" for "timid." The manuscript shows many signs of revision, and the last five lines have been added in place of the original ending: "Seek the San Graal's light." The subtitle also seems to be an afterthought. Other interesting variants include "beggar's" for "wronged one's" on line eight, and "philistine" for "each grocer" on line eleven. Basing the conjecture on his study of Melville's handwriting, Mr. Jay Leyda would date this poem between the composition and the publication of *Clarel,* 1870–76. To Mr. Leyda and Mr. M. M. Sealts, who allowed the materials for this study to be checked against his collection of Melville's literary allusions, the present writer appends his warmest thanks.

The "Persiles" Mystery

MACK SINGLETON

THERE is not sufficient evidence to prove that *Persiles y Sigismunda* (1617) was written during the time of composition of *Don Quixote* (1605 and 1615) or later. The proofs usually adduced have, in general, been built *ex post facto* on Cervantes' statement in 1615 that he hoped to finish the book in four months. His statement does not mean anything. It could mean that he had fifty chapters to write or it could mean that he wished to rewrite the last paragraph of the prologue; and, meaning anything, it means nothing. Where criticism has blundered has been in giving the remark benevolent rather than critical interpretation.

I wish to examine this statement of Cervantes' and some others of similar category to show why I think the dating of *Persiles* has been a scandalous blunder; and I shall present a theory of my own that assumes the facts to have been otherwise.

About the best that has ever been said about *Persiles y Sigismunda* is that it has some well-written pages and pretty images (Menéndez y Pelayo and Azorín), and that it has meaning for us moderns (although Azorín, who claims this in *Al margen de los clásicos,* does not explain exactly what the meaning is). Professor Castro, in the *Pensamiento,* defended *Persiles* as a proper exposition of the *inverosímil,* a concept that is often discussed by Cervantes. Professor Castro did not, however, praise the work.

Were *Persiles* an ordinary book, weak and vague praise of it would not much matter; but it is historically quite extraordinary because it is Cervantes' last published work, and it is always assumed that it was written during the period when he was working on *Don Quixote.* All data have seemed so clearly to point to this being absolutely true that—to my knowledge—no doubt has ever been cast on this chronology—even though it is like saying that *King Lear* and *A Comedy of Errors* could have been written during the same months by a Shakespeare for whom one was as easy as the other.

The amateurish *Persiles* constitutes the principal obstacle that balks any attempt to construct a plausible pattern in Cervantes' artistic and intellectual development. For example, Savj-López, the Italian critic, finds that the lateness of *Persiles* confirms the late date of composition of other weak works of Cervantes. The work he particularly mentions is the short story "La española inglesa," which is not very good. He sees positively no connection between Cervantes' artistic maturity and the date of composition of his works—which is a way of saying that there is no development at all in Cervantes and that he *was* the genius-by-accident people talk about. Cervantes therefore becomes a simple, ignorant, doddering writer of meaningless narratives, who dashed off page after page without understanding a word he wrote—before he wrote it, while he wrote it, or after he had written it. Mr. Krutch has been led by such ideas to think that *Don Quixote* was hastily and carelessly written. I do not think there is any basis for assuming this to be true. People like Menéndez y Pelayo have encouraged this sort of thing by referring to *Persiles* as the child of Cervantes' old age, implying, of course, that the senility of the author is responsible for the superficiality of the work. If *Persiles is* the work of a doddering old man, how then are we to explain the precision, depth, and vigor of *Don Quixote* (Part II), which was, as everybody knows, written during the same lapse into "senility"?

To combine the views just mentioned, we should have this intellectual portrait of one of the greatest minds in European art: Cervantes was static. Between 1585 (*Galatea*) and 1616 (when it is assumed *Persiles* was finished) he learned nothing and forgot nothing; and after a vigorous and active youth of sixty-five-odd years he declined into most lamentable senility during his last months in the year 1616.

I believe this is all wrong. I hold to the theory that the artistic and intellectual life of Cervantes will eventually be clearly shown to have been a slow, conscious, and completely coherent progress. I believe that Cervantes painfully rejected, piece by piece, the static, pictorial, surface aesthetic theories that underlie *Galatea* and proceeded quite as painfully to invent the complex aesthetic devices and intellectual patterns that make of *Don Quixote* the first great speculative, dynamic, *symphonic* work of modern art. And he did *not* deny all this, after he had achieved it, by writing the vapid *Persiles* in a senility he did not experience.

Professor Entwistle, in his *Cervantes* (1940), presents a theory about the stages of composition of *Persiles*. I wish to discuss it because it is a good summary of the latest ideas about *Persiles,* and is based on the best opinions now current. Professor Entwistle attaches the date 1609 to the opening chapters, because in that year the Inca, Garcilaso de la Vega, published a book that is supposed to have influenced the composition of *Persiles*. Sixteen hundred nine is "valid also for the eleventh chapter of the third book, where the expulsion of the Moriscos is considered imminent. It is probable," Professor Entwistle continues, "that the book was begun in 1609 and at least roughed out. It was far enough advanced in 1612 to be announced for future publication, and in 1615 it lacked only four months of completion" (p. 176). (I do not think the first three statements are based on ideas that can be proved. The last two items—Cervantes' statements in two prologues previous to *Persiles*—are not *necessarily* any more reliable than a great many other things Cervantes says in his prologues. I shall discuss these matters later.) Professor Entwistle then acknowledges that these dates do not necessarily apply to other parts of the novel: "It would seem that Cervantes swept the contents of his note-books into this compendious frame." In a word, Professor Entwistle is really saying that he actually doesn't know *when Persiles* was written. He is quite frank about it, and merely repeats the conventional embroidery out of politeness. I assume that he inclines toward the opinion that *Persiles* represents Cervantes' thought and a record of reading over a period of ten, fifteen, or twenty years before 1609.

We now have two ideas about the writing of *Persiles*. The first—the "senility" theory of Menéndez y Pelayo—assumes that *Persiles* was written in one piece during the very last years of Cervantes' life; the second assumes that although the parts of *Persiles* were apparently put together after 1609, the composition of much of it represents the scattered effort of Cervantes before and after that date. I do not think the "note-book" theory will stand up very well after examination.

It is very striking that if Cervantes swept the contents of his note-books into *Persiles,* there should have been in these note-books almost nothing that pre-occupied the mature Cervantes, who was writing or had written the *Novelas ejemplares* and *Don Quixote.* We should expect to find a very great many things—plots, types, events, language—to remind us of the two major works; but, oddly enough, this is not so. *Persiles* is so terribly alien to *Don Quixote* that, if somebody else had signed his name to *Persiles,* I can't imagine that any critic would work very hard to attribute it to Cervantes.

In subject, form, and language, *Persiles* is as different from *Don Quixote* as a soap-opera is from *Faust. Don Quixote* is a long evolution. When we study it chapter by chapter, we can see clearly when Cervantes first rejects theatrical devices, the merely episodic, caricature, low comedy, tagged characters, symmetrical plots. The apparently real, visual world loses a stubborn fight to maintain itself against a universe that is mind, emotion, energy, and evolution. The Medieval and Renaissance worlds of fixed geometrical images are shattered by submerged dynamic *forces* that create and destroy in an endless process. *Don Quixote* destroys both the rationalized Medieval cosmos and the neat world of forms that the Italians had proclaimed. It is a long metaphysical dialogue. In it each character has his own world at any given moment; there is no absolute truth, no absolute universe. Man *discovers* himself and his universe over and over. In *Don Quixote* the European man renounces post-Roman civilization, which like Don Quixote, or Hamlet, had ended in chaos. In the cave of Montesinos, Don Quixote discovers *time,* evolution, and the historical sense. *From his own subconscious* comes the denial of his system, which is based on the real existence of rigid extra-temporal, and therefore eternal, absolutes. Tremendous forces are loosed in the book; and Time eventually conquers Space, after terrible struggles between worlds and otherworlds, the living and the dead, and the essential cultures of two thousand years.

Technically the book is an amazing advance beyond anything that had ever been done in fiction. For example, the concept of character as dynamic development first appears here (although I believe it had been partially formulated in the *Celestina*). Don Quixote and Sancho are the first complex, evolving characters in fiction, beside whom the great characters of Antiquity and the Middle Ages seem like mere sketches. Cervantes here destroyed completely the theory of the "faceless," idealized, one-emotion personality. Character is now not something you see; it exists as development *and only as development;* and—a most remarkable invention—the external world as observed and commented on by the character becomes the index of character-development. We must never say that Don Quixote is something or other unless we say when and in relation to what; and we must never make statements about other phenomena unless we say when and in relation to what. The basic texture of *Don Quixote* is philosophical in the academic sense of that word—so much so that a very great many of the raw philosophical problems that have kept the nineteenth and twentieth centuries busy are to be found sketched, implied, or stated in *Don Quixote.* The great to-do about pragmatism, Kierkegaard, and existentialism, for instance, seems sort of unnecessary to anyone who has followed these attitudes through *Don Quixote,* and (despite Unamuno) watched them decay.

Well, there is nothing like this in *Persiles*—nothing remotely like it. Its world is a "seen" world—a hysterical procession of violent images. The exterior world of appearance is *pictured* as absolutely final; there is no room for speculation about it. The only psychological problems grow out of the erotic. There is only reference to emotion—not communication of it. *Persiles* is a string of visually observed and (as in early Renaissance painting) ideally presented scenes, one-motif characters, poses, exaggerations, unwarranted perfections, emotions pursued to their theatrical extremes, and fortuitous solutions. The ancestor of *Persiles* is *Orlando* (there are direct steals); it is only a little more down to earth than *Os Lusíadas.* It is, in a word, a work that strives very hard to follow the pattern of the best Renaissance lyrical narrative. And this is precisely the pattern that Cervantes in *Don Quixote* works very hard to discredit.

If *Persiles* is the great note-book kept by the master, where are the Moors and the Turks? Where is the Andalusian period? Where is the physical and human Castilian landscape? Where are the little boys, the animals—dogs, donkeys, horses (major characters in Cervantes)—the simple people, the low-comedy types? Where the miniature beauty of the chivalry matter, the Vergilian pastoral landscapes and the rococo shepherds, the sterling good taste that marks the gaiety of *La gitanilla?* Where are the wit and learning that distinguish the dialogue of Don Quixote and Sancho, of Rinconete and Cortadillo and the little dogs? Where is the deep knowledge of the anatomy of language, that makes even a few lines of the late prologue of *Persiles* superior to the rest of the book? Where is the technically and intellectually complex *humor*—the great Cervantine fusion of comedy and tragedy that denies that the two theatrical extremes can exist aesthetically isolated? Where is there in *Persiles* a reflection of the synthetic texture-of-narrative that in *Don Quixote* permits the introduction of *any* matter affecting the human creature?

Well, in *Persiles* we can find only stale maxims that look as if they had been copied out of a quotation-book, only a few elementary attempts at humor by Bartolomé the Manchegan, and, as a show of learning and wisdom, some commonplace observations on astronomy, geography, and witchcraft copied out of mid-sixteenth-century books. Once in a while you do feel that here or there, Cervantes has begun to think about something that years later might take form —as, for instance, the character of Bartolomé or an interest in the primitive man. But nothing *happens;* there is no development. In the case of Sancho Panza— the great summary of Cervantes' thought about the primitive, natural man—a lot happens; such a great deal, indeed, that criticism has not yet got around to seeing how very much does happen, and still resigns itself to calling Sancho a simple, amiable fellow. It ought to be said in passing that Sancho Panza comes to be the only person in the book who has the intellectual, moral, and temperamental qualities that are required for administering successfully, wisely, and justly a world that very much stands in need of those abilities and attitudes. The Island is Cervantes' Republic or Utopia; and Sancho, unlike Don Quixote, does not suffer defeat in his own heart, but is *physically* destroyed by the overwhelming forces of evil and chaos from without.

Now, why should all these things that we know preoccupied Cervantes for twenty years (at least) be missing from the "note-books"? I can see only one answer: Cervantes when he wrote *Persiles* knew nothing about all the things that form the texture of all his great work and decorate it. He had not acquired or invented his techniques and atmospheres, he had not learned to think in philosophic terms, and he had not created the wonderfully complex and subtle linguistic instrument with which he was finally able to create an authentic and everlasting work of genius.

The reasons for thinking that Persiles *is not the last work of Cervantes are so compelling that it is amazing no one has hitherto questioned the standard chronology.* The "senility" theory does not make sense, and the long-elaboration "note-book" theory is nothing but an observation. What is left?

Persiles *must, as a unit, be an early work.*

My own theory, which I can formulate only by rejecting previous theories, is that *Los trabajos de Persiles y Sigismunda: Historia setentrional* is actually one of Cervantes' earliest works—perhaps about the only thing left in his trunk after he had published, in more or less reverse order of composition, practically everything he had preserved from his apprentice days.

If we examine the cases cited by Schevill and Bonilla, in their edition of *Persiles,* in an unsuccessful effort to fix a date for the composition of the book, we shall discover that most historical references are to events in the reign of Charles V or the early part of the reign of Philip II (1556–1598). The *bárbaro* Antonio fought under Charles V; Mauricio says he saw Charles V at a monastery, apparently at the time of the abdication; reference is made to the death of the Emperor and to his wars in Transylvania; and reference is made to the recent publication of the works of Garcilaso de la Vega (which took place in 1543). Most of these things indicate that the people in the story are talking around 1560.

But there are references apparently to the years 1581, 1606, and 1609. As far as I know, these are the only textual obstacles to pushing *Persiles* back in time of composition. Let us examine these references.

1581. This date is not too late to upset my theory, certainly. However, this date ought not be cited to show that *Persiles* had to be written after 1581. It may have been written before that. Cervantes does *not* make reference to the publication of Tasso's *Jerusalem Delivered,* as critics always say he does. Cervantes has a seer prophesy that there was going to be a great poet, by the name of Torquato Tasso, who was going to sing the recovery of Jerusalem better than anybody else had ever sung it. The obvious next remark will be: If Cervantes says that, he must have seen the book (1581) in print. Perhaps he did. He doesn't say so. The essential thing to note is this: It is common knowledge that *Jerusalem Delivered* was finished in 1574 and was a matter of discussion and debate years before its publication in 1581. For Cervantes to attempt a scoop about a work published thirty-five years before, would be about as exciting as to write a novel now, and predict with much fanfare that there was going to be a First World War. What Cervantes says suggests that at the time this part (at least) of *Persiles* was written, *Jerusalem Delivered* had not been published. The prediction looked at from this angle *is* a prediction and has a certain excitement about it. Otherwise it seems pretty dull stuff. And of all things *Persiles* tries hard not to be dull.

1606. The editors say that Cervantes alludes to the return of the court of Philip III to Madrid in that year. *"Intenté* [says a character, relating the story of his life] *venir a Madrid, donde estaba recién venida la corte del gran Felipe tercero."* ("I decided to come to Madrid, where the Court of the great Philip III had recently come.") Then eleven pages later, reference is made to the works of Garcilaso de la Vega (not the Inca): *"por haber mostrádole a la luz del mundo aquellos días las famosas obras del jamás alabado como se debe Garcilaso de la Vega."* (" . . . because the famous works of Garcilaso de la Vega, who will never be praised as much as he deserves, had appeared in those days.") Periandro (Persiles) quotes from Garcilaso as if quoting from the latest sensation. Now, either 1606—the return of the Court—is wrong, or 1543—the date of publication of Garcilaso—is wrong. The time of the publication of the works of Garcilaso is not something to be delayed for sixty years. Even the "late," "Romantic," "senile" Cervantes was not that stupid. And the confusion cannot be attributed to ignorance, for Cervantes had specifically been mentioning Garcilaso, and quoting him, ever since *Galatea*. If the date 1543 fits reasonably well with the other times mentioned in the story—and it does—then the references to Philip III, the return of the Court, and the year 1606 (not mentioned in the text) look like a slip—not senility.

Note that the text does not say, as the editors interpret it to say, *vuelta* ("return"). It says *venida* ("come"), which may be a return or it may not. When did the Court *come* to Madrid? The Court came to Madrid in 1560, when Philip *II* established the capital there for the first time. Everything is all right if we could get rid of that word *tercero*. It seems easy to imagine that somebody reading the manuscript might have felt Cervantes had made a slip and, with the coming of Philip III fresh in his mind, might have made an unnecessary correction. I do not imagine Cervantes himself made the change (if a change was, of course, made), because he had many opportunities to bring his book up to date (1616), and obviously has not done so. My theory is that in the original the words were: *"del gran Felipe"* without the number—without any number, because Philip II was the *gran Felipe,* the only real Philip who had actually been king *at the time* Cervantes was writing *Persiles.* However, the printer's reader (for the printer apparently did not look at the manuscript but had it read to him) when he came to *el gran Felipe* naturally must have paused and asked: "Isn't something missing? *Which* "gran Felipe?" And the simplest answer would have been: "The Third, naturally. You know what happened just ten years ago, don't you? That's what Cervantes is talking about obviously, so throw in a *tercero*." I am quite aware that I have no basis for this conversation between printers; I am also quite aware that I am juggling text. But either you have a man in your 1947 novel refer excitedly to the works of Walt Whitman that are just hot off the press—or you get rid of that word *tercero*.

1609. This is the date of the expulsion of the *moriscos*, to which editors say Cervantes makes reference. He does nothing of the sort. He has a rhapsodic character say, in a long, hysterical speech, that the *moriscos* are bad people and *ought* to be expelled—something that people had been saying for a century before 1609. It should be recalled that the great rebellion of the *moriscos* dates as far back as 1567–1570. Nowhere in the *Persiles* passage does Cervantes make anything like a reference to the expulsion itself.

Now let me summarize this section of my inquiry: Does Cervantes specifically refer to anything that had to happen after any of these three dates? With the exception of the word *tercero*, everything could have happened a good forty to fifty years before it is assumed by critics that *Persiles* had to be written. I have tried to show that the reasons for throwing *tercero* out are stronger than the reasons for keeping it in.

In the matter of sources the editors insist that Cervantes read the Inca Garcilaso de la Vega carefully to prepare himself for the writing of *Persiles*. This Garcilaso's *Comentarios reales* came out in 1609. The cases of influence cited are: the incident of a man who, after a shipwreck, swam to an island and stayed there three years, the sacrifice of living victims, the use of poisons as charms, the wearing of skins, the practice of witchcraft and prophecy, the tying together of rafts to form bridges, and the making of fire by rubbing sticks together. None of these things seems so strange or novel to me that I should feel I had to accept Cervantes' borrowing them from Garcilaso and only Garcilaso. However, that they should occur in both works does seem suggestive —though I cannot see that the parallels *prove* borrowing. Let us assume that Cervantes had a written source for these details. Does the source have to be Garcilaso? The footnote on page xxvii of the Schevill and Bonilla introduction is interesting: Garcilaso copied, they remark, quite a lot ("bastante") from other historians (Cieza de León, Gómara, Acosta, Agustín de Zárate) without ever specifying his source. Cieza de León published part of his *Chronicle of Peru* in 1553; Gómara, the first two parts of his *History of the Indies* in 1552; Acosta, the *History . . . of the Indies* in 1590; Agustín de Zárate, his *History of the Discovery . . . of Peru* in 1555. I do not know whether Cervantes read these works or not, or whether he got from them the details he is supposed to have got from Garcilaso. But perhaps he did. In a word, I cannot see that it has been proved that Cervantes used Garcilaso's book. It seems quite as plausible to think that the young Cervantes read some of the historians mentioned not long after their books came out. (Observe the dates: 1552, 1553, 1555. I should have to assume he did not know Acosta.)

While we are about it, it might be a good idea to list other works mentioned by the editors as sources in some way or other, in order to see when *they* were written. Here are most of them: *Historia de Clareo y Florisea* (1552); the Italian work of Zeno (el menor) (1558); the works of Olao Magno (1539, 1555 and specifically 1565); the *Jardín de flores* of Antonio de Torquemada (1570?); *El libro de las costumbres de todas las gentes del mundo* of Francisco Thamara (1556); *De las cosas maravillosas del mundo* of Julio Solino (translated 1573); Pedro Mejía's *Silva de varia lección* (1540 and 1547); Gil Polo's *Diana* (1564); *Amadís de Gaula* (from 1508 on); the stories of Giraldi Cinthio (1565)—Cervantes apparently imitated one story in the sixth decade directly from the Italian, for the Spanish translation of 1590 contains only ten stories of the introduction and the first two decades; possibly *La isla bárbara* of the *divino* Miguel Sánchez (no date given); possibly three words from a ballad by Juan de la Cueva (no date given). It is strange too that Cervantes' Mauricio, apparently an Irishman, is thought to refer to the Irish rebel Fitzmaurice, who offered the crown of that kingdom to Don Juan of Austria in 1577. There seems also to be a reference to the death of an Ali Pasha (1571) and to the death of Dom Sebastião of Portugal (1578). After this enumeration of sources, the editors devote a couple of pages to similarities of style and thought to be found in *Persiles* and *Galatea* (1585). The editors are particularly struck by these parallels —as I suppose anybody would be, if he stopped to think that Cervantes would thus be imitating his manner of thirty years before. "Even sentences are at times identical," the editors observe. I find this easy to explain. *Galatea* and *Persiles* are both works of Cervantes' first period. It would therefore be extraordinary if there were *not* a great number of parallels. Whether *Galatea* came first or not I should not want to say now. My purely personal reaction is that *Galatea* has a polish and coherence I have never been able to find in *Persiles*—in spite of Menéndez y Pelayo's phrase about "the noble style of *Persiles*."

In the Schevill and Bonilla notes (II, 76) there is a fairly long reference to an incident that happened in Seville in 1565, which it is thought Cervantes might have witnessed. It seems pretty hard to imagine that between 1609 and 1616 Cervantes, after quite a full life, should be so barren that he had to search his boyhood memory for this sort of minor detail. To a young man writing not long after 1565, however, the detail may very well have seemed significant.

If the reader will look back at the dates of the works listed as sources he must be struck by one thing: The author of *Don Quixote* apparently stopped reading

around 1570. Aside from the Inca Garcilaso no writer writing after 1600 has
been mentioned. I have been perfectly fair in listing the sources proposed by the
editors; I have not, to the best of my knowledge, omitted books or writers that
would not fit my theory. To judge, then, from current criticism of *Persiles*, we
should be required to say that with the exception of perhaps one book, the
Comentarios reales, Cervantes read absolutely nothing for at least thirty years;
but to supply this deficiency his photographic mind recalled everything he had
read *more* than thirty years before.

There are some interesting biographical aspects that could be discussed. One
is the story of the young man who felt he had been improperly addressed, had
a fight, and fled. This theme occurs also in Cervantes' "Gallardo español." It
is thought to be like something that occurred to Cervantes himself (around
1570). That it occurs in *Persiles* agrees perfectly well with my theory. There is
a reference by the editors to a possible connection between an incident in *Persiles*
and the Ezpeleta scandal (1605) at Cervantes' house. In the first place, a reading
of the text and a study of the data about the scandal will show that the incidents
are only slightly similar, about all they have in common being that a wounded
man is brought into a strange house where he dies. I cannot believe that
Cervantes would in any circumstance have made reference to a matter that was
so delicate and compromising, involving as it did the reputation of the ladies
in Cervantes' own family. I do not see how it can be proved that there is any
connection between the two incidents.

To summarize what has been learned about dates: The events in the story,
historical references, and sources, indicate that *Persiles* could have been written
in the 60's, 70's, and 80's. It cannot be proved that any incident, historical reference—except the word *tercero*—, or source used *must* refer to events later than
the 80's. It is my opinion that eventually it may be shown that *Persiles* (much
of it, at any rate) antedates *Galatea* by a good ten or fifteen years.

In conclusion, I should like to consider Cervantes' own statements about
Persiles.

In the prologue of the *Novelas ejemplares* (1613) Cervantes mentions *Persiles*
(without *Sigismunda*), which he says he hopes will rival Cliodoro. (That is
what the text says. It is always emended to read Heliodoro.) The mention of
Heliodorus—if indeed Cervantes wrote *Eliodoro*—is a little odd because it is
pretty generally admitted that the book doesn't seem to be too much like
Heliodorus. At any rate, Cervantes says he will offer his readers this book,
which he refers to as "daring" (*atrevido*); then in the dedication of *Don Quixote*
(Part II) he says he hopes to finish *Persilis* (so spelled) in four months. Now,
I contend that these statements do not mean anything. Prologues and dedica-
tions are by definition not matters of scientific accuracy. They are blurbs. If

Persiles were old stuff and Cervantes *had* just taken it out of the trunk, is it likely that he would have cared for his patron to know it? It is like a professor who, at the end of his career, had nothing to publish but an old sophomore theme—he would certainly never tell the Dean *that*. The weird statement about the merit of the book is interesting. Cervantes writes that it will be the worst or the best of books of entertainment in the language, though he regrets to have said that it would be the worst, because his friends assure him it will reach the "extreme of possible goodness." All of which does not mean very much, even though it is widely quoted to show that Cervantes had no critical sense. I think that a penetrating critical mind is precisely one of the qualities that make Cervantes great. Cervantes could not have had much use for *Persiles* except perhaps to feel that it was not a bad job for a boy to do. Cervantes does not say it is a good book; he says his *friends* say it is a good book. At least they say it will be as good as it possibly can be (*extremo de bondad posible*)—which doesn't mean very much. Now, who said it was the *worst* book ever written? Cervantes did. I know of nothing like it in all history: A man writes a book and says, "This is the worst book ever written—the worst of its kind, I mean— although my friends think it will be as good as it possibly can be." Critics have given great—very great—weight to these words to prove that Cervantes was a hack. I contend that either the passage means nothing at all or that it means the opposite of what it is said to mean. Can he really then be saying with magnificent circumlocution that *Persiles* is terrible, awful, and that he is encouraged to publish it only because his friends (his family?) want him to? I don't know, I don't think anybody else knows, and I think it is high time for people to stop quoting it as if they *did* know.

Cervantes could be very wily at times. If anybody thinks he is not being wily when he defends the *Novelas ejemplares* as being exemplary in a Counter-Reformation society, I think he is wrong. *Rinconete* is, I imagine, the cleverest satire ever written on monastic life—yet Cervantes could always say: "It may *seem* to you to be so, but I had no intention of saying what you say I say. Show me the actual words." The protestation about wanting to ruin the chivalry-novel market is a good example of Cervantes defending himself against people who would say, "You have attacked the fundamental nature of Christian society, you have attacked two thousand years of European civilization." Even in matters of observable fact Cervantes seems highly unreliable. In the prologue of the *Novelas* you read that he *"perdió en la batalla naval de Lepanto la mano izquierda."* Now, *perdió* meant to at least one person—Avellaneda, in the apocryphal *Quixote*—that Cervantes had only one hand, because Avellaneda says that Cervantes has only one hand; and so it is not our ignorance of seventeenth century language that obscures this. Yet in the prologue of *Persiles* (three or four years later) a student hastens forward to clasp him by the left hand ("*asirme de la mano izquierda*"). I find it very hard at times to understand what Cervantes means.

The *Persiles* prologue—a very beautiful piece of writing—looks as sober and real as a doctor's chart temperature. Cervantes tells how he met a student who praised his work, recommended a change of diet, and then went his way. But this is all pure invention, for the paragraphs about the student are a reworking of a similar incident and student in the *Adjunta al Parnaso*.

Briefly, I think these details should put us on guard against accepting literally anything found in the prologues.

The dedication and prologue of *Persiles* are very strange documents. *No reference is made in them to the book itself*. The dedication is more of a letter of welcome to a patron than a dedication; and the prologue seems to have nothing to do with *Persiles*. It could be used with utmost propriety for any book, except that in it Cervantes says that he is dying. Is it not an extraordinary thing that only after having received extreme unction, Cervantes should finally come around to writing the prologue of this peculiar book? Is it not strange that the book in toto should be finished and ready for the printer after he was convinced that he was going to die? *What is the prologue trying to tell us?* What is the purpose of resurrecting a character out of another book—a student whose ruff is always falling askew, who gives the most facile advice, who takes Cervantes by the left hand that he three years before had publicly said he had lost? The prologue is beyond any doubt cryptic. Is Cervantes trying to say in it: "I would never dare face my enemies . . . or my friends, if *Persiles* came off the press while I was alive. *Persiles* would ruin me if I lived. Now that I am dying it doesn't matter. The family will get some money out of it before the public catches on. And who is the student? *I* am the student; I was just like that when I was his age and was writing *Persiles*." "*Lo que se dirá de mi suceso, tendrá la fama cuidado, mis amigos gana de decirlo, y yo mayor gana de escucharlo*." Does he mean that somebody will explain what has happened—later—that his friends will defend his reputation by telling the truth about *Persiles*?

He must have published *Persiles* for somebody else's profit. I can imagine that he had promised his family to publish everything he could . . . eventually. He had stalled as long as he could. After his death *Persiles* could do him no harm. When he was sure—*sure*—death was upon him he surrendered, and wrote a kind of dedication and preface; and four days later died.

Thematic Design

PAVEL I. NOVITSKY

CERVANTES' novel is directed against the literature of his period, against the universal passion for the romance of chivalry, which had by this time assumed disastrous proportions. It ridiculed both the exalted authors of these romances and their credulous readers who were trying to escape from a living world of reality into a dead world of fiction—into an empty world of illusions and castles in the air. Cervantes repeatedly underscored this thematic design. He says in the preface, through the mouth of his friend, that his book is an uninterrupted disparagement of all the romances of chivalry ever written, that he "aims at nothing more than to destroy the authority and influence which books of chivalry have in the world and with the public." He finishes his novel with the following assertion: "For my desire has been no other than to deliver over to the detestation of mankind the false and foolish tales of the books of chivalry."[1] Cervantes parodies the style of these romances, ridicules the endless narratives of endless adventures, and misses no opportunity to emphasize the harmful effects of an unrestrained imagination that forgets reality. Satirically and ironically, he points out how books can destroy the last link with the living and concrete world of reality, how they can befog life, how they can substitute hallucinations of fiction for reality. He warns against a slavish attitude towards books, against those fanatics and maniacs whose counterpart was to worry Anatole France. "Lovers of books," remarked France, "are like hasheesh fiends. The subtle fumes of the poison which penetrates their brain causes them to become insensible to the world of reality and delivers them into the power of enchanting and terrible phantoms. Books are the opium of the West. They devour us. The day will come when we will all turn into bibliophiles, and that will be the end of everything."[2]

But Cervantes did not confine himself to exposing the harmful influence of the romances of chivalry and the slavish attitude toward books. His *Don Quixote* has a more profound theme, a more far-reaching aim. In the introductory poem, Urganda, which prefaces the first edition, Cervantes hides behind a mask of

239

subtlest irony and intentional obscurity. He denies that his purpose—upon which he is so insistent in the preface—has been merely to ridicule the romances of chivalry. Let the fools who are under the delusion that they have understood all the motivations of the novel smack their lips. These motivations are far more profound than they have any conception of. *"Don Quixote" is the greatest lampoon on the aristocratic culture of the nobility, the greatest satirical exposé of the historical limitations and spiritual contradictions which gave birth to the age it represents.* On the one hand, the novel depicts scenes of the extravagant madness, the castle-building fancifulness, and the social schism which was characteristic of the poverty-stricken provincial gentry and university students. These latter had broken with reality. They lived in a world of phantoms because they could not reconcile themselves to their uselessness. They craved activity, they wanted to play an important role in the formation of the new period. But they were capable only of foolish activities which harmed them and those around them; of escapades, suicide, and death. On the other hand, the novel presents an unvarnished picture of the authentic life: the dull, animal, vegetative existence of the peasants, the commercial bustle of the merchants, the greed of the innkeepers, and the dull cynicism and decadent cruelty of the ducal courts. The senseless and disastrous romanticism of these madmen is only one aspect of cruel social reality. Monks, strolling players, and galley slaves pass along the high road. The song of the youth whom "poverty and need are driving to war" can be heard. Folk-lore episodes are followed by adventure stories. Life—rich, succulent, spicy—forms the basis of every occurrence. *In this way the satirical, the folk, and the genre elements are intertwined.* The lunatic is united to the prosaic, the artificial to the natural.

This sane, passionate book glorifies the smell of the earth—the ravenous, animal forces of life. It is rooted in the same soil that had nourished the full-blooded Flemish painting, the empirical philosophy and the bourgeois drama of England. The physical life of man, the physiological functions of the human organism arrest Cervantes' attention. With unsparing and naive naturalism he describes the bodily functions of Sancho (Part I, chapters XVIII and XX), without fear of revolting the reader. The satirical and folk novel is the finest specimen of literary naturalism.

The thematic design of the novel, however, is not limited only to these aspects of life. Cervantes was not content to write merely a satirical and folk novel. Had he no broader aim than the exposure of the contemporary literature of manners, had the basic thematic design of his novel been nothing more than the depiction of the overwhelming contradictions and the ideological range of his epoch—an epoch in which fantastic utopian dreams rubbed shoulders with a restricted, common-sense existence—his novel would now be nothing more than an interesting historical document of the period whose significance would not extend beyond the boundaries of its own age. The significance of Cervantes' novel is much broader, for it raised the ideo-psychological experience of the age to great artistic heights. He deepened, by force of generalizations, the significance of the chief heroes of his novel until they assumed gigantic symbolic proportions. *His novel is not a lampoon on the Spanish gentry of the sixteenth century, but a record of the fate of a culture centuries old.*

Don Quixote lives in the past. That is the most important thing to remember. He is completely unaware of contemporary reality. He is blinded by the dazzling phantoms of feudal days, living only for their enchanting visions. He has slept through the fall of Feudalism and the advent of an unromantic age which had nothing of knighthood in it. Thus he lacks all feeling for reality. He despises the coarse impulses of Sancho Panza whom lack of imagination chains to earth. He does not welcome the reality of vegetable gardens and pigsties. Had he lived in the age of knightly tournaments, single combats, and wars, he would have rejected the cruel, brutal, bloody reality of knighthood as definitely as he rejects the reality of his own age. *The present is unbearable to him.* He can exist only in a world of an imaginary illusory reality, and in dreams of days long past. He refuses to take cognizance of the present. It is just this attitude that is responsible for all his adventures, all his suffering, all his failures, and all his humiliations. He never takes circumstances or his environment into account because they do not exist for him. The past lures him with its dreams because he never came in contact with its reality. *He quarrels boldly with his age in the name of the past,* as our later knights—Agrippa d'Aubigné, Carlyle, Leo Tolstoy—quarreled with theirs. And were not all the others who rebelled against everyday life transformed into Don Quixotes as soon as they tore themselves away from solid reality and consequently lost their perspectives—Byron, Heine, Blok?

Only for the sake of the future is it permissible to quarrel with one's age, to reject the present, and to vanquish one's epoch. Ideals must not be disembodied spirits, incapable of ever becoming corporeal reality. Barren dreams which can never be fulfilled only succeed in discrediting one's ideal and making it ludicrous! One must be able to realize the ideal, to establish it by changing the present and controlling the future through struggle and realistic activity. Heine did not understand this and opposed the drab reality of the present by individual heroism and insurgence.

Don Quixote did not understand this either. He possessed an unrestrained imagination. To him reality was the world of dreams his fancy had created. He substituted for life the inspiration of an unheard of madness. Everything he saw, every adventure he had, he transformed into a dream. An inn was to him a castle with four turrets, steeples of shining silver, a draw-bridge, and deep moats. The pipings of the swineherd's reed, festive court music; black mouldy bread, white rolls of the finest wheat flour; prostitutes, noble ladies and princesses; windmills, giants swinging their arms; Benedictine monks, magicians who had spirited away the princesses; merchants, knights errant; two flocks of sheep, two opposing armies led by the emperor Alifanfarron and the King of Guermantes; the barber's basin, Mambrino's magic helmet; and the buxom Aldonza Lorenzo was the delicate, ethereal Dulcinea. The loss of all feeling for reality turned Don Quixote into a madman, a maniac. It made a laughingstock of him. Yet there was a method in his madness. He was fully aware of the fact that no reality, no matter how lofty, could ever equal the illusory world created by his imagination. Therefore he answered one of Sancho's questions by saying:

"It is not to be supposed that all those poets who sang the praise of ladies under the fancy names they give them, had any such mistresses. Thinkest thou that the Amarillises, the Phillises, the Sylvias, the Dianas, the Galateas, the Filidas, and all the rest of them, that the books, the ballads, the barbers' shops, the theatres are full of, were really and truly ladies of flesh and blood, and mistresses of those that glorify and have glorified them? Nothing of the kind, they only invent them for the most part to furnish a subject for their verses, and that they may pass as lovers, or for them who have some pretensions to be so; and so it is enough for me to think and believe that the good Aldonza Lorenzo is fair and virtuous. . . . To put the whole thing in a nutshell, I persuade myself that all I say is as I say, neither more or less, and I picture her in my imagination as I would have her to be, as well in beauty as in condition; Helen approaches her not nor does Lucretia come up to her, nor any other of the famous women of times past, Greek, Barbarian, or Latin; and let each say what he will, for if in this I am taken to task by the ignorant, I shall not be censured by the critical."[3]

Don Quixote despises the dull and platitudinous mentality of churls like Sancho Panza, who believe the transfiguration of the universe to be but madness and arrant nonsense and can see only the inns and the pigsties. He, Don Quixote, wants to be mad with no ulterior motive. Disinterestedly and aimlessly mad. When Sancho, puzzled, wants to know the reason for this madness—all other knights who had lost their minds always had some justification for their insane actions, they had either been rejected by their ladies, or their ladies had proved unfaithful—Don Quixote answers:

"There is the point, and that is the beauty of this business of mine; no thanks to a knight-errant for going mad when he has cause; the thing is to turn crazy without any provocation, and to let my lady know, if I do this in the dry, what I would do in the moist. . . . Is it possible that all this time thou hast been going about with me thou hast never found out that all things belonging to knights-errant seem to be illusions and nonsense and ravings, and to go always by contraries? And not because it really is so, but because there is always a swarm of enchanters in attendance upon us that change and alter everything with us, and turn things as they please, and according as they are disposed to aid or destroy us."[4]

The self-inspired madness of Don Quixote can accomplish only one thing— the transfiguration of the world. Its absurdity lies in its lack of direction. It is true that Don Quixote is often under the delusion that he is helping the oppressed and routing the oppressors. But his whole pathetic idealism, his lofty romanticism, and his noble enthusiasm are senseless, even harmful, when their application effects negative results, when *they are without social justification*. Euthusiasm is one of the most powerful moral weapons with which to fight the decadent skepticism and pessimistic individualism of bourgeois culture. But *aimless enthusiasm, unmotivated enthusiasm, misplaced enthusiasm,* is false and ridiculous. Enthusiasm must be justified by reality. It must have a positive aim. If it has not, it turns into a game, into a pose, into self-indulgence.

Don Quixote, who profoundly and sincerely desired to fight for the truth and to protect the oppressed, is, nevertheless, guilty of injustice at every move he makes. He harms those he wants to save. He stops a peasant from flogging a shepherd lad. But no sooner does he ride out of sight than the peasant again ties the boy to the oak-tree and flogs him into unconsciousness. When Don Quixote meets the lad again, he is greeted not with words of gratitude but with curses:

"For the love of God, sir knight-errant, if you ever meet me again, though you may see them cutting me to pieces, give me no aid or succour, but leave me to my misfortune, which will not be so great but that a greater will come to me by being helped by your worship, on whom, and all the knights-errant that have ever been born, God send his curse."[5]

Another time Don Quixote meets a funeral procession escorting the corpse of a nobleman to its grave. Under the impression that the procession is a band of brigands who had carried off the body of the dead knight, he rushes at the unarmed priests and throws one of them to the ground. In falling, the priest breaks a leg. Introducing himself to the wounded man as a knight-errant who is restoring justice to earth and righting wrongs, he hears in response the bitter laments that the worst evil and greatest misfortune that could possibly befall an unfortunate man is to meet the ill-fated knight. Still another time Don Quixote frees the convicts of a chain-gang. They turn upon their rescuer and beat him unmercifully. In a word, the admirable forces of heroism and self-sacrifice, when directed aimlessly and senselessly, bring only harm. Everything depends *on the direction, on the application, on the purposeful assignment of these forces.*

Don Quixote's eulogists forget the incentives and aims which motivated his actions and exploits. These exploits were not always manifestations of Don Quixote's humanity and altruistic disinterestedness. They were often performed in the name of the formal execution of the rules of the knightly code, and as often inspired by the swagger typical of the petty nobility, by social prejudices, by a petulant thirst for glory, and by desire to earn the favors of his fair lady. Don Quixote is boastful, vain as a peacock.

"I am he for whom perils, mighty achievements, and valiant deeds are reserved; I am, I say again, he who is to revive the knights of the Round Table, the Twelve of France and the Nine Worthies; and he who is to consign to oblivion the Platirs, the Tablantes, the Olivantes and Tirantes, the Phoebuses and Belianises, with the whole herd of famous knight-errant of days gone by, performing in these in which I live such exploits, marvels, and feats of arms as shall obscure the brightest deeds."[6]

Similar speeches are scattered throughout the novel. Don Quixote often refuses to help the "lower classes," because the code of chivalry forbids him to unsheathe his sword against anyone who has not taken the knightly vows. He fights only knights; the rabble, the riff-raff, he leaves to Sancho. He refers to the plebeians with contempt. They excel the illustrious nobles who are blessed with all the virtues, all the riches and all the generosity in the world, only in their contributions to the multiplication of the population of the earth, "and their greatness deserves no other fame or praise."[7] Once, purely out of vanity, he risks his own life and exposes the whole neighboring population to mortal danger by forcing a lion-keeper to open the cage of the lions that were being brought to the Spanish King. Then, to the terror of all around him, he challenges the lions to combat. By a lucky accident, however, they turn their backs on the madman and refuse the challenge. Don Quixote is at the height of his bliss and demands a certificate testifying to his valor.

Don Quixote finally forgets all his humane ideals completely when Merlin, the sorcerer, demands that Sancho give himself three thousand three hundred lashes to pay for the restoration of the real countenance of the enchanted Dulcinea. He forgets all the hardships Sancho had undergone with him, forgets all justice and fairness, and is vigorously insistent that Sancho carry out Merlin's orders, threatening, if he refuse, to tie his squire to a tree and flog him twice as hard with his own hands. It is well that Sancho preferred to flog the tree instead of himself; had he not, he would have had to bid farewell to life.

All this merely proves how relative Don Quixote's enthusiasm and humaneness are and how the results they produce can be sharply negative. Only socially directed enthusiasm and socially justified heroism are admirable and capable of transforming and purifying life. *Senseless, self-sufficing heroism, empty vanity and fruitless day-dreaming can never change anything;* they can only sustain and strengthen social slavery and oppression. "This heroism, this high-mindedness, this devotion—all these beautiful, lofty, and noble qualities, if only they had been directed towards a definite goal, and at the right time—what a truly great man Don Quixote would have been!"[8]

NOTES

[1] Part II, chapter LXXIV (Ormsby's translation)—*A.F.*
[2] Henri Bordeaux: *Ames modernes*, p. 221. Paris, 1912.
[3] Part I, chapter XXV (Ormsby's translation).
[4] *Ibid.*
[5] Part I, chapter XXXI (Ormsby's translation).
[6] Part I, chapter XX (Ormsby's translation).
[7] Cf. Raskolnikov's theory about the division of people into the "common and uncommon" in Dostoevsky's *Crime and Punishment*. The common people exist solely for the propagation of others like themselves.
[8] V. G. Belinsky: *Collected Works*, (in Russian) 3 vols., edited by Ivanov-Razumnik (St. Petersburg: 1913)—in his article "Tarantas: The Writings of Count V. A. Sologub" is to be found a brilliant characterization of both Don Quixote and quixotism, p. 966.

The Apocryphal "Quixote"

STEPHEN GILMAN

S any reader of Cervantes knows, in the 59th chapter of the second part of their adventures, Don Quixote and Sancho make a frightening discovery. They learn that they have been imitated, that caricatures of themselves have been unloosed upon the hapless towns of Spain, and that that part of their beings which exists in the minds of others, that very essential part which is known as fame, stands in immediate danger of destruction. For Don Quixote and Sancho Panza, living men within a literary environment, the appearance of the *Apocryphal Quixote* is clearly a case of calumny. Their reaction is natural: in order to distinguish themselves from their infamous imitators, they decide to change their plans, to alter their futures—to go to Barcelona, instead of to the jousts at Zaragoza, as they previously had intended. Later, when Don Quixote meets Don Alvaro Tarfe, a person from the rival history who had known his counterpart, he has him take a written oath affirming their lack of identity. It is a problem, like many of the other problems of Cervantes' second part, of being and will.

For Cervantes, the appearance of the *Apocryphal Quixote* had even more personal implications. Apparently without any forewarning, in the midst of the creation of the second part, he was confronted with a rival author who not only copied the first part of his book, but who also seemed to have a strange prescience as to the manuscript then in his hands, who in some way had managed to imitate and corrupt the adventures not yet published.[1] Furthermore, this unknown Alonso Fernández de Avellaneda, whoever he might be, had had the effrontery to preface his work with a series of insults to him. Cervantes was called "complaining, gossipy, impatient, and choleric as are all prisoners," and was taunted for his age, and even for his maimed hand, that glorious proof of his participation in the battle of Lepanto. Avellaneda even went so far as to gloat over the thought that his book might ruin the sale of the real second part and so cheat Cervantes of some much needed income. In addition to the spiritual trespass and the insults, there was the admitted intention of physical robbery.

246

Cervantes' reaction was not natural as had been that of Don Quixote and Sancho; it was typically Cervantine. After pointing out, in his own prologue, the injustice of some of his rival's remarks, he makes it clear that he disdains the polemic which was expected of him. He prefers to encompass Avellaneda in a web of irony. Hence, the anecdotes of the madman and the dogs in the same prologue; the introduction and annihilation of Avellaneda's story within his own; and the finality of Don Quixote's death at the end of the book. Perhaps the darkest stain upon Avellaneda's soul is not the writing of his own version nor even his attacks upon Cervantes, but his share in the death of Don Quixote, his share in the death of meaning for man. In any case, it was not Cervantes but Cid Hamete Benengelí who permitted himself the luxury of polemic reply, and called his fellow "historian," "presumptuous," and "perverse."

If Don Quixote and Sancho and if Cervantes had their own reactions to the *Apocryphal Quixote,* what has been and what should be the reaction of Cervantes' readers? In the first place, in 1614, when the false version appeared they were better equipped to judge its counterfeit nature than either Don Quixote or Sancho had dared to hope. Only one edition was printed before the appearance of the genuine second part in 1615, and none was printed afterwards. In the eighteenth century certain neo-classic critics, both in Spain and France, inspired by Lesage's translations, were not so sure. They seemed to feel that Avellaneda's caricatures, in that they did not develop and change novelistically with their circumstances, in that they were dead rather than living, were more "true to the truth" than the originals. The counter-quality of decorum must certainly have been rather difficult for them to find amid the extravagance and obscenity of the Avellanedan world.

The reaction of the nineteenth century was again typical; it represented an exaggeration not of doctrinaire but of positivistic criticism. Alonso Fernández de Avellaneda was not seen as a man with a pen in his hand who might imitate, who might criticize, or who, in doing both, might recreate. He became above all a problem, a mystery, a playground for erudites. Well over a hundred articles and books were published, naming this or that seventeenth-century figure as the unknown author, and almost every known personage of the time from Lope de Vega to Cervantes himself was accorded the dubious honor. It was a subject about which "cervantistas" could become passionate, and many long and bitter arguments were waged. Although from time to time, disparaging remarks were directed against the *Apocryphal Quixote,* very few critics took the trouble to judge the work on its own terms. If they had done so, they might have been surprised to find abundant support for the oldest theory of them all, that Avellaneda was a Dominican from Aragon.

Judging from the excesses of past criticism of Avellaneda's extraordinary book, it is perhaps now time to outline a fresh approach. The possibility that the imitation may surpass the imitated has long been discarded, and, on the basis of available evidence, the hazardous identifications of the artist have come to no conclusion. A major problem remains, however, among others. What is the imitative technique of Avellaneda? What does he discard and what does he keep and why? Or to state the problem differently, how can Avellaneda's changes be made to throw new light upon the way of Cervantes' creativity? When Menéndez y Pelayo called the *Apocryphal Quixote* a point of comparison which might serve for the "estimation" of the genius of Cervantes, he foresaw this problem, but unfortunately he did not investigate it. He returned instead to his generation's ceaseless quest for the name of Avellaneda.

If the problem of the *Apocryphal Quixote* is so to be redefined by the contemporary reader of Cervantes, he must first become aware of the centuries-old imitative tradition in Castilian literature that preceded Avellaneda. From the time of the medieval "juglar," like Juan Ruiz, who could dedicate his *Book of Good Love* to all and to anyone "who may add or change as he pleases," until that of the "comedia," with its numerous revisions and borrowings, imitation had become an accepted practice in the peninsula. As Avellaneda himself says:

> Let nobody be surprised that this second part should come from a different author, for it is not a new thing for different persons to pursue a single history. How many have spoken of Angelica's loves and of her fortunes? Arcadias have been written by many, and the *Diana* is not all from a single pen.[2]

It is a tradition which, according to Menéndez Pidal, corresponds integrally to the "popular" essence of Spanish culture. The reader is more important than the writer. The artist, as Avellaneda defines him above, becomes an historian and a servile one at that.

But Avellaneda has other things to say in his vicious prologue. In the first place, he modifies his self-justification, as the heir of a long tradition of imitation, by his attacks on Cervantes. Why insult the original author and at the same time admit his merit by the very fact of continuing his narrative? It is a delicate problem; Juan Ruiz certainly did not expect such treatment at the hands of the "juglares" who, he hoped, would carry on his inspiration. A further modification is the surprising statement by Avellaneda: "This part is somewhat different from his first, because I am of opposite humour to his . . ." He admits an antipathy here of such depth that it affects the creative process itself. He has gone beyond mere imitation, he says; he has recreated according to his own "humor," a humor profoundly hostile to that of Cervantes. The changes, then, that the reader will find in the apocryphal version correspond to something more than the incompetency of an imitator lacking Cervantes' genius; they represent a distinct artistic intent. It would be idle to deny that Avellaneda imitates and that, when he does so, he yields to the inevitable tendency of all those who copy, which is to caricature. Yet, if these were the only changes, consideration of the *Apocryphal Quixote* would merely emphasize Cervantes' poetic skill. It is when Avellaneda recreates that he throws light upon his rival's full poetic genius. It is possible to make a vital as well as a mechanical comparison.

The scope of this essay[3] does not allow for anything approaching a complete exploration of the Avellanedan world; it will be possible only to survey a few of its isolated landscapes, to sense the texture of its scenery, and to suggest routes for its future travelers. Although later the divergence of the two creative intents will be examined as they bring into relief different values from Don Quixote's familiar delusion that inns are castles, it would perhaps first be better to examine the initial escapade of the spurious knight. It holds a key to his future conduct. Don Quixote has buckled on a suit of new armor left in his care by Don Alvaro Tarfe, a gentleman who has recently passed through Argamasilla, and he stands before the mirror admiring himself for Sancho's benefit:

> "What do you think, Sancho? Does it look well on me? Do you not admire my gallantry and my warlike aspect?" This he said while walking up and down the room making faces and striking poses. . . . after which such an accident suddenly occurred within his fancy, that, putting his hand to sword with all speed, he drew near to Sancho with visible anger, saying: "Wait, cursed dragon, serpent of Libya, infernal basilisk; you shall know by experience the valor of Don Quixote, a second Saint George in strength . . ." Sancho, who saw him coming so ruthlessly, began to run around the room . . . fleeing from the fury of his master . . . Don Quixote meanwhile followed poor Sancho around the bed launching a thousand insults at him and with each one taking a long swing at him with his sword; and if the bed had not been as wide as it was, poor Sancho would have had a bad time of it.

Sancho then pleads for mercy, which is granted him only after he has promised to relinquish all his enchanted damsels and hidden treasures. When Don Quixote ultimately reverts to his senses, his explanation for the outburst is curious:

> "Can you not see, Sancho, that it was feigned, in order that you might witness my great strength in combat, my skill in laying low my enemies, my craftiness in the charge?"

Here is a Don Quixote who, unlike the Knight-of-the-Rueful Countenance, could feign his vocation, could play-act. He needs no inward belief, no comforting stimulus from aspectual reality; he could compose variations on the theme of knighthood with apt talent and dismiss the resulting tense situation a moment later as mere pretending. Here is to be the basic rhythm of the *Apocryphal Quixote;* a sudden aberration, an intensity of conflict, and an artificial dismissal of the whole matter. As soon as this scene has been played out, both Don Quixote and Sancho seem to have forgotten it and converse awkwardly about going home to eat. But, as Avellaneda is careful to point out, the exaggeration of Don Quixote's madness corresponds to basic psychological change. The knight is now possessed of a crippled mind. As a literary character, he is not only imitated badly; he is conceived differently, and his madness now results from accidents "within the fancy." These are accidents which are to modify the very foundation of the novel.

The original Don Quixote's frequent delusion that inns were castles, when imitated by Avellaneda, will further illustrate the artistic metamorphosis. In the fourth chapter of the apocryphal version, the knight and the squire perceive an inn in the distance, where the inhabitants and their adventures are reminiscent of the inn of Juan Palomeque "the left-handed," and of Maritornes. In both cases the two disagree as to the identity of the building before them, but Avellaneda's hero is not interested, as is Cervantes', in defending the exactness of his perception. He sees, instead, an opportunity to fabricate, to take an imaginary inventory of insane details. He says to Sancho:

> "Stupid fool, can you not see from here the high turrets, the famous drawbridge, and the two very fierce griffins who forbid entrance to those who wish to enter against the will of the seneschal? . . . It would be well, Sancho, if you went up to that castle as if you were a real spy and if you noted with great care the width, height, and depth of the moat, the disposition of the gates and drawbridges, the towers, the platforms, the covered causeways, the dikes, the counter-dikes, the trenches, the portcullises, the sentry boxes, the parade grounds and guard posts that are there and the artillery possessed by the defenders . . ."

Just as in the attack on Sancho, the reaction overwhelms the slight original stimulus. Each incident and each encounter provokes an outpouring of absurd monologue in such proportions that Don Quixote's illusion that he is a knight, and the restricted set of chivalresque patterns that this belief can encompass, are lost from sight. The need for variation of entertainment that is the inherent problem of both *Quixotes* is solved in this way, by Avellaneda, in terms of quantity. (Cervantes, on the other hand, found a qualitative solution by interpolating other generic patterns, pastoral, picaresque, etc., and by allowing Don Quixote, still faithful to his vocation, to live in and react against them.) Thus the apocryphal Don Quixote is more comic madman than knight-errant.

Sancho Panza, too, is conceived of as an entertainer and has his own form of comic monologue. His speech is a blend of witticisms, puns, and simplicities which permit of no more interruption than the follies of his master, and consequently there can be no dialogue between them. Lacking the human understanding, the perspectivism, implied by Cervantes' dialogue technique, Avellaneda's protagonists can only exchange their interminable monologues. The fool fails to understand and the madman fails to heed. Don Quixote, for example, when flatly told by Sancho that his castle is only an inn, is unperturbed: "To the devil with you, then, for it is what I say, in spite of the whole world." He is neither saddened nor angered but stubborn; he does not argue, but holds his ground, even in the face of such an absolute contradiction. Later, after Don Quixote has entered the inn, he refuses to take off his helmet, stubbornly insisting the while that his hosts are "untrustworthy pagans." It is one of those innumerable minor crises that threaten to halt the forward movement of the narrative, and it has a typical solution. Sancho breaks down his master's perverse immovability by "repeated demanding." Don Quixote and Sancho may demand but they cannot argue; they may talk for the amusement of the reader, but cannot converse the one with the other. Their adoption by Avellaneda has affected the depths of their beings.

The inn itself, as Avellaneda portrays it, has very different contours from its Cervantean counterpart. Cervantes' frightful picaresque makeshift of a couch becomes a "reasonable bed"; Maritornes, with her almost sprightly ugliness, becomes a colorless Galician prostitute; Juan Palomeque "the left-handed," with all his jesting rascality, becomes an innkeeper whose only living reaction to Don Quixote is anger at his failure to pay for his lodging. Although the Galician girl solicits both Don Quixote and Sancho during the night, it is only a faint reverberation of the alarms and excursions of the Cervantean episode. Thus the counterpoint of picaresque versus chivalresque patterns, the ironic artistry of "being" as opposed to "seeming," that constituted the texture of the original incident, is lost. Don Quixote's make-believe is not inserted into a circumstance created for him, a circumstance of literature, but into a world having no relationship whatsoever with himself. Although Menéndez y Pelayo has compared the *Apocryphal Quixote* to the novels of Zola, such terms as "realism" or "naturalism" are not adequate for the world here presented. It is rather a world which is unevaluated, uncreated, in a sense unloved, the world of an historian but not of an artist. Of neither Zola nor Balzac can this be said. The frequent obscenity and filth of Don Quixote's surroundings is then, like the Galician prostitute, merely coincident with their meaninglessness. The "reasonableness" of the bed is a purely casual phenomenon; it could have as easily been, as it was so often to be, unspeakable. It is a world alien to Don Quixote in that it appears completely out of his, and his author's, artistic control.

So it seems that the spurious knight is ideally suited to the place of his existence. His stubborn insanity needs no carefully prepared excuses, no artificial configurations of circumstance for its delusions; and none are there. He needs no reference to enchanters to explain his failures, as in the first part, for he never admits them. He can desert Cervantes' pastoral countryside and travel through cities without risking the growing disillusion of the second part, because there is no continuity to his experience. His damaged "fancy" overrides his senses, and any too evident contradiction from the outside world can be dismissed merely by changing the subject. Without some dominant motivation which can give a functional value to his memory, it becomes unstrung, a kaleidoscope of past impressions and information. There can be no accumulation of disillusion, no experience in the novelistic sense. It is not that the false Don Quixote is clinically insane, as might first have been supposed, but that some stabilizer, some internal gyroscope of constant faith has been removed from his spiritual mechanism. But what is the name of the motivation, the stabilizer, the faith, that Avellaneda seems to have cut from the soul of Don Quixote? The name is Dulcinea. Avellaneda's knight no longer loves Dulcinea, and he changes his name to symbolize this new basis of his existence. He is not now the Knight-of-the-Rueful Countenance but the Knight-without-Love (el Caballero Desamorado). When the real Don Quixote hears of this, his reaction demonstrates the immediacy of the coupling of his love and his memory: "Neither can the peerless Dulcinea del Toboso be forgotten, nor can forgetfulness exist in Don Quixote," he cries out. The Knight-without-Love, in contrast, must necessarily forget. He has nothing with which to evaluate the contents of his memory.

The deep purposefulness of Avellaneda's creative intent is made evident by this new title for Don Quixote. Avellaneda has not only imitated the *Quixote;* he has remade it by removing the basis of its transcendence. He has situated a loveless hero within a loveless world, a negative creation which helps to explain so much of the human consolation of Cervantes. Avellaneda's work can thus be considered as the other side of the Cervantean tapestry, and a comparison of the two reveals not the inspiration of the weaver but the excellence of what was woven.[4]

NOTES

[1] The general scheme of the stay in the Duke's palace is present in Avellaneda's work, as well as that of such minor adventures as the puppet show of Ginés de Pasamonte. Rather than admit the unlikely and unsatisfactory explanation advanced by Menéndez Pidal to the effect that Cervantes imitated Avellaneda in parts, I prefer to accept the supposition of Fitzmaurice Kelly that Cervantes read chapters of his work in progress to his friends and that Avellaneda learned of his rival's plans through the consequent, and perhaps nationwide, gossip about what was going on.

[2] Available translations of the *Apocryphal Quixote* in English are taken from Lesage's French version. The passages quoted here represent my own translation from the original.

[3] From this point forward the material presented is a condensation and general revision of an article of mine published in Spanish in the *Revista de filología hispánica*, Buenos Aires, 1943.

[4] The reason why Avellaneda built a Don Quixote without a heart, why he despised the man he imitated, why he created a world without value, and perhaps these are all parts of the same question, cannot be answered here. I hope, however, to be able to answer it in the future.

Musical Settings to Cervantes Texts

CHARLES HAYWOOD

I. *DON QUIXOTE*

A. *Operas and Ballets*

Sajon, Carlo (c. 1650–   ?)

Il Don Chisciot della Mancia.

Dramma per musica da representarsi nel Teatro di Canal Regio. L'anno MDCLXXX. 3 acts by Marco Morosini, Venice, 1680.

> In a postscript, the composer adds the following bit of information about the opera: "che è stato composto nel ristretto termine di soli giorni quattro."

Förtsch, Johann Philip (1652–1732)

Der Irrende Ritter Don Quixote de la Mancha.

Text by Marco Morosini. Hamburg, 1690.

Purcell, Henry (1658–1695), and Eccles, John (1650–1735)

Comical History of Don Quixote.

Book by Thomas d'Urfey. Dorset Garden Theatre, 1694. Second part, same year; and a third part in 1696. Purcell contributed the music to the first two parts only. Some of his songs are the well-known: "Let the dreadful engines," and "From Rosie Bowers."

Conti, Francesco (1681–1732)

Don Chisciotte in Sierra Morena

Tragicommedia per musica, da rappresentarsi nella Cesarea Corte— nel carnevale dell'anno MDCCXIX. Five acts, by Apostolo Zeno and Pietro Pariati. Vienna, Feb. 11, 1719.

Treu, Daniel Gottlieb (1695–1749)

Don Chisciotto

Breslau, 1727.

Caldara, Antonio (1670–1736)

Don Chisciotte in Corte Della duchessa.

254

Opera seria ridicola per musica da rappresentarsi alla Cesarea Corte —nel Carnevale dell'anno MDCCXXVII. La poesia e del Sig. abate Giovan. Claudio Pasquini. Five acts. Nicola Matteis was the composer of the ballet music. Vienna, February 6, 1727.

Ristori, Giovanni Alberto (1692–1753)
Un Pazzo Ne Fa Cento (Il Don Chisciotte). Text by Pallavicini. Three acts. Dresden, February 2, 1729.

Ackeroyd, Samuel (c. 1650–   ?)
The Comical History of Don Quixote.
London, 1729.

Gilliers, Jean Claude (1667–1737)
Sancho Pança, Governeur, Ou, La Bagatelle.
Paris, 1730.

Martini, "Padre" Giovanni Battista (1706–1784)
Don Chisciotto, Intermezzo.
Bologna, 1730.

Caldara, Antonio (1670–1736)
Sancio Panza, Governatore dell'Isola Barataria.
Text by G. C. Pasquini. Comedia per Musica. 3 acts. Vienna, 1733.

Silva, Antonio José (c. 1707–   ?)
La Vida do Grande Don Quixote de Mancha.
Lisbon, 1733.

Fielding, Henry (author) (1707–1754)
Don Quixote in England. A Comedy
As it is acted at the New Theatre in the Hay-Market,
London, 1734.

Feo, Francesco (1685–1745)
Don Chisciotte della Mancia, Intermezzo.
Naples, 1740.

Ayres, James
Sancho at Court, or, The Mock Governor.
By a gentleman late of Trinity College, Dublin. As it was design'd to be acted at Drury Lane, London. 3 acts. Ballad opera. 1741.

Leo, Leonardo (1694–1744)
Il Fantastico od Il Nuovo Don Chisciotte.
Naples, 1743.

Boismortier, Joseph Bodin de (1691–1765)
Don Quichotte chez la Duchesse.

Opera-ballet. Book by Favart. 3 acts. Paris: Académie Royale de
Musique, 1743.

Holzbauer, Ignaz (1711–1783)
Don Chisciotto.
Mannheim, 1755.

Philidor, François André Danican (1726–1795)
Sancho Pança, Gouverneur dans l'isle de Barataria.
Opéra bouffon représenté sur le Théâtre de la Comédie Italienne et
à Fontainbleu devant La Majesté 1762. Les paroles sont de M.
Poinsinet le Jeune.

Gassman, Florian Leopold (1729–1774)
Un Pazzo Ne Fa Cento (Don Chisciotte).
Dramma giocoso per musica, da rappresentarsi nel teatro Giustiniani
in S. Moisé, il presente autunno MDCCLXII, text by G. Foppa.
Venice, 1762.

Paisiello, Giovanni (1741–1816)
Don Chisciotte della Mancia.
Commedia per musica di Gianbattista Lorenzi, P. A. Da rappresen-
tarsi nel Teatro de' Fiorentini nell'esta de quest'anno, 1769.

Piccinni, Niccola (1728–1800)
Don Chisciotto.
Naples, 1770.

Salieri, Antonio (1750–1825)
Don Chisciotto alle Nozzi di Gamazzo. Festa Musicale,
Libretto di Boccherini. 1 act. Vienna, 1771.

Schack, Benedict (1728–1826)
Don Chisciotto.
Vienna, 1785.

Beecke, Ignaz von (1733–1803)
Don Quixote.
Operette in drei acten. Berlin, 1788.

Zaccharelli, —— (1759–   ?)
Le Nouveau Don Quichotte.
Paris, 1789.

Champein, Stanislaus (1753–1830)
Le Nouveau Don Quichotte.
Opéra en deux acts, paroles du C. Boisset, représenté sur le Théâtre
des Thuilleries le Mai 1789.

Spindler, Fritz (1759–1820)
Ritter Don Quixote: Das Abenteuer am Hofe.
Kommisch-romantische oper. 1790.

Tarchi, Angelo (1760–1814)
Don Chisciotte.
Paris, 1791.

Hubatschek, —— (c. 1760–   ?)
Don Quichotte.
3 acts. Hermannstadt, 1791.

Pitrot, Antonio (author)
Don Chisciotte.
Comic ballet. (Composer's name not known)
Milano, 1792.

Dittersdorf, Karl Ditters von (1739–1799)
Don Quixotte der Zweite.
Ein komisches singspiel aus dem Italienischen, in zwei aufzugen.
Die musik ist vom herrn von Dittersdorf.
Oels, Hoftheater, February 4, 1795.

Mayr, Johann Simon (1763–1845)
Un Pazzo Ne Fa Cento (Il Don Chisciotte).
3 acts. Text by Giuseppe Foppa, Venice, 1796, "Nel Nobilissimo
Teatro S. Samuele."

Arnold, Dr. Samuel (1740–1802)
The Mountaineers:
An opera in three acts, by G. Colman, the younger, as performed at
the theatres—New York, Philadelphia, and Baltimore. With remarks
by Mrs. Inchbald. Based on the adventures of Cardenio in Don
Quixote. The music by S. Arnold. London, 1795.

Navoigeville, Guillaume E. J. (1745–1811)
L'Empire de la Folie (La Mort et l'apothéose de Don Quichotte).
Pantomime, 3 acts. Paris, 1799.

Lefébre, Louis F. H. (1754–1840)
Les Noces de Gamache.
Libretto de Milon. Paris, 1800.

Mueller, Wenzel (1767–1835)
Ritter Don Quixote.
3 acts. Text by Von Hensler. Leopolstadter Theater.
Wien, 1802.

Generali, Pietro (1783–1832)
Don Chisciotte. Libretto di Rossi.
Milan, 1805.

Miari, Antoine Compte de (1787–1854)
Don Quichotte.
Venice, 1810.

Seidel, Friedrich Ludwig (1765–1831)
Die Abenteur des Ritter Don Quixote de la Mancha.
Berlin, 1811.

Bochsa, Robert Nicolus Charles (1789–1856)
Les Noces de Gamache.
3 acts. Paris, 1815.

Mendelssohn-Bartholdy, Felix (1809–1847)
Die Hochzeit des Camacho.
Komische oper in 2 acten. Op. 10. Libretto by Klingemann. Berlin
Opera, April 29, 1827. The composer later referred to this work as
"my old sin of Camachos' wedding."

Garcia, Manuel del Popolo Vicente (1775–1832)
Don Chisciotte.
2 acts. New York, 1827.

Mercadante, Giuseppe Saverio R. (1795–1870)
Don Chisciotto.
Cadix, 1829.

Donizetti, Gaetano (1797–1848)
Il Furioso nell'Isola di San Domingo.
Text by G. Ferreti. 2 acts. Rome, 1833.
Founded on an episode in Don Quixote.

Rodwell, George Herbert Bonaparte (1800–1852)
Don Quixote, operetta.
London, Adelphi Theatre, 1835.

Mazzucato, Alberto (1813–1877)
Don Chisciotte.
Milano, 1836.

Gährich, Wenzel (1794–1865)
Don Quixote. Ballet.
Berlin, 1840.

Macfarren, George Alexander (1813–1887)
Don Quichotte.
London, 1845.

Moniuszko, Stanislau (1819–1872)
The New Don Quixote.
Text by Count Fredro. 3 acts. Wilna, 1847.

Clapisson, Antoine L. (1808–1866)
Don Quichotte et Sancho. Operetta.
Paris. December 11, 1847.

"Ronger" (Hervé, Florimond) (1825–1892)
Don Quichotte et Sancho Pansa, Operetta. 1 act.
Paris, Opéra National, 1848.

Boulanger, Ernest, H. A. (1815–1900)
Don Quichotte.
Opéra-comique. 3 acts. Book by Jules Barbier and Michel Carré.
Paris, Théâtre Lyrique, 1869.

Minkus, Aloysius Fyodorvich (1827–1890)
Don Quichotte: Ballet in 4 acts and 4 scenes and a prologue. Book
and choreography by Marius Petipa. First performed at the Bolshoy
Theatre, Moscow, Dec. 14–26, 1869.

Pessard, Émile (1843–1917)
Don Quichotte.
Operette-bouffe. 1 act. Book by M. J. Deschamps.
Paris, Salle Érard, 1874.

Offenbach, Jacques (1819–1880)
Don Quichotte.
Book by Sardou. Pantomime. Paris, 1874.

Clay, Frederick (1840–1889)
Princess Toto and Don Quixote.
Comic opera. London, 1875.

Menendorff, A. (1843–1897)
Don Quixote.

Roth, Philipp (1853–1898), and Weinzierl, Max Ritter von (1841–1898)
Don Quixote.
Operetta. Vienna, 1879.

Ricci, Luigi (1852–1906)
Don Chisciotte.

Opera Heroi-comique. Text by Fiorentino and Gallo.
Venice, Feb. 4, 1881.

Lucantini, Giovanni (1825–1902)
Don Chisciotto.
Ballet. 2 acts. Milan, December 26, 1884.

Chapí y Lorente, Ruperto (1851–1909)
La Venta de Don Quijote.

Roth, Luigi (1849–c1914)
Don Chichotte.
Budapest, 1888.

De Koven, Reginald (1859–1920)
Don Quixote.
Boston, 1889.

Jacques-Dalcroze, Emile (1865–   )
Sancho.
Comédie lyrique en 4 acts et 8 tableaux. Poème de R. Yve-Plessis.
Geneva, 1897.

Rauchenecker, Georg W. (1844–1906)
Don Quixote.
Elberfield, 1897.

Kienzl, Wilhelm (1857–1941)
Don Quixote.
Eine musikalische Tragikomödie in drei aufzugen.
Dichtung and musik von Kienzl. Op. 50. 1898.

Beer-Walbrunn, Anton (1864–1929)
Don Quijote.
der sinnreiche Juncker von der Mancha: Musikalische Tragikomödie in 3 aufzugen von Georg Fuchs. München, 1908.

Besi, Simone.
Don Chisciotto della Mancia.
San Sepolcro. April 18, 1908.

Massenet, Jules Emile Fréderic (1842–1912)
Don Quichotte.
Comédie héroique en cinq actes. Poème de Henri Cain, d'après Le
Lorrain. Monte Carlo Theatre, Feb. 19, 1910.

Pasini, Francesco.
Don Chisciotto della Mancia.
Florence. April 9, 1910.

Falla, Manuel de (1876–1946)
El Retablo de Maese Pedro.
Adaptación musical y escénica de un episodio de "El ingenioso caballero Don Quijote de la Mancha" de Miguel de Cervantes. Seville, 1923.

B. *Orchestral Compositions*

Telemann, George Philipp (1681–1767)
Don Quichotte Suite.

Gandolfo, E.
Marche Héroique de Don Quichotte.
Pour instruments à cordes.
Nice, Paul Décourcelle, 1892. 3 pp.

Kienzl, Wilhelm (1857–1941)
Don Quixote's Phantasticher Ausritt und Seine Traurige Heimkehr.
Miteinander verbundene u. zum konzert-vortrage eingerichtete symphonische zwischenspiele für grosses orchester aus der musikalischen tragikomödie Don Quixote. Op. 50.
Berlin, Ed. Bote & Bock, 1899. 47 pp.

Rubinstein, Anton Gregorievich (1829–1894)
Don Quixote.
Musikalisches Characterbild. Humoreske für orchester. Op. 87.
Leipzig, Verlag von Bartholf Senff, 1871. 99 pp.

Chapí y Lorente, Ruperto (1851–1909)
Scherzo.
Symphonic poem based on an episode of Don Quixote.

Strauss, Richard (1864–   )
Don Quixote.
(Introduzione, tema con variazioni e finale.)
Fantastische Variationen über ein thema ritterlichen characters für grosses orchester. Op. 35. München, Jos. Aibl, 1898. 94 pp.

Gherard, Roberto.
Don Quijote.
Incidental music. Radio presentation.
London, 1945.

II. *NOVELAS EJEMPLARES*

A. *Operas*

Dibdin, Charles (1745–1814)
The Padlock.
Text by I. Bickerstaffe. Two acts. Based on "El celoso extremeño."
London, 1768.

Auber, Daniel François-Esprit (1782–1871)
Leocadie.
Text by P. A. Wolff. Romantische Schauspiel mit musik. 4 acts.
Based on "La gitanilla." Berlin, 1821.

Weber, Carl Maria von (1786–1826)
Preciosa.
Text by P. A. Wolff. Romantisches Schauspiel mit musik. Four acts.
Based on "La gitanilla." Berlin, 1821.

Chapí y Lorente, Ruperto (1851–1909)
La Gitanilla.

Orbón, Julián (1925–   )
Incidental music to La gitanilla. Hábana, 1944

Laparra, Raoul (1876–1943)
L'Illustre Fregona.
Text by composer. Zarzuela. Three acts. Paris, 1931.

III. *ENTREMESES*

A. *Operas*

Winter, Peter von (1754–1825)
Der Bettelstudent oder Das Donnerwetter
Text by Weidmann. Two acts. Based on "La cueva de Salamanca."
Münich, 1785.

Paumgartner, Bernhard (1887–   )
Die Höhle von Salamanca
Opera Buffa in einem Akt nach dem gleichnamigen swischenspiel
des Cervantes. Klavierauszug von Meinhard Zallinger. Wien,
Wiener Philharmonischer Verlag, 1923. 187 pp. Dresden, 1923.

Lattuanda, Felice (1882–   )
La Caverna di Salamanca, Opera seria
Text by Piccoli. One act. Genoa, 1938.

Offenbach, Jacques (1819–1880)
Les Bavards

Opera bouffe en deux actes. Paroles de Ch. Nuittier. (pseud.); 2 actes. Ems, 1863. Based on "Los dos habladores."

IV. *SONGS: VOICE AND PIANO*

Obradors, Fernando J.
Consejo
from Historia del "Curioso impertinente" de *El Ingenioso Hidalgo Don Quijote de la Mancha.*
Madrid, Union Musical Española, 1930.

Ravel, Maurice (1875–1937)
Don Quichotte à Dulcinée
Chanson romantique
Chanson épique
Chanson à boire
3 songs. Text by P. Morand

V. *OPERAS BASED ON CERVANTES LIFE*

Lassen, Eduard (1830–1904)
Le Captif
Text by E. Cormon. Brussels, 1865. One act.
Deals with an incident in the life of Cervantes.

Strauss, Johann (1825–1899)
Das Spitzentuch Der Königin
Text by H. Horrmann-Riegen and R. Genee. 3 acts.
Vienna, 1880.
The librettist invented a plot, without any basis in fact, involving Cervantes with the King and Queen of Portugal.

PART FOUR

PART FOUR

Cervantes and English Literature

EDWIN B. KNOWLES

AS one looks back over three hundred and forty-odd years, the adventures of *Don Quixote* in English literature command attention because the book came to achieve great popularity and also because it reflects the changing literary tastes of many generations of English readers. The lesser popularity and influence of Cervantes' *Novelas, Persiles y Sigismunda,* and other works reduce them to a very small part of the general scene. It is *Don Quixote* which must occupy the centre of the stage in the following survey, a survey which will necessarily be superficial, both for lack of space and because in the fields of the 18th and 19th centuries very little scholarly research has ever been done.[1]

In addition to setting down a brief story of the borrowings and influence that has been uncovered, this essay will seek to demonstrate that there have been four relatively distinct English interpretations of the novel and its hero: that of the 17th century, which emphasized only the surface farce; that of the 18th century, which, while enjoying the comic values, chiefly esteemed the serious satire; that of the 19th century romantic period, which deprecated both the comedy and satire in order to exalt the deep spiritual implications; and that of the late 19th and 20th centuries, which—most eclectic of all—embraces the earlier views in a more just proportion and sees in the book an eternal human classic of a richly complex nature. There are, of course, no sharply cut lines between periods. The earlier modes flow into the later, and, though superseded in popularity, persist to our own day. Like miners, successive generations of English readers have penetrated deeper and deeper into the inexhaustible riches of *Don Quixote* and found new veins of ideas to work. But the old galleries near the surface continue to yield good ore. The situation bears interesting analogies to a different kind of universality described by Sansón Carrasco in Part II, when he says, " . . . the children turn its leaves; the young people read it, the grown men understand it, and the old folks praise."

In 1612, seven years after the printing of *Don Quixote,* Part I, in Madrid,

Thomas Shelton's translation was published in London—*The History of the valorous and wittie Knight-Errant, Don Quixote of the Mancha*. It was the first complete version in any foreign language. The translator's statement that it had been done for a friend rather than for the public is probably true, for though complete, it is a hurried, often very careless job. Shelton's colloquial vocabulary was vivid, but in general he lacked sufficient knowledge of Spanish, and he had the bad habit of translating Spanish words into English homonyms (*e. g., trance* to trance). Though marred by amusing blunders, his rendition has charm and flavor, particularly for readers with a knowledge of and taste for the English of Cervantes' and Shakespeare's time. A translation of Part II was published in 1620 (also by Shelton), together with a new edition of Part I. Shelton was reprinted twice before 1700 (1652, 1675). The only other translation in this period was a facetious rendition by John Phillips, to be discussed later. This paucity of English versions during the first ninety-five years of *Don Quixote's* existence should be borne in mind when one reads overheated statements about the way the book was enthusiastically received in England. There were fourteen editions of translations in France during the same period.[2]

The direct imitations or borrowings from *Don Quixote* between 1605 and the Restoration in 1660 are misleadingly impressive when listed. First is Beaumont and Fletcher's *The Knight of the Burning Pestle* (c. 1611). Hailed originally (and persistently by German scholars) as a direct and important imitation, this play is now considered to be only very slightly and vaguely related to the Spanish novel. Massinger's *The Second Maiden's Tragedy* (1611) is directly adapted from *El Curioso Impertinente*, but without making any use of *Don Quixote* as a whole. Probably in the same year appeared Field's *Amends for Ladies*, which to a less extent borrows plot ideas from "El Curioso Impertinente," or at second-hand from Massinger's play. It may well be shown some day that both these plays derived from Baudouin's French version of Cervantes' story (Paris 1608), rather than from the original Spanish.

In 1613, the year after Shelton's translation, there was acted at the English court a play entitled *Cardenno*, written by Fletcher and, perhaps, Shakespeare. It has generally been assumed that this was an adaptation of the Cardenio story, but it is impossible to be certain for the play has disappeared. However, the whole matter has been extensively debated in relation to the eighteenth-century dramatization of the Cardenio story by Theobald in his *Double Falsehood* (1727). E. H. C. Oliphant and Walter Graham are the champions of the thesis that Theobald reworked a play originally written by Fletcher and Shakespeare. As yet, Shakespeare's collaboration has not been widely accepted. Fletcher and Massinger's play *The Double Marriage* (c. 1620) lifts the scene of Sancho's unhappy dinner as governor and fits it into a play otherwise unrelated to the Spanish. In Fletcher's *The Pilgrim* (1621) a character retells the anecdote told by Cervantes in his introduction to Part II about the madman who almost talked himself out of the madhouse.

The first use of major characters occurs in 1630 as a minor comic element in D'Avenant's *The Cruel Brother*. A silly country gentleman, Lothario, and his farmer servant, Boraccio, "a bundle of proverbs," bear a general resemblance to the Don and Sancho. However, Lothario soon loses this resemblance as he develops into a scheming courtier. Boraccio remains like Sancho for at least two acts: his attitude towards his master, his plans for rising in the world, his proverbs, his amusing comments all echo Sancho—but in outline and as from a great distance. Another brief and strictly farcical appearance of Quixote and Sancho is made in Shirley's masque *The Triumph of Peace* (1634). Shirley thus describes the action of his pantomime:

> After the *Dotterels* [silly birds] are caught by several imitations, enter a Windmill, a fantastic *Knight* and his *Squire* armed. The fantastic adventurer with his lance makes many attempts upon the windmill, which his squire imitates: to them enter a *Country-Gentleman* and his *Servant*. These are assaulted by the Knight and His Squire, but are sent off lame for their folly. Then enter four Bowlers, who shew much variety of sport in their postures . . .[3]

In the same vein as the Shirley use, but much larger and more significant, is Edmund Gayton's *Pleasant Notes upon Don Quixote* (republished in 1768 and 1771 as *The Festivous Notes*. . .). Gayton was a "superior beadle in arts and physic" at Oxford until his royalist sympathies reduced him during the Commonwealth to the impoverished life of a hack writer in London. For a person with no feeling for the greatness of Cervantes' work, the book is, in the words of the *D.N.B.*, "a gossipy and anecdotal commentary . . . spiritedly written." However, the admirer of Cervantes is more apt to be disgusted by Gayton's misguided joking and triviality. Using Shelton's translation, Gayton goes through Part I chapter by chapter, selecting short passages and commenting on them facetiously, or relating some joke suggested by them. Much of the story is summarized in doggerel verse. The following are typical:

> *There stood at the Inne by the door, two women adventurers likewise.* These I beleeve had been budd'd and dubb'd againe, and had devises in their Targets, for hotter adventures then ever the Don assailed; it was strange that the *Don* (but that strong imagination is irresistible) being *gaunt,* (not *John a Gaunt* I meane) but fasting, and therefore of more

exquisite sense, had not smelt out their profession from the evaporations of their salt-pits: or that *Rosinante* had not by a merry neighing, discovered the approaches of two over-ridden jades. Their standing at the Inne door, was a sign of themselves and the house, and (though they were bound for *Sevil*) that their behavior was not so.

* * * *

> Happy that age, which called was the golden,
> Not because gold (which doth so much embolden
> Men in this Iron age) was plenty store;
> Alas (good men) they had nor coyn, nor oar;
> But because all things were in common to 'un,
> And those two filthy words, *meum* and *tuum,*
> Were not i' the World, but each mans heart and house
> Were open, they kept gen'ral rendevouse.

Prefixed to Gayton's book was the usual antechamber of commendatory poems. It is significant, though not surprising, that Gayton's friends consider his comment superior to the original text; more startling is the discovery that Gayton had made an obscure work intelligible. Each of the following is from a different poem.

> If solid heads may judge the Text is good,
> It will improve much now, being understood.

* * * *

> Your Clavis makes his History to be
> The unveiled Cabala of chivalrie.

* * * *

> So thou, considering what befits this age,
> Hast brought thy *Don* unridled on our stage;
> And with thy rayes illustrating his shade,
> Hast a clear mirrour of a night-piece made.

* * * *

> Were *Don* alive againe, he would be vext
> To see a Comment better then his Text.

Gayton's concept of Don Quixote as reflected in the *Notes* is no complimentary one. The Manchegan Knight is called "a sly coward," "an unabashed liar," "a vagabond," "hypocritical thief," "sly fox," a "mealy-mouthed courtier." On several occasions his chastity is leered at. In fact, there was absolutely nothing in the Knight's character as Gayton saw it to prevent the English wit from using it as a hatrack on which to hang any sort of facetious story that he dared to print. For him Don Quixote had no ideals. He was an amusing old fool whom Gayton hoped to make more amusing by the addition of jokes. Sancho is similarly shorn of his personality. Dulcinea is only a subject for jest. Of awareness of Cervantes' satirical purpose there is none. Though it is an extreme example of the farcial interpretation, Gayton's is not particularly out of line with his age; further, he set the prevailing fashion for the next fifty years.

In the period down to 1660 there are two other large uses of *Don Quixote*. The first is a play—"the *History of Donquixot, or, the Knight of the illfavoured face,* a comedy"—advertised by Nathaniel Brook, bookseller, as one of several "in the presse and ready for printing." The advertisement appeared three times: in *The New World of English Words* (1658), *Wit and Drollery* (1661), and *Tom Tyler and His Wife* (1661). Unfortunately there is no record that the drama ever reached the stage or was actually printed. The other use is a scene in William Chamberlayne's *Pharonnida* (1659), a very long, obscure heroic poem. As a brief comic interlude Chamberlayne introduces an aged pair of platonic lovers, who, as a result of reading romances, go around in peculiar costumes and make senile love, strictly according to the code of chivalry. Also, a group of courtiers, like the Duke and Duchess in the novel, play a practical joke on the pair for the amusement of the court. The influence is tenuous and general.

For the period down to 1660 the allusions to *Don Quixote,* as distinguished from the ten larger borrowings just discussed, confirm the picture of both the slow growth in popularity and the interpretation as farce. The thirty allusions discovered by Fitzmaurice-Kelly, Becker, and others have now been pushed up to eighty.[4] The first occurs in 1607, with four more before 1612. By 1620 four others had appeared, and from then they occur at the rate of one a year until 1629. From then on the number each year increases gradually to the seven found in 1659.

Parallel to this gradual growth in numbers is the development of the allusions themselves. Read in sequence they almost seem to have been written by one composite author who, year by year, read further into the book and gradually understood it better. The first ones are very simple. Typical is this from George Wilkin's play *The Miseries of Enforced Marriage* (1607): a drunken roisterer shouts to his page boy, "Now am I armed to fight with a windmill." Commonly Cervantes' satire is linked with the books it satirized or distinguished from them only by being comic. Such is Kastril's slur in *The Alchemist* of Ben Johnson:

> It is my humour: you are a pimp and a trig, and an *Amadis de Gaul* or a *Don Quixote.*

Francis Lenton in *The Young Gallants Whirligigg* (1629) sets forth, as the preface tells us, "the inordinate affections, absurd actions, and profuse expenses of unbridled and affected youth." As an example of thriftless reading he couples the *Don* with the most popular penny-dreadful of the time:

> Now thinkes his father, here's a goodly sonne,
> That hath approached unto Littleton, [studied law]
> But never lookt on't—for instead of that
> Perhaps hee's playing of a game at Cat.
> No, no, good man, hee reades not Littleton,
> But *Don Quix-Zot* or els *The Knight o' the Sun*.

Serious discussions, criticisms, appraisals of Cervantes' novel, of which a substantial number exist in French, are non-existent in England during this time. The reason is not far to seek. The uncordial social and religious affiliations between Spain and England of this era need no elaboration. Cervantes had no critical reputation in his homeland to force his name on the attention of serious readers. In fact, his name is mentioned in English in only five known places before 1660. More important, *Don Quixote* was at first grouped with the cheap romances which were popular with the untutored and scorned by the literary élite. Richard Braithwaite has this to say in his *The Schollers Medley* (1614); he is speaking of proper reading for the young:

> And last of all (which in my judgment is worst of all) others which the phantasticke writings of some supposed knights (Don Quixotte transformed into a knight with the *Golden Pestle*) with many other fruitless inventions moulded *only for delight without profit*. These histories I altogether exclude my economy or private family. I have culled out more beneficial discourses for youths to employ themselves withall . . . not from the brain of every Quacksalver that runs out his inventions by selling lyes at grosse-sale.

Cervantes realism and his rich humor went begging at a time when a facetious sort of wit, called "drolling," was coming into vogue through the pens of Smith, Mennes, Flecknoe, and Gayton, a style that after the Restoration blended with the stream of burlesque and parody made popular by Scarron and others.

And what of Cervantes' other works? *La Galatea* was not translated into English until the 18th century and there is no record of its being known earlier. *Los Trabajos de Persiles y Sigismunda* was anonymously translated from the French in 1619 and was seized at once by Fletcher and Massinger for *The Custom of the Country* (1620). Parts of the plot are patched into a play which contains some loose parallels in dialogue. However, the characters and atmosphere have been transformed from innocence to one of the most indecent of Jacobean comedies. The *Ocho Comedias y Ocho Entremeses* have never been entirely done into English, and none were translated in this century. *Los Baños de Argel* has been claimed as the source of Massinger's *The*

Renegado (1624), but on entirely unconvincing evidence. Similarly, there are no grounds for the statement that Massinger and Field's *The Fatal Dowry* (1619) is indebted to *El Viejo Celoso*. The *Novelas Ejemplares* were available in a French translation in 1615. Six of the twelve were Englished by Mabbe in 1640 (with no reference to their author). In keeping with the taste of the times was his selection of the more slickly plotted, Italianate tales rather than *El Coloquio de los Perros* or *Rinconete*. As a translation, it is excellent.

However, certain English dramatists hawking for plots did not wait for the English of Mabbe; the French translation satisfied their needs. Of the eight plays which various scholars have considered indebted to the *Novelas*, three should be rejected on grounds of insufficient evidence: *The Queen of Corinth, The Beggar's Bush,* and *A Very Woman*. Of the other five there is no question. *Love's Pilgrimage* (c. 1615) by Beaumont and Fletcher takes part of its plot and some of the dialogue from *Las Dos Doncellas*. The same is true of Fletcher's *The Chances* (c. 1615), adapted from *La Señora Cornelia*. *The Spanish Gypsy* (1623) by Middleton and Rowley, cleverly combines material from *La Fuerza de la Sangre* and *La Gitanilla*. Fletcher's *Rule a Wife and Have a Wife* (1624) derives its subplot from *El Casamiento Engañoso,* and the same author's *The Fair Maid of the Inn* (c. 1625) draws directly from *La Ilustre Fregona.*

We see, then, that during the first half of the 17th century there is no evidence of borrowing from Cervantes' *Galatea,* his *Comedias,* or his *Entremeses.* One play was based on sections of the *Persiles,* and five, in varying degrees, owe clear allegiance to *Novelas.* In every instance, so far as the evidence goes, the French translation was used. It can be said in common of the six plays that the element sought was plot; that the borrowing is always clear, in every case parallel wording being present; that Spanish, or Cervantic, literary qualities disappear; that the adaptors added characters, scenes, changed details; that the moral or ethical tone is always lowered, in some cases to the point of degrading the original; that the dramatic quality is generally heightened and improved. Cervantes is never mentioned. In the broad sense, the resulting plays are so thoroughly English that it is difficult to see anything which could be called influence.

The situation in England from 1605 to 1660 has been treated in more detail than will later periods for two reasons: it is the only period which has been thoroughly combed for Cervantes' influence; and, paradoxically, it is the period about which the most incorrect generalizations are commonly made. Anyone familiar with the writings about Cervantes in England knows that over and over again it is glowingly declared that *Don Quixote* was immediately popular, was at once accepted as a great classic, and, by implication, at once had an important influence. The preceding pages should go a long way to proving this notion a myth.[5]

Cervantes' masterpiece stole into England, but not as a masterpiece. It was read first by the readers of romances (for the most part uncritical folk), by dramatists in search of plot material, and by those with a penchant for the curious (like Burton) and the facetious (like Gayton). Its popularity developed gradually, for its appeal suffered because the book was not appreciated for what it is, because there was no critical push behind it, and because for a long while people tended to assume that it was "just another" romance. Its influence was slight from any point of view; none of the uses made of it were important. This reception, far from being unusual, is just what the social, political, and literary conditions during the first half of the 17th century make most natural.

. The forty years from the Restoration to 1700 saw the misbegotten, farcical approach to *Don Quixote* reach its full flowering. They also saw a growing serious interest which culminated in a burst of new translations and widespread critical interest in the opening years of the 18th century. Then the belittling interpretation of Gayton, Phillips, and Ward finally gave way before the view that Cervantes' novel was a masterpiece of serious satire. In addition to the normal growth in readers enjoyed by any worthy book, there were at least two special impulses behind these changes. First was the return of the Cavaliers from their exile in France, where, as has been said, *Don Quixote* enjoyed a high repute. Second, the great popularity of *Hudibras* must have sent many an Englishman in search of a copy of the book so often mentioned as its origin.

There is no disagreement about the definite, though limited, indebtedness of Samuel Butler's *Hudibras* (1663, 1664, and 1678) to *Don Quixote*. In many superficial aspects the Presbyterian fanatic resembles the Spanish knight—his physical appearance, his sorry nag, his certainty of his calling, his preconceptions which blind him to reality, his ill-success as a fighter, his long discussions with his squire Ralph. The squire is more of a knave and sophist than Sancho, more nearly on an equal footing with his master; and, unlike Sancho, he deserts his knight. But the differences outweigh the similarities. Butler's mock-heroic poem has for its central characters a pair of self-seeking, hypocritical, puritanical rogues. The reader never wastes any sympathy on them. The satire—merry, punishing, keen—so completely demolishes its butts that there is no residue left of ennobling idealism or appealing human nature. The sparkling brilliance of the tetrameter couplets creates a mood and tempo entirely unCervantic. To the extravagance and bite of the travesty Rabelais and Scarron contributed rather than Cervantes. From the Spaniard came the broad suggestions for the main characers, their general relationship, the pattern of their wanderings. This kinship weakens as Butler's poem moves into Part III. The qualities of genius in *Hudibras* are original, and a similarity to *Don Quixote* in any deep sense does not exist. However, because Butler's fellows were, more than we, under the influence of the Gayton conception, they undoubtedly saw Butler, "the English Cervantes," as more closely imitative of *Don Quixote* than is possible for us.

Even more completely in the Gayton line is the only new translation to be made before 1700. It was the work of John Phillips (one of the nephews Milton educated) and was done in the most *à-la-mode* style of travesty. Phillips had already worked in this vein: he was probably the translator of Scarron's *Typhon* (1665) and certainly the author of *Moronides, or Virgil Travestie . . . in Burlesque Verse* (1672). In 1687 appeared his *Don Quixote* "now made English according to the humour of our Modern Language." Phillips worked from Shelton and omitted relatively little. But his folio of 616 pages contains almost nothing that has not undergone a sea-change. Space will admit of only one quotation; following is Phillips' rendition of that part of Chapter XXV where the Don and Sancho discuss who Dulcinea really is:

> And I question [says Quixote] whether she herself ever took notice that ever I looked upon her, so strict a watch did old Richard Hogg of Stanwel, her Father, and Joan Hogg her Mother, keep over her.
> Cuds-bobs, cryed Sancho, and is Dulcinea del Toboso the Daughter of Dick Fogg of Stamwel, otherwise Nan Hogg? Uds sish, I know her as well as her Mother that bore her; she's a Strapper y' faith, and pitches the Bar with e're a young Fellow i' the Villiage. The very same, quo Don Quixote, that's she, and she that deserves to be Mistress of the whole Earth. Is that she, quo Sancho! She's a Bouncer, Begar law; and one that will keep her Chin out O' the Mire, I warrant her, in despite of the best Knight Errant that wears a Head. Long Megg of Westminster was a Dwarf to her. One day I remember, she stood upon the top of our Steeple to call the Plough men home to dinner, that were at work above half a League off; yet they heard her as plain, as if they had been just under the Sun-dial. The best thing I know in her, is, that she is not Coy, but will bid he kiss the top of her Nock as briskly as e're a Coggshall Wench that goes to Market; there's ne're a Water-man upon the Thames can out-rally her.

Although we would probably not look in one translator for an unbiased appraisal of his predecessors, in this instance Motteux's comment on Phillips' work is no overstatement:

> "[He] changed the Sense, ridiculed the most serious and moving Passages, remov'd all the scandalous places in London into the middle of Spain, and all the Language of Billingsgate into the mouths of Spanish

Ladies and Noblemen. He has confounded the characters and the Countries, and added a world of Obscenity and fribbling Conceits.

The climax of the Gayton-Phillips approach is reached in Thomas D'Urfey's trilogy of plays, *The Comical History of Don Quixote,* Parts I and II in 1694 and Part III in 1696. It is one of the crowning ironies of literature that Cervantes' moral and dignified novel should have been the source of plays so immodest that they were among those selected for condemnation by Jeremy Collier in his *A Short View of the Immorality and Profaneness of the English Stage* (1698), and the cause of their author's prosecution for profanity.

Part I centers its action in the Cardenio and Dorothea stories with comic scenes for Don Quixote about the windmills, the wineskins, Mambrino's helmet, the galley slaves, and the enchanted cage. The order of events is transposed for a better-knit plot and some scenes with Sancho's wife are moved in from Cervantes' Part II. The second play uses scenes from the second half of the novel at the Duke's estate, with Sancho's governorship and a much enlarged part for Marcella. In the third play appear the adventure with the lions, Camacho's wedding, Sancho's whippings for the disenchantment of Dulcinea, the puppet play, and a fat part for "Mary the buxome," Sancho's daughter. D'Urfey supplies her with a rustic lover and a foul wit. As plays these are mediocre, the first being the best and containing the least objectionable material. Of them one must say what has already been said of Gayton's *Notes* and Phillips' translation: Don Quixote throughout is nothing but an amusing crackpot; Sancho is a sharp-tongued, irreligious, rude English country boor. Altisidora, Marcella, and Mary are in various ways unpleasantly suggestive. The general atmosphere is no more that of Cervantes and Spain than is that of Wycherley's *The Country Wife* or *Congreve's Love for Love,* which were equally condemned by Collier.[6]

To complete what is perhaps a too extensive survey of Gayton's progeny of false Quixotes, it will be necessary to jump ahead to 1711 and Ned Ward's *The Life and Notable Adventures of that renowned Knight Don Quixote de la Mancha, Merrily translated into Hudibrastic Verse.* Ward, a London tavern-keeper, did some vividly realistic scketches of London life and enjoyed a considerable reputation as a wit. His wit and Cervantes' humor have little in common, as a brief sample from Chapter I of his "translation" will show:

> The *Don* in this abstemious life,
> Without a mistress or a wife,
> Except the keeper of his house,
> Supply'd the office of a spouse,
> And when she tucked him in at night
> Received the nipple of delight.

The poem runs for thirty-nine cantos, carrying Part I of the novel as far as the assumption by Dorothea of the rôle of Princess Micomicona. A sentence from Ward's dedication offers interesting evidence of how far *Don Quixote* had progressed in England in almost 100 years:

> Besides, the universal approbation the original has obtained in all the courts of Europe, and the step it has made towards a venerable antiquity, has not only given a kind of sanctity to the work, but has procured for its author a monument of fame, not inferior to that which is so justly due to the flourishing memory of our own English Butler.

Phillips in his preface had made a similar statement about the book's popularity "in all the Learned parts of Europe." But the book's reputation abroad and the "sanctity" afforded by its antiquity could lead Ward to no higher praise than to compare its author with Butler. That was undoubtedly no mean compliment in Ward's eyes, but it hardly satisfies the modern reader.

Our picture of the 17th century will be completed by the mention of three plays that relate to *El Curioso Impertinente*. Aphra Behn's *The Amorous Prince, or, The Curious Husband* (1671) bases its subplot on the Spanish story. The same is true of Sotherne's *The Disappointment* (1684). Crowne's *The Married Beau, or, The Curious Impertinent,* (1694) is a farcical treatment of the same tale—a tale which up to this date was certainly the most copied portion of *Don Quixote*.

Cervantes was by now becoming well enough known to be a fair risk for publishers. In the 1680's and -90's the public was offered no less than four abridgments of the novel, the smallest a 24-page chapbook with illustrations. The *Novelas Ejemplares* were also beginning to circulate. *The Spanish Decameron* (1687) contained translations of five of the stories, stolen by Roger L'Estrange from Mabbe's earlier work. *Select Novels,* "The first six written in Spanish by Miguel Cervantes Sayavedra, author of that Famous History Don Quixote de la Mancha" (1694) has new but somewhat condensed translations by Dr. Pope of six tales. Five of Pope's selection were the same stories offered by L'Estrange and Mabbe: *Las Dos Doncellas, La Señora Cornelia, El Amante Liberal, La Fuerza de la Sangre,* and *La Española Inglesa.*

In spite of his uncertain spelling, Dr. Pope's reference to Cervantes as "the author of that Famous History" speaks volumes. Though good business in 1694, it would have been an unthinkable statement in the first half of the century. By the end of the 17th century *Cervantes* had begun to be a name worth mentioning.

II

No better evidence of the now burgeoning interest in *Don Quixote* could be found than the appearance in 1700 of two translations, and—in the century as a whole—of four additional translations, the first good Spanish text, the first scholarly commentary, and a flood of second, fourth, sixth, and tenth editions of the popular translations. The first of the pair in 1700 was a thorough refurbishing of Shelton's translation by that ardent hispanophile, Capt. John Stevens. His volume III contained the first Englishing of Avellaneda's spurious continuation. More important, because it has been reprinted down into the twentieth century, was the new translation by Peter Motteux (he of the Motteux-Urquhart Rabelais) and "several hands." To a very real extent the curse of Gayton's biased view can still be felt here, felt in Motteux's practice of heightening and anglicizing the comical coloring of the original. He is occasionally as inaccurate as Shelton in details of idiom and he has no hesitancy about adding or removing modifying adjectives. His Sancho has a strong English flavor. As a whole, the work is lively and sprightly, qualities which go a long way to explain its continuous popularity.

Even more popular than Motteux's version was that by Charles Jarvis, or Jervas, the portrait painter and friend of Pope, published in 1742. In England and America it has been reprinted in well over one hundred editions. Jarvis, in order to avoid Motteux's facetiousness, leaned over backwards to be literal. For accuracy, his version is a real improvement, but it is rather wooden and at times ponderous. With the proverbs Jarvis' literalness is most objectionable; in general, it is a faithful but uninspired performance. The translation by Smollett (1755) has been much argued about. Later opinion grants him more knowledge of Spanish and a smaller indebtedness to Jarvis than did his contemporary critics. It was a popular translation in its own period (thirteen editions), but has been little used since. The other two "translations," both really versions of Jarvis and Smollett, are by George Kelly (1769) and C. H. Wilmot (1774). Neither deserves further comment. A fascinating by-path, unexplored here, is the illustrations which accompany many of the eighteenth-century editions.

A further mark of serious English concern was the publication in 1738 of the *Vida y hechos del ingenioso hidalgo Don Quixote de la Mancha* in four handsome volumes. This is the first edition anywhere that attempted to treat the book as a classic worthy of a handsome format and a correct text. In volume one appeared the first *vida* of Cervantes, by Gregorio Mayans y Siscar. No less a matter for English pride is the edition of the Rev. John Bowle (1781), whose four volumes of *Anotaciones* comprise the first scholarly work of any moment on the *Quixote*. According to Fitzmaurice-Kelly (1905), Bowle "has done more to elucidate Cervantes' masterpiece than any other commentator, with the possible exception of Clemencín."

There was no complete translation of the *Novelas* in this century, but many of them received a greatly increased circulation. In 1709 Ozell brought out five, together with the "The Captive's Story" and "The Curious Impertinent." Samuel Croxall's *A Select Collection of Novels* contained three in the edition of 1720, six in that of 1722, and eight in 1729. *A Collection of Select Novels* (1742) included six, newly translated by Harry Bridges. In the same year the *Instructive and Entertaining Novels* (twice republished) offered six. Finally, in 1741, appeared for the first time in English the stories of Scipio and Rinconete, printed separately as *Two Humorous Novels,* with later editions in 1747 and 1767. There were no editions of Cervantes' other works.

In making a survey of the reaction to *Don Quixote* in the first three quarters of the 18th century, the student is embarrassed with riches. No longer does he have to poke around in the odd corners of English writing to discover an occasional allusion. Here it is the famous names that appear as commentators and devotees. Pope makes several references to the book, including one to Avellaneda; it was enjoyed by Dr. Johnson, Steele, Addison, Temple, Wharton, Garrick, Fielding, Smollett, Sterne, Swift, Defoe, Hume, Locke, Arbuthnot, and Lady Montague (who, "though a mere piddler in the Spanish language . . . would rather take pains to understand him in the original"). There are still no thorough critical discussions such as the following century yields, but the number of brief comments is so great that only a small sampling can be offered here.

To begin with, Cervantes is now recognized as one of the world's great writers—something not true in the era just past. Sir William Temple's statement in "An Essay of Ancient and Modern Learning" (1692) can be offered as typical.

> The great Wits among the Moderns have been, in my Opinion, and in their several Kinds, of the Italians, Boccace, Machievel, and Padre Paolo; among the Spaniards, Cervantes (who wrote Don Quixot) and Guevara; among the French, Rablais, and Montagne; among the English, Sir Philip Sidney, Bacon, and Selden.

(Alas, for poor Shakespeare!) Rabelais among the moderns and Lucian among the ancients are the writers with whom Cervantes is most often compared. Temple, in "Of Poetry," prefers Cervantes to Rabelais as a writer of ridicule because he lacks the maliciousness, smut, and profanity of the Frenchman and "seems to be the best and highest strain that ever was, or will be reached in that vein." Wharton, in *The Adventurer,* No. 133 (1754) believes Cervantes superior to Lucian because of "his solemn and important air with which the most idle and ridiculous actions are related." Addison, Steele, Fielding, Johnson and others similarly group the Spaniard with the great humorous writers of all time.

Not only was Cervantes placed among the elect, he was credited with having been unusually successful in the purpose of his satire against the books of chivalry—so successful, in fact, that the morale of Spanish nobility had suffered a serious decline. Probably of Spanish origin, so far as I can find out, this idea first reached England in Rapin's *Reflections sur la Poetique de ce Temps,* which was widely read after the Restoration. The preface to Motteux's translation contains a clear statement of this notion:

> The character of Don Quixote must speak its own praise: 'tis an original without a Precedent, and will be a Pattern without a Copy; its greatest fault was its too great beauty, by which some think it answer'd the Design too effectually: Many men being still of opinion that the wonderful Declension of the Spanish Bravery and Greatness in this last Century may be attributed very much to his carrying the Jest too far, by not only ridiculing their Romantic love and Errantry, but by laughing them also out of their Honour and Courage.

The same idea finds expression in Shaftesbury's *Characteristics,* in Steele's *Tatler,* No. 219, in Defoe's *Memoirs of Captain Carleton,* and in other writers less well known.

Such an assumption about the devastating effects of Cervantes' satire led to the use of his novel to lend weight to arguments—very prevalent in the 1720's and -30's—against the widespread use of ridicule. For example, Lord Boling-broke in No. 14 of *The Craftsman* (1727):

> A man who has lived but half as long in the World as I have done, cannot avoid having a great many melancholy reflections, on seeing things of the most *serious* and *solemn* nature turned into *Ridicule.* This method of writing was first introduced by *Cervantes* in *Spain* and *Rabelais* in *France;* from whence it was brought into *England* by King *Charles II* at his Restoration. It is evident to every Reader of the meanest capacity, that the author of this curious piece [a Whig pamphlet] proceeds on the model of those writers, and that his design is to ridicule *Statesmen* and *political* Matters in the same manner that *Cervantes* exposes books of *Chivalry* . . .

Addison in *The Spectator,* No. 249, and Shaftesbury echo this thought.

Blended with this eighteenth-century recognition of Cervantes' greatness as a satirist and the belief that, in Byron's phrase, he had "smiled Spain's chivalry away," is a third new and important concept. Again Motteux's preface yields the earliest clear statement:

> Every man has something of Don Quixote in his *Humour,* some darling Dulcinea of his Thoughts, that sets him very often upon mad Adventures. What Quixotes does not every Age produce in Politics and Religion, who

fancying themselves to be in the right of something, which all the world tells 'em is wrong, make very good sport to the Public, and show that themselves need the chiefest ammendment.

So, too, Steele in *The Tatler,* No. 178 (1710):

As much as the case of this distempered Knight is received by all the readers of his history as the most incurable and ridiculous of all phrensies, it is very certain that we have crowds among us far gone in as visible a madness as his, though they are not observed to be in that condition.

And Dr. Johnson in *The Rambler,* No. 2 (1750):

. . . very few readers, amidst their mirth or pity, can deny that they have admitted visions of the same kind [as Quixote's and Sancho's]; though they have not, perhaps, expected events equally strange, or by means equally inadequate. When we pity him, we reflect on our own disappointments; and when we laugh, our hearts inform us that he is not more ridiculous than ourselves, except that he tells what we have only thought.

If the reader's recollection is sharp, he will have remarked that nowhere up to this last quotation has he seen the word *pity* used in connection with Don Quixote. That Dr. Johnson was not romantically inclined is surely an understatement. However, in his admiration and appreciation for a book "to which," he says, "the mind of the greatest powers may be indebted without disgrace," he anticipates the more tender sentiments yet to come. As "a book of entertainment," he thought *Don Quixote* "the greatest in the world . . . after Homer's *Iliad."* Elsewhere he remarked, "Was there ever yet anything written by mere man that was wished longer by its readers, excepting *Don Quixote, Robinson Crusoe,* and *The Pilgrim's Progress?"*

Turning to matters of influence, it is naturally Henry Fielding who first comes to mind. As Wilbur Cross has said, apropos of *Joseph Andrews,* "Fielding was so saturated with Cervantes that analysis, beyond exteriors, is rendered almost helpless."[7] Though his knowledge of *Don Quixote* may have been more extensive than that of his contemporaries, Fielding does not differ from them in the main aspects of his interpretation. He, too, saw Cervantes as a great social-moral force; his remarks in the *Covent-Garden Journal,* No. 10 (1752) show this clearly:

These authors [Lucian, Cervantes, Swift] I shall ever hold in the highest degree of esteem; not indeed for that wit and humour alone which they all so eminently possessed, but because they all endeavoured, with the utmost force of their wit and humour to expose and extirpate those follies and vices which chiefly prevailed in their several countries.

As both Brown and D'Urfey have been discussed in this paper, Fielding's couplet-motto for his essay has special flavor:

> In former times, this tasteless, silly Town
> Too fondly prais'd Tom D'Urfey and Tom Brown.

Fielding's first use of Cervantes' novel is the comedy (or ballad-opera) *Don Quixote in England*. Sketched out by Fielding while he was a law student in Leyden, aged twenty-one, the play was laid aside until 1729, when Cibber and Booth refused to buy it. Five years later, at the request of the Drury Lane actors, Fielding added new material and it was produced with reasonable success. The English writer has transported Don Quixote and Sancho to an English Inn. The plot and all the other characters are English. The obvious intent of the play is to satirize—by contrasting the "mad" but upright Quixote with the "sane" but venal citizens—the corruption in county politics. The Knight and Sancho have only a few broad traits. The former is mad on all subjects relating to knight-errantry (inns for castles, ladies for princesses, coachmen for giants, etc.) but an honorable gentleman the rest of the time. The transitions back and forth from one state to the other are so sudden as to be sheer farce. Sancho is little more than a proverb-cracking glutton. Fielding does not vulgarize the character of Don Quixote as D'Urfey had, but he does present him with farcical simplicity. The play concludes with a speech by the "mad" Spaniard which illustrates Fielding's agreement with the common eighteenth-century opinion, already described, that there's a little Quixote in the best of us.

> I've heard Thee [Drench, an inept doctor], thou ignorant wretch, throw
> that word [mad] in my face, with patience; for, alas, cou'd it be prov'd,
> what were it more than almost all mankind in some degree deserve?
> Who would doubt the noisy boist'rous squire [Badger], who was here
> just now, to be mad? Must not this noble knight [Sir Thomas] have
> been mad to think of marrying his daughter to such a wretch? You,
> doctor, are mad, too, tho' not so mad as your patients. The lawyer, here,
> is mad, or he wou'd not have gone into a scuffle, when it is the business
> of his profession to set other men by the ears, and keep clear themselves.

The curtain is rung down by a song, "All mankind is mad, 'tis plain," which, after itemizing various common forms of madnesses, concludes:

> Since your madness is so plain
> Each spectator
> Of good nature
> With applause will entertain
> His brother of La Mancha.

Fielding, as his preface indicates, was dissatisfied with the immaturity of his adaptation. Except for Squire Badger (the first draft of Squire Western), the play is a lively farce with little to recommend it but its comment on corruption in local politics.

With *Joseph Andrews,* written, as the title-page tells us, "in imitation of the manner of Cervantes," we have not only mature work but also a closer and more complex relationship to the Spanish novel. There are many surface "correspondencies" (to use Cross's word): the grouping of characters in four books in epic style, the facetious chapter headings and the chapter endings that entice the reader on, the mock-heroic style in appropriate situations (which Fielding carries much farther than Cervantes), the absurd and ridiculous episodes, many of them full of rough horseplay, the framework of two companions traveling the highway from inn to inn, and others. The Rev. Mr. Abraham Adams is an English Don Quixote, differing sharply from the Spaniard in details, but close to him in what is basically comic. The English parson, with a deep knowledge of classical literature and a pure, naïve, and generous disposition, like Quixote, tried to apply to the real world a set of bookish values which were not operative there. His physical strength, his absent-mindedness, his voracious appetite, his wife and children are, among others, all details peculiar to himself. Peculiar, too, to the English novel, are those aspects of the plot and characters which relate to the book's function as a parody of Richardson's *Pamela.* Even more than Don Quixote, Adams is presented sympathetically. His degree of madness is never as extreme as the Spaniard's. Though more lovable, he never rises to Quixote's stature. The Don is presented in a much more richly complex series of adventures and conversations, and reacts to a much more richly complex variety of ideas. The English parson (though the closest adaptation of Cervantes' character in English literature) lacks the depth and nobility of its prototype for the very good reason—though not the only one—that Fielding, being a man of his age, failed to see what was highest and deepest in the Don, in spite of his sincere admiration for him. In other words, though Fielding would have been the first to acclaim the superiority of the Spanish knight as a character, he would not, it seems to me, recognize as great an essential difference in kind, or quality, between the two heroes as does the modern reader.

In *Tom Jones* the Cervantic echoes are softer. Most obvious is the use again of a pair of traveling companions who meet adventures on the highways and in the inns that border it. Young Tom, in his idealism, his naïveté, his good intentions, his relations to Partridge, and for a time to his temporary Dulcinea, Molly, shows his kinship to Don Quixote. Partridge, the schoolmaster-barber, in his relationship to Tom, in his superstition and garrulity, and his dreams of advancement reminds us not a little of Sancho. Again we find long inserted stories and mock-heroic passages. Here, too, it is possible to believe (as in *Joseph Andrews*) that Fielding learned something about the use of realism and humor from his Spanish master, though this is impossible of proof.

In these three works of Fielding there is to be seen a natural change in Cervantes' influence. In his youthful drama Fielding presented Don Quixote and Sancho in rough outline, directly transposed into an English setting and plot; in *Joseph Andrews* there is a deeper infusion of influence thoroughly blended with much that is pure Fielding; in *Tom Jones* there are slight Cervantic traces amid the richness of Fielding's own genius. If Fielding came closer to Cervantes than any other English writer, it is essentially because there were many traits of personality that made the Englishman *simpatico* to the Spaniard.

With Smollett, the novelist who translated *Don Quixote,* we have a writer who knew the novel as well as Fielding but on whom the influence is smaller and more superficial, partly because Smollett's personality was so different and partly because Le Sage was more his master. Tom Bowling in *Roderick Random* and Hawser Trunnion in *Peregrine Pickle* are both quixotic eccentrics of a likeable sort. Clearer are the similarities in Lismahago of *Humphrey Clinker:* the Scotch soldier's physical appearance, his ideals, his arguments, his horse, and the action of an occasional scene recall *Don Quixote*. Matthew Bramble, of the same novel, is of the family of Bowling and Trunnion. *Sir Lancelot Greaves,* Smollett's most direct imitation, is one of the most unsuccessful of his writings. Superficially similar in station in life and in appearance to Quixote, Greaves lacks the Spaniard's madness, his greatness, and his humanity. In personality he reminds one more of Hudibras than the Don. Crabshaw, the squire, has many of Sancho's obvious traits, but not his goodness of heart. His relationship to his master recalls the surly outspoken hardness of D'Urfey's Sancho. Whether Smollett had *Hudibras* in mind is not certain, but the end result is a work which in spirit is closer to the comic poem or D'Urfey's travesties than to the Spanish original. Smollett's violence and hardness made him constitutionally unfit to see anything but comic satire in *Don Quixote*. He comes closest to the Don, not in Greaves, but in the general quality of such kindly eccentrics as Trunnion and Lismahago.

Laurence Sterne knew *Don Quixote* and admired it highly, as allusions in his letters and in *Tristram Shandy* testify, but what influence the Spanish book exerted is difficult of definition, more so than for *Gargantua and Pantagruel.* From Sterne's use of the phrase "Cervantic gravity" to describe Walter Shandy's method of discussion (III:10), it is not unfair to presume a limited imitation of a stylistic quality conspicuous in *Don Quixote*. The character of Uncle Toby has quixotic overtones, and Corporal Trim, in his relationship to Toby and some of his conversations with him, reminds us of Sancho. Even more does Walter Shandy's vast store of useless knowledge recall Quixote's fund of romance lore. Larger, but more nebulous, is a similarity in the way Sterne and Cervantes couple the comic with a warm appreciation for a character. There is a gentleness and lack of bite in Sterne's laughter, so different from Smollett's, which come close to scenes in the Spanish novel. Like Quixote, Toby, Walter, and Trim have a complete goodness of heart and unspoiled humanity. But, obviously, they are drawn with a sentimentality, an eccentricity and self-conscious funniness which is foreign to Cervantes.

Of Don Quixote's relation to works of lesser interest in this period space permits only the briefest mention. Becker has shown that the unfinished *Memoirs of Martinus Scriblerus* (1741), written by Pope, Swift, and, chiefly, Arbuthnot is somewhat indebted for the general outlines of Scriblerus and Crambe to Cervantes' leading characters. Mrs. Charlotte Lennox's *The Female Quixote* (1752) has in Arabella a central character who has been misled by her reading; however, the book as a whole resembles *Tom Jones* much more than its title would indicate. Richard Graves' novel *The Spiritual Quixote* (1772) takes *Don Quixote* for its model in the best Fielding manner and sets out to redeem Englishmen from the folly of Methodism. As the author says,

> Nay, I am convinced that Don Quixote or Gil Blas, Clarissa or Sir Charles Grandison, will furnish more hints for correcting the follies and regulating the morals of young persons, and impress them more forcibly on their minds, than volumes of severe precepts seriously delivered and dogmatically enforced.

Wildgoose and Tugwell are a pair of superficial imitations, but for general qualities, *Tom Jones* again provides a closer kinship. A third-rate "opera comedy," *Sancho At Court* (1742) was made by James Ayres out of one scene in Part II. Its quality is suggested by the presence among the Spanish characters of Colonel At Wit, Lord Smart, Never Out, and Lord Sparkish. Two plays of the period, Charles Johnson's comedy, *The Generous Husband* (1713) and Isaac Bickerstaff's comic opera *The Padlock* (1768), went to "El celoso extremeño" for plot material.

During the ages of Pope and Johnson, as we have seen, *Don Quixote* and its author rose out of the slough of Gayton, Phillips, and D'Urfey to the eminence of world masterpiece and comic genius respectively. Praised for its comedy and the effectiveness of its satire, the novel was widely interpreted (in true neo-classical fashion) as presenting the portrait of one universal type of madness. The influence of *Don Quixote* (for none has been claimed for Cervantes' other works) followed three general lines: blending with the more purely picaresque tradition, *Don Quixote* provided stimulus for the writing of long, peripatetic novels with inserted short stories; secondly, in a satire-loving age, it provided the most conspicuously cited model (as they saw it) of moral, or social, satire done in a vein at once kindly and elevated; most obviously it stimulated—and was in part the model for—a number of lovable eccentrics and charming crackpots. As compared to his master's personality, the richness of Sancho's character was as yet relatively unappreciated. It is hardly necessary to say that none of the various partial imitations is a serious rival of the Spanish masterpiece.

III

The romantic period in England, and particularly in Germany, discovered new virtues in *Don Quixote*. The farce and satire were recognized but played down. Nobility, pathos, and the tragic dichotomy of life were the admired traits. The word *sad* was frequently applied to the book, and Christ Himself was not too exalted a figure to be used for comparison with the Don. (Think what D'Urfey, or Fielding, or Dr. Johnson would have thought of such a comparison!) Although there are a number of English works which make use of *Don Quixote* in their titles, none is of lasting interest and none is by an author of importance. The periods of direct borrowing appear to be over, giving way gradually to interpretive essays in the reviews and quarterlies.

Wordsworth read our novel as a schoolboy and makes use of it by name in *The Prelude* (V:56), but his comments shed light only on personal problems, giving us no evaluation of the book other than that he enjoyed it enough to reread it. Sir Walter Scott knew *Don Quixote* well. He read it in the original, and apparently used it as a Baedeker for his extended tour into the land of romance books. From one of his letters to Constable it is clear that at one time he seriously contemplated doing an English translation. This interest and certain parallels in personality and style have fostered vague suggestions of influence, but the closest situation to a direct parallel that has been seen in his novels (by Grierson) occurs in the opening chapters of *Waverley;* there the reader is prepared for the hero's romantic adventures by a description of his over-indulgence in the reading of romances. In my opinion, the misguided Jacobite hero of *Redgauntlet* bears a much closer affinity to the Don. Lockhart describes how one evening shortly before Scott's death (while Wordsworth was visiting him) the group listened to a reading of Cervantes' beautiful preface to the *Persiles y Sigismunda*. It is a scene that teases one out of thought.

As so often happens, it was a poet who struck off the one phrase in this period which has embedded itself in the general consciousness—Byron's "smiled Spain's chivalry away." The same author's lines in *Don Juan* (XIII:viii) suggest a thoroughly un-eighteenth-century view:

> Of all tales 'tis the saddest—and more sad,
>   Because he makes us smile: the hero's right,
> And still pursues the right;—to curb the bad
>   His only object, and 'gainst odds to fight
> His guerdon: 'tis his virtue makes him mad!
>   But his adventures form a sorry sight;—
> A sorrier still is the great moral taught
> By that real epic unto all who have thought.

In the same vein is gentle Charles Lamb's comment in "The Barrenness of the Imaginative Faculty in the Productions of Modern Art":

> Deeply corporealized and enchained hopelessly in the grovelling fetters of externality must be the mind to which, in its better moments, the image of the high-souled, high-intelligenced Quixote (the errant Star of Knighthood, made more tender by eclipse) has never presented itself divested from the unhallowed accompaniment of a Sancho, or a rabblement at the heels of Rosinante. That man has read the book by halves; he has laughed, mistaking the author's purpose, which was tears.

With this attitude, it is no wonder that Lamb failed to enjoy Part II. That he personally suffered with Don Quixote as the latter suffered at the hands of the Duke is apparent from the violence of his language:

> Why, Goneril would have blushed to practice upon the abdicated king [Lear] at this rate, and the she-wolf Regan not have endured to play the pranks upon his fled wits which thou has made thy Quixote suffer in Duchesses' halls at the hands of that unworthy nobleman.

One of the best examples of the Byron-Lamb interpretation in a work imitating the novel is the *Alonzo Quixano, Otherwise Don Quixote* of E. G. Morrison (Elkin Mathews). Though written and produced at the end of the century (1895), this play is purely romantic in its interpretation. Perhaps because of that fact it would, I think, provide much more palatable theatrical fare to a modern audience than Fielding's or D'Urfey's dramas. The plot is a new combination of scenes from Part I and Part II plus some of Morrison's own. The emotional pivot of the play is the deep affection that exists between the Don and his niece, Antonia, whom Morrison makes a major figure. New, too, is an evil inn-keeper who loves Antonia, and hopes to force Quixote to let him marry the girl, in payment for the debts naïvely incurred by Quixote over the years when he needed money to buy romances. Of course, the villain is foiled in the end. The windmills, the wineskins, Mambrino's helmet, the governorship of Sancho all appear. Interesting is a scene "At the Duke's Pleasaunce," where all the people Don Quixote has injured, plus the officers of the Holy Brotherhood, gather to denounce him before the Duke. In the last scene Quixote comes to his senses before dying; the Duke has the evil inn-keeper punished and pays all debts as a penance for having helped mislead one of nature's noblemen. Quixote's death is much more pathetic than in the original. Though too sentimental to be an accurate copy of the Spanish *hidalgo,* Morrison's Don Quixote has much more personal reality than Fielding's or D'Urfey's just because he does stir some emotion in the reader.

Morrison's preface shows his interpretation clearly:

> Though Cervantes sat down with no thought but that of recording the pranks of an elderly lunatic, he did not rise till he had created the Christ of fiction.

> The Quixote I attempt to reproduce is not the Quixote Cervantes started with, but the Quixote he finished with . . . Alonso Quixano, the same whom the world, for his fair and honest life, was pleased to surname The Good.

> It [the play] is, for one thing, too sombre, but it is at least reverential, and remembering the paltry and degraded uses to which Quixote has been so often put, I am not without hope that those who share my reverence will forgive my errours.

One who apparently shared this "reverence" was Percy Addleshaw, who reviewed the play very sympathetically in the *Academy* (XLVIII:44). Though only moderately enthusiastic about Morrison's verse, he gave unstinted praise for the author's efforts "not to falsify" the Don. In the same vein, though even more illogically tearful and un-comic are Henri Cain's "heroic-comedy" opera (1911), Englished by Claude Aveling, for which Massenet composed the music, and in the 1920's the moving picture version in which Chaliapin was the pictorially perfect and very moving hero—all nobility and sentiment. In the average audience it would produce a few rueful smiles and a great many tears.

Returning to the earlier part of the century, we find in Samuel Taylor Coleridge a critic who only slightly shared his contemporaries' morbid view of *Don Quixote.* Perhaps it is flattering our own perspicacity too much to say that most of his views are so sound that they seem quite modern. He was the first in England to interpret in any detail the personalities of the two leading characters, and many of his observations have become platitudes. He admired Cervantes' "acuteness." He points out that Cervantes did not wish to destroy romances "but to cause them to be read as romances,—that is, for their merits as poetry." He praises the descriptions of nature [an entirely new approach], and sees in the episode of the galley slaves the one place where the author "slips the mask of his hero and speaks for himself." He observes that "Sancho's selfishness is modified by his involuntary goodness of heart, and Don Quixote's flighty goodness is debased by the involuntary or unconscious selfishness of his vanity and self-applause." Cervantes' preface "is a model of gentle, everywhere intelligible irony at its best." Of the style: "Equally natural and easy, Cervantes is more spirited than Addison; whilst he blends with the terseness of Swift an exquisite flow and music of style, and, above all, contrasts with the latter by the sweet temper of a superior mind, which saw the follies of mankind, and was even at the moment suffering severely under hard mistreatment, and yet seems everywhere to have but one thought as the undersong—'Brethren! With all your faults I love you still!' " The Don "is reason divested of the judgment and understanding," and Sancho "is common sense without reason or imagination . . . put him and his master together and they form a perfect intellect. These two characters possess the world, alternately and interchangeably the cheater and the cheated. To impersonate them, and to combine the permanent with the individual, is one of the highest creations of genius, and has been achieved by Shakespeare and Cervantes, almost alone.[8]

This section on the romantics will be rounded out with the opinions of one other famous English writer, one out of many who might be used. John Ruskin's reaction is interesting because he changed from an initial appreciation to a peculiarly unfriendly view. In the first part of *Modern Painters* (1843) are the sentiments familiar in this era:

> Take Don Quixote for example. The lowest mind would find in it perpetual and brutish amusement in the misfortunes of the knight, and perpetual pleasure in sympathy with the squire. A mind of average intelligence would perceive the satirical meaning and force of the book, would appreciate its wit, its elegance, and its truth. But only elevated and peculiar minds discover, in addition to all this, the full moral beauty of the love and truth which are the constant associates of all that is even most weak and erring in the character of its hero, and pass over the rude adventure and scurrile just in haste—perhaps in pain, to penetrate beneath the rusty corselet, and catch from the wandering glance the evidence and expression of fortitude, self-devotion, and universal love.

But only a decade later in his *Letters on Architecture and Painting,* and subsequently elsewhere, he expresses a conviction which is a curious exaggeration of an eighteenth-century misconception illustrated earlier:

> . . . and if you were to ask me who of all powerful and popular writers in the cause of error had wrought most harm to their race . . . [Voltaire, Byron, Schopenhauer] rather Cervantes, for he cast scorn upon the holiest principles of humanity—he, of all men, most helped forward the terrible change in the soldiers of Europe, from the spirit of Bayard to the spirit of Bonaparte, helped to change loyalty into license, protection

into plunder, truth into treachery, chivalry into selfishness; and, since his time, the purest impulses and the noblest purposes have perhaps been oftener stayed by the devil, under the name of Quixotism, than under any other base name or false allegation.

IV

The last period gets under way at the end of Victoria's reign. It is dominated by scholarly and critical essays, with no notable examples of imitation. During the 1880's and -90's, culminating in the tercentennial year of 1905, there occurred in England—as elsewhere—unusual activity in things Cervantic. As in the somewhat comparable period at the turn of the 18th century, there were new translations. The first of these, in 1881, was the least successful. Alexander James Duffield's three fat volumes, with biographical sketch, notes, and an introduction, are a monument to his industry and eccentricity. The verse was skilfully translated by J. Y. Gibson, but Duffield's prose is less happy. He was haunted by the past treatment of the work (even as Morrison) as "a vulgar piece of unmatched buffoonery." Dedicated to Gladstone, the introduction commences with an unconsciously amusing colloquy between the translator (on his knees) and an angel, in which Duffield avers that "not one graceless or unchaste word of mine intrudes itself." This Victorian bias for the chaste and the moral throws some of Duffield's comments and parts of his translation off center. In 1885 appeared the second new translation, this by John Ormsby, also with biographical and historical introductions, notes, and helpful bibliographies of romances and editions of the novel. Suffice it to say here that this translation has been denominated by the great majority of competent critics as the best in the English language. The third new Englishing was by Henry Edward Watts in 1888, again replete with introductions and bibliographies. Though free from Duffield's eccentricities, it was Mr. Watts' misfortune to follow a better man. Like Duffield's, his work has been completely, and rightly, over-shadowed by Ormsby's. These new versions by no means throttled the old ones. During the last quarter of the nineteenth century and the first of the twentieth, new editions of Motteux, Jarvis, and Shelton appeared so regularly on both sides of the Atlantic that one wonders how they could have been absorbed. Many were beautiful examples of fine bookmaking, illustrated by such artists as Doré, Cruikshank, Johannot, Schoff, and Gilbert. Many were prefaced with helpful, if not brilliant essays; the most commonly reprinted was that by John G. Lockhart, first published with an Edinburgh edition of Motteux in 1865.

In 1892 appeared the first important work of Sir James Fitzmaurice-Kelly, a scholar to whom all later students of Cervantes are indebted. His *Life,* in 1892, was outstanding in its time, with the first attempt at something like a complete bibliography. Subsequently revised, it is a standard work. Four years later he edited the Tudor Translations reprint of Shelton's translation, with an excellent introduction which contained, among other things, the first spade work on Cervantes' influence in England—material which in expanded form appears in his address before the British Academy in 1905. In 1902 he edited, with another excellent introduction, the Maccoll translation of the *Exemplary Novels,* which is the standard English version. His other and latter services in the cause of Cervantes in England are well known.

In the same fruitful period was published the first Iconography, by Ashbee, in 1895, antedating the more monumental work of Rius by a year; the same author argued in the *Revue Hispanique* (1899) for a general, though vague, influence of Cervantes on Dickens. In 1897 George Meredith in his famous *An Essay on Comedy* makes many references to *Don Quixote*. "Heart and mind laugh at Don Quixote, and still you brood on him." He finds "the loftiest moods of humor, fusing the tragic sentiment with the comic narrative. The stroke of the great humorist is world-wide, with lights of tragedy in his laughter."

Also in 1897, the poet Francis Thompson wrote a short study of the novel for *The Academy* that is typical of the modern interpretation of *Don Quixote* as a many-faceted masterpiece.

> It has a core of scornful and melancholy protest, set about with a pulp of satire, and outside a kind of thick burlesque . . . With all the inward gravity of his irony, Cervantes has abundantly provided that we need not take his seriousness too seriously; there is laughter even for those who enter deepest into that grave core.

Arthur Machen, in *Hieroglyphics* (1923), in his own way strikes the same chord: It is "the finest prose romance in existence," with at least five aspects. First, its "essence" is "man's eternal quest for the unknown, his longing for infinity." Second is its "moral," "the strife between temporal and eternal, soul and body, spiritual and corporeal, the great antimony of life." Third is "the burlesque," "the best ever." Fourth, it is "the institute of cynicism, the reduction of every generous impulse to absurdity." Finally, it is "Cervantes' mouthpiece," particularly (unlike Coleridge) near the end of Part II, "where Cervantes comments on men and affairs in Spain." So, too, Sir Walter Raleigh in his very able essay "Don Quixote" (1916): "The truth is that the book is so many-sided that all kinds of tastes and beliefs can find their warrant there. The soul of it is an irony so profound that but few of its readers have explored it." Professor Bailey's illuminating address, "The Continuity of Letters" (Oxford, 1916) finds a classic quality in this diverse appeal. Like all great classics *Don Quixote* "gives us a sense of the indestructible continuity of human life" and "has in it the whole of our human nature, a whole which transcends the differences of time and nationality . . . it is in the strictest sense a classic, which is by definition a book that is at once universal and immortal."

In rounding out these scattered references to distinguished modern studies, mention must be made of W. P. Ker's "Don Quixote," read first before the Royal Society of Glasgow in 1908, an essay too long and diverse to suggest by brief quotations. Its most rewarding sections contain Professor Ker's defense of the essential rightness of Hegel's analysis of *Don Quixote* in his *Aesthetik*. Subtly ingenious are those chapters in Wyndam Lewis' *The Lion and the Fox* which contain his analyses and comparisons of Shakespeare and Cervantes. He is particularly interested in the clash of medieval and renaissance thought as revealed in the two writers, and his comparison of Shakespeare's knight, Falstaff, with the Spanish Don is stimulating and fresh. He believes that Schelling's romantic interpretation of *Don Quixote* as a philosophical novel that delineates the conflict of the ideal and the real is the only one "compatible with the great beauty of the book." Equally rewarding is Sir Herbert Grierson's "Don Quixote, Some Wartime Reflections on Its Character and Influence" (English Association Pamphlet No. 48, 1921). In addition to a penetrating analysis the essay is unusually rich in revealing comparisons made between Cervantes' novel and masterpieces of English and other literatures. Of more narrowly scholarly investigations into details of Cervantes' life, education, and the bibliography of his works no mention can be made here. A splendid example of how the dusty lore of fact-grubbing can be vitally re-interpreted so that new knowledge about the author's life helps to explain the creation, growth, and meaning of his work is Professor William J. Entwistle's little book *Cervantes* (1940).

The temptation to be resisted in writing a conclusion to the foregoing remarks is that of overstatement. Too many good essays on this theme have wound up in a state of emotional exaggeration based on national pride. That England welcomed *Don Quixote* promptly cannot be denied. However, that the welcome was conspicuously intelligent remains to be proved. As soon as the book escaped from the unfortunate gang of "wits" who first took it up, its inherent greatness assured its vast popularity with all classes. Along with the Bible, Bunyan, and Shakespeare it has been a book that almost every literate Englishman for the past two hundred years has read, at least in part. That it has had great influence has yet to be proved. Like most truly great works it is unique and inimitable. As has been shown, it was pilfered for plots, as were the *Exemplary Novels,* but in a way which preserved little or nothing of the peculiar qualities of the original. If *Don Quixote* helped shape the course of the English novel, it was done in conjunction with other works and hence uncertain of proof. It did, it seems to me, assist materially in the development of one type of English humorous character from the 18th century on—about the only real "influence" that can be claimed for it. But more important, its very real popularity has created for hundreds of thousands of English readers the occasion for coming in contact with one of mankind's greatest artists, and perceiving something of the soul of Spain.

NOTES

[1] Cervantes' influence in England has been generally studied in terms of single authors or plays, *e.g.,* Fletcher or Fielding, or *The Knight of the Burning Pestle.* There are few general surveys: most dependable are Fitzmaurice-Kelly's *Cervantes in England* (1905), Becker's *Die Aufnahme des Don Quijote in die englische Litteratur, 1605–1770* (1906), Knowles' *The Vogue of Don Quixote in England, 1605–1660* (1938, unpub. diss., N.Y.U.). The relevant sections in Hume's *Spanish Influence on English Literature* (1906) and Armas y Cardenas' *Cervantes en la literatura inglesa* (1906) are often unsound. The materials, without the comment, are to be found most completely in Ford-Lansing, *Cervantes, A Tentative Bibliography* (1931) and Pane, *English Translations from the Spanish* (1944).

[2] See E. J. Crooks, *The Influence of Cervantes in France in the Seventeenth Century* (1931).

[3] *The Dramatic Works and Poems of Shirley,* ed. Dyce (1833), VI, 272.

[4] See the author's "Allusions to *Don Quixote* before 1660," *P.Q.,* XX, 573.

[5] An excellent short antedote to the myth is Rudolph Schevill's "On the Influence of Spanish Literature upon English in the Early Seventeenth Century," *Romanische Forschungen,* I (1907), 604.

[6] See R. S. Forsythe, *A Study of the Plays of Thomas D'Urfey,* 1916.

[7] *The History of Henry Fielding* (1918), p. 323. The reader is referred to this excellent study for more details than can be given here, particularly of *Joseph Andrews* and *Tom Jones.*

[8] See *Literary Remains* (1836), I, 113–131; also his analysis of humor.

Translations of Cervantes into French

ESTHER J. CROOKS

CERVANTES appeared on the literary horizon at a moment favorable to his acceptance by the currently Hispanophile French: when the adoption of Spanish dress and manners, the study of the Spanish language, the playing of Spanish drama-companies, and the publication of Spanish religious works were all in high fashion in France.

In 1607, just two years after the appearance of the first part of *Don Quixote* in Madrid, the novel was reprinted in the original in Brussels to meet the demands of the Spaniards in the Low Countries. In 1608, an excerpt from it ("El curioso impertinente") was published in Paris in a French version. The translator, Nicolas Baudouin, apparently tried to simplify the language, but at times used rather cumbersome phrases to explain the meaning. The following year another excerpt (the Marcela-Grisóstomo episode) was published in Paris in a bilingual Spanish-French edition, when the pastoral vogue was at its height. The anonymous adapter changed the name of Grisóstomo to the pastoral name Philidon, and made various other alterations.

César Oudin, a leading figure in the introduction of Cervantes to France, who as early as 1608 included "El curioso impertinente" in an edition of Julian de Medrano's *Silva curiosa,* published *La Galatea* in Paris in 1611, in Spanish— it was not translated into French until 1783. This earnest Cervantist made the first translation into French (1614) of Part I of *Don Quixote*. An attempt at a word-by-word rendering, this faithful version is quite tiresome; nevertheless, the translation was reprinted in 1616, 1620, 1625, 1632, 1639, 1646, and 1665. The last three editions included François de Rosset's translation of the second part of *Don Quixote,* which had been published in 1618. De Rosset had less regard for Cervantes' style than Oudin, and greater facility of expression, but his translation contains numerous inexactitudes and pedantic expressions. Nevertheless, the Oudin-de Rosset translation, which made *Don Quixote* known in France, was a great success. In 1884 it was chosen as the model for a new version by Emile Gebhart, and even as late as 1936, by Jean Cassou.

In 1677–78 Filleau de Saint-Martin made a very free translation of *Don Quixote*, adapting it to French taste. The liberties taken in this first complete version of *Don Quixote* in French did not please Florian, who made a translation in 1794; Filleau de Saint-Martin, he said, used any synonym that he happened to find in the dictionary. Nevertheless, this translation has been published many times, even appearing in our own day (1935).[1] Louis Viardot, who translated *Don Quixote* into French in 1836, prepared himself for his task by rereading Montaigne, for the similarity between early seventeenth-century French and Spanish was very close. For Viardot, translation was a matter of conscience; nothing should be omitted or added, and the plain effect of each sentence and each word should be given. Oudin and de Rosset, according to J. B. François Biedermann, who wrote *Don Quichotte et la tâche de ses traducteurs* the following year (1837), produced only an inadequate literal version, "avec une confusion continuelle des différentes significations des mots et de leurs valeurs diverses dans la composition des phrases." Literalism is discussed by Francis Miomandre in the preface to his modern French version of *Don Quixote* (1935). Literalism, he holds, is both absolute and relative; absolute for the vocabulary and relative for the syntax. The word-for-word method is foolish. "La véritable loyauté pour un traducteur ne peut consister qu'en une seule chose: donner, en français, l'impression que procure le texte original. On ne peut pas tout sauver. C'est le sens, c'est la forme, c'est la couleur . . ."

The *Novelas ejemplares* were published in French early in 1615, only sixteen months after the first edition appeared in Madrid. This work has the distinction of being the first rendering of the *Novelas ejemplares* into any foreign tongue. The translator of the first six stories was François de Rosset, who three years later translated the second part of *Don Quixote;* the other six stories were translated by Vital d'Audiguier, who had already produced among other works some original novels modeled on the Spanish *Amadís*. These men worked at a speed that was not conducive to the best results. De Rosset had his mind fixed on an exact translation, while d'Audiguier proposed to keep the spirit of Cervantes' pages but not the wording, at times trying to improve upon the language. In this edition of the *Novelas ejemplares* each story is preceded by the argument; for, as Allesandro Novilieri, the translator of the *Novelas ejemplares* into Italian, remarked, a summary is to a story what the eye is to the body. At least six reprintings of this translation were made by 1665 (1618, 1620–21, 1626, 1633, 1640, 1665) and it continued to be used for subsequent translations, even though publication-permission was supposed to have stopped in 1670. It formed the basis of the "new translation" of Cotolendi (1678), who decided that certain changes were necessary in order to please French taste. In his opinion, verses expressing deep religious feeling were not appropriate for a gypsy fortune-teller and dancer, and he therefore substituted a poem of lighter vein in the opening pages of "La gitanilla." As he did not like the thought nor the style of some of the other poems, he inserted verses of his own invention. In the 18th century there were more than twenty versions which in reality stem from the original translation of de Rosset and d'Audiguier.[2] These men also gave the French public a version of *Persiles y Sigismundo* (1618).

In the first half of the 17th century there are many French allusions to Cervantes' writings, and they are almost entirely laudatory.[3] The most abundant and most interesting of these references deal with *Don Quixote*. The episodes most often mentioned are Don Quixote's attack upon the windmills, the burning of his books, his retirement into Sierra Morena, and the stories of Cardenio and the "Curioso impertinente." D'Aubigné, the *précieux* Voiture and Sarrazin, the burlesquing Saint-Amant and Scarron, among others, all gave evidence that Cervantes was appreciated in his own epoch by French people of literary discernment.

One of the early and significant borrowings in prose from *Don Quixote* was Charles Sorel's *Berger extravagant* (1627), an attack upon the pastoral novel. Sorel's hero has gone mad reading pastoral novels, he has these books burned, and demonstrates his ambitions in extreme fashion. Cervantes, in ridiculing chivalric adventures, came to love the knight whom he started to parody, and bestowed upon him a generous, noble soul. Sorel, however, does not develop the agent of his satire, but maintains him as a madman throughout his fourteen books.

In his *Berger extravagant,* Sorel makes objection to *Don Quixote* on the ground that it is not probable that a duke and a duchess would spend so much money making sport of an eccentric knight-errant, or that a place so large in population as the "insula Barataria" would accept the rustic Sancho Panza as governor, or that the priest would leave his church, or the barber and Carrasco their village to follow Don Quixote; he also complains that while Cervantes set out to ridicule the novels of chivalry he confined that matter to four pages and filled the rest of the book with strange adventures. In *De la Connoissance des bons livres, ou Examen de plusieurs autheurs* (1671) Sorel laments the fact that *Don Quixote* was causing young men to neglect their studies. . . .

Three other novels of Sorel's period which show the influence of *Don Quixote* are *Dom Quixote Gascon* (1630) by the Count de Cramail, the *Chevalier hypocondriaque* (1632) by du Verdier, and the *Gascon extravagant* by du Vail. The second is most like the Spanish novel; it has a satiric purpose and is not a mere following of the burlesque features.

Cervantes' novel was often dramatized in this period. H. C. Lancaster has called attention to Cervantes' influence on *L'Heureux désespéré* (1613) by C. A. Seigneur de C., an unidentified author. The Cervantine influence is also discernible in Nicolas Chrestien's *Amantes ou la grande pastorelle* (1613); Pichou's *Folies de Cardenio* (1630), which ran through five editions in five years; and the Guérin de Bouscal comedies, *Don Quixote de la Manche* (1639) and *Gouvernement de Sanche Pansa* (1641). Guérin de Bouscal, in putting these plays on the stage, was the first to use the Don as a theatrical protagonist, and to adapt material from the second part of the novel; he showed, as well, that he could invent dramatic episodes and lines in the Cervantine manner.

The Classic Age (1660–1700) is more indifferent to *Don Quixote;* but the work is read, enjoyed, and referred to by leading writers. For example, in the correspondence between Boileau and Racine in 1687, there are several comparisons of Boileau's household with that of Don Quixote,[4] and Madame de Sevigné also refers to the Spanish knight in her letters.[5] In the *Combat de Cyrano de Bergerac avec le singe de Brioche* (ed. 1704), probably written by d'Assoucy, Cyrano is described as "plus brave que Dom Quixote de la Manche."[6] The fineness of Don Quixote's spirit is appreciated in Scarron's *Faux Alexandre,* and Cervantes' work is praised by Segrais, Huet, and P. Rapin.

The attraction of *Don Quixote* led the French to an interest in the *Novelas ejemplares,* which became a rich source of material for dramatists. With their romantic stories, psychological tales, references to customs, and humorous incidents they were well suited to this purpose. The most popular were the character studies of "La señora Cornelia," "La fuerza de la sangre," and "Las dos doncellas"; the adventures in Mohammedan lands of "El amante liberal"; and the gypsy experiences of "La gitanilla."

The dramatic possibilities of the *Novelas ejemplares* were first demonstrated by Alexandre Hardy, who based on them three of his eleven extant tragicomedies. His first borrowing in 1625, *Cornélie* (from "La señora Cornelia"), antedated by about three years any French play derived from *Don Quixote;* and his *Belle Egyptienne* (1628) influenced a tragi-comedy of the same title (1642) by Sallebray, whose knowledge of the original text is evident from the language. One sign of influence may be the introduction of songs, as in Cervantes' *novela.* This play uses the popular ballet, a feature to be repeated in a number of adaptations and imitations of Cervantes, especially of *Don Quixote.* The episode of Andrés from "La gitanilla" is in Molière's *Étourdi* (represented 1655).

Hardy's successor in the use of the *Novelas ejemplares* was Jean Rotrou, in *Les deux Pucelles,* represented about 1636. Following rather closely the plot, the ideas, and the lines of "Las dos doncellas" he more nearly approached the spirit of Cervantes than did Hardy. In 1652, seventeen years after the appearance of Rotrou's tragi-comedy, Philippe Quinault modeled on it a comedy, *Les Rivales,* as has been shown by Étienne Gros in his work on this dramatist (1926)

Almost all the *Novelas ejemplares* were adapted to the French theater in the 17th century. Some of the leading playwrights proudly acknowledged their source in the preface or by preserving the original title. The *Novelas* lent themselves especially to tragi-comedy; as the popularity of this form waned and comedy came into vogue, these short novels were less useful, though Quinault did employ them in a comedy.

French novelists, too, drew from the *Novelas ejemplares.* Charles Sorel, while regretting certain romanesque elements in these stories, cites Cervantes as an author who made the short novel a popular type. As Hainsworth has pointed out, certain stories in Sorel's *Nouvelles françoises* (1623) are reminiscent of "El Celoso extremeño," "El Amante liberal" and "La Ilustre fregona"; and in the works of Jean-Pierre Camus, minor elements of material and method may have come from the above-mentioned stories, as well as from "La fuerza de la sangre" and "La gitanilla." Scarron expresses the opinion that if "l'on faisoit des nouvelles en françois aussi bien faites que quelques-unes de celles de Michel de Cervantes elles auroient cours autant que les romans héroiques."

The approval of Scarron is one indication that even greater than Cervantes' external influence upon the novel and the theater is his internal influence upon the composition of French short novels. The *Novelas ejemplares* served to deflect the French public's attention from the Italian *novella,* which was popular in France in the 16th century, and to turn it, in the middle and latter part of the 17th century, toward Cervantes' successors in Spain.

Unlike *Don Quixote* and the *Novelas ejemplares,* Cervantes' plays, so full of complexities and abstractions, were little used in France, with the possible exception of the *entremeses.* Their amusing, lively scenes from everyday life may have suggested incidents and conversations to Molière, as S. G. Morley has pointed out.[7] G. Huszar in *Molière et l'Espagne* (1907) suggests that Molière may have had in mind Cervantes' *entremés,* "Los dos habladores," when he wrote the part of Sganarelle in *Don Juan.* Cervantes' "La cueva de Salamanca" is called to mind by a one-act comedy, *Le Bon Soldat,* which F. C. Dancourt in 1691 arranged from Poisson's three-act comedy, *Les Foux divertissans* (represented 1680). Armando Cotarelo in *El teatro de Cervantes* (1915) explains how through the French theater Cervantes' "La cueva de Salamanca" went into Germany. So France in this instance, as well as in others, acted as intermediary in extending the influence of Cervantes.

If Cervantes suffered something of an eclipse in France during the second half of the 17th century as compared with the first, under the Regency and until 1730, he regained his initial place. This reversal of French opinion has been attributed to the fact that conditions in France at the end of the 17th century and the beginning of the 18th resembled those of a hundred years before: political defeats abroad and poverty at home. In the decline of Louis XIV, the War of the Spanish Succession was a potent factor, and all eyes turned toward the Court of Madrid. Accounts of travel in Spain, books of Spanish history, and translations from the Spanish abounded.

The most important translator of *Don Quixote* in the 18th century is Florian. He explains his task thus: "Le principal but de mon travail a été l'espoir de faire sentir une vérité qui ne me semble pas assez connue; c'est que don Quichotte, indépendamment de sa gaieté, de son comique, est rempli de cette philosophie naturelle qui, en livrant au ridicule de vains préjugés, n'en respecte que plus la saine morale. Don Quixote est fou dès qu'il agit, il est sage dès qu'il raisonne."

"N'espérant point faire passer dans ma langue les continuelles beautés qui compensent si fort ces taches légères, j'ai cru devoir les affaiblir, en adoucissant certains images, en changeant quelquefois des vers trop éloignés de notre goût, surtout abrégeant des digressions" (pp. 2, 5 of the Preface). Because he admires Don Quixote and wishes to give the French translation the same grâce it has in the original, he has taken liberties.

Florian's translation of *Don Quixote* (finished in 1794 and published in 1799), as well as his translation of two of the "Novelas ejemplares," met with varying degrees of approval. Louis Viardot in the introduction to his *Don Quichotte* (1836) says: "C'est vraiment une pitié que de voir les oeuvres d'un si grand génie audacieusement maniées, écourtées et mutilées par un si petit bel esprit." The *Spectateur du Nord,* however, felt that Florian's alterations enhanced the glory of the author. In general, the public of Florian's time, influenced by a century and a half of classicism, accepted this weakened and humorless Cervantes.

The 18th century, carefully studied by Maurice Bardon in his work on this and the preceding century, shows a variety of influences. Among the authors who mention the paladin of La Mancha are Fontenelle, who places the hero of Cervantes against Lisis, the hero of Charles Sorel; and Madame de Lambert, who charged Cervantes with contributing to the disorganization of the Spanish monarchy by ridiculing Spanish valor.

The Spanish knight also enters the Quarrel between the Ancients and the Moderns. A user of his lance is Charles Perrault, who, thinking Antiquity "n'a rien de la mesme nature qu'elle puisse opposer a *Don Quichot* et au *Roman comique,*" declares that there is in those works "un sel plus fin et plus piquant que tout celuy d'Athenes." He praises highly the amusing touches of *Don Quixote*. De Callières, as well, in his *Histoire poëtique de la guerre nouvellement declarée entre les Anciens et les Modernes* (1688) inquires if there is not room to hope that "celuy qui avoit si heureusement defait tous les Amadis et les autres Romans de l'ancienne Chevalerie, par son roman inimitable de *Don Quiote* (sic) *de la Mancha,* pourroit encore vaincre Ciceron et Demosthenes?"

These are the typical opinions: *Don Quixote* is either an amusing tale, or a powerful literary satire.

Now comes a new departure in Cervantine history in France. Le Sage makes in 1704 a translation of Avellaneda's false *Don Quixote.* More than that, he writes a continuation of the tale. Although long, and without originality in the development of Sancho, the book has a spirited style and served to revive interest in the story of Don Quixote.

In a vein similar to that of Cervantes, Marivaux wrote two novels: *Pharsamon* (written about 1712, and printed in 1737), which is a parody of the romanesque type, and *la Voiture embourbée* (1713), with its tale of the *Avantures du fameux Amador.* Marivaux' dramatic work, *le Prince travesti* (1724), is also influenced by the Spanish author.

Don Quixote was apparently indispensable to many dramatists. It provided Destouches with the title of his *Curieux impertinent* (played in 1710), wherein he modified the story and, attempting to prove the fidelity of a fiancée instead of the wife, made the test more probable but less interesting. More fortunate was Charles-Antoine Coypel with his *Folies de Cardenio* (1721). The artistic talent which is evident in his twenty-eight Gobelin tapestry designs from Don Quixote is seen again in his stage settings for this play. Here, rather than in the composition, lies its merit. Still more successful, with its exact and spirited interpretation of Cervantes' story of Camacho's wedding, is the tragi-comedy *Basile et Quitterie* (1723), by Gaultier. Another imitator of this tale, as well as that of the *Curioso impertinente,* is Fuselier.

Not only the minor characters of the novel but also Don Quixote and Sancho appear on the stage in this period. *Le Sancho-Pança, Gouverneur* (1712) of Dancourt, derived from the comedy by the same title by Guérin de Bouscal as well as from the original, is not without interest. Among others, Favart stands out, who was twice influenced in *Don Quichotte chez la Duchesse* and *Le Caprice amoureux ou Ninette à la Cour.* A very unusual Don Quixote, only thirteen years of age, was invented by Carmontelle for his fanciful and pleasing *Petit Dom Quichotte* (1774). This youthful marquis, on bended knee before a supposed shepherdess, pleads for the hand of the ten-year-old Astrée, and when discovered in this act by the romantic grandfather of the boy and the sentimental grandmother of the girl, they are so deeply moved that they themselves marry.

Ballets in which the "Ilustre Chevalier de la Manche" figured were popular in this century. Among these an important one is *Don Quichotte chez la Duchesse* (1734) by Pannard. The dramatist Poinsinet and the musician Philidor present Sancho and his wife Teresa in a gay "opéra-buffon," *Sancho Pança dans son isle* (1762).

As the popularity of Spanish things waned during the reign of Louis XV and English influence gained the ascendancy, the French set themselves to criticizing the Spanish. The Marquis Boyer d'Argens in his *Lettres Juives* (1738), complains of the Spaniards' jealousy, pride, laziness, and superstition, as well as of the Spanish Inquisition; nevertheless he thinks that there is more moral teaching in *Don Quixote* than in all the philosophic treatises published by professors. Among the Encyclopedists, Diderot, d'Alembert, and Voltaire point up their criticism by alluding to Don Quixote. Voltaire, for his part, when he feels he has become a sort of Don Quixote and a corrector of wrongs, fears that he will be no more successful than Don Quixote. In the political realm he condemns quixotism, as he points out in judging Charles XII of Sweden. He also used the name of Don Quixote to characterize St. Ignatius Loyola.

Don Quixote is cited in the period of the Revolution, when Marat, Robespierre, and C. Desmoulins call their enemies Don Quixotes, and the Royalists do the same.

The pre-romantic period (1800–1815), very favorable to Cervantes, furnishes a translation of *Don Quixote* and *Persiles* in 1807 by Bouchon Dubournial. In his preface he states the method that he will follow: " . . . la langue espagnole du temps de Cervantès, ne se prête, qu'en très peu de cas, à la traduction littérale en français. Il fallait donc, pour rendre fidellement Cervantès, s'attacher essentiellement à bien pénétrer toutes ses idees, et à bien sentir toutes ses beautés; et sans égard, ni aux mots, ni aux tournures de phrases dont il se servit, écrire tout se qu'il a pensé, et dit en espagnol, comme il l'aurait fait, si, avec la touche qui lui est propre, il eût écrit en français. C'est d'après ce principe, qu'est travaillée la traduction que je présente au public." His is a mistaken method because a faithful translator must consider the vocabulary and the phrase as well as the meaning. In his translation there are many omissions and suppressions. Interpreting and paraphrasing, Bouchon Dubournial, like Florian, weakened the vigorous Spanish text. But the edition found buyers, probably because it was a complete translation, while the preceding one of Florian was only an abridgment.

In the period of this translation the attitude is not entirely favorable to Cervantes. Mme. de Staël does not even mention him when dealing with Spain in her *De la littérature* (1800). Napoleon, upon reading *Don Quixote* while at Sainte-Hélène, calls the knight's adventures "babioles."

Chateaubriand, like Rousseau, hints at the coming Romantic sympathy with the suffering indicated in *Don Quixote* when he speaks of its "gaiété cruelle." In the numerous dramatic borrowings from the Spanish author the misfortunes of Cervantes are deplored in the *Portrait de Michel Cervantes* (1802) by Michel Dieulafoy. This work was translated into German the following year by F. L. Schmidt, and Tieck mentions seeing it played in London in 1817.

The Romantic attitude of pity, and the conception of *Don Quixote* as a work of art lend a new importance to the Spanish novelist. Bernardin de Saint-Pierre says that Rabelais and Cervantes have served mankind by freeing it from two great oppressors—the priest and the knight. Victor Hugo asserts that Cervantes gives "les deux profils de l'homme, parodie tout l'homme, sans plus pitié pour la partie sublime que pour la partie grotesque de notre nature." Théophile Gautier, who visited Spain and was familiar with the spirit of the people, emphasizes the sadness and the symbolism of the masterpiece.

In the revolt against romanticism the Castilian paladin is subjected to ridicule by A. Gandais in his *Don Quichotte romantique ou Voyage du Docteur Syntaxe* (1821), and by R. P. Castel in his *Nebulos ou le don Quichotte romantique* (1831).

In the political struggle for liberalism and freedom of the press Bouchon Dubornial (who, as stated above, made a translation of *Don Quixote*) employed the Spanish hero in his *Don Quichotte et Sancho Pansa a Paris en 1828*. He also expresses political and philosophical thoughts of the type of the squire's in a communication to the National Assembly, *Constitution octroyée par Sancho Pansa aux insulaires de l'Ile Barataria, ou Almanach constitutionnel de Sancho pour l'année 1849*.

Three outstanding novelists of the 19th century—Stendhal, Balzac, and Flaubert—were influenced by Don Quixote, but their interest was based neither on the combative value of the knight and his servant nor the amusement often provoked by their ridiculous figures. As Maurice Bardon has observed, they penetrated more deeply into the novel.[8] Stendhal reproduces Cervantes' zeal in *Le Rouge et le noir* and *La Chartreuse de Parme*. The quixotic Balzac compares himself to the Spanish knight: "Je suis comme don Quichotte, j'aime à prendre la défense du faible contre la fort!" The protagonist of his *Recherches de l'absolu* is engrossed in his pursuit of the absolute, and that of his *Cousin Pons* in his love of the aesthetic. Flaubert, in addition to many allusions in his *Correspondance,* puts the frustration of Don Quixote into Frédéric Moreau, the hero of his *Education sentimentale,* and the common sense of Sancho into Charles Deslauriers. The two figures of *Bouvard et Péchuchet* possess corresponding traits. As the search of Bouvard in the mental realm is reminiscent of Don Quixote's quest, so is that of Madame Bovary for ideal love.

The nineteenth-century critic, Sainte-Beuve, in his *Nouveaux Lundis,* says that for him the greatest worth of *Don Quixote* is its lively invention. Anatole France thinks that the Spanish novel inspires a laughing serenity. Barrès finds a profound lesson in the ability of the Spanish people to simplify and refine. The position of the French in regard to Cervantes has been clarified by such well-known scholars as A. de Puibusque, Paul de Saint-Victor, E. Littré, P. Chasles, Victor Fournel, E. Chasles, Paul Morillot, Morel-Fatio, Prosper Mérimée, and Émile Gebhart, who wrote a preface to the reprinting (1884) of the first translation by Oudin and Rosset. Gebhart later expressed his views on Cervantes in two important studies: *La Renaissance italienne et la philosophie de l'histoire* (1887) and *De Panurge à Sancho Pança* (1911), which appeared first in the *Journal des Débats,* June 21, July 21, and August 28, 1897. He says that of all foreign works *Don Quixote* has been the most popular in France because it contains the philosophy of the human heart, expressed by a mind that reasons accurately. Nothing to which Cervantes put his hand turned out well for him at the time. *Don Quixote* is the tragic cry of the unfortunate great writer. "Ici," writes Gebhart, "domine la comedie. Don Quichotte seul est profondément serieux et convaincu. Il marche, avec une allure magnifique, le front perdu dans les nuages."

The meaning of the great Spaniard for our day has been expressed by André Suares in his *Cervantès* (1916). He writes: "Je ne vous distingue plus, Don Quichotte et Cervantès. Vous êtes aussi beaux l'un que l'autre. Votre grandeur est inimitable: elle devrait faire pleurer et elle fait rire. Rien de bas ne peut tenir devant vous: Cervantès se moque ou s'indigne; et Don Quichotte court sus, avec sa grande âme qu'il lance devant soi comme une faulx." . . . "L'égalite dans la noblesse, la liberté dans le beau service, et l'amitié chrétienne, tel est Don Quichotte. Telle est l'âme de la France: la charité de la justice." "La liberté de Don Quichotte est sans bornes. Rabelais et Montaigne seuls, en ce temps-là, sont libres comme lui. Don Quichotte a la fureur de la liberté."

Another important interpreter of Cervantes for our present time is Paul Hazard. In clear and charming style, he shows us Cervantes as an individual, as a Spaniard, as a European, in all his human relations. Hazard reveals the influence of Américo Castro's epoch-making book, *El pensamiento de Cervantes* (1925);[9] and finds Cervantes' most striking traits, "facility, ease, pleasure in the game, the simplicity of the strong." Hazard, together with Ernest Martinenche, Gustave Reynier, and F. Baldensperger, not only contributed valuable studies in this field, but inspired the research of a number of Frenchmen. Notable examples are J. -J. A. Bertrand's *Cervantes et le romantisme allemande* (1914), M. G. Hainsworth's *"Novelas exemplares" en France au XVIIe siècle* (1933) and M. Maurice Bardon's *"Don Quichotte" en France au XVIIe et au XVIIIe siècle* (1931).

NOTES

[1] A detailed discussion of the translations of *Don Quixote* into French in the 17th and 18th centuries, as well as a thorough study of the influence of this Spanish novel in France in these two centuries, may be found in *"Don Quichotte" en France au XVIIᵉ et au XIIIᵉ siècle* (1605–1815) by Maurice Bardon (1931).

[2] The importance of the version of de Rosset and d'Audiguier has been stressed by G. Hainsworth in his *"Novelas exemplares" de Cervantes en France au XVIIᵉ siècle* (1933).

[3] Of the judgments concerning *Don Quixote* and the adaptations and imitations of it Paul Hazard in 1930 gave information in his penetrating study, *Don Quichotte;* the following year Maurice Bardon brought out his definitive work on *"Don Quichotte" en France au XVIIᵉ et au XVIIIᵉ siècle,* and three years later in the introduction to an edition of chapters from *Don Quixote* he extended to the present time an outline of French impressions of the master novel. Cervantes' tales were considered, through the 17th century, by M. G. Hainsworth in *Les "Novelas exemplares" de Cervantes en France au XVIIᵉ siècle* (1933). Hainsworth has an important section, entitled "La Nouvelle espagnole et l'Evolution du genre en France," in which he contends that the techniques introduced from Spain overshadowed those that had been coming in from Italy. But on this point, as R. H. Williams showed in his review of the book in the *Romanic Review* (1936, p. 298–305), it must be kept in mind that the Spanish novelists still continued to lean heavily upon Boccaccio and his countrymen for plots, so that they were really transmitting a diluted influence. With reason, however, Hainsworth gives prominence to Cervantes and his school and insists upon their importance in the cultivation of the short novel.

[4] *Oeuvres complètes de Boileau.* Paris: Garnier, 1870–3, Vol. IV, pp. 295–6.

[5] *Lettres.* Paris, 1862, Vol. VI, pp. 209–210, Vol. VII, p. 271.

[6] *Histoire comique des etats et empires de la lune et du soleil.* Paris: Garnier, s.d., P. lxviii.

[7] "Notes on Spanish Sources of Molière," *PMLA,* Vol. XIX, 1904.

[8] *"Don Quixote* et le roman réaliste français," *Révue de Littérature Comparée,* January–March 1936.

[9] This work received a discerning review by Marcel Bataillon in the *Revue de Littérature Comparée,* April–June 1928.

Cervantes in Germany

LIENHARD BERGEL

WHETHER Spain had ever had a Renaissance was a favorite topic of discussion among German scholars and writers during and after the First World War. The newly awakened enthusiasm for Spanish literature was due largely to the belief that Spain was a "country without a Renaissance," that Spain, like Germany, had succeeded in keeping herself free of the corrupting influences which had proved so fateful to England, France, and Italy in the 15th and 16th centuries. The tenor of intellectual development in Germany during the recent half-century, her effort to purge herself of "Western" ideas and influences, is also reflected in her attitude toward the literature of foreign countries. Since the days of Romanticism, Spain had always been particularly dear to the Germans, for it was then that critics and historians made the surprising discovery that Spain was the most "Germanic" of all romance countries because she had preserved her medieval character longer than any other, and because a particularly large amount of "Gothic" blood flowed in the veins of Spaniards.

If the German conception of Spain as a "country without a Renaissance" has no foundation in history, this designation can, nevertheless, be applied with some justification to Germany. Here the Renaissance remained on the whole the concern of a small group of learned humanists, who had little or no contact with the masses, while the popular literature retained in form and spirit much of the late medieval tradition and assimilated into this style whatever it took over from the Humanistic and Renaissance sphere.

This peculiar, dualistic structure of German literary life in the 16th and 17th centuries is reflected in the earliest reception of Cervantes. The first work of Cervantes which was translated into German was not *Don Quixote,* or any of the "novelas" in the Renaissance style, but *Rinconete y Cortadillo,* for this story seemed to have the closest affinity with the indigenous popular *genre* of jest-books. The German *Isaac Winckelfelder und Jobst von der Schneidt* of 1617 is not a translation in the strict sense of the term, but a transposition of the story

305

into German conditions. As the title shows, the names of the heroes are rendered
in German, the locality is Prague, the spirit and the language of the original
are transformed into a German rogue's tale. The translator was probably a pious
Catholic, for he omits all references which might give offense to the Church.
His work was extremely successful; there are numerous allusions to details of
it in the books of other writers of the time; Grimmelshausen, the author of the
most important German picaresque novel *Simplizissimus,* is thoroughly familiar
with it.

Isaac Winckelfelder und Jobst von der Schneidt was succeeded by a translation of the *Curioso impertinente.* It follows the Spanish text more closely than
its predecessor, but in spirit is far removed from it. Here no trace is left of the
Renaissance elegance of the original. However, this loss is not compensated for
by the charm of racy, popular idiom which distinguished the German *Rinconete
y Cortadillo.* The translation is written in the clumsy style of the moralizing
prose novels of middle-class inspiration which had made their first appearance
in the 16th century in Germany. The subtitle stresses the lesson to be taught:
"A new and nice story in which is painted the untimely curiousness of some
men, and the weakness of women, and the death of both; good and useful
to read."

The moralizing mission of this version is completely sacrificed in favor of
coarse entertainment in a dramatization it underwent a few years later. The play
became part of the repertoire of the "English Comedians," wandering troupes
of professional actors who originally came from England. Though the German
play preserves the outline of the original plot, in spirit it is worlds apart from
the Spanish *novela.* The subtle psychology and moral dignity of Cervantes'
story is completely destroyed; in its stead we find vulgar comicality.

The interest in Cervantes' novelas as mere sources of subject-matter, with
complete disregard for their artistic qualities, continues through the century,
even with authors who catered to an audience more educated than that for
which *Isaac Winckelfelder* and the play of the English Comedians were written.
In the middle of the century, the Nuremberg patrician Philip Harsdörffer, a
man well versed in the principal European literatures, and one of the most
active literary intermediaries of his time, included in his vast collections of stories
and plays of foreign origin also a number of novelas by Cervantes. His versions
are not more than excerpts, recounting the main action of the originals.
Cervantes' novelas had to wait until the end of the 18th century to find an
adequate reception in Germany.

A few years after the publication of Harsdörffer's collections, the *Gitanilla*
was rendered into German from a Dutch version in verse. This translation
deserves mention mainly because it is the only known example of Holland

serving as an intermediary for Cervantes, in contrast to the important rôle Holland played in transmitting the Spanish drama to Germany. Of greater curiosity than this version from the Dutch is the form in which the *Licenciado Vidriera* first reached Germany. A Rhenish humanist, Caspar Ens, included this novel in his Latin collection of edifying stories under the impressive title of *Phantasio-Cratumnius sive homo vitreus*. This translation of a work of modern literature into Latin was at that time nothing unusual; it is an example of the survival of humanist traditions in the 17th century. The *Homo vitreus* is, however, the only work by Cervantes to be honored in Germany by being elevated into the highest literary sphere; it is doubtful whether its author would have fully appreciated this distinction.

While the novelas were thus exploited as sources for literary entertainment and moral improvement, it was not until the middle of the century that *Don Quixote* was presented to the German reading public. This does not mean, however, that before this date it was entirely unknown in Germany. *Don Quixote* is mentioned in Germany for the first time on the occasion of the marriage celebrations of a German prince with an English princess, in Heidelberg, in 1613. As part of the entertainment, Don Quixote and Sancho Panza, in archaic German, challenge the assembled guests to admit that Dulcinea is the most beautiful woman in the world; the audience must have been sufficiently familiar with the story to appreciate the dramatization of this episode.

As long as a translation into their own language was lacking, the Germans read the novel in French. Philip Harsdörffer, speaking about the French translations available in Germany, finds Rosset's version especially popular. Even after the German translation had finally appeared in 1648, its French equivalents were still used for a long time, for the German version contains only the first twenty-three chapters of the original. This translation is remarkable in many respects. Its publication had been announced for the year 1621, but unfavorable circumstances delayed it for more than a quarter of a century. The translator hides himself behind a pseudonym which has not yet been satisfactorily explained, but the most widely accepted theory identifies him with a humanist who has several other translations from the romance literatures to his credit.

In his preface the author shows himself to be familiar with the English and French translations of *Don Quixote*. A comparison of these versions with his own leads him to some acute observations on the differences among the main European languages and on the problems of translation. The sound principles enunciated in his preface he applies intelligently to his practice. It is significant for his attitude toward the literary merits of the original that he omits what he considers to be boring: the prologue, and most of the poems and novelistic episodes. He wishes to concentrate on the "real story" about Don Quixote.

Thus begins a tendency which only in Romanticism was brought to an end: that of dealing with two Cervantes who have practically nothing in common: the author of the novelas, and the author of *Don Quixote,* shorn of its novelistic portions.

We do not know why the unknown translator did not finish his work. Nevertheless, this fragment renders the spirit of the original better than any other version. The best-known German translation, that of Ludwig Tieck, whatever its merits may be, cannot compare with it. His translation has nothing of the *grandezza* of the original, for it flows too smoothly, it reads like a nonchalant, discursive improvisation in the style of a romantic travel novel. The translator of 1648 accomplished much better the preservation of the satirical bitterness and the sharp thrusts of the original. Fortunately, others have used his fragment as a model, especially Ludwig Braunfels in his translation of 1884, who makes a consistent effort to write in the style of the first German *Don Quixote.*

In 1683 a complete translation was finally given to Germany. It is inferior to its predecessor, partly because the French text of Filleau de Saint Martin was used as the basis for the translation; not until 1775 did the Germans return to the original. France was in the 17th century the most important intermediary for Cervantes, because it furnished not only the texts for translations, but also other literary products derived from him.

Aside from these translations and adaptations, what is the critical attitude of the German Baroque toward *Don Quixote?* For the reading public of this time, *Don Quixote* is mainly a book of entertainment and amusement; it is often classified with the popular jest-books of the 16th century.

There were only a few voices during this period which did not share the general view, and which anticipated the attitude toward *Don Quixote* which was to prevail in the following century. The polyhistor Daniel Morhof is perhaps the first German to see in *Don Quixote* "a charming satire." Another scholar of the late 17th century, Christian Thomasius, assigns *Don Quixote* a place in the neighborhood of the *Roman Comique.* He stresses the universal applicability of *Don Quixote,* and sees in the actions of the hero a symbol of confused idealism. To the author of the first complete German version of *Don Quixote,* the book is more than a satire; for, as he points out, its hero, in matters not pertaining to his particular obsession, has the most reasonable opinions. The translator of 1683 represents the most enlightened judgment on *Don Quixote* in the whole period.

The history of Cervantes in Germany during the next half-century is, to a large extent at least, in a field different from that of translations, adaptations and criticism. Before Don Quixote assumed the grave function of chastizing the follies and shortcomings of German life in many different guises as the hero of satirical novels, he played a delightful interlude on the German stage. Hamburg, at that time the center of German operatic art, witnessed in 1690 the performance of the first German opera which had Don Quixote as its main character. Christian Heinrich Postel, at that time one of the most successful writers of *libretti* for the Hamburg opera, was also an admirer and connoisseur of Spanish literature and did much to spread its fame. For a long time after him, Hamburg remained the German city best informed on Spanish matters in general. The example of Hamburg in exploiting *Don Quixote* as a source for *libretti* was followed by other stages; the extraordinary popularity of *Don Quixote* in German during the 18th century, a vogue which surpassed that of any other work of foreign literature, is not to a small extent due to the large number of plays and operas based on this novel. It is not surprising that the serious intentions of Cervantes were largely forgotten in this form of entertainment.

In addition to the stage career of *Don Quixote,* two main trends, not always neatly separable in time and character, may be observed in the history of Cervantes during the 18th century. *Don Quixote* is used as an instrument in the hands of enlightened and rationalistic writers and critics of society, but at the same time, new ways of evaluating Cervantes begin to outline themselves which prepare for the criticism of the romanticists.

Two features are characteristic of the attitude of Enlightenment toward Cervantes: its dependence on the literature of France and England, and the concentration on *Don Quixote* alone, disregarding Cervantes' other works.

The critical opinion on *Don Quixote* is practically unanimous in considering it essentially a satire. The intention of its author is interpreted as an attack on everything illusionary, fantastic, and not in accord with reason and experience. Viewed in this light, *Don Quixote* becomes a favorite book of this period. The natural predilection of the age for satire may also account for the fact that the "romantic" and novelistic sections of Cervantes' work arouse hardly any interest. Critical utterances on *Don Quixote* are rare.

It was later in the century that *Don Quixote* reached the height of its popularity; never afterwards, not even in Romanticism, was its influence stronger. Practically every aspect and phase of German life between 1750 and 1800, so far as it is reflected in literature, is directly or indirectly related to *Don Quixote.*

Don Quixote would have been unable to perform this all-embracing function in Germany without an impetus from the English novel literature, which had taken its inspiration from Cervantes. The history of *Don Quixote* in Germany in the 18th century is intimately interwoven with the reception of Fielding. It is often difficult to determine whether *Don Quixote* itself or its English derivatives had served as a model; most frequently they act simultaneously. The comparison between Cervantes and Fielding is a favorite topic of the critics of the time, as for instance Möser and Lichtenberg. The Germans saw *Don Quixote* through English eyes, and from English books they took the courage to apply it to their own concerns.

The tenor of all these imitations of *Don Quixote* is best exemplified in a novel by Wieland, *Don Sylvio von Rosalva.* Wieland, the most important German novelist in the 18th century before Goethe, in his youth had fallen under the influence of a religious sentimentalism and idealistic fervor which was inclined to a dreamy, self-centered enthusiasm and which looked contemptuously upon reality and practical matters. This sentimentalism was a European phenomenon, but it found particularly favorable conditions in Germany, where it was nourished by the survival of mystical currents related to the Reformation. This connection between sentimentalism and the 16th century can be observed in the history of the word most frequently used to denote the enthusiastic idealism of the time: "Schwärmerei." The word originally symbolized the humming sound of bees and other insects in flight; later it assumed the connotation of "bacchic turmoil" which prepared the new meaning of "religious ecstasy." Radical sects of the Reformation which did not submit to church discipline, were called "Schwarmgeister." The linear descendants of these are the pietists of the 18th century; the German sentimentalism of the time is in many respects a secularized pietism. Klopstock's and Wieland's background, as well as that of most non-Catholic writers in the 18th century, is that of pietism. Wieland speaks of his sentimental youth as of the "seraphic" period in his life. But his nature was much too complex, his gifts too manifold, and his personal and literary contacts too varied for him to remain an idealistic "angel." In the process of disengaging himself from his saintly beginnings, he found the reading of *Don Quixote* a most helpful antidote against fevers of the soul. This conception of *Don Quixote* as medicine against sentimental "fevers" is typical of the time. Wieland's application of this cure to himself resulted in his writing *Don Sylvio von Rosalva.*

The principal theme of this book is expressed in the subtitle of the first edition, which was later omitted: "The triumph of reason over dreaming" ("Schwärmerei"). The author himself explains in a note that with the hero's predilection for fairy tales he aimed principally at the "zoroastric, plotinic, paracelsic and rosicrucian errors," the "pythagorean-cabalistic philosophy" which was closely connected with the extravagances of the pietists and sentimenta... Since the days of Paracelsus and the alchemists, mystical efforts to unite with God and pseudo-scientific experiments to unlock the secrets of Nature with the help of magic were intimately interwoven; the symbols of the alchemists always had, in addition to their chemical, a religious meaning. The preoccupation with mystical and magical problems assumed in the 18th century in Germany the proportions of an epidemic; sincerity and charlatanism had become inextricably intermingled, and beclouded the brains of many well-meaning persons.

Like the hero of Cervantes, Don Sylvio is at bottom a noble character; it was his good-nature which made him so easily yield to misleading influences. His yearning for a world of fairies, foolish as it may be, is essentially idealistic and therefore worthy of the reward of marriage with a beautiful, though very real lady. He does not criticize the capability for enthusiasm and feeling as such, but merely those sentiments which are based on abstractions. Don Sylvio's great weakness, typical of the young, is his excessive impressionability; a good dose of experience and some friendly advice help him to overcome it. Thus the book is related to the educational novel, so popular at the time of Wieland and so characteristic of German literature.

In *Don Sylvio von Rosalva* practically all motifs of the novels written under the inspiration of *Don Quixote* are anticipated. The satire on occultism is a most frequent subject in books of this kind.

In other novels of this group the relation to *Don Quixote* is not so direct. The main link with their model is the thesis that the folly of the hero is caused by too much reading, and that he now tries to transpose his book world into life; the plot is based on the clash between imagination and reality. In many of these books, the place which the Amadis-novels occupied in *Don Quixote* is taken by the sentimental writings of Richardson and his followers, and here the influence of Fielding is unmistakable.

The best-known representative of this kind of novel is *Der deutsche Grandison,* by Wieland's friend Musaeus. Musaeus made use of the framework offered by *Don Quixote* in another novel, which is at least as important as the parody on Richardson. His *Physiognomische Reisen* are a satire on the most wide-spread psychological fad of the 18th century, Lavater's doctrine of the relation between shape of skull and cut of features to character and personality.

Closely related to this travesty of psychological theories are books which are aimed at the educational doctrines of the time. Here the satirists struck a particularly fertile subject, education being the quixotic enterprise *par excellence*. The common feature of all these works is the pernicious influence of literature and abstract theories on the hero.

The satire on the aristocracy of the time, which had been a minor motif in Wieland's *Don Sylvio von Rosalva,* becomes the principal theme in one of the best comical novels of the German 18th century, a book that in freshness and directness of characterization can be compared only to those of Hippel and Jean

Paul. Johann Gottwerth Müller, a friend of Lichtenberg, chooses a Prussian Junker as the hero for his *Siegfried von Lindenberg*. This "Pomeranian Don Quixote," as the author calls him, has been so much impressed by the story of of the Germanic hero that he intends to equal him. After he has once begun to imitate what he has found in a book, he extends his efforts and applies them to whatever is recounted in printed form. He conceives the idea of introducing into his backward little realm everything about which he has heard in the newspapers (he cannot read them himself and has his schoolmaster read him the daily news). "His pride urged him on at least to equal the greatest personages on earth, if not to surpass them."

Like Don Quixote, his Pomeranian counterpart completely lacks originality. If it is one of Don Quixote's main concerns whether his actions and attitudes correspond closely to those of his models in the chivalric novels, Lindenberg is constantly worrying whether his projects are according to "Kustühm." After he has assured himself of this, he will duplicate that which is "customary" on a bigger and better scale. Though the similarities with *Don Quixote* in general inspiration and in detail are not numerous, *Siegfried von Lindenberg* belongs to the distant progeny of the Spanish novel, particularly if we consider that some interpreters have seen the basic objective of *Don Quixote* as a criticism of *hidalguismo*, the Spanish equivalent of Prussian Junkerdom. This parallelism occurred not only to the author of *Siegfried von Lindenberg,* but also to the critic, novelist, and political writer of "Young Germany," Ludwig Boerne, who calls Pomerania "The German Asturias." *Siegfried von Lindenberg* opens a series of novels on the pattern of *Don Quixote* which satirize German nobility and German nationalism, and most of which are now forgotten.

The significance of these imitations of *Don Quixote* lies not only in the fact that they mirror some of the principal tendencies of German life during the 18th century, but that they also give an indication of the way in which *Don Quixote* was then interpreted. In most of these novels the intentions of the hero appear foolish and as mere whims. His dreams do not possess any ideal value, they only serve to block the access to reality. He does not appeal to the reader's sympathy, but is simply ridiculous. On the other hand, the optimism of the time does not permit the hero's illusions to be more than a thin layer on the surface, which is not deeply rooted in his personality; a good dose of experience and reason suffices to remove them. Usually a catharsis is effected, and after the hero has abandoned his fantasies, he is happier than before.

There are only two novels which deviate from this set pattern. As we had seen, Don Sylvio's belief in fairies is not merely ridiculous, it is a misguided aspiration toward an ideal. In Wieland's novel the ending is still optimistic. However, a different tone is sounded for the first time in Johann Karl Wezel's novel, *Tobias Knaut*. Here the character resembling Don Quixote is conceived as basically tragic. The author, whose other works often show a furious pessimism and who, like Swift, ended in insanity, makes his creature suffer and become destroyed by the clash between ideal and reality. Wezel sympathizes with him and takes his side. Selmann, the master of Tobias Knaut, is a "psychological knight-errant." "Because of his reading he is always with his head in the land of fantasy. There he finds his own impetuous imagination, his own sensitivity, his ethereal principles, ideal stories, seraphic poems." When he sets out to discover in reality people who would correspond to his high expectations, he meets nothing but baseness and vulgarity. The academic circles and pious societies with which Selmann has most contact are represented as thoroughly detestable. Selmann's unwillingness to compromise with his ideals, which leads to his premature death, has heroic qualities. Thus the romantic interpretation of *Don Quixote* is adumbrated in this novel.

Meanwhile, a new attitude toward *Don Quixote* was also slowly maturing in the critical appraisals of Cervantes. Bodmer, the opponent of Gottsched, and paternal friend of Wieland, who opened so many new vistas in the evaluation of literature, is probably the first German critic to make himself independent of the English interpretation of *Don Quixote,* which saw in Cervantes principally a forerunner of Fielding. For Bodmer, *Don Quixote* is not so much a satire as a representation of complicated psychological states. Don Quixote demonstrates to him the intricate interaction among imagination, feeling, and reason in human nature. Don Quixote is a fascinating example for the process of rationalization of irrational impulses. He is not a victim of illusions; what may give this appearance, is in reality an essential part of his character, its irrational side. Instead of condemning Don Quixote for sacrificing his rational abilities to his irrational proclivities and for making his reason serve his feelings, he proclaims in words resembling those of Pascal that "imagination and feeling have their own logic" and are of equal value with reason. New also is the emphasis which Bodmer lays on Cervantes as a conscious artist; he mentions particularly the way in which Cervantes develops the contrast between Don Quixote and Sancho Panza.

Compared with the discoveries of Bodmer, the critical opinions of Lessing, his much more famous contemporary, are insignificant. The fact that most of his utterances on Cervantes are scattered in reviews of *Don Quixote*—imitations, are an indication that Lessing was not particularly interested in the subject. His only remarks on *Don Quixote* worthy of notice are that Cervantes "knew the art of hiding a most serious moral behind amusing incidents" and that "Cervantes had a serious way of joking."

Of infinitely greater importance is the attitude of Herder toward Cervantes.

Herder studied *Don Quixote* during his whole life, and his opinions on the novel underwent many changes. These shifts in his appraisal not only summarize the typical attitudes of the 18th century toward Cervantes, but, like Bodmer's criticism, they prepare the romantic conception of *Don Quixote*. The young Herder, brought up in pious and sentimental surroundings, is a "Schwärmer" of the purest breed, and he is conscious of it. In this frame of mind he reads *Don Quixote*. In a letter to his bride he describes his impressions of the book: "The main character, however perfectly drawn, I never liked, . . . for it offended something in myself which is quixotic; my feelings were hurt that the author ridicules a person who possesses so many great and noble traits." For this reason he prefers "the quiet, good-natured, always satisfied Sancho Panza."

Thirty years later Herder had almost completely reversed his opinion. Now he mentions *Don Quixote* together with Butler's *Hudibras,* a parallel which was frequently drawn in the criticism of the time, and he notes with satisfaction that *Don Quixote* put an end to the novels of chivalry, just as *Hudibras* rid the age of "Schwärmerei." In an essay of 1801 about "Romantic Characters" he reveals himself an outspoken opponent of all forms of "Schwärmerei," particularly that variety which had been bred by the reading of unrealistic, idealizing books; Don Quixote, the first victim of novel reading, might have served as a warning example for the future. To this repetition of traditional views Herder adds his original contribution, a socio-historical approach to *Don Quixote* which foreshadows Hegel's interpretation. In Herder's eyes, Don Quixote becomes the symbol of the reactionary, of the man who has lost contact with the necessities of historical reality and confuses yesterday with the present. Herder speaks of "the pucks of history who are still riding in broad daylight without realizing that their hour is past." Viewed from this angle, Cervantes' part in destroying the popular taste for chivalric novels appears in a new light. These novels, with their eccentric enterprises, originated in a time of barbarism and deserve condemnation for this reason alone. Herder finds particular occasion for criticism, however, in the stress these novels laid on class distinctions. Here the democratic inclinations of Herder, so frequently interspersed in his work and arbitrarily suppressed by his modern nationalistic interpreters, come to the fore. The romantic spirit of these novels seems to him related to an aristocratic order of society, and to the tendency of isolated individuals toward the extravagant. Yet the exceptional, in whatever form, must submit to reason and to the divinely established order of nature which makes for harmony among all its constituents. The unrestrained individual's willful quests for the impossible must give way to moderation and the observance of the limits set by socio-historical reality. In this essay, Herder gave the theoretical foundation to what was felt and expressed in narrative form by Gottwerth Müller and the authors of other novels, who took as their target the decaying aristocracy of their time.

This disregard for reality Herder finds also in the philosophy of his old teacher, Kant. We cannot discuss here the implications and merits of the philosophical conflict between the two former friends—it is pertinent to our investigation, however, that Herder puts Kant's philosophy of transcendental idealism, his "onto-logico-cosmologico-physico-theological" efforts to find a basic principle beyond experience, to penetrate to the "immaculate conception of reason" on the same level as Don Quixote's sublime intentions. Kant reminds him of Don Quixote's riding Clavileño: both are blindfolded in order not to be disturbed by brutal empirical facts. Kant appears to Herder as a new kind of "Schwärmer."

In another article dealing with *Don Quixote,* Herder gives a more explicit expression to the democratic convictions which were at least implied in his essay on "Romantic Characters." In 1802 he translated for his periodical *Adastrea,* from Brooke's "Fool of Quality," the conversation on *Don Quixote* between the author and his friend. The conclusion that Herder identified himself largely with its content is justified. The English author's attacks on wanton destruction in the name of heroic, aristocratic individualism, and his praise for the unspectacular, unselfish, humble Sancho Panza as governor of Barataria, must have struck a sympathetic chord in Herder, the unrelenting critic of the barbarities perpetrated by the Prussian invaders on Slavonic soil. Herder had, in another context, praised the wisdom of Sancho Panza, who, with his proverbs, would have been a better ruler than the statesmen in power, with their clever tricks.

Herder's veneration for Sancho Panza is shared by one of his contemporaries, Maximilian Klinger. Klinger, the friend of young Goethe, author of the play *Sturm und Drang* which later gave its name ("Storm and Stress") to the whole period, after his unruly youth, had become a high administrative officer in the Czarist government. In his "Reflections on World and Literature" of 1803, written at a time when he had gained much direct insight into the workings of absolutist government, Klinger confronts Sancho Panza, as governor, with the rulers he had known; the comparison is entirely in Sancho Panza's favor. The overheated, idealistic hate of tyrants and injustice which had inspired Klinger in his youth now had given way to a more realistic attitude of resignation, and this is also reflected in his opinions on *Don Quixote*. He has not completely abandoned his early ideals, but he despairs of their ever being carried out in practice. Thus he finds occasion to praise and criticize Don Quixote at the same time. He lauds his noble convictions but finds fault with the intransigence with which Don Quixote wants to convert others. He concludes on the pessimistic note that all virtue and all purity of intention contain an element of quixotism. Klinger is among those who pave the way for a positive evaluation of Don Quixote's character. As early as 1766, the poet and critic Gerstenberg had timidly expressed such an opinion when he observed that "the 'Schwärmerei' of Don Quixote can easily appear ridiculous, but never contemptible."

Herder and Klinger stand alone in their time with their high esteem for Sancho Panza. To most other contemporary critics Sancho Panza is a grotesque and coarse figure. The opinion of Lichtenberg is typical: "Sancho Panza is a person whose only concerns are money and food." This is also the way in which the novels imitating *Don Quixote* present the companion of the hero. Herder's and Klinger's predilection for Sancho Panza is surpassed, however, in an amusing way by a minor writer; the satirist, author of fables, and friend of Klopstock, Rabener. His favorite among the characters in *Don Quixote* is Sancho Panza's donkey. For Rabener, this animal is the symbol of equanimity, that middle-class virtue which Gellert and his circle put above all other perfections. The stoical calmness with which the donkey accepts his misfortunes appears to Rabener as a model of behavior. In this respect the *rucio* is perhaps the model of the German middle class altogether, and suggests Edwin Allan's poem on "middle-class-assitude." Herder, the irritable and temperamental, whose malicious gibes were feared even by Goethe, undoubtedly did not include the *rucio* in his admiration.

In his interpretation of Cervantes, Herder transcends his time in more than one way. He was the initiator not only of the historical approach to *Don Quixote,* but also of a more refined æsthetic appreciation of the book. Even in his seraphic period, when Cervantes' irony repulsed him, Herder was sensitive to the peculiar atmosphere in the novel. He finds in it "something strange, half fairy-like and mysterious." He anticipates a favorite dogma of the Romanticists when he declares *Don Quixote* to be the "national novel" of Spain, but, unsatisfied with such a vague generality, he later corrects himself and emphasizes that the only possible approach to *Don Quixote* is the effort to understand the artistic individuality of its author.

It is surprising that the century which read *Don Quixote* with such eagerness, interpreted the novel with such originality, and connected it in so many ways with its own concerns, did not produce a translation of the book from the original until the end of the period. This delay may be explained by the fact that in Germany the art of translation from languages other than Latin and French developed rather late, only after such writers as Bodmer, Wieland, and Herder had shown the way. The first full German translation of *Don Quixote* from the Spanish, that by Bertuch, was undertaken with Wieland's encouragement. Bertuch's version of 1775 is not complete in the strict philological sense of the term, for he, like many of his predecessors in France, omitted all novelistic and romantic parts in which he saw only as superfluous insertions.

Bertuch's opinions on *Don Quixote,* as he expressed them in the preface to his translation, are typical of his time. He sees in Don Quixote "the image and mirror of the Schwärmer," the "typical fool," while Sancho Panza represents "the common people." With these rough classifications he does not come near Bodmer's subtle psychological analysis. His sympathies, like those of Herder, are on the side of Sancho Panza. This personal predilection was not without influence on the translation itself. Not only is Bertuch more successful in rendering the speeches of the servant than those of the master, but the tone of the whole book is more fitting for the squire than for the knight.

In contrast to the 17th century, the interest of the period of Enlightenment in Cervantes was almost exclusively limited to *Don Quixote.* The two main characters of the novel lent themselves as convenient symbols for the oppositions dominating the time, while the picturesque world of the *novelas* was rejected. The only exception is the *Coloquio de los Perros,* which was welcomed because of its satirical purpose, and was frequently imitated. Toward the end of the century, however, the horizon broadened again to admit other works of Cervantes. A translation of *Persiles and Sigismunda* from the French, made around 1750, had received little notice, but now the wide success of Bertuch's *Don Quixote* attracted attention to Cervantes' work as a whole. A pupil of Bertuch, Soden, rendered all the *novelas* and *Persiles* into German from the original. Though Bertuch himself considered only *Don Quixote* acceptable to the taste of his contemporaries, he published two of Cervantes' plays in his periodical devoted to Spanish and Portuguese literature. Thus all sides of Cervantes' literary activity were now presented to the German public, with the exception of the *Galatea,* a gap which was filled in 1787, when Mylius rendered into German Florian's version of the Spanish pastoral. While the interest in the *novelas* and in *Persiles* was mainly that of antiquarian and philological curiosity, Mylius' translation is more directly related to the literary currents of the time. One of the forms in which 18th century sentimentalism found expression was the revived genre of bucolic poetry. The *Idylls* of the Swiss Salomon Gessner gained acclaim the world over. Gessner was acquainted with the Spanish work and appreciated it. Florian was among the many admirers of Gessner and in correspondence with him; Gessner's style, as he observes himself, served him as a model in his version of *Galatea.*

Thus the ground was prepared for a new approach to Cervantes. Bertuch had gained direct access to Cervantes' works in the original, and the monopoly *Don Quixote* had possessed in the 18th century was broken. Herder had opened new vistas with his interpretations. Beside Herder, Goethe forms the most important link between the enlightened attitude toward Cervantes and that of Romanticism. Like Herder, Goethe in his youth had been a "Schwärmer" of the purest strain; the *Sorrows of Young Werther* are the authentic expression of Goethe's "sentimental" period. Again like Herder, Goethe outgrew this mood and became its severe critic, proclaiming this new, mature attitude in a series of short, farcical plays which ridiculed the extreme forms of "Schwärmerei." The most significant piece of this group, *Der Triumph der Empfindsamkeit,* owes some features to Cervantes. The sentimental prince Oronaro adores a doll, which, as revealed by later inspection, is stuffed with books fashionable at the time, among them *The Sorrows of Young Werther*. These writings are the cause of the prince's sentimental disease. The behavior of the prince toward the puppet resembles in many respects that of Don Quixote toward Dulcinea. Just as Don Quixote, in the Sierra Morena, engages in long monologues about the cruelty of his lady, so the prince acts out long monodramas in which he pours forth his devotion to the marionette. Like Don Quixote, he is conscious of the theatrical element in it, but he does not allow this thought to interfere with his performance: "There exists an intimate bond between the stage and our nature." The resemblance between these lines and some famous verses of the young Hofmannsthal is not accidental; the "fool" of Hofmannsthal's play is not entirely free from quixotic features. The moral of the play which the king proclaims at the end, would also be fitting for *Don Quixote:* "Only then is a fool really deceived when he imagines in his folly to heed the voice of reason or to obey the gods."

Though Goethe's critical utterances on *Don Quixote* are scarce, they attest to his detailed and continued study of the novel. It is significant that he mentions *Don Quixote* most frequently in the years following the sentimental crisis of his youth, at the time when he disciplined himself into taking the complete opposite of his former attitude. Among these opinions one in particular is often quoted: "The novel loses its interest at the point when the hero is merely the victim of hoaxes and impositions of others." Usually this statement is interpreted as referring to the genuine second part of the novel. It is entirely possible, however, that Goethe rather had in mind Avellaneda-Lesage's continuation which was appended to Bertuch's translation. Though Goethe was able to read Spanish haltingly and possessed copies of the book in the original, he probably read *Don Quixote* most often in Bertuch's version, which was very popular at the Weimar Court.

Of greater importance than these occasional remarks is a short essay in which Goethe propounds his views on the central theme in *Don Quixote*. This article was written in the last decade of Goethe's life and shows unmistakably the influence of romantic criticism of Cervantes, which was fully developed by that time. While the 18th century saw in *Don Quixote* the opposition between two psychological tendencies, "Schwärmerei" on the one hand, and a respect for reason and experience on the other, the romanticists shifted the interpretation to the philosophical field. *Don Quixote* symbolized for them the speculative and dialectical relationship between idea and reality. This new conception is also at the bottom of Goethe's essay. It was written as a review of a translation of Spanish romances. Goethe begins with a short description of what in his opinion constitutes the basic trait of the Spanish national character, the tendency "to transpose the idea directly into concrete reality." Don Quixote's conduct is in harmony with the predisposition of his nation. The theme of the novel is the struggle between idea and reality: "When the idea enters directly into life, it will be received either as something tragic and serious, or as mere fancy, and the idea becomes actually perverted into a play of fancy if it is not able to preserve its original sublime purity; even the form in which the idea manifests itself is destroyed in the effort of preserving the original purity. If, on the other hand, the idea appears merely as something fantastic, then it has lost its value; this is the reason why the fantastic, when it is destroyed in a clash with reality, does not arouse our sympathy but rather becomes ridiculous. For the fantastic in action produces comical situations which give only too much pleasure to gleefully malicious minds." In this passage, complicated as it may be, Goethe delineated the philosophical premises for the romantic criticism of Cervantes more clearly than the romantic philosophers themselves ever did. His evaluation of the Don Quixote problem has the additional advantage of preserving a just balance between idea and reality, the sublime and the fantastic, an equilibrium which the romanticists tend to upset in favor of the "idea."

In his attitude toward Cervantes, Goethe was indebted to the romanticists in more than one respect. It was through them that his interest in the *novelas* was aroused. The intensive study they had devoted to Boccaccio and the *novelas ejemplares* had resulted in new theories on the "Novelle," that narrative form typical of nineteenth-century German literature. Goethe followed these æsthetic discussions attentively and utilized them for his own writing. The novelettes of his maturity, those which compose the *Unterhaltungen deutscher Ausgewanderten,* and those inserted in the second part of *Wilhelm Meister,* have Cervantes *novelas* as their model.

Beside the question of Goethe's opinions on Cervantes and that of possible influences, there exists the broader problem of potential affinities between the two poets. The most acute observations on this matter, which also was a favorite topic of romantic criticism, were made by Heine. Heine finds the common element between the two to be their "humoristic irony." He explains this trait in both as resulting from the lack of political liberty during their lifetimes:

"Just as Cervantes, at the time of the Inquisition, had to take recourse to humoristic irony in order to hint at his real convictions, without giving open offense to the representatives of the Holy Office, Goethe chose the tone of humoristic irony for that which he, the courtier and minister of state, did not dare to express frankly. Goethe never concealed truth; instead, whenever he was prevented from showing it nakedly, he clad it in humor and irony. Writers who smart under censorship and mental compulsion of all kinds, are particularly dependent on the ironic and humorous form of expression. This is the only recourse left for intellectual honesty, and in the humoristically ironic disguise this honesty reveals itself most impressively."

Heine complements his observations by a comparison between the prose style of the two artists which is equally perspicacious: "Goethe resembles Cervantes even in stylistic details, in his comfortably and leisurely flowing prose which is permeated by a sweet and ingratiating irony. They are akin to one another even in their stylistic vices, in the prolixity of some of their periods which are comparable to a train of royal equipages. Often a single idea only is embodied in such an extended period, which rides along like a large, gilded court coach pulled by six decorated horses. But this single idea is always exalted, if not the sovereign himself."[1]

While Goethe was influenced by the romantic criticism of Cervantes, but exerted little immediate influence himself, the opposite holds true for two of his closest friends, Schiller and Wilhelm von Humboldt. The outstanding feature of Wilhelm von Humboldt's attitude toward Cervantes is the fact that he based his interpretation of *Don Quixote* on direct acquaintance with the country of its origin. Toward the end of the 18th century it had become fashionable among European travelers to include Spain in their "grand tour." Wilhelm von Humboldt's Spanish trip was not exclusively motivated by this vogue, but he was among the first to relate his impressions of the country with his reading of Cervantes. *Don Quixote* appeals to him mainly as a book full of local color, a rich picture of Spanish life. He believes to have seen innumerable Don Quixotes, followed by their Sancho Panzas, crossing slowly the barren mountains and arid plains of Spain. He claims that only he who has traveled in Spain and observed its people can understand *Don Quixote* correctly. His position is the opposite of that of the 18th century, which had attributed to *Don Quixote* a universal meaning.

Schiller's importance in the development of the romantic views on Cervantes can hardly be overestimated. Though he wrote little on Cervantes, his theories of literary types and literary development created the foundations for the critical edifice erected by the romanticists, in which Cervantes occupies such a prominent place. In addition, *Don Quixote* played a not insignificant part in

the genesis of Schiller's first drama, *The Robbers*. The author himself acknowledged that the figure of the generous bandit Roque Guinart in the second part
of *Don Quixote* had contributed to the conception of his hero. This influence
is of secondary importance, however, compared to that exerted by the character
of Don Quixote himself. In a preface to his play Schiller points out the similarities between Don Quixote and Karl Moor, giving at the same time his own
interpretation of the novel: "The hero's false conception of his abilities and his
power, his overabundance of energy which overflows all limits set by law—such
qualities must collide inevitably with the established institutions of society and
lead to a catastrophe, and if to these enthusiastic dreams of greatness and
unbounded activity is added a feeling of bitterness against the world because
of its imperfection and its remoteness from ideals, then we possess the complete
picture of the strange Don Quixote whom we abhor and love, admire and pity
in the robber Karl Moor."

This passage is rich with implications. The 18th century had ventured only
timidly to find anything praiseworthy in Don Quixote's dreams. Schiller, however, without hesitation represents Don Quixote as the noble idealist who
suffers from the imperfections of the world. Instead of being a ridiculous figure,
he appears now in a heroic light. Schiller alters also the foundation on which
up to this time the concept of the quixotic character had rested. The new Don
Quixote is no longer a victim of too much reading, who tries to transpose the
book-world into reality, or who aims at the restoration of antiquated institutions.
Schiller's hero no longer requires books to conceive an ideal world, he is the
creator of his own inspirations. If Karl Moor reads Plutarch, he does so merely
to confirm his own longings; the book is no longer their source. The new Don
Quixote, instead of dreaming of an ideal past, gazes into an ideal future for
which he works; the boundary between the reactionary and the progressive
visionary becomes tenuous and finally disappears. From now on the Don
Quixote interpretation divides into two main currents: Don Quixote is understood either as a restoration-minded reactionary or as a radical utopian. Schiller
himself created the prototype for the latter in his *Marquis Posa*.

Schiller's literary production was essentially an illustration, in the form of
poems or plays, of his philosophical system. His positive historical importance
lies, therefore, not in his dramas, which are for the most part barren of any
poetical quality, but in his essays. Here the conflicts which had found a pompous
and rhetorical expression in *The Robbers* and *Don Carlos* are presented in less
adulterated form. Schiller's philosophical investigations contributed indirectly
to the romantic interpretation of *Don Quixote*.

Schiller's central problem is the relationship between the finite and the infinite,
between "idea" and "reality." This polarity underlies all other pairs of opposites

established by Schiller, those of "naïve" and "sentimental," of "Greek" and "modern." The romanticists built upon these antitheses in their own æsthetic and historical theories. It is the heritage of Schiller, often unfortunate, but typically German, if the romantic critics of Cervantes are usually more concerned with the discovery of philosophical relationships in the novel than with its artistic values.

Schelling's interpretation of *Don Quixote* shows more clearly than that of any other romanticist how a work of art is sacrificed for the sake of serving as an illustration to a philosophical system. His thinking is based on the concept of an original identity of idea and appearance or reality, an identity which was destroyed through a fall similar to that of Adam and Eve; life consists of an effort to restore the paradisiac state of harmony. For Schelling, *Don Quixote* is a "mythical saga" which symbolizes "the inevitable struggle between the ideal and the real, a conflict typical of our world, which has lost the identity between the two."

Other romanticists played numerous variations on this basic theme. Novalis sees in *Don Quixote* the conflict between dream and reality. For Adam Müller, the Catholic thinker whose social theories were partly resurrected by National-Socialism, *Don Quixote* represents the contrast between mind and body. The epigone of romantic philosophy, Friedrich Theodor Vischer, shifts Schelling's antithesis between the ideal and the real back into the psychological field: he sees the attitudes of idealism and realism personified in the two main characters of the novel. In general, Sancho Panza, the favorite of the 18th century, now has a bad press. He is constantly scolded for his "materialism" and narrow-mindedness. On the other hand, Don Quixote grows more and more into the proportions of a tragic hero, who succumbs to the stupidity of his inferior surroundings. The extremes of this attitude were reached by two noblemen, Adalbert von Chamisso and Friedrich von Sallet. In a poem, Chamisso takes the side of Don Quixote against Sancho Panza in the windmill episode, and Sallet sympathizes with Don Quixote, whose only fault it was to imagine the world as beautiful, and to overlook its baseness. Both are outraged at the thought that Sancho Panza, a mere servant, and therefore unable to conceive high-flown ideals, should laugh at his master.

Extreme flights of fancy like those of Chamisso and Sallet, though they were not meant as objective criticism but are rather lyrical outbursts, show the fatal consequences of the attempt to interpret *Don Quixote* by the methods of German idealism. The possibility that *Don Quixote* might have an anti-idealistic tendency did not occur to the romanticists, or, it was purposely ruled out because it would have disturbed their system. The philologist Eugen Lerch has given a keen description of the dilemma with which *Don Quixote* confronted the German romanticists: The eighteenth-century view of the book was naturally unacceptable to them, and therefore "they tried, through an allegorical interpretation, to render harmless that which they could not annihilate by useless protests . . . Thus the tendency developed subconsciously to deprive the beast of its fangs, to dissolve the vigorous life of the novel into harmless philosophical speculation."[2]

The same abstract method which they applied to the content of *Don Quixote* the romanticists used also in scrutinizing the artistic form of the novel and the *novelas*.

Cervantes was useful to the romanticists for filling a number of positions on the map of literature they had drawn up. After having assigned to Shakespeare the foremost place in the drama, they needed a counterpart for "the novel"; Cervantes conveniently served this purpose. The romanticists determined first theoretically what a novel should be, and then searched for books which could fulfil their requirements. Practically every romantic critic of Cervantes began with a definition of "the novel" and then scrutinized Cervantes for the qualifications necessary to a novelist; usually Cervantes passed the examination with a good mark.

The romanticists were not only anxious to press Cervantes into the forms of metaphysical and æsthetic speculation, they also fitted him by force into their scheme of literary development. To the antithetical pairs applied by Schiller to literary history, they added a new polarity, the romantic and "poetic" principle on the one hand, and the "prosaic" and realistic on the other. Thus Don Quixote appears to A. W. Schlegel as the representative of the "poetry of chivalry," while Sancho Panza represents mere prose. His brother saw in these antinomies the basis for a historical conflict. The "poetic" or "romantic" is the ideal state which is threatened by the "prosaic." The ideal condition is historically identified with the Middle Ages, "the epoch of knights, love, and romance." To the Schlegels and other romanticists, *Don Quixote* is primarily a "chivalric poem," Cervantes a "romantic poet." "The romantic poet was surrounded on all sides by a poetic reality in which he was rooted and which completely permeated him . . . This applies also to Cervantes, although his poetry is affected by the growing discrepancy between a reality which has become unpoetical, and the chivalric imagination."[3] The "poetic" world in *Don Quixote* is not the product of fancy, but a picture of real life, for "life in Spain was at that time still chivalric and romantic." Thus *Don Quixote* is not only a "romantic" poem, but an expression of the national genius, a *Nationalwerk*. As a "romantic poem," *Don Quixote* possesses universal meaning, but at the same time it is a reflection of the "Spanish soul."

This transformation of *Don Quixote* into a "romantic poem" could be accomplished only if its principal component, the Don Quixote-action proper, was relegated to a minor position. To many romanticists the *novelas* inserted in the novel are of greater importance than the hero of the book. They are fascinated by the picturesque elements in the *novelas:* violent passions, shepherds, Moors, beautiful women in flight. *Don Quixote* is, for them, mainly a colorful book. Friedrich Schlegel perceived the dangers inherent in such a concept of the "romantic," when he remarked ironically that "romantic" tends to become identical with "what is against the police regulations," though he himself had declared that "the absence of a well-regulated system of public order" at the time of Cervantes had contributed favorably to the poetry of his books. With the new emphasis on the novelistic components of *Don Quixote* and the neglect of the satirical main action, the attitude prevailing in the 18th century is completely reversed. The explosive possibilities contained in the novel were diverted into harmless channels; the discovery of *Don Quixote* as a "romantic poem" is another way of "drawing the fangs of the beast."

The beast having been slain, it was now ready to be prepared into an exquisite dish for literary gourmets. The most accomplished master in these culinary operations is Friedrich Schlegel. For him, *Don Quixote* is a product of the "romantic wit," that intellectual activity which sees in life and art nothing but an opportunity for irresponsible play, and to which the romanticists assigned the highest rank among man's abilities. Cervantes' art in *Don Quixote* consists in the delectable intertwining of episodes and in the invention of constantly changing contrasts which should be enjoyed merely for the sake of variety. *Don Quixote* is now a book for literary connoisseurs. It is an "arabesque," an "artistically arranged confusion, a charming symmetry of contradictions in its rhythmical alterations between enthusiasm and irony." "Like all true poetry" it reflects "in the infinite variations of its music . . . the original chaos of human nature."[4] The emasculation of a profound work of art cannot be carried further than in these remarks of Schlegel.

Yet, in spite of its capriciousness, romantic criticism made some contributions to a better understanding of Cervantes. For this the very faults of the romantic approach are partly responsible. Though the philosophical-allegorical interpretation of *Don Quixote* could only lead to an impasse, the literary epicureanism of the Schlegels contained some fruitful germs. They took delight in the style of Cervantes and were the first to describe the linguistic finesse of his writings. They appreciated the metrical and rhythmic qualities of the poems interspersed in *Don Quixote*. Friedrich Schlegel's *aperçu* of the "arabesque" led to a better comprehension of structure of the novel. A. W. Schlegel's analysis of the book as an interplay of "romantic and parodistic complexes," in his review of Tieck's translation, is one of the most satisfying pieces of romantic criticism.

In this translation the critical efforts of the romanticists bore fruit. The brothers Schlegel had treated *Don Quixote* as an organic whole and thus invalidated the arguments of Tieck's predecessor, Bertuch, against the inclusion of the *novelas*. Tieck's translation is complete. Others had raised the significance of Don Quixote by making him a heroic character worthy of sympathy. Tieck's translation does better justice to the sections dealing with Don Quixote than did that of Bertuch, which excelled in its rendition of Sancho Panza.

While Tieck, encouraged and assisted by the Schlegels, worked at his translation, another German hispanophile, Soltau, announced a forthcoming translation of his own. This declaration led to unpleasant quarrels between the two main literary camps of the time, the romanticists and the older school, which was greatly disturbed by the extravaganzas and the challenges offered by the young group of critics. An impartial comparison of the finished products, however, must attribute considerable merit to both translations.

Tieck is the central figure in the romantic criticism of *Don Quixote*. Although he uses the romantic position as his point of departure, the results are his own. He answers the question of the relation between the "poetical" and the "unpoetical" in *Don Quixote,* which had so seriously concerned the Schlegels, by asserting that "one need not assume a fundamental opposition between the two," and he finds that "in *Don Quixote* and in the *novelas* the representation of ordinary life is at the same time miraculous and poetical." Tieck takes a similar view in regard to the other opposition which the romanticists had applied to *Don Quixote,* that between ideal and reality. He does not blindly side with Don Quixote the "idealist," but concludes that "he is deserving of both veneration and laughter." He sympathizes with Don Quixote's ideals, but observes that nevertheless "he is completely mistaken in his choice of means for putting them into practice."

It is in regard to this problem that Tieck gives his most profound views on *Don Quixote*. In the last period of his career he had turned from a champion of romanticism in literature and life into a critic of many of its excesses, of those of its aspects which Croce calls "moral and sentimental romanticism." In the novelette *Eine Sommerreise,* Tieck takes up the tradition of the satirical *Don Quixote* novels of the 18th century. Here he chastises the quixotic behavior he had observed among his contemporaries, and the new forms of "Schwärmerei." The characters in this story shrink back from reality for the sake of a vaguely conceived ideal which is located in the past. One of them dreams of restoring classical antiquity in its perfection, while the hero of the story is about to become a convert to Catholicism. Tieck's main criticism is directed against this typically romantic form of "Schwärmerei." Ferdinand, like Don Quixote, has drawn his inspiration merely from books. His friend warns him that, if he observes Catholicism in reality, he will be rudely disappointed, and he gives some examples. In order to dissuade him more forcefully from his intentions, his friends discuss *Don Quixote* with him. Don Quixote tried to give full, concrete realization to his ideal, and failed, because ideal and reality can never be completely identified. Instead of indulging in sterile lamentations over this fact, man can transplant at·least part of his ideals into reality, and find consolation in practical activity. In this interpretation, and in the remedy he recommends against the romantic *malaise,* Tieck is close to Goethe.

A remarkable feature of the discussion on *Don Quixote* in *Eine Sommerreise* is the ingenious way in which the story of the *Curioso impertinente* is related to the main action: "The story of the *Curioso impertinente,* which has been criticized as being superfluous, is really a subtle counterpart to the main plot, for it serves to illustrate the folly of Don Quixote from a different side. Anselmo, like Don Quixote, wishes to hold visibly, corporeally, in his hands, that which is invisible and which we possess only through an act of faith. He desires something unsubstantial and terrestrial to represent the eternal and celestial."

Tieck stood practically alone among his contemporaries in this conception of *Don Quixote.* His and Goethe's views found their nearest equivalent in the opinions of Friedrich Bouterwek. A philologist and historian of literature, Bouterwek utilized some of the romantic discoveries, though he did not share their basic theories, but rather continued the traditions of the 18th century. In Germany he is almost totally forgotten. As happens so frequently in the history of literary relations, other more original works than those of Bouterwek were not translated, while accidental translations of his books helped to establish for him a reputation outside his country which is out of proportion to his actual merits. Bouterwek's opinions on *Don Quixote* are not original. To him, "Don Quixote is the immortal representative of those fantastic characters who, in spite of the most magnificent enthusiasm, become fools, because they cannot resist the temptation of succumbing to a self-deception in which they consider themselves chosen for a mission." With this psychological interpretation Bouterwek returns to the eighteenth-century views. Bodmer's analysis comes close to that of Bouterwek, and it has also some similarity with Schiller's conception.

In his anti-romantic interpretation of *Don Quixote,* Tieck was joined by a writer who was in great favor with the romanticists, Jean Paul. Jean Paul occupies an important place in the history of the reception of Cervantes in Germany, both as a critic and as the author of a satirical novel in the vein of *Don Quixote.*

In his *Vorschule der Aesthetik* of 1804, Jean Paul operates with the polar concepts of German idealistic philosophy and their literary adaptations. He introduces, however, an important new element. According to Jean Paul, the conflict between the finite and the infinite, between appearance and idea, results in "humor"; *Don Quixote* is the outstanding example of this. "Humor, being the sublime in reverse, does not nullify that which is individual, but rather that which is finite, by contrasting it with the idea. Humor does not recognize any individual folly or any individual fools, it recognizes only folly as such, a world consisting of folly . . . Humor humbles that which is grand by confronting it with the insignificant, it elevates the insignificant by confronting it with the grand, and thus it nullifies both, for in the eyes of infinity everything is equally *nil* . . . Cervantes' genius was too great for composing only a protracted farce about a harmless folly and a frequently encountered silliness. Therefore, always keeping before his eyes the equation between the finite and the infinite, he carried to its full conclusion the humoristic parallel between realism and idealism, between body and soul; his twin stars of folly shine over the fate of humanity as a whole."

Jean Paul's concept of "humor" should not be confused with Friedrich Schlegel's notion of "romantic irony." The romantic "wit" is a purely subjective element, while humor results from a conflict of objective metaphysical principles and is therefore related to the tragic. Jean Paul is far from approving the lack of responsibility exhibited in the theory of the "romantic" wit; on the contrary, the unbounded subjectivity of the romanticists meets with his sharpest opposition. He chastises severely the romantic flight into a "poetic" world. The advocates of a poetry of dream he confronts with the example of Shakespeare and Cervantes, both of whom "were furrowed and ploughed by life, before the seeds of their poetic flora opened and unfolded."

The conflict between dream and reality, between the vagaries of pure subjectivity, and the demands of the concrete present, is the theme of Jean Paul's last great novel, *Der Komet, oder Nikolaus Markgraf.* The author himself acknowledges that during the writing of this book "he constantly recharged himself at the galvanic cells of Rabelais and Cervantes." More important than the numerous direct references to *Don Quixote* which are found in the novel, is the similarity of inspiration between the two books. Nikolaus Markgraf, resembling Don Quixote, "puts, like an actor, a foreign soul in place of his own." There is, however, a significant difference between Don Quixote and his German descendant. The Spanish knight clings firmly to the rôle he once selected for himself, while his German pupil acts out whatever part has been suggested to him by his latest reading. He is the typical romantic dilettante in borrowed sentiments. The ever-changing whims of his hero afford the author an opportunity to chastise those sides of contemporary romanticism which he finds particularly repellent. Nikolaus, after having read the legends dealing with his namesake saint, believes himself to be a saint and falls into religious ecstasies. In the ridiculous episodes dealing with Markgraf's sainthood, Jean Paul aims at the book-nourished flirtations with Catholicism which were so widespread at his time. The author congratulates himself for having found a hero who, in competition with other fools, can always prove his superiority, a task which is not easy "in this decade of super-Christianity and super-poetry." He observes that the places most fertile in fools are "the abodes of mystical poets, mystical preachers, and mystical professors." Thus *Der Komet* resumes the function the *Don Quixote* novels had in the 18th century, satirizing the follies of the time.

The affinity between *Der Komet* and some of the eighteenth-century imitations of *Don Quixote* can be seen also in another respect. Like the heroes of the pedagogical novels of that time, Markgraf has far-reaching philanthropic plans. He is a Don Quixote of the progressive variety and the victim of an elaborate self-deception. "I should like to find the man who, after having read how Nikolaus Markgraf fooled himself and others in the same breath, would still feel himself capable of distinguishing in the speeches of Mohammed, Rienzi, Thomas Münster, Loyola, Cromwell, and Napoleon, where these men, intoxicated with their mission as they were, hoodwinked others and where they hoodwinked themselves." Thus Markgraf becomes the symbol for the religious and political fanatic.

Jean Paul's importance in the history of *Don Quixote* is two-fold. His critical views were further developed in the philosophy of Solger and Hegel, and *Der Komet* prepared the way for the last great German novel written under the inspiration of *Don Quixote*, Immermann's *Münchhausen*.

Solger was a close friend of Tieck, and an influential propagator of romantic æsthetic theories. In his interpretation of *Don Quixote*, he starts from the romantic premises of the conflict between idea and reality and adds to them Jean Paul's concept of humor as the dissolution of the finite in the moment of its confrontation with the infinite. Instead of "humor," Solger uses the term "higher wit." In Solger's exegesis the time of chivalry appears no longer as a vague region of poetry and perfection, but as a specific manifestation of the infinite in historical form, which is to be succeeded by other forms in which the idea reveals itself. This new concept is later more fully developed by Hegel. With this historical approach, the problem of the relationship between idea and reality appears in a new light. In addition, Solger gives the romantic concept of "wit" a new meaning and removes it definitely from the sphere of irresponsible subjectivity.

The final blow to the traditional romantic interpretation of *Don Quixote* was delivered by Friedrich Hegel. Hegel himself acknowledged the services rendered to æsthetics by Solger. He was contemptuous of the pseudo-philosophical attitudes assumed by Friedrich Schlegel and had in general little liking for the two brothers, who "were always eager for something new, and always anxious to make themselves noticed by some extravaganza." His main criticism was directed, however, against their perversion of Fichtean idealism into the famous theory of "romantic irony."

It was Hegel's principal concern to oppose the capricious explosions of romantic egocentricity by a new sense of what he calls the "substantial," objective values. According to Hegel, the adventurous individual who is the hero of the books of chivalry lacks any "substantial content"; "law and order have not yet any meaning and purpose in themselves, but are merely subjective whims." It is the historical significance of Ariosto and Cervantes to have portrayed this medieval world in the process of dissolution. Don Quixote is a character who has been overtaken by historical development and left behind. He remains "the subjective character in its extreme form" at a time when objective norms have gradually come into existence. "Poetic" subjectivity has been replaced by a prosaic world order, which imposes on the individual restrictions on all sides. If Hegel had lived in our time, he might have written that Don Quixote represented a Republican under the New Deal. Don Quixote's comicality consists in "the contrast between a rationally organized world and an isolated individual who tries to create for himself order and stability."[5] Thus Don Quixote ceases to be a tragic figure, a superior individual who suffers from the lack of comprehension of his contemporaries. He deserves ridicule and harsh treatment, not so much because by chance he proved incapable of keeping in step with the progress of the time, but because he represents a lower form of ideal in the face of a higher one. On the other hand, Hegel does not become an uncritical admirer of prosaic modernity. He is not insensitive to the human greatness of Cervantes' hero. His steadfast belief in the ideals of chivalry "rises in its noble aspects above the childishness and superficiality, the lack of conviction and the general inferiority of the new prosaic reality and thus demonstrates impressively its shortcomings." Hegel's sense for historical reality protects him from both a lachrymose idealization of the past, and a boisterous adulation of the present.

Hegel gives new significance also to the romantic concept of *Don Quixote* as the prototype of the modern novel. Both have as their main theme the clash "between the chimeric, subjective ideals of love, honor, ambition or world improvement, and the prosaic reality of the existing order" which is represented by the "established laws of state and society, by the police, the courts and the army." The subjective state of mind is characteristic for youth; "young people are the modern Don Quixotes."[6]

The breadth and originality of Hegel's interpretation finds its only counterpart in that of Herder, who had anticipated it in some respects. Hegel's views, however, did not find the wide attention they deserved; the typically romantic attitude toward *Don Quixote* prevailed through most of the 19th century. Some feeble echoes of Hegel's opinions can be observed in the writings of the Hegelian school, e.g., those of Rosenkranz, but nowhere were Hegel's ideas developed more in detail. Usually they were amalgamated with the traditional romantic conceptions. The most noteworthy of these compromises was accomplished by the poet Eichendorff.

In his interpretation of *Don Quixote*, Hegel had declared it his task to "mediate between heart and reality." Beside him, Goethe, Tieck, and Jean Paul had shown the way in which the conflict could be harmonized, and had demonstrated it on *Don Quixote*. The majority of the Romanticists, however, were unwilling to follow this road. They clung to their attitude of desperate, subjective idealism for which Don Quixote was the heroic symbol. It was inevitable, however, that sooner or later the moment would come when the idealistic tension became unbearable, and the pleasure of assuming a heroic posture was no longer a sufficient palliative. Then the disillusioned idealist turns into a pessimist. This point was reached earlier in France and England than in Germany. In France, Sismondi was perhaps the first to draw the final consequences from the romantic attitude toward *Don Quixote*. Sismondi was personally acquainted with A. W. Schlegel and fully conversant with the theories of the two brothers. It had been their example which directed him toward the study of the Southern European literatures. For Sismondi, *Don Quixote* is a melancholy book: "Cervantes has shown us the vanity of greatness of character and the illusion of heroism in a satire written without bitterness." In England, Byron represents an attitude toward *Don Quixote* similar to that of Sismondi. Tieck was acquainted with Byron's stanzas on Cervantes and disagreed with them. For him, *Don Quixote* does not symbolize the futility of nobly inspired enthusiasm, but opposes the wrong direction this enthusiasm had taken.

The first German who adopted Byron's views without reservation was Franz Grillparzer. In Byron's lines about the reasons for the decadence of Spain he finds "more truth than in all the silly things Mr. Tieck had said about poetry and the poets." The German writer who comes closest to Byron's views is the young Nietzsche. In a letter to his friend, Erwin Rohde, he writes: *"Don Quixote* is the bitterest reading I know. Here everything solemn and inspiring appears as nonsensical. It is good to keep this lesson in mind for special circumstances, but normally one would do better not to think of it." Here Nietzsche reveals himself as the hyper-sensitive idealist that he actually is.

The central figure in the post-romantic interpretation of Cervantes in Germany is undoubtedly Heinrich Heine, and this not so much owing to the originality of his criticism, but because he combines practically every shade of opinion on *Don Quixote* current in the 19th century. It is therefore impossible to summarize Heine's views in a simple formula. They changed considerably in the course of his life and are full of contradictions, for they are more in the character of lyrical outpourings than of systematic critical effort.

In his earliest published opinions on *Don Quixote, Reisebilder,* Heine approaches the attitude of the young Schiller; Don Quixote is for him the symbol of idealistic martyrdom. With typical vanity, Heine identifies himself with the hero of Cervantes and recalls his own sufferings in the service of ideals. He differentiates, however, between the reactionary utopianism of Don Quixote, and his own brand of humanitarian fervor: "Don Quixote was intent on restoring the declining institution of chivalry, while I, on the other hand, wish to destroy completely any remnant from this age." After he has made this distinction, he loses sight of it and places the idealism of Don Quixote side by side with the programs of social reformers, the Roman Gracchi, Robespierre, and Saint-Juste. Don Quixote's enthusiasm for the world of chivalry corresponds to his own devotion to the ideals of the French Revolution. The books of Rousseau and Mirabeau have played the same part in his life as did *Amadis* for Don Quixote. Thus Heine's attitude does not differ essentially from that of the romantics. He merely gives the vague romantic idealism a different and more specific content.

Heine's essays on German romanticism, which he wrote a few years later, contain his most mature observations on Cervantes. It is in these essays that Heine, in comparing Goethe with Cervantes, makes the discovery of the humoristic irony in both. He has somewhat changed the opinions he had expressed in the *Reisebilder.* He is now doubtful whether the romanticists were right in their interpretation of *Don Quixote* as a symbol of frenetic idealism, and, like Byron, he asks himself whether, after all, "Cervantes intended to make fun of those who are struggling and suffering for an idea."

Heine's best-known piece of writing on Cervantes, his introduction written in 1837 to a new translation of *Don Quixote,* is perhaps his weakest, most incoherent utterance on the subject. In it he incorporated almost literally sections of his previous writings on the subject without any attempt at harmonizing them with his latest views. He has now fully adopted the Byronic attitude and sees in *Don Quixote* "the greatest satire against human enthusiasm." This opinion, which had been adumbrated before, unfolds in the new context its full meaning. Heine speaks of the "irony with which God had endowed the world when he created it, and which the poet (Cervantes) imitated in his book creation." Here the concept of irony is invested with a new meaning. With Friedrich Schlegel it had no bitter connotation. Heine gives it a pessimistic turn. He understands by the god-created irony the forces of internal contradiction ruling the world, which on the one hand implant in man an idealistic longing for perfection, and which on the other constantly and effectively thwart these aspirations. Heine's views have some similarity with Camus' conception of Sisyphus as the symbol of humanity. Heine seems to imply that the only road open to man, after he has exhausted his energies in a vain struggle for the realization of his ideals, in order to gain relief from the tension between ideal and reality, is to rid himself of all vestiges of his dreams by ridiculing them in self-irony; and that this is what Cervantes intended in *Don Quixote*. Heine applies this new interpretation immediately to himself, when he concludes: "I have found, by bitter experience, that the effort to call back to life a long dead past is just as thankless folly as the attempt to introduce the future too early into the present." Heine assumes here the part of a despairing Marquis Posa.

This dejected attitude leads to strange consequences. He accepts now, without hesitation, some of the romantic concepts in *Don Quixote*. While in his earlier essay, he had celebrated the skill with which Cervantes had circumvented the oppressive controls of state and church, he now praises him for "having devoted his youth to Philip II, the greatest champion of Catholicism." To this faithful adherence to the Church, and the resulting freedom from enervating doubts, Cervantes "owes that unshakable serenity of his epic style." Cervantes was attached with equal devotion to the ideals of absolutist government, which he glorified in poetic form: "He gladly sacrificed his individual freedom for the purpose of helping to satisfy the Castilian national ambitions." This is a far cry from the attitude of the intrepid champion of human rights, the part which Heine chose to play earlier.

Heine widens even further the gulf separating him from his former ideals. He explains Cervantes' personal misfortunes as the inevitable sufferings of the genius who is misunderstood by the masses. "Society is a republic. It hates every form of distinction, whether it be material or intellectual. This is the lesson the July Revolution has taught us . . . The republicans supporting that revolution wanted to level the intellectual differences between men." Heine implies through the context that the plebeian republicans of the Spanish absolute monarchy were responsible for Cervantes' miseries! The exaltation of the lonely genius at the expense of the vulgar, uncultured masses is one of the heritages of romantic thought. Heine's confusion in his introduction to *Don Quixote* has its counterpart in Friedrich Schlegel's meandering vagaries. His essay is an unpleasant compound of vanity and self-commiseration, of pompous self-righteousness and of sheer posing.

The last great figure in the history of Cervantes' reception in Germany is Karl Immermann. In his critical views he does not go beyond the romantic position; his importance is rather to be found in the way in which he developed the Don Quixote theme in his own writings. The historical circumstances surrounding Immermann has many resemblances to the time of Cervantes. In the political field, the Metternich era of Restoration may well be compared to the Counter-Reformation. In literature, the products of the romantic epigones, their monotonous rehashing of medieval material, and their decadent glorification of a miraculous past at the expense of present-day reality, bears some analogy to the romances of chivalry. Immermann and Cervantes are alike in the seriousness with which they put themselves to the task of penetrating the artificiality of their times to that which is "substantial" in literature and life. Thus the object of Immermann's writings, like that of Cervantes in *Don Quixote,* is a criticism of false attitudes toward reality and the portrayal of reality itself. Compared with this fundamental affinity between these two poets, Immermann's numerous borrowings of details from Cervantes appear unessential.

The culmination of Immermann's work is his great novel *Münchhausen.* Here the principal motives of the German Don Quixote imitations and of the critical views on *Don Quixote* enter into a new synthesis. Here we find satire on the decadent nobility, on the enthusiasm for pure teutonism, on the German inclination for bootlicking, their eagerness for titles. Here female sentimentality and female flirtations with literary vogues, the blindness of teachers and administrators who try to make reality conform to their theories, are ridiculed. This similarity with the Don Quixote novels of the 18th century is not accidental; Immermann was well acquainted with many of them, particularly with *Don Sylvio von Rosalva* and with *Siegfried von Lindenberg.* To the satire on social groups and individuals who cling to the past or live in a fictitious world, Immermann adds the persiflage of the "progressive" and humanitarian type of Don Quixotes, which had found its first important literary representation in Jean Paul's *Der Komet.* The character who gives the book its title, the Baron von Münchhausen, is full of projects similar to those of Johann Markgraf. Yet *Münchhausen* is more than a broad panorama of the ridiculous aspects of German life in the first three decades of the 19th century, just as Cervantes' novel is more than a parody on the books of chivalry. Among all German novels of the progeny of *Don Quixote, Münchhausen* is the only one which in its fundamental conception comes close to its prototype, for here irony and satire are balanced by a portrayal of reality, and both form an organic whole.

With Heine and Immermann ends the period in which Cervantes was an active ingredient in German life. The second half of the 19th century produces no more original interpretations or adaptations of Cervantes, but restricts itself to academic variations and combinations of the traditional views. While formerly Cervantes was widely read in the original, and the knowledge of Spanish was almost as widespread as that of English and French, Cervantes becomes now almost exclusively the object of philological specialists. Toward the end of the century Richard Strauss' tone poem attracts renewed attention to *Don Quixote*. The quatrocentenary of Cervantes' death is the occasion for a flood of articles, most of which are without importance. Even the revitalization of romance philology in Germany which was instituted by Karl Vossler and his followers, brought less profit to Cervantes than might have been expected. The most valuable contribution made by the school of "idealistic philology" to the study of Cervantes is a number of investigations on his style and technique, such as those by Hatzfeld, Spitzer, and Harry Meier, but these minute dissections were written for specialists and never transcended the academic sphere. Thus in Harry Meier's analysis of *La Gitanilla*[7] the Spanish text serves mainly to illustrate a broad linguistic problem, that of word order. The members of the school of "idealistic philology" do not offer any new integral interpretation of Cervantes. The initiator and guiding spirit of this group, Karl Vossler, returns to the romantic conceptions of *Don Quixote*. He sees in this figure the "typical" Spaniard, who is full of utopian projects and who separates forever ideal and reality.[8] Don Quixote is the symbol of true heroism in its struggle against mediocrity. For Vossler, as for the romanticists, Don Quixote is a "anachronistically spontaneous and original personality," the representative of an aristocratic view of the world and of the Spain of the conquistadores.[9] *Don Quixote* is not a satire; Cervantes merely intends to criticize in this novel the exaggerations of heroic idealism. He was actually fond of the novels of chivalry, and his parody of them is a form of admiring emulation. According to Vossler, the time of Cervantes was a period of perfection, and Cervantes the flower of his age. For Vossler, Cervantes forms part of the idyllic picture he draws of the happy times of the Counter-Reformation. His panorama of the *siglo de oro* comes dangerously close to what the Spanish call "una españolada," a highly romanticized and idealized picture of things Spanish, drawn by a foreigner.

The ambiguity of Vossler's attitude toward the *siglo de oro* has been recently pointed out by his pupil, Leo Spitzer.[10] Yet Spitzer's own opinions on Cervantes do not differ materially from those of his former master. For Spitzer, Cervantes is first and foremost a Catholic poet. This interpretation necessarily brought Spitzer into conflict with that of Américo Castro. Spitzer's most important views on Cervantes are found in his polemics with Castro. In general, *El pensamiento de Cervantes* was received in Germany with little enthusiasm. Vossler merely praised it condescendingly as a "solid piece of scholarship" and did not delve into the deeper implications of the book. Spitzer, however, opened a full-fledged attack on Castro's conception of Cervantes.[11] The immediate occasion was the question of Cervantes' "hypocrisy," which Castro had discussed in his book and in subsequent articles. For Spitzer it is beyond doubt that hypocrisy is totally absent in Cervantes' writings; on the contrary, "his attitude is medieval in its faithful devotion to the national religion." In the characters of the *novelas,* Spitzer sees "cornerstones of a theocratic world order"; they are "dependent on the world beyond . . . determined from above."[12] In his search for a religious interpretation of *Don Quixote* and in his Germanic obtuseness to the grotesque satire of the novel, Spitzer sometimes makes amazing discoveries. When Don Quixote, in the Sierra Morena, acts out the part of a lover driven to madness by the cruelty of his lady, Spitzer believes this performance to signify "the Christian attitude of uninterested morality, an *'acte gratuit.'* " Equally surprising is the choice Spitzer makes for the nearest counterpart to Cervantes among German writers. He compares him to Adalbert Stifter, the Austrian writer whose brilliant gifts were stunted and frustrated by his time, the period of Metternich, and who sought refuge from reality in his idyllic writings.

Though Ludwig Pfandl does not belong directly to the school of "idealistic philology," his views on Cervantes are close to those of Vossler and are approved by Spitzer. The romantic origin of Pfandl's attitude toward Cervantes is easily discernible.[13] Like Eichendorff, Pfandl believes that *Don Quixote* was intended as a mirror of true chivalry at a time of degeneration; the hero "is combating the growing proletarianization of ideals." Don Quixote, Ignatius of Loyola, and Saint Theresa are the three Spanish heroes who fought for the same cause. In his effort to explain the satirical features of the book which do not fit his interpretation, Pfandl uses a clumsy *tour de main:* though Cervantes was in fundamental agreement with the ideals of his hero, he was forced to make fun of him, because this was the only way by which he could hope to find any readers; the satirical and farcical elements in *Don Quixote* are nothing but the sugar coating for the moral pill of teaching sublime idealism. Cervantes merely followed the Horatian principle of *delectare et prodesse.* The comicality of *Don Quixote* and the *novelas* inserted in the novel were simply meant for entertainment. Yet Pfandl destroys his own thesis and returns to Heine's position when he sees in Don Quixote's conversion to sanity before his end "the greatest *desengaño* imaginable . . . Cervantes admits that noble efforts in the service of the common good are delusions."

Also, outside the field of philological specialists, the romantic tradition continues to dominate the German attitude toward Cervantes. In his essay "Seereise mit Don Quixote"[14] Thomas Mann interweaves his impressions of a trip to America with his observations on *Don Quixote*. He read the book in Tieck's translation and was therefore from the beginning under a romantic influence. For Thomas Mann, as for Friedrich Schlegel and Heine, Cervantes is a faithful son of the Church and a loyal subject of his king. For Mann, Cervantes is still the *"ingenio lego"* who is not conscious of either his art or his fundamental convictions. This is also why Mann prefers the first part of *Don Quixote* to the second. There he misses the "happy naïveté of the first part, in which one can observe how a conception which was originally simple and unpretentious, a lively, amusing satire without any plan and literary ambition, can grow, *par hazard et par génie,* into a symbol of humanity."

Thomas Mann follows the romantic precedent also in other details. He accepts the stenciled view of the Spanish as a nation of *"grandezza,* idealism, ill-placed magnanimity, and unlucrative chivalry," and he sees in Don Quixote the symbol of these traits. This conception naturally leaves many features of the novel unexplained. Mann is startled by the cruelty with which the author punishes every magnanimous intention or action of his hero. The solution he offers for this apparent contradiction is similar to that of Byron and Heine: *Don Quixote* "is the melancholic travesty and *reductio ad absurdum* of the classical Spanish traits"; in *Don Quixote* the author ironizes and castigates himself. "It seems to me that in this book the author, after many disappointments, forsook and ridiculed his faith in the idea, in man, and in the possibility of ever ennobling him, and that this bitter and disillusioned submission to vulgar reality is the essence of humor." In this definition of humor as a capitulation before the baseness of life, Mann differs from Jean Paul. For the latter, humor implies merely recognition of the inadequacy of the limited and concrete in face of the infinite, while Mann's interpretation is essentially pessimistic. He speaks of the discrepancy between Don Quixote's rational opinions, and his nonsensical actions. He believes that Cervantes intended this incongruity as a symbol for the "natural and unavoidable antinomy which dominates the higher forms of ethical activity." Therefore, the attitude of Cervantes toward his hero is ambivalent: he is ready at the same time to humiliate and to exalt him, and this psychological contradiction Mann explains as the outgrowth of Christian sentiments. He returns to the pre-Hegelian views on *Don Quixote* when he sympathizes unreservedly with the hero's "blind magnanimity, even though it may make its thrusts into empty space." Hegel had given a historical criticism of these "thrusts into emptiness." Mann gives a special reason, however, for his sympathy with Don Quixote. He contrasts Don Quixote's incorrigible optimism with a different kind of fanaticism, that of an "anti-idealistic, somber, and pessimistic Don Quixote, who is a zealot of violence and of brutality and who would yet remain a Don Quixote." Mann is obviously thinking of the main characters in the *Magic Mountain.* Settembrini is a Don Quixote *à la* Marquis Posa, while Naphtha is the systematic advocate of chaos and destruction. Mann's definition for the character of Don Quixote could be easily applied also to Settembrini: "What supports and ennobles him, is the spirit in form of a spleen."

Thomas Mann continues the nineteenth-century views in other respects also. Like Grillparzer, whose opinion on *Don Quixote* he shares in various ways, he is bewildered by the novelas inserted in the book. If *Don Quixote* is merely the expression of self-irony of a disappointed idealist, then the novelistic pictures of reality must be without significance in the structure of the whole novel. For similar reasons Mann is dissatisfied with the way in which Don Quixote's end is treated by Cervantes. Mann regrets the conversion of the hero to a sane realism before his death. He tries to justify this conclusion of the novel by means which are ingenious, but unconvincing: Cervantes wished to protect himself from another Avellaneda; Don Quixote had to die as a normal person out of literary jealousy, while the sincere intention of the author would have been to uphold the "magnanimous spleen" of his hero to the last breath. This forced diversion of the narrative from its natural path was unsuccessful, for "in order to make the hero's rational conversion more palatable, the author should not have made his folly so attractive." Mann is also shocked by the unsentimental behavior of Don Quixote's friends after his death; he fails to see any artistic purpose in these scenes, which are an indirect condemnation of the hero by his author, and explains them simply as "humor."

In an article on Thomas Mann's essay,[15] Leo Spitzer dealt again with the question of the end of Don Quixote. Spitzer agrees in general with Mann's interpretation of the novel, but gives a different explanation for its conclusion. He believes that Mann's dissatisfaction with the commonplace death of Don Quixote springs from a residue of unconquered irrationalism, which would prefer a fantastic and extraordinary finale, to sober bourgeois regularity. Spitzer believes that Cervantes purposely brought about a sharp break in the artistic climate of *Don Quixote,* in order to express his opposition to romantic embellishments of reality by fiction-writers. Cervantes made use of "deliberate prosaicness" when he let his hero die so unceremoniously, for he was anxious to demonstrate this way the presumptuousness of composing fiction in the face of reality.

In the same year in which Mann published his essay, there appeared also the Cervantes novel of his friend Bruno Frank, the main merit of which consists of lively descriptions of the period and of the immediate biographical background of Cervantes' writings. For Bruno Frank, *Don Quixote* is the outgrowth of the author's reflections on his own life, with its frequent idealistic enterprises which always met with failure: "the baseness of life always proved too powerful for the dreamer." Cervantes glorifies in *Don Quixote* "the unconquerable persistency in building a realm of noble illusions." Thus Don Quixote becomes the symbol for the great illusionists of Cervantes' time, for Don Juan d'Austria, "the last foolish and brilliant knight," for Philip II, and finally for Spain herself, the country which "in magnanimous blindness clung to the past while the world around her discovered new realities." In these views the survival of romantic conceptions and the similarity with Mann's interpretation are obvious.

The romantic attitude toward *Don Quixote* in modern form, as represented by Vossler, Spitzer, and Mann, though it was widely shared, did not remain unopposed. A pupil of Vossler and a romance philologist of renown, Eugen Lerch, laid bare the fundamental weaknesses of the romantic approach to Cervantes. It was he who attracted attention to the embarrassing position in which *Don Quixote* had put the romantic critics.[16] In the same article Lerch exposed the typical errors into which German readers of *Don Quixote* are likely to fall. One of them is the confusion inherent in the biographical approach. "They asked themselves the question of how it was possible that an old, miserable man could write a book full of light buffoonery. They found in the novelas the remark that despair is man's greatest sin. From this they concluded that in *Don Quixote*, Cervantes had drawn a picture of himself, and that his irony was the most profound of all, namely irony directed against himself. Since that time Cervantes was looked upon as the predecessor of Jean Paul and Gottfried Keller, of Theodor Fontane and Wilhelm Raabe. They discovered in Cervantes something like a profound German soul and a sensitive German heart. Yet the gentle tear in *Don Quixote* is pure imagination."

A much sharper attack on the romantic interpretation of *Don Quixote* is made in the only article worthy of attention among the many which were written in Germany on the occasion of the 300th anniversary of the publication of *Don Quixote* (1905), that by Florens Christian Rang.[17] The author, a former Protestant minister, possesses a broad knowledge of the Spanish and the European literatures of Cervantes' time, and of the political, ecclesiastical, and economic history of the period. In spite of some exaggerated conclusions, his essay is one of the most remarkable *Don Quixote* interpretations Germany ever produced. Rang breaks completely with the romantic conception by redefining the relation between the poet and his hero: Cervantes did not sympathize with, but abhorred Don Quixote. The novel has a direct political significance: through it the author gave vent to his repugnance against the basic political ideals and practices of his time. His assertion that the purpose of his book was to ridicule the novels of chivalry was a pretense which was made necessary by the strict censorship State and Church then exercised. The blows which were supposed to be directed against the follies caused by the chivalric novels were really meant for the fantastic fanaticism which inspired State and Church of the Counter-Reformation. Cervantes does not criticize isolated instances of shortcomings in the society of his time, but he attacks the roots of the whole system. Don Quixote's zeal for reviving the order of knight-errants symbolizes Spain's policy of aggressive intolerance, the resuscitated spirit of the crusades. Yet this religious fanaticism appears to Cervantes not only unjustified in itself, it is not even purely religious. It merely serves for rationalizing predatory instinct, providing a convenient cloak for the policy of the conquistadores. Rang quotes the words of Don Quixote: "With their booty we shall lay the foundations for making ourselves rich; for this is an honest war."

Rang compares Don Quixote to Loyola, as had done others before him, but he gives this parallel a different meaning. He believes that Cervantes criticized indirectly in *Don Quixote* two features of Jesuitism. The author intended Don Quixote's veneration for Dulcinea as a parody on the cult of the Holy Virgin, and in Don Quixote's theories on withcraft he travestied the Jesuit practice of presenting religious beliefs concerning the invisible world in grossly concrete forms. Rang goes even further: he interprets the scene in which Don Quixote asks Sancho Panza to apply to himself three thousand blows in order to free Dulcinea from her bewitchment, as a concealed attack on the Christian dogma of vicarious atonement. In Rang's opinion, Cervantes had none of Christian humility, but was rather possessed of a pre-Christian stoicism and fatalism, which accepts reality in all its aspects. From this point of view, the final scenes of *Don Quixote* are represented to him in a new light. Here he sees the culmination of Cervantes' art and the most comprehensive expression of his attitude toward the world. Don Quixote's admission of his errors before his end is fully convincing. He does not die a death of despair over the destruction of his ideals, but he realizes that his folly was part of his character, as nature had created it, and that therefore he was not responsible for his actions. He feels that the core of his personality is not touched by his deeds, that "our soul is good in spite of our actions," that "soul and character are independent of one another." "His actions and opinions are foolish and often coarse, they call for laughter if not for tears, but his inner being is essentially good and worthy of veneration. Cervantes, the writer who laid bare the aberrations of his nation in political, ecclesiastical, and economic matters, the corruption of its thinking and even of its instincts, was also the one to discover the fundamental goodness of human nature, a goodness unfathomable and indestructible, whatever the actions may be by which it manifests itself. Cervantes revealed to mankind the nobility of its fate and taught it reverence for this distinction. His discovery is more important than that of America, for it contains the possibility for becoming the fountainhead of a new humanity." This revelation elevates Cervantes even above Shakespeare, the only other poet who can stand a comparison with him.

Rang's essay, in spite of its many exaggerations so richly suggestive, remained completely unnoticed. It was not until a third of a century later that a Swiss writer, probably without knowing of his predecessor, offered an interpretation of *Don Quixote* which has much in common with that of Rang. Although R. J.

Humm's essay[18] is not the work of a philologist or a historian, but primarily a pamphlet on the political conflicts of our days, it is not without value. According to Humm, the political and social implications of *Don Quixote* overshadow the purely literary significance of the novel. Probably independent of Morel-Fatio's book, Humm sees the purpose of *Don Quixote* to be a criticism of the outdated social institution of *hidalgismo,* and of the part Spain played in world politics of the 16th century. With obvious reference to contemporary events, Humm writes: "Wherever the Spanish appeared, they behaved like Junkers; convinced of their special prerogatives, they lived from the products of the industry of the people they suppressed. They never succeeded in constructing anything permanent." Humm likens Don Quixote to Loyola in his "reactionary romanticism." He believes that Cervantes saw the reasons for Spain's decline in her religious and racial intolerance, and, drawing a hidden analogy with National-Socialist Germany, he gives special attention to the Ricote episode. He discerns irony in the way in which Cervantes tells the story, and sees in it "an example for opposing, at least in writing, the 'greatness and heroism' of the rulers of a nation."

Yet Humm is not consistent in his interpretation. He attaches special significance to Don Quixote's speech to the shepherds about the "golden age," and, like Spitzer, he believes that Cervantes intended these words to be understood as a positive message. For Humm, Don Quixote symbolizes not only national arrogance and religious fanaticism, but also the best traits of European civilization: "idealism, individualism, and eternal protestantism." He draws a fantastic parallel between the Islamic world of Cervantes' time, and twentieth-century Russia. He believes that Cervantes, who suffered from and fought against oriental despotism, can offer spiritual support in the coming struggle between East and West. The second half of Humm's essay is worthy of the imagination of Cervantes' hero, and reminds one of Don Quixote's dissertations on witchcraft.

Humm's essay has some affinity with Joseph Bickermann's book on *Don Quixote und Faust.*[19] This book is the most ambitious and comprehensive venture in Cervantes criticism undertaken in Germany during the last half-century. The author is a Russian Jew who left his native country because of his opposition to the Soviet régime. Bickermann's political experiences and sympathies are reflected to some extent in his interpretation of *Don Quixote.* Don Quixote appears to him as the typical utopian world reformer, who believes himself to be in possession of a simple formula which will explain the universe, and who is convinced that with the help of an equally simple recipe, he can cure all of the world's ills. In spite of this oversimplification and the partisan spirit in which it is written, Bickermann's book is not totally lacking in merit, for the particular point of view of the author led him to analyze some aspects of Don Quixote's character which, at least in Germany, were hardly noticed before. While for the romanticists and for Vossler in their following, Don Quixote represented the spontaneous and original individual who is restricted by mechanical and unpersonal routine, Bickermann emphasizes his ritualism and dogmatism: "Don Quixote is the prisoner of a ready-made scheme; he is the very opposite of a dreamer." Bickermann draws a detailed psychological picture of a man caught in a net of formulas and preconceived notions, and exemplifies it in Don Quixote. Like Bodmer, he points out Don Quixote's skillful rationalizations in order to support his convictions. This web of artificial arguments becomes so strong that it finally paralyzes Don Quixote's ability to distinguish truth from falsehood, and leads him into a state of abysmal insincerity. "Don Quixote is a symbol of the most powerful reaction against the lack of conscience in intellectual matters." Bickermann studies the problem of the incongruity between the many sensible opinions of Don Quixote, and his foolish actions, but, unlike Thomas Mann, he asserts that the author, in disregard of the fundamental character of his hero, often made him the mouthpiece of his own opinions.

Bickermann's views on Don Quixote are to some extent paralleled by those of Max Kommerall.[20] He formulates the two basic assumptions on which the interpretation of Don Quixote can rest. One may either suppose that Cervantes detached himself from the fundamental concepts of Catholic Christianity, or that he remained essentially a son of the Church. Kommerell decides for the latter. He sees in Don Quixote one of the "most Christian" books in world literature. According to him, it was Cervantes' intention to portray a character who overreaches himself, who has arrogated to himself a mission which is *hybris* in the eyes of God. Don Quixote's *desengaño* before his death destroys his presumptuous pride and thus makes him worthy to receive the grace of God. Kommerell's views have their most direct ancestor in Bouterwek and Fouqué.

Kommerell implied in his essay that the alternate approach to Don Quixote, the one he excluded, would lead to a pessimistic interpretation similar to that of Heine and Thomas Mann. That this is not necessarily so, was demonstrated by Georg von Lukacs. Lukacs' views on Cervantes form part of his book on the Theory of the Novel.[21] According to Lukacs, Don Quixote is intimately related to the progressing disintegration of transcendental Christianity, and forms one of the earliest artistic expressions of this historical process. Don Quixote represents the prototype of modern subjectivism, in which the objective values formerly safeguarded by a transcendental realism are replaced by an immanent idealism. Thus Cervantes' hero is the ancestor of Schiller's Marquis Posa, and is surrounded with the same aura of ambiguity as is Schiller's figure. In Lukacs' interpretation, many of the approaches to Don Quixote, which were tried before, meet and are fused into a new synthesis. Here we find the historical method of Herder and Hegel, here is also the romantic view on Don Quixote as the idealist in a hostile world, but it is divested of the sentimentality and the pathos which the romanticists never failed to read into the novel. Here the pessimistic, post-romantic conception of *Don Quixote* is at least touched upon, but it is immediately discarded in favor of a virile, cool analysis of man's fate in a world without transcendental support. Lukacs' interpretation, though written a quarter of a century ago, is thoroughly modern.

NOTES

[1] Introduction to *Don Quixote*, 1837.
[2] "Don Quixote im Spiegel," *Die Neue Rundschau*, 1916, pp. 1103–1114.
[3] Friedrich Schlegel in a review of Goethe's works in 1808.
[4] "Rede über die Mythologie" in *Gespräch über die Poesie*.
[5] *Vorlesungen über Aesthetik*, Vol. 2, p. 214.
[6] *Ibid.*, p. 216.
[7] *Romanische Forschungen*, Vol. 51, 1937.
[8] *Algunos caracteres de la cultura española*, p. 60.
[9] *Introducciòn a la literatura española del siglo de oro*, Madrid, 1934, p. 83.
[10] *Monatshefte für den deutschen Unterricht*, Vol. 37, 1945, p. 480.
[11] "Zur Frage der Heuchelei des Cervantes," *Zeitschrift für romanische Philologie*, Vol. 56, 1936, p. 138 ff.
[12] "Das Gefüge einer cervantinischen Novelle," *Zeitschrift für romanische Philologie*, Vol. 51, 1931, pp. 194–225.
[13] *Geschichte der spanischen Nationalliteratur in ihrer Blütezeit*, Freiburg im Breisgau, 1929.
[14] *Leiden und Grösse der Meister*, Wien, 1936.
[15] "Thomas Mann y la muerte de Don Quijote," *Revista de Filología hispanicá*, Vol. 2, 1940, pp. 46–48.
[16] Cf. note 2.
[17] "Don Quixote: Politik und Seele," *Preussische Jahrbücher*, Vol. 120, 1905, pp. 387–493.
[18] *Don Quixote und der Traum vom goldenen Zeitalter*, Olten, 1939.
[19] Berlin, 1929.
[20] "Humoristische Personifikation im Don Quixote," *Die Neue Rundschau*, Vol. 49, 1938, pp. 209–232.
[21] *Theorie der Novelle*, Berlin, 1920.

Cervantes in Russia

LUDMILLA B. TURKEVICH

THE age of Catherine the Great saw the first translations of Spanish literature into Russian. The Empress herself translated parts of Calderón's *El Escondido y la tapada*. In 1769 appeared *Istoria o slavnom Lamankhskom rytsare Don Kishote,* done by N. Osipov from the currently popular French version of Filleau de Saint-Martin. The *Istoria* belongs to Osipov's school days and this is amply evident in the verbose, clumsy, and occasionally ungrammatical style. Serious mistranslations and omissions resulting from inexperience and carelessness abound; neither was the original version selected a particularly good one. Later, Osipov revised it somewhat and published it in 1791 with the new heading of *Neslykhanny chudodei* . . .[1] and again in 1812.[2] In spite of all the defects of this version,[3] it did introduce *Don Quixote* to the Russian public and for thirty-five years was the only Russian translation.

The second rendition of the *Quixote, Don Kishot La Mankhski,*[4] belongs to the twenty-one-year-old poet Vasili Zhukovski. It was done from Florian's version.[5] The young poet esteemed Florian highly and faithfully followed his principles of translation. Consequently, in working on the translation of the *Quixote* he altered, toned down, and expurgated the already mutilated text. This, of course, led to numerous changes in the thoughts of the novel. This divergence goes farther. Zhukovski, in an unsuccessful attempt to give his work the smoothness and purity recommended by Florian, fell into the error of substituting racy familiarity for the classic dignity of Cervantes' prose. Little of the Cervantine spirit was preserved in the Florian translation; none remains in Zhukovski's work. Curiously, the poetry of the translation is better than Cervantes'. Zhukovski was an exceptionally gifted poet and this talent is reflected in the verses of his translation. Excellent though they may be, their sentiment, ideas, and tone have nothing in common with the original. The love poems, even Altisidora's crude and mocking plaint, are all charming lyrics of ardent young love.

343

This translation went through two and possibly three editions. The first appeared in 1804–6, the second, "revised," in 1815[6], and the third, according to Fitzmaurice-Kelly, in 1820.[7]

A new translation of the *Quixote* was published either in 1831 or 1837. It was done from the French text of S. de Chaplet.[8]

In 1838[9] we have the first translation of the *Quixote* done directly from the Spanish by the Hispanist and author, Konstantin Masalsky. It shows great care, ability, and good taste but suffers from excessive literalness which deprives the version of that verbal expressiveness so vital in the original. There are errors, of course, yet for a first attempt this version is as good as its reputation.

To the same period (1763–1850) belong various other translations of Cervantes such as *Las Dos doncellas* in 1763,[10] followed by another edition in 1769,[11] In 1795 we have *La Gitanilla,*[12] in 1805 Kabrit's *Novelas ejemplares,*[13] then *La Fuerza de la sangre*[14] and another *La Gitanilla,*[15] printed in 1839 and 1842 respectively. All of these *novelas* were done from the French, as was *Galatea*[16] which enjoyed two translations, one by Aleksei Pechenegov 1790 and another by A. Khanenko in 1799.

The middle of the century saw a new translation of *Don Quixote* done by V. Karelin.[17] It is prefaced by a short biography which is as imaginative as it is inaccurate. The text is complete with the exception of the dedications and prologue. The author claims that it was done from the Spanish, but the peculiar rendition of the text and the gallicized forms of the proper names suggest a French rather than a Spanish source. Grammatical changes and errors resulting from the author's excessive liberty with the text are numerous and often seriously distort the meaning. Karelin's work, however, is redeemed by its excellent style which conveys much of the charm and flavor of the *Quixote*. The proverbs and *dichos,* so important in the book, are rendered by well-chosen Russian parallels. When this is impossible Karelin gives a good translation of them.

During this period (1850–1881) this translation went through three editions (1866, 1873, 1881), the last prefaced by the essay *Don Quixotism and Demonism*. Unfortunately this intriguing and promising title heads an exceptionally poor study that is long, badly constructed, full of digressions, and abounding in excellent suggestive material which stands weakly developed. But its value, a coordination and conciliation of the philosophical and sociological interpretations of Don Quixote, must be remarked.

A. N. Ostrovski, the creator of the Russian theater, translated all Cervantes' interludes in 1879. The work was done hurriedly, seven to ten days an interlude, and consequently done poorly. Ostrovski had planned to revise them but evidently he did not do so, for when Vainberg, the publisher of *Izyschnaya*

Literatura, bought them there was not much time for making the version as graceful "as the name of the author deserves." Certainly the text, as it appeared in the journal, is no credit to the great dramatist. It is in prose and often does convey the general idea of the original correctly, but there are numerous inexplicable grammatical rearrangements and distortions. *Izyaschnaya Literatura*[18] did not exist long enough to publish all Ostrovski's *entremeses* and only forty-two copies of the limited edition of Ostrovski's *Complete Works*[19] were offered to the public. Thus the *entremeses,* even in this version so deeply regretted by the translator, were kept from the Russian public till the producers Evreinov and Meierhold brought them to the theater at the beginning of the 20th century.

Señora Cornelia[20] was translated by A. Kirpichnikov from Brockhaus' *Colección de autores españoles* (vol. XXV). In comparison with Ostrovski's work and many of the other current Cervantine translations, this is excellent. Since the author was a professor in Western European literature, however, we can be more exacting. The style is good, sacrificing literalness, and occasionally meaning, to grace and clarity. More attention to modifiers, tenses, dependent clauses, and actual meaning of words would have been desirable since it would have resulted in a closer translation without necessarily spoiling the style.

A revised edition of Karelin's work done by V. Zotov appeared in 1893.[21] The editor substituted the prologues by a literal translation from the original and broke up the chapters according to the Spanish text, giving them corresponding titles. He did not touch the actual text or correct its footnotes. His translation of the prologues is no improvement on Karelin, for the style is clumsier and the craftsmanship careless.

This version is now followed by Mark Basanin's *Bezpodobny rytsar Don Kikhot Lamanchski,*[22] translated from the Spanish, with introduction, notes, and a biography of Cervantes. The biography, in spite of some inaccuracies, is much better than Karelin's but the text of the novel is inferior. It is more literal and often much more accurate than Karelin's translation but it lacks the suppleness of good style. Obviously aware of the deficiency, Basanin tried to enliven the text, which resulted in over-adornment often not in the best of taste.

N. V. Tulupov's *Don Kikhot Lamanchski* (Moscow, 1904)[23] was purportedly done from the Spanish but actually it was made from the French. It is very poor.

A landmark in the history of Cervantes in Russia is M. V. Vatson's *Ostroumno izobretatlny idalgo Don Kikhot Lamanchski.*[24] It is the first really complete and accurate translation done with deep respect and love for the *Quixote* by a highly responsible person. She uses the 1898 Fitzmaurice-Kelly edition for her text and explains her choice in a preface. Then she gives a good biography of Cervantes and a survey of his works based on sound Spanish sources. The text is handled literally, which is both the translation's main virtue and its greatest defect, for in Vatson's effort at precision and completeness some of the *Quixote's* artistic value is dissipated. When she feels that her version does not convey all the shades of meaning necessary for a good reading, she supplements it with good notes. The names are all consistently transcribed from the Spanish, with the exception of Don Quixote. *Don Kikhot,* the current Russian form of the name, is retained. This translation went through five editions (Petrograd 1917, Moscow-Leningrad 1924, 1929, 1930, 1933). It enjoyed great popularity until it was supplanted by a newer and better translation by Krzhevsky and Smirnov in 1929.

There are several other translations, apparently complete ones, concerning which we have little data: an Odessa version of 1899,[25] the ones done by Murakhina,[26] Chistyakov,[27] and S. M.[28]

Contemporaneously with these *Quixote* versions we have several translations of Cervantes' other works. There is the Glivenko translation of *El Celoso extremeño,*[29] done from the Spanish. It is literal and essentially complete, but in details the translator occasionally preferred concision to fidelity. *El Licenciado Vidriera,*[30] by the Hispanist L. Y. Shepelevich, is thorough and scholarly. M. V. Vatson's renditions of *El Celoso extremeño, El Amante liberal,* and *La Ilustre fregona*[31] show the same conscientious workmanship that characterized her *Don Kikhot Lamanchski.* The 1892 edition of *Rinconete y Cortadillo*[32] and L. B. Khavkina's translations of *Rinconete y Cortadillo* and *El Licenciado Vidriera*[33] (Moscow 1913 and 1916) have not been available.

Since the founding of the "Academia" of the Soviet Union in the late 'twenties the Russian book mart has brought out a lavish as well as attractive array of books. This group of scholars has worked diligently producing new editions and translations of great masterpieces. As a rule, the new work surpasses in quality anything previously done in Russia. The same can be said of the "Academia" *Khitroumny idalgo Don Kikhot Lamanchski.*[34] The work on the new edition was done mainly by Krzhevski, whose task was the interpretation of the text, and Smirnov, whose work was the artistic rendition. The poetry was by Lozinski and Kuzmin. As far as the actual language of the text is concerned, they sought for the golden mean, between the archaic and the modern, favoring slightly the latter, since their avowed purpose was to create a live artistic text just as comprehensible to the man today as it was to Cervantes' contemporaries. Above all, their efforts were directed toward the concreteness, plasticity, and dynamics of words, expressions, and images, an inherent trait of Cervantes' style.[35] On the whole, this text is much better than Karelin's and

Vatson's, though sometimes it falls short of the goal the translators had set for themselves. The version is literal and careful. When possible, proverbs and idioms are rendered by well-chosen parallels carrying the flavor of the *Quixote* to the Russians. Furthermore, allusions that are obscure to readers carry notes. These are concise and are mainly derived from Rodriguez Marín's *Don Quixote*, edition of 1915–1916. For the greater part they are correct, with the exception of obvious typographical errors in figures and spelling. Nevertheless, these, as well as the more serious mistakes in the main text, should have been corrected by the time the book reached its third edition. Preceding the translation there are several interesting articles done from the Marxist point of view.

The first complete translation of the *Novelas ejemplares*[36] appeared in 1934 (Moscow-Leningrad) by B. A. Krzhevski. They were done from the texts of Schevill-Bonilla, Rodríguez Marín, the latter's special edition of *Rinconete y Cortadillo* (Madrid, 1905), Foulché Delbosc's and Cortes' editions of *El Licenciado Vidriera* (1899 and 1916 respectively), Amezúa's *Casamiento engañoso* (Madrid, 1912) and Wolf's *Tía fingida* (Berlin, 1818). They are printed in the sequence of the 1613 edition and also include the *Tía fingida*. The translation is literal, the proverbs are given Russian equivalents, the texture of the original language is preserved as much as possible, and still the reader does not feel that he is reading a translation. At the end of each volume there are notes taken mainly from Rodríguez Marín's edition of the novels. These explain fully many of the allusions made in the text. They have not the flaws found in the notes to the *Quixote* translation of the "Academia." Our only comment on them is that several more notes could have been added, especially where there is a play on words.

Two individual *novelas* preceded this "Academia" collection. They are *Rinconete y Cortadillo*[37] and *El Licenciado Vidriera*.[38] Though issued in large quantities neither has been available to us. This period also offers new editions of some of Ostrovski's interlude translations: *Los Habladores, El Viejo celoso, La Cueva de Salamanca* (all three in 1919) and *El Rufián viudo* (in 1923). A new translation of the last interlude was made by B. A. Krzhevski in 1923.[39]

Now for a recapitulation: From 1763 to the Second World War *Don Quixote* had had forty-one more or less complete Russian editions. Of these, notable was Osipov's because it was the first translation, then Masalski's, because it was the first to have been made from the Spanish. This one was superseded by the more graceful Karelin version which, in turn was replaced by the more accurate Vatson and then "Academia" renditions. In addition to these, *Don Quixote* in abbreviated versions or adaptations for children appeared in thirty-nine editions whose printing ranged from some 2,000 to 10,000 copies. Here we might also note a Ukrainian version by M. O. Ivanov (Kharkov, 1927). For the *entremeses* Russia must still look to A. N. Ostrovski's version with the exception of *El Rufián viudo. Galatea's* early popularity waned with the passing of the sentimental school and the 18th century. The *Novelas ejemplares,* on the other hand, are now enjoying increased attention.

II INFLUENCE

Penetration of Cervantine influence into Russian *belles lettres* began during the era of Catherine the Great. It is in a minor scene from A. N. Radischev's *Journey from Petersburg to Moscow* where we find a re-enactment of the famous scene of the galley slaves. A traveler of the quixotic type meets a group of shackled men who through bureaucratic injustice are being taken into the army. Incensed, the gentleman approaches the poor devils and tells them how to escape their menacing fate. Thereupon the guards pounce upon him and drive him away, but the mischief has been done.

The great poet Pushkin, who combined in a brilliant synthesis the literary heritage of Russia with the best of Western literature, traced his artistic gene-alogy back to the Golden Age, to Shakespeare, Dante, Camöens, Villon, Cervantes, and others. And a study of Pushkin's writings shows reflections of these writers at various points of his life. Cervantes he particularly admired and it is, therefore, not surprising to find Cervantes' influence in Pushkin's works.

This is evident in his great narrative poem *Yevgeni Onegin,* a story of a St. Petersburg dandy living in the country, where he meets the sensitive and intro-spective girl Tatyana. She falls in love with him, but he spurns her. Subsequent events, a stupid duel, necessitate his departure from the estate but several years later their paths meet again. Now Tatyana's mature beauty, poise, and charm so overwhelm him that he pleads for her love. Though loving Yevgeni, she rejects him and remains with her husband.

Tatyana of the first part of the story has much in common with Don Quixote. She is a person of more than average intelligence, imagination, and will-power. She likes to read, but all that current literature has to offer is the sentimental novels, with their wonderful and eternally faithful heroes. These so excite her youthful imagination that she withdraws from the natural pastimes of child-hood into the emotionally satisfying retreat of day-dreaming. These books create for her a new pattern of life which she follows with quixotic fidelity. As Don Quixote is inspired by the compellingly marvelous Amadís, so Tatyana is guided by the beguilingly lachrimose Clarissa, Julia, and Delphine.

The result in both cases is a logical sequence to the reading. Don Quixote becomes a knight-errant, Tatyana a pining heroine. As Don Quixote endows the peasant Aldonza with supreme feminine beauty and nobility, so Tatyana attributes to the cynical Byronic Yevgeni all the exalted qualities of her literary heroes. Reality's disillusioning impact when finally recognized by Don Quixote has a sobering effect, but its shattering intensity kills the old man. Sobering, too, is Tatyana's recognition of reality's contradiction, but her youth makes adjustment to saner things easier and possible. For her the revelation is not an overwhelming catastrophe, rather a heaven-sent boon.

Yevgeni Onegin is more than a tale of a quixotic maiden. It is an indictment of the preceding literary *genre*. Like *Don Quixote,* which ridicules the novels of chivalry with their fantastic heroes, so *Yevgeni Onegin* satirizes the senti-mental novel, with its equally unreal heroines. Upon this rests the organic relationship between the two works. In addition there is the social indictment against the reading habits of the public. People either did not read or else indulged in the reading of the sentimental novels, which, at best, wasted their time or else produced dire results. It is the folly resulting from excessive reading of the absurdities contained in this *genre* that Pushkin depicts in young Tatyana.

The ballad, *Lived a Knight Once,* shows a much more profound handling of Don Quixote's image. Whereas Tatyana was light, supple, surrounded with the delicate aura of romanticism, here in the knight the original magnificence is retained. The hero, like his prototype, is solid, grave, and dramatic adorned with feudal elegance.

> Lived a knight once, poor and simple,
> Pale of face with glance austere,
> Spare of speech, but with a spirit
> Proud, intolerant of fear.
> He had had a wondrous vision:
> Ne'er could feeble human art
> Gauge its deep, mysterious meaning,
> It was graven on his heart.
> And since then his soul had quivered
> With an all-consuming fire,
> Never more he looked on women,
> Speech with them did not desire.
> But he dropped his scarf thenceforward,
> Wore a chaplet in its place,
> And no more in sight of any
> Raised the visor from his face.
> Filled with purest love and fervour,
> Faith which he sweet dream did yield,
> In his blood he traced the letters
> A. M. G.[1] upon his shield.
> When the Paladins proclaiming

> Ladies' names as true love's sign,
> Hurled themselves into the battle
> On the plains of Palestine,
> *Lumen coeli, Sancta Rosa!*
> Shouted he with flaming glance,
> And the fury of his menace
> Checked the Mussulman's advance.
> Then returning to his castle
> In far distant country side,
> Silent, sad, bereft of reason,
> In his solitude he died.

The similarity between this knight and Don Quixote is patent. Both the heroes are poor, but proud and fearless knights. Both are impelled by an ideal incomprehensible to the ordinary mind, which involves a pure love for humanity. The atmosphere of noble self-sacrifice and dynamic optimism of the beginning of the work is displaced in the finale by tragic sadness and solitude, a change experienced by both heroes. The obvious influence of Don Quixote is heightened by the poet's concentration on the hero's inner grandeur which is effectively expressed in the rhythm, the music, and the subtle nuances of Pushkin's language.

In addition to these manifestations of Cervantine influence, we have evidence that Pushkin had in mind a subject based on *Don Quixote* "from which he had wished to develop something on the order of a poem," but instead he gave this idea to Gogol. This was the theme of *Dead Souls*.[2] Another instance of Cervantes' inspiration is found in the *Gypsies,* whose basic pattern is that of "La Gitanilla." Then, too, there is the framing device used in the *Tales of Belkin* that recalls the fictitious papers of Cid Hamed Benengeli.

Don Quixote, in the light of philosophical and metaphysical interpretation, appears in the pattern of Odoyevski's *Segeliel, Don Quixote of XIX century*. "The basic thought of this poem is to show the social status of an individual in whom love for mankind is brought to an extreme. The author wished to combine in one personality all the philanthropic dreams of our age and to contrast them with the real conditions of life. In short, he sought to do for philanthropy, this knighthood of our times, what Cervantes did for knighthood, the philanthropy of his era, to portray its noble and comical aspects."[3] Though this work was not completed, the romantic interpretation of Don Quixote is inherent in its imaginative conception. Into its execution entered other influences, such as Goethe's *Faust,* Milton's *Paradise Lost,* and Klopstock's *Messiad,* giving the original theme new contours.

There is a fundamental similarity between Don Quixote and Segeliel. The hero is an idealist who, like Don Quixote, is moved by an aspiration never satisfied with detached observation of human sorrows but by active and helpful participation. For this purpose he descends to the terrestrial spheres. With an eagerness equalled only by his prototype, Segeliel sacrifices himself to his ideal, never abandoning it even in the face of ridicule and abuse. Both take every opportunity, good or bad, to preach their ideal, which in both cases is the concept of good. Segeliel, like Don Quixote, is misunderstood by all and is called a madman.

Don Quixote, the symbol of ethical behavior, is here set into a frame confusing in its clashing combination of the real with the fantastic. On the one hand we have a very vivid nineteenth-century reality, and on the other, the romantic presence of Lucifer, Segeliel's vague and unearthly origin and his mystifying metamorphoses. It is indeed unfortunate that the work was not completed, for it has great possibilities.

Gogol's *Dead Souls,* the greatest satire in Russian literature, was influenced by *Don Quixote.* Chichikov, the hero, is an inversion of the *hidalgo* set into the mechanical frame of episodes derived from the Spanish novel and projected against the backdrop of contemporary Russia. The result, an overwhelming picture of human baseness and stupidity, evokes the same "laughter through tears" that is produced by the *Quixote.* It is a saga of an arch-swindler, who travels through Russia for the purpose of mending his fortunes by the doubtful procedure of purchasing dead souls. His plan is to mortgage this non-existent commodity and for the cold cash acquire real, live souls, as serfs. With this intent he arrives in a small town and calls on the local "potentates." His airs of importance and refinement so impress the country folk that soon he is the social lion. Meanwhile he wastes no time and shops for dead souls. All goes well, until the rascal Nozdryov and the chatterbox Korobochka start rumors which lead to Chichikov's undoing. Gogol cleverly exploits the episodic character of the novel's plan and presents as clear a picture of the hero and his *milieu* as one finds in the *Quixote.*

As we have said, Chichikov is a faithful inversion of Don Quixote. Don Quixote's spiritual perfection becomes in Gogol's hero utter depravity. From this fundamental inversion naturally stem all the other qualities which are true negatives of the positive. The only exceptions to this are the hero's will and perseverance. These qualities both heroes possess in abundance, and by virtue of them, both follow their respective inclinations undaunted by failure, privation, or fatigue.

The inversion is first of all indicated in the external features of the heroes. The peculiar-looking, poorly attired elderly gentleman of the Quixote emerges in *Dead Souls* as a modishly dressed young man. Don Quixote's *hidalguía* suggests good heredity. This is reversed in the picture of Chichikov's father, who is a thief and a pervert. Chichikov's moral constitution, low by heredity, is further debased by unhealthy education. This is a direct contrast to Don Quixote, whose naturally noble character is so enhanced by the cultivation of the more refined qualities that he conceives the idea of liberating humanity from its yoke. In Chichikov, this ideal takes the form of complete exploitation of society for his own ends.

In the development of the Cervantine theme Gogol shows also a complete comprehension and application of Cervantes' portrayal of the dual nature of life, the universal and the individual. Like Cervantes he so formulates the universal aspirations of humanity that, upon closer analysis, they show the flesh of the individual ambitions. On the other hand, his delineation of the individual aspirations forms a panorama of the universal longing.

The universal desire for self-assertion, the desire to leave one's imprint upon this world, may find expression in a variety of forms. In Don Quixote, this ambition takes the form of knight-errantry, his path to glory and fame. In Chichikov, this urge is different. Since he is of low moral and intellectual stratum his longing takes the most primitive form of expression. He toils endlessly to acquire property upon which to settle and have children. It is almost pathetic to watch him in the midst of shady transactions, sitting and dreaming of litle Chichikovs. His many failings make him almost a caricature, but his dreams make him human.

Another universal desire delineated in Don Quixote is the human struggle to dominate reality. The *hidalgo's* heart is set on chivalry, but this he cannot realize, hence he resorts to fancy. Chichikov accomplishes this by treachery and unscrupulousness.

Amid these broad aspirations Cervantes presents the individual ones. His hero strives to reduce suffering, to obliterate injustice, to fulfill his social and moral obligations to society and to restore knighthood. In Chichikov the universal longings are accompanied by petty personal ones, to swindle, to exploit society, to acquire wealth and position.

There is similarity as well in the method of character development. Both Cervantes and Gogol describe their characters with amazing minuteness and stress effectively their peculiarities. They both tend to burlesque, but in this Gogol exceeds Cervantes. In the Spaniard the burlesque is focused upon one victim, the hero. Some of the other figures also suffer from it but only superficially. Gogol's ridicule hits every character of *Dead Souls* except Konstanzhoglo and his wife. This ridicule pierces into the Russian types, venomously exposing the mentality, the habits, and other internal features of the person, creating thereby a grotesque.[4]

In *Rudin,* the combination of Turgenev technique with Cervantes' thematic material is elegant and aesthetically perfect. The stress falls on the futility of impractical idealism and on the significance of liberty. The drama of the story centers on the hero Rudin, who portrays the tragedy of the preceding genera-tion, a generation of idealists who for all their pioneering courage and strength of conviction lacked comprehension of the important things in actual life.

The plot of the novel is briefly this: An eloquent and idealistic guest (Rudin) appears on a charming estate of the idle gentry. He wins the favor of most, including that of the heiress Natalya. He becomes very much interested in her, and she is completely enthralled by his ideas and personality. Matters come to a point where he must decide between marriage or departure from the estate. Natalya, with youthful enthusiasm, offers to sacrifice all to be with Rudin. He, though genuinely honorable, does not appreciate either the situation, or the greatness of the girl's offer, or life's demands. He decides to withdraw alone, saying to his admirer, "Do you remember what Don Quixote says to his squire when he is leaving the court of the duchess? 'Freedom,' he says, 'my friend Sancho, is one of the most precious possessions of a man, and happy is he to whom Heaven has given a bit of bread and who need not be indebted to anyone.' What Don Quixote felt then I feel now . . ."[5] For Rudin his visit at the Lazunski's is just an episode comparable to Don Quixote's stay at the duchess'. On this estate lies all the promise for a happy life. Rudin is assured love, com-fort, prestige, and success of a less exalted nature than that of Don Quixote, but his price is also freedom. Like Don Quixote, he chooses liberty, and goes to live a life equally fantastic, equally unreasonable, as his.

Rudin, without family, without money, without a clearly marked plan, wanders through the country in much the same manner that Don Quixote did. The futility of impractical idealism is best revealed in his conversation with Lezhnev at the end of the book. He relates the story of his life after his departure from the Lazunski home. In the course of his endless peregrinations, he met an eccentric lover of science, whose resources he tried to utilize in rendering service to the world. He tells Lezhnev, "My plans, brother, were great; I dreamed of various improvements and innovations." He first enters upon an agricultural venture. The initial enthusiasm is colossal, but constant reason-ing with himself kills his faith in that particular enterprise, and the result is that two years of work come to nothing. After sacrificing all for this scheme, he fails, but this and other disappointments do not kill his idealism. Like Don Quixote, he falls, then rises; and right ahead, falls again, only to rise anew. After many impractical projects Rudin finally dies in the French Revolution— significantly fighting for freedom, a lost cause.

When Turgenev creates a strong male character one can always trace it to outside influences. Just such a character is Bazarov, the hero of *Fathers and Sons*. In him we find the Nihilist ideology superimposed on the image of a certain doctor, who in turn is given a psychological pattern derived from the *Quixote*.

It is startling to consider negation, that is, Nihilism, as a form of idealism, yet once it is seen in this light the underlying pattern of *Fathers and Sons* becomes apparent. Bazarov saturates himself with nihilistic precepts in much the same manner that Don Quixote absorbs the chivalric lore. He wins over a fellow-traveler in Arkadi Kirsanov, and sets out to disseminate and practice these dogmas. From this point he follows his ideal with the same persistence, faith, self-abnegation, and logic that we find in Don Quixote. There are many points of divergence between the two characters but they spring from the different nature of the ideal. The execution is the same in character. Like Don Quixote, Bazarov brings upon himself unwarranted suffering. He denies himself the comforts of the parental roof, the joys of love and marriage and aesthetic pleasures. Just like his prototype, he embraces an ideal whole heartedly, but when he discovers that it is a "phantom" he dies. On his deathbed Don Quixote openly concedes that the pursuit of his ideal was madness. Although Bazarov does not admit it, the heavy pall of disappointment that hangs over the final scene suggests a similar opinion.

A. N. Ostrovski, the playwright and translator of Cervantes' interludes, is the author of *Forest,* one of Russia's better dramas of manners. Its heroes, inspired by Don Quixote and Sancho, are Gennadi Neschastlivtsev (Mr. Unhappy), a seedy provincial tragedian, and Arkadi Schastlivtsev (Mr. Happy), a tattered provincial comedian. Hungry, penniless, and homeless, they meet on a lonely road. A conversation ensues, banal in content but rich in suggestive quality and Cervantine in tone and mood. From it Neschastlivtsev emerges as a grim, imperious, impulsive, bombastic individual lofty in ideas, speech, and action. Schastlivtsev, like Sancho, is his companion's counterpart. He is simple, good-natured, witty, modest in ambition, keenly sensitive to the exigencies of life, and possesses a remarkable ability to use what little he has to the greatest personal advantage. In this short dialogue their mutual relationship is established. Neschastlivtsev is condescending and domineering; Schastlivtsev is subservient and tractable. Though socially and professionally they are equal, morally Neschastlivtsev is the master, and his companion the servant.

This marvelous team is set against the background of mid-nineteenth-century Russian provincial society which presents a disheartening picture of smallness, meanness, and baseness. In this setting the pair dreams and acts now grandiloquent, now pathetic, now comic, but always irresistible. Thus they lead the reader to a brilliant climax where, by the dramatic rejection of a much-needed sum of 1,000 roubles, they sustain and reaffirm the essential goodness of man and the greatness of freedom.

Dostoyevski was deeply impressed by *Don Quixote*. "A more profound and a more powerful work than this one [Don Quixote] is not to be found," he says. "It is the final and the greatest utterance of the human mind. It is the bitterest irony that only man could express." It is the key to life showing "how man's purity, wisdom, simplicity, benignity, manliness, and finally his great mind . . . go to waste, go without benefit to mankind and are even turned to ridicule . . . only because all these highly noble and lavish gifts . . . lack but one final gift—namely the genius to manage and to guide all this power along the road of truth and not of fantasy and madness, along the path that is for the benefit of humanity."[6] This becomes the final theme of Dostoyevski's *Idiot*.

As he began work on the *Idiot,* Dostoyevski wrote,

> The idea of the novel is to present a positively beautiful character. There is nothing more difficult . . . There is only one positively beautiful figure —Christ, and therefore, the appearance of this immeasurably, infinitely wonderful personality is indeed an unquestionable miracle . . . I will merely mention that of the beautiful characters in Christian literature Don Quixote is the most complete. But he is excellent only because at the same time he is comical. Dickens' Pickwick . . . is also ridiculous and succeeds by virtue of this fact. Pity is evoked for that ridiculed and beautiful figure who does not know his worth, and consequently sympathy is aroused in the reader. This stimulation of pity is the secret of humor . . .[7]

It was with this idea that Dostoyevski set to writing the *Idiot*.

The complete story of the genesis of the Idiot, Prince Myshkin, is involved and not necessary here. Suffice it to say that between the writing of the sixth and the seventh drafts this character, conceived as a clinical case of the lowest order, changed into an image of spiritual perfection possessing a dream-like vitality. The character has only one fault—the inability to apply usefully all that selfless compassion, intuitive wisdom, and glowing purity that is his.

This attractive person belongs to an old family, and is returning to Russia to assume his responsibilities as a land-owner. He is soon surrounded by a group of restless people, among whom is the engaging Aglaya Epanchin and the exciting Nastasya Filipovna. Both women fall in love with him and he reciprocates the attentions of both, much to the bewilderment of all but the ladies concerned. He is torn between the two women—proposing to Aglaya at one moment, and waiting at the altar for Nastasya Filipovna, the next. In the resulting conflict emerges the sharp contrast between Nastasya's frantic, demanding passion and Aglaya's deep, pure devotion. This triangle (perhaps this is too sordid a word to apply to the situation) turns into a merciless circle by the entrance of Nastasya's other suitor, Rogozhin, who solves the impasse by murdering her. Myshkin "escapes" from the squalid tragedy by retreating into idiocy, Rogozhin goes to Siberia, and Aglaya marries an adventurer.

Two personalities helped form the pattern for Myshkin. Christ was the main model; Don Quixote was the secondary one. Because of the fundamental similarity between these models it is in the variants of the primary one that one sees the influence of Don Quixote on Myshkin. It appears in the motivating force of the character, the rôle of women in his life, his attitude toward society, and his manner of facing adversity.

The lives of all three—Christ, Don Quixote, and Myshkin—are impelled by a desire to help man. Myshkin, emerging from the Swiss sanitarium, is a humble and idealistic spirit that seeks to do good to all. He comes up against a world of sorrow, but the cause of his tragedy, as of Don Quixote's, lies in the fact that he is not aware of this reality. (Christ knew reality only too well.) All Myshkin's efforts of kindness are scorned or returned with detestable meanness, comparable to the numerous similar reverses suffered by the *hidalgo*.

In the *Idiot* the love motif is very important. It is based on a deep emotion, pure in quality, and just as inseparable from the hero's ideal as it is in the *Quixote*. It is, however, more complicated in that it involves two women, each representing an aspect of the *idée fixe*. Aglaya parallels Dulcinea, the ideal of perfection, while Nastasya represents suffering humanity. Together they portray the same ideal that guides Don Quixote.

Myshkin's gentle attitude toward the world, derived from Christ, is in direct contrast to Don Quixote's militant one. There is, however, one variation. Christ was meek not through innocence, for he was well aware of human nature, while Myshkin and Don Quixote are both infants when confronted with the human factor. Christ was a realist with a mission, whereas Don Quixote and Myshkin are dreamers with ideals. Christ's purpose in life was within him. He was the ideal and therefore the ideal was flexible. Myshkin's and Don Quixote's ideals are without them, and consequently less pliable. Therefore when life does not fit into their design they have to compensate psychologically for the frustration.

Both Don Quixote's and Myshkin's faith in the ideal resists the attacks of reality remarkably well. Don Quixote has the supplementary re-enforcing device —his madness; Myshkin—epilepsy. In crises, Don Quixote defends his ideal by a fantastic explanation, Myshkin by an epileptic fit. Myshkin does see the failures but denies this recognition entrance into his consciousness. A clash between his ideal and reality produces emotional conflicts which unresolved are augmented by others and culminate in a stroke, a form of revenge. These strokes come at moments when his *idée fixe* is endangered. Thus epilepsy, playing this vital rôle in the life of Myshkin's ideal, parallels Don Quixote's madness. This is obviously the function that Dostoyevski planned for it.[8]

Idealism, solid as it may be, cannot resist, indefinitely, the battering of reality. When the final crash comes and Don Quixote is deprived of his mania, he falls into apathy and dies. In madness life was full; now there is devastating emptiness. The same is true for Myshkin. So long as he had his concept of beauty, he lived for it, but when Nastasva's flight and death wrench it from him, he sinks into idiocy—a living death.

The manner in which Dostoyevski handles the Cervantine theme is intense and harrowing. An atmosphere of tragedy hangs over the hero from the very first pages, and it thickens as the story advances, breaking into a raging storm of blood and horror. The novel closes like a cry of anguish amidst the destruction resulting from an unequal though valiant fight.

Cervantine influence assumes an interesting form during the reign of symbolism. The emphasis shifts from the heroic Don Quixote to the ephemeral Dulcinea. It is to the search and homage of such a mysterious and intangible lady that Sologub, Blok, and Solovyov devote their lives and works. Solovyov seeks Sofia (wisdom), Blok—Prekrasnaya Dama or Neznakomka (the Lovely Lady and the Unknown Lady), and Sologub—Dulcinea.

F. Sologub developed an early and lasting admiration for *Don Quixote*. The preface of his famous novel *The Litle Demon* is modeled directly after the concluding pages of the first part of the *Quixote*. But a more profound expression of his admiration for Cervantes is seen in the fact that the Symbolist drew on the tale of Don Quixote's transformation of Aldonza into Dulcinea to express his own literary credo. Dulcinea is for him the symbol of Beauty which man seeks. She, the dream (mechta) so strange, unselfish, and beautiful, hovers about man pleading for him to recognize and crown her as Dulcinea, but he, the blind slave of the world of Evil, does not see her beside him. He looks for her in the earthly realm and what he thinks to be Dulcinea turns out to be a vulgar Aldonza.

A version of this theme is Sologub's *Triumph of Death* where Aldonza-Dulcinea appears in just this unappreciated and mistreated though deeply touching guise. Another variant of this theme is the *Hostages of Life,* which presents the eternal discord between thought and reality, art and life, the Dulcineas and Aldonzas. The work is fraught with symbolism. The creative basis of life is portrayed by Mikhail, and the earthly life by Katya. They are in love with each other but circumstances prevent their union. Katya marries Sukhov (Mr. Dry), the symbol of uncreativeness and miserliness, while Mikhail is left to make his career. The emptiness in his life, however, is filled by the lunar, ecstatic Lilith (Dulcinea), the idealistic basis of life. She loves Mikhail for his creativeness, and demanding nothing she remains with him as long as he needs her. The tragedy comes at the end of the play, when Katya and Mikhail are reunited and remain life's hostages, while Lilith stands alone, unrecognized, uncrowned by them.

To us this is a very curious manifestation of Cervantine influence, for we have here the paradoxical situation of a Symbolist, a writer of dream and fantasy comparable in a way to the writers of chivalric lore, using materials from the *Quixote.*

In the vast output of D. Merezhkovski, Cervantine influence plays a rather small part. It is palpable in a minor character of *Peter and Alexis.* Pastor Gluck, nicknamed "the Don Quixote of astronomy" is a kind, clever, and peculiar man engaged in the writing of commentaries on Newton's *Commentaries on the Apocalypse,* an endeavor truly worthy of his namesake. This involved task leads the poor old man into confusing metaphysical debates with himself, reminiscent of similar scenes in the *Quixote.* Merezhkovski also has a three-page descriptive poem, *Don Quixote,* which he concludes with these words, "Both love and faith are sacred, and by this faith are moved all great madmen, all prophets, and poets."

There are two dramatic works derived from *Don Quixote* by the Soviet writers Lunacharski and Chulkov. Lunacharski's *Liberated Don Quixote* employs Cervantine material—the sixteenth-century ducal palace in Spain, some of the main characters, and minor episodes—to depict the Social Revolution and the attitude of the "intelligentsia" toward it and thereby to defend the new government's conduct in the matter. In the play, as in the novel, Don Quixote is a heroic dreamer who is forced to play the clown by sadistic courtiers, symbols of the old regime. The play is well done, presenting Don Quixote in a very touching light.

Chulkov's play *Don Quixote* focuses on the ethical aspect of Don Quixote. The playwright sets out "to reveal both the abstract dreaminess of Don Quixote and the equally abstract rationalism of Carrasco." This play draws copiously on the *Quixote* and yet it is by no means a mere dramatization of the novel. Chulkov takes the characters, sets the scene in the castle of the Dukes, and telescopes various other episodes from the novel that help develop his fundamental thesis. The Cervantine sociological and critical implications are completely suppressed.

A glance at this brief survey of the penetration of Cervantes into Russian creative writing reveals several very significant facts. First, the writers most sensitive to Cervantes' influence are some of the great authors of Russia. Secondly, in most cases, it is a major work of the writer that manifests the inspiration of Cervantes. Thirdly, it is obvious that for Cervantes, changing political, sociological, and literary beliefs in Russia never constitute a barrier, for the autocrat Catherine, the Westerner Turgenev, the Slavophil Dostoyevski, and the Marxist Lunacharski all show a great feeling for and appreciation of Cervantes.

III. CRITICISM

High esteem for Cervantes and his *Don Quixote* characterizes the general attitude of Russian critics. Long before criticism became an established branch of Russian letters, opinions on books and authors were expressed in private correspondence, papers, and journal articles and it is among these that we find such writers as Sumarokov and Karamzin referring to Cervantes as a great author.[1] Then came the Golden Age with its Pushkin, Polevoi, and Kukhelbeker who hail Cervantes as one of their literary forefathers.[2]

Russian criticism began in the 1840's under the leadership of Vissarion Belinski. It is, therefore, interesting that this critic should also be the author of the first critical essay on Don Quixote. The article is actually a review of Count V. A. Sollogub's *Tarantas,*[3] but there is a long digression which is a discussion of Don Quixote from the point of view of romantic idealism.

> Don Quixote is the most excellent and the most noble of men . . . a true knight . . . Notwithstanding the fact that he is comical from head to foot . . . you cannot consider him stupid. On the contrary, he is very wise . . . Whether because of his own nature, or his education, or the conditions of his life . . . fantasy took dominance over all other abilities and made of him the laughing-stock of all nations and all ages . . . We do not propose to reconcile this contradiction, but it is clear to us that such paradoxical characters are very numerous (in real life). They are wise, but only in the world of illusion . . . Everything is comprehensible to them except reality.[4]

These are some of the highlights of the article. Belinski has fully grasped both the essence of Don Quixote and understood the public's reaction to his antics. He concludes that in the creation of this eternal and generic character is manifest the greatness of Cervantes' genius.[5]

In the essay *Hamlet and Don Quixote,* Turgenev, the great exponent of Russian Realism, adopts the romantic point of view. He interprets Don Quixote as an expression of ethical behavior of a certain intellectual type. He says,

> It seems to us that in these two types (Don Quixote and Hamlet) are embodied two opposite fundamental peculiarities of human nature—the two poles of an axis about which it revolves. We think that all people belong more or less to one of these two types . . . All people live con-

sciously or unconsciously by an ideal, which they accept in totum, or subject it to minute examination; the ideal may be within the man—being his "I," or without him—something also that he considers superior.[6]

Don Quixote represents faith in something eternal, in something outside the individual—in truth, which is attainable only by constant devotion and sacrifice. Hamlet represents egotism, and skepticism.

> The man who sets out to sacrifice himself with careful forethought and consideration of all consequences . . . is hardly capable of self-sacrifice. . . . Only he who is led by the heart reaches the ultimate goal. . . . It seems to us, therefore, that the principal thing in life is sincerity and strength of conviction,—the result lies in the hands of faith.[7]

Among the extensive commentary[8] inspired by this article we have A. Lvov's *Hamlet and Don Quixote*.[9] Lvov attacks Turgenev's attempt to classify humanity into two types as useless and conventional, and he asserts that the novelist confused faith in an ideal with faith in truth. Lvov then proceeds to expound his own views, which are steeped in positivism. He does not consider Don Quixote a model of idealistic heroism, but rather a madman and an egoist who fights windmills because in this he sees his own betterment. With regard to Don Quixote's love for Dulcinea, which Turgenev calls "ideally chaste," Lvov says that Don Quixote loves his ideal, which happens to be Dulcinea. As for Sancho, he is but a typical picaresque figure. In opposition to Turgenev, Lvov says that "Cervantes' only purpose was the destruction of the novels of chivalry and the misinterpreted spirit of chivalry." This Cervantes accomplished, and upon this rests his fame and historical importance.

A. Hornfeld, a Soviet critic, in commenting on Turgenev's parallel says that Turgenev did not appreciate the idealist in Hamlet. The Danish Prince, like Don Quixote, wanted to uproot evil, but his was a task far more difficult, for he was aware of his own limitations and need of external assistance. Don Quixote's problem is solved by him alone, while Hamlet's requires the cooperation of all mankind."[10]

The philosophical approach to Don Quixote is again found in Karelin's *Don Quixotism and Demonism*. It centers on the ethical behavior manifest in Don Quixote and Milton's Satan—the protest of a strong creative personality against unwholesome surroundings. Both are typified by a complete renunciation of the sensual "I" and dwell in the spiritual heights with all their forces concentrated upon the idea adopted by them. In contrast to this form of human behavior, is the form completely devoted to the sensual interests of the individual. This is exemplified by Sancho. Between these two extremes or poles—lies the mass of mankind. Some individuals approach one pole, others the opposite. Only the exceptional personalities are at the very poles. "But, alas, they are so few in number because life . . . . claims its own. 'Tis but one small step from the great to the ridiculous."[11] And it is the tragedy of this dangerous proximity that Cervantes revealed in his Don Quixote. Greatness could have been Don Quixote's, but the putrefying social atmosphere about him diverted this potential greatness into abnormal channels, and transformed it into absurdity. Such tragedy is not peculiar to individuals, continues Karelin, but also is true of society itself at certain moments of political history.[12] There is much that is valuable and interesting in this article, but the construction of the essay could have been better. Karelin frequently goes off on a tangent, such as the comparison between Sancho and Richard III, or in discussion of other aspects of Don Quixote.[13] Though this has nothing to do with the original antithesis, these irrelevancies constitute the article's main value, because in them Karelin deals with aspects of the novel itself, something hitherto neglected by the Russian critics.

Dostoyevski was also attracted by the ideological and philosophical aspects of Don Quixote, as a commentary on life and a revelation of the human heart. In his Diary of an Author he dwells on the hidalgo's bewilderment when he considered the impossibility of one knight's annihilating a host of warriors in a brief time.

> The fantastic man suddenly became homesick for realism. It was not the appearance of the fantastic hosts that disturbed him. Oh, this was not open to doubt . . . No, it was not the ideal that confused him, but only that very precise . . . observation that regardless of how the knight waved his sword . . . it was impossible to conquer an army of a hundred thousand in several hours . . . He conceives a hundred diabolical men with bodies of lizards . . . Realism is thereby sustained, and truth is saved, and now, of course it is possible to believe indubitably in the first fundamental dream . . . Here, the great poet . . . marked one of the most profound and mysterious aspects of human nature . . . And such observations . . . one finds on every page.[14]

All the articles heretofore have presupposed the reader's acquaintance with the novel. They discuss the hero but little is said about the author or the actual work. In this respect V. G. Avseyenko's study, the Origin of the Novel[15] is different. Simply and logically he acquaints the readers with Cervantes' literary career and his works, then he proceeds to a discussion of the purely literary aspects of Don Quixote, such as the realism of the heroes, Cervantes' artistic tone—his humor and irony, and the book as a vehicle of aesthetic philosophy.

N. I. Storozhenko's Philosophy of Don Quixote is divided into three parts: Part one is a survey of the earlier critical attitudes toward the Cervantine novel.

In part two, Storozhenko considers Don Quixote in the original mould of Cervantes' novel. In so doing he combines the ideas proposed by the philosophic school with those of the realists giving them a well-rounded form. He discusses the social and political conditions that led up to Cervantes' writing a satire on the books of chivalry and the author's familiarity with these books. "The author of *Don Quixote* did not ridicule enthusiasm for good and truth, but the extravagant form of its manifestation, its caricature induced by the novels of chivalry which was not at all suitable to the spirit of the times."[16] For greater convincingness of the satire Cervantes selected an intelligent hero who has but one weakness, a pathologically developed fantasy and a passionate interest in human sorrow. From this stems a dualism which shows Cervantes' artistic greatness.[17] The third part of the essay is purely informative, containing the seeds for the thorough studies on the social, religious, and historical significance of *Don Quixote* later to be written by Shepelevich and others.

Storozhenko's article leads us to three new paths of criticism, the Symbolist, the scholarly, and the Marxist. To the first group belong the works of D. Merezhkovski, Iv. Iv., V. Ivanov and S. Botkin. Merezhkovski in *Eternal Companions*[18] considers the *Quixote* as a satire on man's defect (inactivity of the brain) and the hero as a ridicule of the deficiencies of medieval culture. He then plunges into developing an antithesis from which Don Quixote emerges as the representative of the cold North, and Sancho, of the warm South, with its humor and kindness. Merezhkovski here gives Sancho a long-deserved character analysis, and concludes by saying that Sancho and Don Quixote present an example where opposites attract and live together in complete understanding and love.

Iv. Iv. in his essay *The Famous Knight Don Quixote* says, "The most valuable and lasting are those works in which the hero incarnates the personality of the author and thereby represents his intimate spiritual aspirations, his thoughts, and his relation to contemporary reality."[19] He then shows how Don Quixote is Cervantes' *alter ego*.

V. Ivanov's highly technical article the *Crisis of Individualism*[20] ventures to trace and explain the evolution of individualism using Don Quixote, King Lear, Macbeth, and Hamlet as expressions of its demands, struggle, and tragic antimony.

S. Botkin, in his *Cervantes*,[21] shows how the novelist's restlessness, his philosophy, his interest in the *pueblo*, and finally, his naturalism all reflect national characteristics and interests.

N. Evreinoff in his book *Theater in Life*[22] presents Don Quixote as an example of the human desire for play-acting or "theater for oneself."

To the group of scholarly critics belong Gvozdev, Petrov, Krzhevski, Smirnov, and Bickermann. A. Gvozdev's article on *Cervantes and the Tragedy of Heroism*[23] deals with *Numancia* which the critic considers to be one of the most important monuments of early Spanish drama. He gives the stories of Numancia, the historical and the Cervantine, and brings out the latter's virtues and faults.

L. Shepelevich was undoubtedly one of the most important, prolific, and inspiring Cervantine scholars to come out of Russia. German-trained in scholarship, he devoted his life to giving his students at Kharkov University and elsewhere accurate information about Cervantes, his works, and his culture. Shepelevich's works are scholarly, using sources and methods that are in the best tradition of Western scholarship.

One of his earliest articles (unfinished) deals with Cervantes' dramatic works, which he classifies into three groups: those of biographical inspiration, those derived from other literary influences, and comedies of manner. In the article that was written he discusses the first group.[24]

This is followed by an article on the spurious *Don Quixote*,[25] and then another, on *Don Quixote and the Novels of Chivalry*, in which he rejects the theory that Don Quixote is a parody on the novels of chivalry, saying that though their influence is obvious in the plot of the individual episodes, in separate psychological moments, and in some of the hero's ideas, the general tone is realistic and therefore foreign to the chivalric novel.[26] In the same year Shepelevich published a bibliography of Russian translations of *Don Quixote*, and a list of critical articles written on the subject by his compatriots.[27] He was also very active in acquainting Russia with new Cervantine works appearing abroad through reviews. His major work, *Don Quixote, the Life of Cervantes and his Works*, has not been available but its second volume was reviewed by another Russian, the Hispanist, Petrov.[28] The contents of the book are distributed in the following manner: Chapter I (pp. 1–8) discusses the editions of the *Quixote* and stresses the merits of the one by Fitzmaurice Kelly (1898). Chapter II (pp. 9–41) characterizes a novel of chivalry, explains its *bytovouyou* worth and its effect on the Spanish customs of the 16th and 17th centuries. This is followed by an analysis of *Amadís de Gaula* and *Don Quixote's* relation to it. Chapter III (pp. 42–67) deals with the influences of Boyardo, Ariosto, and some of the Spanish picaresque novels on *Don Quixote*. Chapter IV (pp. 68–102) is a discussion of Avellaneda's *Don Quixote* and a commentary on the imitations of the *Quixote* in later Spanish literature. Chapter V (pp. 103–120) contains a critical evaluation of Russian literature on *Don Quixote* and the important Russian translations. Chapter VI is devoted to the historical, social, literary, and philosophical significance of the *Quixote*, its autobiographical elements, the self-sufficiency of the novel, and of the features contained in it that link it to Cervantes' other works. The book is followed by two appendices, one of which contains remarks on Cervantes' Russian bibliography and other notes on Shepelevich's own investigations.

The book is impressive for several reasons. The author tried to study his subject from every angle. His chapters on *Amadís* and Avellaneda's spurious *Quixote* will be a well of new information to many a reader. Chapter V is valuable, for it points out the shortcomings of Karelin's translation and introductory articles. Its comments on Merezhkovski's article, Petrov finds, are unusually good, as well as Shepelevich's own interpretation of Don Quixote's and Sancho's psychology.

"Shepelevich points to the wealth of psychological moments which prevent one from regarding the heroes of the novel, as abstract symbols and the novel as a work written *ad hoc*."[29]

Although Chapter VI has no startling originality or depth, it is interesting. The book's most valuable asset is the ardent love of the author for his subject, which pervades the entire work. D. Petrov's review of this book sustains the high level of Hispanic scholarship set by Shepelevich. Carefully Petrov analyses the work of his compatriot and gives criticism or praise wherever it is due.

Shepelevich's article[30] for the 300th anniversary of *Don Quixote's* publication apparently is a summary of his book.

B. Krzhevski's article *Cervantes and his "Novelas ejemplares"*[31] shows the expert handling of a good Spanish scholar. Joseph Bickermann's *Don Quixote and Faust, the Heroes and the Works* is scholarly in preparation and interpretative in execution.[32]

There are also essays on Cervantes and his novel which were written for the general public by V. Fisher, P. Vainberg, A. D. Alferov, Diones, E. During, O. Peterson, A. Yevlakhov, A. Altayev, D. A. Averkyev, Tsomakion, N. Bokardov, L. Chizhikov and N. Bakhtin and an article in *Niva*.[33]

Marxism, which appeared in the intellectual atmosphere of Russia at the end of the 19th century, made its debut in criticism in the writings of Kogan and Friche. As Kogan's early work shows, methods of Marxian criticism were vague at first, but with time became defined into the following scheme—first, an analysis of the economic structure of the given society; secondly, an explanation of its social conditions and its class division; and thirdly, a deduction of the resultant social psychology. This system lies at the bases of the Cervantine literature by Friche, Lunacharski, Beletski, and others.

The first article on Cervantes by a Marxist is Kogan's *Tragedy of Idealism,* wherein the critic approaches the whole novel of Don Quixote as "the history of an ideal existence and the story of its clash with the most varied of life phenomena."[34]

V. Friche in *Shakespeare and Cervantes*[35] discusses the expression of social and political conditions in the attitudes and works of these authors. (Aesthetic aspects are completely ignored.) In doing this he draws an interesting parallel between Don Quixote and Falstaff whom he considers blood relations and manifestations of the same social conditions.

A. Lunacharski, in his interesting section on Cervantes, claims that while Cervantes was laughing feudalism out of existence he was also mourning the disappearance of its finest aspects. He recalls that at the time that Cervantes wrote *Don Quixote* the original Christian, idealistic qualities of early knighthood were vanishing. "And Cervantes, who was himself a noble individual, a Don Quixote . . . was the best representative of the current bourgeoisie in its protest and in its struggle to wrench itself from the claws of falsehood . . . Cervantes worshipped that old ideal . . ." of early knighthood.[36] For men like the *hidalgo* there was no place either in that world or in any succeeding one. Only now, says Lunacharski, can the question of the ideal and the real be solved. "Only we communists are in a state when the highest ideals of mankind do not become Don Quixotism but a reality."

Victor Shklovski, the principal theoretician of Formalism, studies *Don Quixote* in the first sections of his *Development of a Subject*. Rejecting all extraliterary—ideological, sociological, psychological, biographical, and other—elements, he approaches the novel as nothing more than an interplay of devices for the purpose of "ostrannenia" (making strange) of reality. He sees Don Quixote as a device pure and simple, a string upon which episodes and speeches are strung. At first Cervantes planned a series of adventures of a silly old man. But as the story advanced, Cervantes sensed the effectiveness of a contrast between foolishness and wisdom. He then proceeded to exploit this duality, making Don Quixote a "string" for speeches on fame, linguistics, arms, literature whose actual motivations was but slight.[37] "It is curious," he remarks, "that as Don Quixote becomes wiser and wiser an analogous change occurs in Sancho. The point in the matter is that Sancho is the string carrying folkloric wisdom, whereas Don Quixote—book-learning." Shklovski then points to several differences between the two parts of the Quixote and discusses the intercalated *novelas*.

P. Medvedev,[38] an exponent of the Marxist method, attacks Shklovski for disregarding the organic element of the novelistic genre. Unity, he says, is not the result of external devices, but of internal (thematic) coordination. As for Shklovski's hypothesis that Cervantes needed the knight's madness as the motivating element for adventures, Medvedev says that Don Quixote is valuable *per se,* as are all essential elements of the work. With Sancho for contrast this pair comprises the basic thematic concept of the novel, and all episodes, speeches, *novelas* evolving therefrom are subordinate in importance.

P. I. Novitski's article *Cervantes' "Don Quixote"* begins with the premise that "every cultural scheme creates its own artistic forms and genres which are in accordance with the peculiarities of the ruling classes."[39] The Renaissance marks the end of feudalism and the birth of new bourgeois "intelligentsia." The latter with their feeling for the real and the natural create a new genre. Consequently, alongside the old aristocratic genre—the novels of chivalry, we have appearing the germs of the bourgeois genre—satirical parodies, *fabliaux,* moralizing novelas, and political pamphlets. These ultimately yield the satirico-social naturalistic novels. *Don Quixote* is at once the child of this struggle between literary forms and the victor. Expressing new social and cultural forms, it begins the literary history of the naturalistic novel. The purpose of the *Quixote* was not only to discredit the books of chivalry, but to serve as "a forceful pamphlet against aristocratic culture, a revelation of the historical limitations, the internal contradiction of the epoch that bore it." Novitski concludes his essay with the message of *Don Quixote* to the Soviets. *Don Quixote* shows that the present cannot be ameliorated through fancy and chimera but through practical idealism. Genius, enthusiasm, and talent must be given a reason and a goal lying in the present and in the future, and not in the shades of the past.

B. Krzhevski's article *"Don Quixote" on the Background of Spanish Literature of the XVI–XVII Centuries*[40] is a work of a fine Cervantine scholar who is versed in but not exclusively dominated by the Marxian critical method. The work deals with Cervantes' life, literary influences on *Don Quixote,* and the general appreciation of the novel prior to and after Schlegel. Of particular interest is the second part of the essay, the part devoted to chivalric, pastoral, and picaresque novels, their history, inter-relation and their influence on *Don Quixote.*

We also have a short article by A. Smirnov[41] on the translations of *Don Quixote.* He deals with the general value of Karelin's, Basanin's and Vatson's versions and gives a few examples of the type of errors that they make. He then explains the methods employed in the translation done by him and Krzhevski.

In the third volume of the *Literary Encyclopedia* there is a short article on *Don Quixote* by I. Nusinov,[42] which tries to sum up the various readings of Don Quixote and to set up the Marxist interpretations of the image. Nusinov assigns the Cervantes' novel to the category of reactionary literature, because its hero is a representative of the dying feudal world which is struggling for outmoded feudal ideals or utopian dreams of an equally reactionary character.

C. Derjavin's bibliographical article written in Spanish,[43] though incomplete, is valuable in that it informs the non-Russian world of the numerous Russian translations of *Don Quixote* and of many Russian articles dealing with Cervantes that had been unknown to many. Derjavin also published a short book on *Don Quixote* in Russian, where he advances the thesis that *Don Quixote* represents the organic discrepancy and discord of Spanish life of the period. Discussing the social, political, and economic background of *Don Quixote,* the author reveals Spain's paradoxical condition of external grandeur and internal putrefaction. This period of stagnation, says Derjavin,

> found expression in the mysticism of Santa Teresa, Luis de León, in the gloomy pathetics of Calderón, in the skeptical grotesques of Velasquez' canvases, in the annihilating aestheticism of Gongora's poetry, and in the cynical realism of picaresque novel and in the madness of the knight Don Quixote.[44]

The critic then reviews some of the foreign and Russian critical opinions and says,

> Exposing in Don Quixote the ideological essence of his class, Cervantes in defiance of the cruelty and heartlessness of the morals of XVI–XVII century raised his voice in defense of the *déclassées hidalguía* . . . idealized by him as the depository of national prestige, magnanimity, and social justice. The cruelest indictment of the epoch and his class go hand in hand with his ideological glorification (of the hidalguía)—the only and last weapon of class self-defense in conditions of social downfall and inevitable destruction of the petty bourgeois mass. (p. 72).

A. Beletski[45] strips Cervantes of the glamor bestowed upon him by time and over-enthusiastic biographers, and refutes some current ideas about the book, replacing them by others of Marxist orientation. For example, critics have claimed that Cervantes laughed chivalry off this earth by creating the most charming of knights. This is not so, says Beletski. Don Quixote is not in the least charming, but sick, and Cervantes did not love him but condemned him. Alonso Quixano, not comprehending the interests of his class—those of bourgeois development—styled himself as Don Quixote and invoked the phantoms of the past, a malady typical not only of him but of all Spanish politics of the time. Cervantes considers Don Quixote's exploits mad, not great. The first part of the novel is purely negative, but in the second certain positive elements emerge. It ceases to be an indictment and becomes a plan for betterment. These are but a few of the points made by Beletski.

An article devoted to the *Novelas ejemplares,* by F. Kelin,[46] is definitely overambitious. In forty-seven pages the critic attempts to discuss the foreign influence of the *novelas* in England, France, Germany, and Russia, the reasons for their success, the history of the *novela* in Spain, the dating of the *Novelas Ejemplares*, Spanish history, the revolutionary significance of the *Quixote*, and many other topics. And yet, Kelin touches but lightly on what would be most essential in an introduction to the *Novelas*—an explanation of the title. This done from the Marxist angle would have been most interesting.

In conclusion, we wish to mention Emil Midlin who continues the Marxist line of criticism in his article *Cervantes*.[47]

Thus we see that Cervantes and his works have been discussed by most of the important Russian critical schools. We have the philosophical interpretations given by such men as Belinski, Turgenev and Karelin, the positivist by Lvov, the scientific by Storozhenko, the symbolist by Ivanov and Merezhkovski, the historico-cultural by Shepelevich, the formalist by Shklovski, and finally the Marxist by Friche, Lunacharski, Derjavin and others.

NOTES: I

[1] *Neslykhanny chudodei, ili udivitelnia i neobychainia priklyuchenia khrabrago i znamenitago stranstvuyushchagorytsarya Don Kishota*, sochinenie Mikhaila Servantesa, perevel s frantsuzskago N.O., St. Petersburg, 1791.

[2] Bears the same title, Moscow, 1812.

[3] The British Museum has a copy of the 1769 edition, the two volumes are bound in one book.

[4] Moscow, 1804. The whole work covers six vols. in 12° which can be read in its entirety at the Madrid Biblioteca Nacional.

[5] Bardon, Maurice, *"Don Quichotte" en France au XVIIe au XVIIIe siècle, 1605–1815*, Paris, 1931, vol. I, pp. 327 ff. has a detailed analysis of this translation.

[6] Sopikov, V. S. *Opyt Rossiiskoi Bibliografii*, edited by V. N. Rogozhin, in 5 vols., St. Petersburg, 1904–1906, vol. V, #12890.

[7] Fitzmaurice-Kelly, James, *The Life of Miguel de Cervantes Saavedra*, London, 1892, p. 351.

[8] Rius y de Llosellas, Leopoldo, *Bibliografía crítica de las Obras de Miguel de Cervantes Saavedra*, in 3 vols., vol. I, 1895 is cited. #820 and #821.

[9] St. Petersburg. This was carefully reviewed by an unknown author in *Otechestvennie Zapiski*, St. P., 1839, vol. II, 2, pp. 67–86. There were also reviews in other journals. Another 1848 edition is cited by Rius, *op. cit.* #823.

[10] *Dve Lyubovnitsy, Gishpanskaya povest Mikh. Tservantesa Saavedry, avtora Don Kishota*, Moscow, 1763, mentioned in "Redkie i tsennie russkie izdania," #70, Antikvarny katalog, #14 of Mezdunarodnaya Kniga, Moscow, 1932, p. 24, #124.

[11] Same title, Moscow, 1769, Sopikov, V. *Op. cit.*, vol. II, #3104.

[12] *Idem*, vol. V. S. P., 1906, #12546 reads *"Tsyganka (prekrasnaya) Neotsena*, Smolensk, 1795."

[13] *Idem*, vol. IV, St. P., 1905, #8359. *Povesti Mikhaila Servantesa*, Moscow.

[14] *Sila Krovi*, in "Otechestvennie Zapiski," 1839.

[15] *Khitana*, in "Syn Otechestva," 1842.

[16] Sopikov, V. *Op. cit.*, vol. V, #12405, *Galatea, pastusheskaya povest*, Moscow, 1790. *Idem*, #12404, same title, St. Petersburg, 1799.

[17] *Don Kikhot Lamanchski*, sochinenie Miguelya Servantesa Saavedry, perevod V. Karelina, St. P., 1866, cited by Rius *Op. cit.* #825. A copy of the 1873 edition is to be found in the British Museum. The 1881 edition is cited by Rius, *Op. cit.* #828.

[18] *Izyashnaya Literatura,* Dec. 1883, pp. 230–243, July 1884, pp. 1–20, May 1885, pp. 1–22, Jan. 1884, pp. 260–282.

[19] St. Petersburg, 1886. In 1919 *Los habladores, El viejo celoso,* and *La cueva de Salamanca* were reprinted in "Innostranny teatr," Izdanie Teatr. Otd. Narodnago Komissar. po Prosvesch, vols. VIII, IX, and XI respectively. Ostrovski's *El rufián viudo,* which had been omitted from the complete works, was printed in "Sbornik Petrogradskogo Ob-va A. N. Ostrovskogo," Petrograd, 1923.

[20] *Russki Vestnik,* 1872, #8 and 9, pp. 235–269.

[21] The British Museum has a copy of this edition. Other editions of this version were issued in 1895, 1901, and 1910.

[22] St. Petersburg, 1903. An abbreviated and revised edition of this version was printed in Leningrad in 1925.

[23] Kholodnyak, I. D. review this version in "Zhurnal Ministerstva Narodnago Prosveschenia," St. P., 1906, vol. IX, pp. 98–101.

[24] St. Petersburg, 1907. The British Museum has a copy of this edition.

[25] *Katalog Odesskoi Gorodskoi Publichnoi Biblioteki,* vol. II, Odessa, 1903, #1137.

[26] Ford, J. D. M. and Lansing, R. *Cervantes, a tentative bibliography of his works and of the bibliographical and critical material concerning him,* Cambridge, Mass., 1931, p. 83 cites *Don Kikhot Lamanchski,* roman v dvukh chastyakh i risunki Gustava Dore, perevod s ispanskago, L. A. Murakhinoi, Pt. I, Moscow, 1899. Suñé Benages, Juan and Suñé Fonbuena, Juan, *Bibliografía crítica de Ediciones del Quijote impresas desde 1605 hasta 1917, continuada hasta 1937 por el primero de los citados autores.* Edited by J. D. M. Ford and C. T. Keller, Cambridge, Mass., 1939. #1205 cites a Moscow, 1899 edition which could easily belong to Murakhina.

[27] *Knizhnaya Letopis, Gosudarstvennaya Knizhnaya Palata,* St. P.-Moscow issued weekly since 1908, Oct. 25, 1914, #27132 cites *Istoria znamenitago Don Kikhota Lamanchskago,* Servantesa, perevedena pod redaktsieyu M. B. Chistyakova, St. P., 1914. This refers to the fifth edition, a second edition is cited by Rius, *Op. cit.,* #833. No other information has been available.

[28] *Kiizhnaya Letopis,* May 8, 1910, #10365 cites *Slavny rytsar Don Kikhot Lamanchski,* roman v dvukh tomakh. Novy polny perevod S. M. s portretom Servantesa i 75 kartinami Dore . . . Moscow, 1910.

[29] *Vestnik Inostrannoi Literatury,* 1892, #10, pp. 163–198.

[30] In the Homage volume to N. I. Strozhenko, Moscow, 1902.

[31] *Sovremenny Mir,* 1916, no. 4, pp. 91–121, *Severia Zapiski,* 1916, nos. 4–5, pp. 40–88, *Vestnik Yevropy,* 1916, vol. IV, pp. 129–183 respectively.

[32] St. Petersburg, 1892.

[33] Moscow 1913 and again 1916 cited by *Knizhnaya Letopis,* Sept. 10, 1916 #13401.

[34] *Khitroumny idalgo Don Kikhot Lamanchski,* perevod pod reaktsiei s vstoup. statyami B. A. Krzhevskogo i A. A. Smirnova, vvedenie P. I. Novitskogo, Moscow-Leningrad, 1929.

[35] Smirnov, A. A. *O Perevodakh "Don Kikhota,"* pp. lxxxix and xc in *Khitroumny idalgo* . . . cited above.

[36] Turkevich, L. B. a review of *Nazidatelnye Novelly* in "Hispanic Review," VI, 1938, p. 362.

[37] Translated by A. Deich, Moscow, 1927, cited in "Knizhnaya Letopis," Oct. 14, 1927, #16393.

[38] Moscow, 1929, cited in "Knizhnaya Letopis," July 16, 1929, #14111.

[39] Cited by K. Derjavin in BAH, XCIV, 1929, p. 216.

NOTES: II

[1] The translation of this poem is taken from Constance Garnett's rendition of Dostoyevski's *The Idiot* (New York, 1928). We replace the initials N. F. B. used by Aglaya in the novel by A. M. G. of the original Pushkin poem.

[2] P. V. Annenkov, "Materialy dlya biografii Pushkina," in *Sochinenia Pushkina,* St. Petersburg, 1855, p. 367.

[3] A review in "Sbornik na 1838 god," *Literaturnoe pribavlenie k Rus. Inv.* na 1838, XVI, pp. 310–312. Also see P. N. Sakulin, *Iz istorii russkago idealizma, Knyaz V. Odoyevski,* vol. I, pt. II, Moscow, 1913.

[4] Another instance of Cervantes influence is possibly the technique of having two dogs discuss society used in *Zapiski sumashedshego.*

[5] I. Turgenev, *Rudin,* translated by Constance Garnett, London, 1900, p. 195.

[6] F. M. Dostoyevski, "Dnevnik Pisatelya," in *Polnoe Sobranie Sochineni,* St. Petersburg, 1895, pp. 304–308.

[7] "F. M. Dostoyevski v pismakh 1867–1870 godov," in *Russkaya Starina,* July 1885, vol. XLVII, p. 144.

[8] It is important to recall that of all the characteristics given to Myshkin in the first plan of the novel, epilepsy was the only one retained in the finished portrait. The reversal of the original concept of the hero and its subsequent developments was made when the figures of Christ and Don Quixote entered actively into Dostoyevski's creative processes.

NOTES: III

[1] A. P. Sumarokov, *Polnoe Sobranie Sochinenii,* St. Petersburg, 1781, vol. VI, p. 371. M. Pogodin, *N. M. Karamzin, po yego sochineniam, pisman i otzyvam sovremennikov,* Part I, Moscow, 1866, p. 7.

[2] A. S. Pushkin, *Sochinenia,* vol. I, St. Petersburg, 1855, p. 265. N. Polevoi, A review of Schiller's works in *Moskovski Telegraf,* 1825, XIV, p. 289. W. Kukhelbeker, "O Napravleniakh nashei poezii," *Mnemoza,* II, pp. 29–44 passim.

[3] The author here must not be confused with the Symbolist F. Sologub, the author of *The Hostages of Life* discussed in the preceding section.

[4] V. Belinski. "Tarantas, sochinenie Grafa V. A. Solloguba," in *Sochinenia V. I. Belinskago,* Kiev, 1908, IV, pp. 11–12.

[5] *Idem.*

[6] I. Turgenev "Hamlet i Don Kikhot" in *Polnoe Sobranie Sochineni,* St. Petersburg, 1913, X, pp. 451–457, passim.

[7] *Ibid.*

[8] A. Skabichevski, *Sochinenia A. Skabichevskago v 2 tomakh,* St. Petersburg, 1903, II, p. 897. L. N. Tolstoi, *Polnoe Sobranie Sochineni,* LXIII, Moscow-Leningrad, 1934, p. 149. P. I. Novitski, "K sotsiologii zhanra i obraza" in *Don Kikhot,* Moscow-Leningrad, 1932, pp. XXIV–XXV. F. Fedoseyev, "O Realizma Turgeneva," in *Oktyabr,* X, 1933, p. 209.

[9] A. Lvov, *Hamlet i Don Kikhot,* St. Petersburg, 1862.

[10] A. G. Hornfeld *Boyevie otkliki na mirovie temy,* Leningrad, 1924, p. 28. The article was written in 1913.

[11] V. Karelin, "Don Kikhotizm i Demonizm," in *Don Kikhot Lamanchski,* 1893, vol. I, p. 8. Date of the article is 1866.

[12] *Idem,* pp. 16–22.

[13] *Idem,* pp. 26–32.

[14] F. Dostoyevski, "Dnevnik Pisatelyn," in *Polnoe Sobranie Sòchineni,* XI, St. Petersburg, 1895, pp. 304–308.

[15] V. Avseyenko, "Proiskhozhdenie romana: Cervantes," in *Russki Vestnik,* 1877, vol. 131, pt. 9, pp. 95–124, and vol. 132, pt. 2, pp. 442–462.

[16] N. Storozhenko, "Filosofia Don Kikhota," in *Vestnik Yevropy,* St. Petersburg, 1885, V, p. 316.

[17] *Idem,* p. 317.

[18] D. Merezhkovski, "Vechnie Sputniki, Servantes," in *Polnoe Sobranie Sochineni,* XVII, Moscow, 1914, pp. 101–135. Date of the article is 1889.

[19] Iv. Iv. "Servantes, Slavni Rytsar Don Kikhot Lamanchski," in *Mir Bozhi,* 1896, IX, pp. 260–261.

[20] V. Ivanov, "Krisis individualizma," in *Voprosy Zhizni,* 1905, IX, pp. 47–60.

[21] S. Botkin, "Servantes," in *Vestnik Yevropy,* 1916, vol. 299, pp. 77–98.

[22] N. Evreinoff, *The Theater in Life, New York,* 1927, pp. 84ff.

[23] A. Gvozdev, "Servantes i tragedia geroizma," in *Severnia Zapiski*, 1916, V, pp. XXII–XXVIII.

[24] L. Shepelevich, "Dramaticheskia proizvedenia Servantesa," in *Zhurnal Ministerstva Narodnago Prosveschenia*, July, 1899, pp. 277–300.

[25] L. Shepelevich, *Don Kikhot Avelianedy i vopros ob avtore etogo romana*, Kharkov, 1899.

[26] L. Shepelevich, "Don Kikhot i rytsarski roman," in *Obrazovanie*, 1902, nos. 5–9, pp. 70–90, cf. p. 90.

[27] L. Shepelevich, "Russkaya Literatura o Servantese," in *Yubileini Sbornik v Chest N. I. Storozhenka*, Moscow, 1902, pp. 161–165.

[28] L. Shepelevich, *"Don Kikhot" Servantesa, Zhizn Servantesa i yego proizvedenia*, 2 vols., St. Petersburg, 1901–1903. D. Petrov reviews this work in *Zhurnal Ministerstva Narodnago Prosveschenia*, March, 1904, pp. 163–179.

[29] *Idem*, p. 166.

[30] L. Shepelevich, "Trekhsotletie 'Don Kikhote' Servantesa," in *Vestnik Yevropy*, 1905, vol. 233, pp. 238–240.

[31] B. Krzhevski, "Servantes i yego novelly," in *Severnia Zapiski*, 1916, pp. XXIX–XXXIX.

[32] J. Bickermann, *Don Quijote y Fausto, los heroes y las obras*, Barcelona, 1932.

[33] V. Fisher, "Servantes i Don Kikhot," in *Russkaya Mysl*, 1916, V, pp. 1–10. P. Vainberg, "Servantes," in *Mir Bozhi*, 1892, X, pp. 44–61. E. During, *Velikie Lyudi v Literature*, St. Petersburg, 1897. A. Alferov, *Desiat Lektsii po Literature*, 1895. Dioneo, "Miguel Cervantes," in *Russkia Zapiski*, V, 1916, pp. 64–89. The author asserts that Cervantes gave the Spanish writers their slogan—tolerance, respect for word and thought, and struggle against the clergy who had ruined Spain. O. Peterson, *Servantes, yego zhizn i proizvedenia*, St. Petersburg, 1901. A. Yevlakhov, "K trekhsotletiu 'Don Kikhota,'" in *Mir Bozhi*, 1905, V, pp. 47–69. A. Altayev, *Miguel Cervantes*, St. Petersburg, 1907. D. Averkyev, *O Drame*, 1907. Tsomakion, *Zhizn zamechatelnykh lyoudei* (mentioned by N. Storozhenko in his *History of Western European Literature*, p. 215). N. Bokardov, *Istoria zapadno-yevropeiskoi literatury XVI–XVII*, Kiev, 1914. Chichikov and Bakhtin, *Bibliography of Cervantes*, 1914, mentioned in *Literaturnaya Entsiklopedia*, vol. III, p. 385.

[34] P. S. Kogan, "Tragedia idealizma" in *Russkaya Mysl*, 1895, VIII.

[35] V. M. Friche, "Shakspir i Servantes," in Sovremnny Mir, 1916, vol. IV, pp. 110–123.

[36] A. V. Lunacharski, *Istoria zapadno-yevripeiskoi literatury*, Moscow, 1924, Prt. I, pp. 177–178.

[37] V. Shklovski, *Razvertyvanie syuzheta*, Petrograd, 1921, pp. 23–25.

[38] P. N. Medvedev, "Formalny metod v literaturovedenii, Kriticheskoe vvedenie v sotsiologicheskuyu poetiku," in *Priboi*, 1928, pp. 183–187.

[39] P. I. Novitski, "Don Kikhot Servantesa," in *Khitroumny idalgo Don Kikhot Lamanchski*, p. IX. This is the Soviet Academia edition.

[40] B. A. Krzhevski, "Don Kikhot na fone ispanskoi literatury XVI–XVII," in *Khitroumny idalgo Don Kikhot Lamanchski*, pp. XLI–LXXIX.

[41] A. A. Smirnov, "O perevodakh 'Don Kikhota,'" in *Khitroumny idalgo . . .*, pp. LXXXIII–XCI.

[42] I. N. Nosinov, "Don Kikhot" in *Literaturnaya Ensiklopedia*, III, Moscow-Leningrad, 1930.

[43] C. Derjavin, "Crítica cervantina en Rusia," in *Boletín de la Real Academia de la Historia*, XCIV, 1929, pp. 215–238.

[44] C. Derjavin, *Servantes i "Don Kikhot,"* Leningrad, 1933, p. 32.

[45] This article was intended as an introduction to a new translation of *Don Quixote* in the Ukrainian. We were able to read the manuscript through the kindness of the author.

[46] F. V. Kelin, *"Nazidatelnie Novelly" Servantesa*, in vol. I of the "Academia" edition of 1934, pp. 7–47.

[47] E. L. Midlin, "Servantes" in *Almanakh*, XXII, 1939, pp. 388 ff.

NOTES ON CONTRIBUTORS

LIENHARD BERGEL, Chairman of the Department of German, Queens College, is a contributor to the recently published *The Kafka Problem* . . . JOAQUÍN CASAL-DUERO, Professor of Spanish, Smith College, is well known for his critical studies of Galdós and Cervantes. He is now completing a work on the architectural composition of *Don Quixote* . . . MARIO CASELLA, Professor of Spanish, University of Florence, has written widely on Renaissance culture . . . JEAN CASSOU, French novelist, critic, scholar, and translator, is the Director of the National Museum of Art, Paris . . . AMÉRICO CASTRO, formerly Professor at Centro de Estudios Históricos (Madrid) and now Ford Professor of Spanish at Princeton University, is the author of an epoch-making work on the cultural influence of Cervantes: *El Pensamiento de Cervantes* . . . BENEDETTO CROCE, Italy's leading philosopher, requires no introduction to American readers . . . ESTHER J. CROOKS, of Goucher College, wrote her doctoral dissertation on the influence of Cervantes on seventeenth-century France . . . WALDO FRANK, American novelist and essayist, has won the respect of Hispanic readers for his *Virgin Spain* . . . STEPHEN GILMAN, of Princeton University, has published important studies on the Spanish Baroque, the *Celestina,* and de Avellaneda . . . HELMUT HAZTFELD, of The Catholic University, pioneered in stylistic studies of Don Quixote . . . CHARLES HAYWOOD, of Queens College and the Juilliard School of Music, has written widely in musicology and on folk music . . . EDWIN B. KNOWLES, of Queens College, wrote his doctoral dissertation on Cervantes in England before the nineteenth century . . . HARRY LEVIN, Chairman of Comparative Literature, Harvard University, is the author of distinguished studies of Joyce and Stendhal . . . RAMÓN MENÉNDEZ-PIDAL, one of the greatest living Hispanic scholars, has written a number of classic studies, among them *La España del Cid.* Included in the present volume is a translation of his *Un aspecto en la elaboración del Quijote* . . . A. MOREL-FATIO, celebrated French scholar and specialist in Hispanic literature, is the author of *Études sur l'Espagne,* from which our selection is taken . . . PAVEL I. NOVITSKY, Soviet literary critic and Academician, has made some of the finest translations of Cervantes into Russian . . . MACK SINGLETON, Professor of Spanish and Portuguese, University of Wisconsin, has fomented a revolution in Cervantine studies through his revision of chronological data . . . LUDMILLA B. TURKEVICH is a visiting lecturer at Princeton University . . . MIGUEL DE UNAMUNO, novelist, poet, and essayist, is well known to American readers through his many books issued in this country.

A SELECTED BIBLIOGRAPHY

GENERAL

J. D. M. Ford and Ruth Lansing. *Cervantes. A Tentative Bibliography.* Cambridge, 1931.

Juan Suñé. *Bibliography of Don Quixote.* Cambridge, 1939.

EDITIONS

Don Quijote. Mexico. Editorial Séneca, 1943. (A beautifully printed edition, pocket size. Highly recommended.)

The ingenious gentleman Don Quixote of La Mancha. (A translation with introduction and notes by John Ormsby. London. Smith, Elder & Co., 1885. 4 vols. Map.) (Alfred A. Knopf published in 1926 a 2-volume edition of the Ormsby translation.)

BIOGRAPHY

Américo Castro. *Cervantes.* Paris. Les Editions Rieder, 1931. (An excellent interpretation in French of Cervantes' life.)

James Fitzmaurice-Kelly. *Miguel de Cervantes Saavedra. A Memoir.* Oxford. Clarendon Press, 1913. (As a factual reference work this biography is indispensable.)

Bruno Frank. *A man called Cervantes.* The Viking Press, 1935. (A good biographical novel.)

GENERAL STUDIES

Aubrey F. G. Bell. *Cervantes.* University of Oklahoma Press, 1947.

William J. Entwistle. *Cervantes.* Oxford. Clarendon Press, 1940.

Cesare de Lollis. *Cervantes reazionario.* Rome, Fratelli Treves, 1924.

Paolo Savj-Lopez. *Cervantes.* Naples. R. Ricciardi, 1913. (There is a fine Spanish translation of this work by Antonio G. Solalinde, Madrid, 1917.)

Rudolph Schevill. *Cervantes.* New York. Duffield, 1919.

CRITICAL STUDIES—DON QUIXOTE

Maurice Bardon. *Don Quichotte en France au XVIIe et au XVIIIe siècle, 1605-815.* Paris. Libraire Ancienne Honoré Champion, 1931.

J. J. A. Bertrand. *Cervantes et le romantisme allemand.* Paris. F. Alcan, 1914.

Joseph Bickermann. *Don Quijote und Faust.* Berlin. Colignon, 1929. (Spanish translation by P. Félix García, Barcelona. Casa Editorial Araluce, 1932.)

Joaquín Casalduero. "La composición del Quijote," in *Revista de Filología Hispanica,* Buenos Aires, 1940, II, pp. 323-369.

Mario Casella. *Cervantes, Il Chisciotte*. Florence. Felice Le Monnier, 1936. 2 vols.

Américo Castro. *El pensamiento de Cervantes*. Madrid. Centro de Estudios Históricos, 1925.

Esther J. Crooks. "The Influence of Cervantes in France in the Seventeenth Century." Paris, Les Belles-Lettres, 1931.

Ambrosio Czakó. "Don Quijote, a commentary." Winnipeg, The Christian Press, 1943.

Élie Faure. *Montaigne et ses trois premiers-nés*. Paris. G. Crès et Cie., 1926.

James Fitzmaurice-Kelly. *Cervantes in England*. London. H. Henry Frowle, 1905.

R. Flacomio. *La fortuna del D. Q. in Italia nei secoli XVII et XVIII*. Palermo, 1928.

Helmut Hatzfeld. *"Don Quijote" als wortkunstwerk. Die Einzelnen Stilmittel und ihr Sinn*. Leipzig. Verlag und Druck von B. G. Teubner, 1927.

Paul Hazard. *Don Quichotte de Cervantes. Étude et Analyse*. Paris. Librairie Mellottée, 193?.

Hispania. A Teachers' Journal. Cervantes Quadricentennial Number. Menasha, Wisconsin. August 1947.

Thomas Mann. *A bordo con Don Quijote*. Buenos Aires. Losada, 1943.

D. de Merejkowski. "Cervantes," in *Hispania*. Paris, 1921. IV, pp. 97-124.

Pavel I. Novitsky. *Cervantes and Don Quijote*. New York, 1936.

David Rubio. *¿Hay una filosofía en el Quijote?* New York. Instituto de las Españas, Columbia University, 1924.

Ivan Turgenev. "Hamlet and Don Quijote." (See *The Anatomy of Don Quixote. A Symposium*. Edited by M. J. Benardete and Angel Flores, Ithaca, N. Y. The Dragon Press, 1932, pp. 98-120.)

MODERN SPANISH LITERARY CRITICISM

Francisco Ayala. "Nota sobre la Creación del Quijote," in *Cuadernos Americanos* (Mexico), 1947. No. 5.

Manuel Azaña. *La invención del Quijote y otros ensayos*. Madrid, 1934.

Azorín. *La ruta de Don Quijote*. Madrid, 1905; Buenos Aires, 1938.

Salvador de Madariaga. *Guía del lector del Quijote*. Madrid, 1926; Buenos Aires, 1943. (English version, *Don Quixote, An Introductory Essay in Psychology*, N. Y. Oxford University Press, 1939.)

Ramiro de Maeztu. *Don Quijote, Don Juan y la Celestina*. Madrid, 1926; Buenos Aires, 1941.

Marcelino Menéndez y Pelayo. "Cultura literaria de . . . Cervantes y elaboración del Quijote," in *Revista de Archivos*, XII, year IX, 5, pp. 309-339.

José Ortega y Gasset. *Meditaciones del Quijote*. Madrid, 1914.

Angel Sánchez Rivero. "Las Ventas del Quijote," in *Revista de Occidente*, 1927, pp. 1-22.

Miguel de Unamuno. *Vida de Don Quijote y Sancho*. Madrid, 1905; Buenos Aires, 1940. (English version, New York, 1927.)